Petrogradskaya
See pp66–75

PETROGRADSKAYA

Bol Nevka *Бол Невка*

Neva *Нева*

PALACE
EMBANKMENT

GOSTINYY DVOR

0 metres 600
0 yards 600

Palace Embankment
See pp76–97

Gostinyy Dvor
See pp98–115

EYEWITNESS TRAVEL

St Petersburg

DK EYEWITNESS TRAVEL

St Petersburg

Main Contributors **Catherine Phillips**
Christopher and Melanie Rice

Penguin
Random
House

Project Editor Anna Streiffert
Art Editor Marisa Renzullo
Editor Ella Milroy
Designers Gillian Andrews, Carolyn
Hewitson, Paul Jackson, Elly King,
Nicola Rodway
Visualizer Joy Fitzsimmons
Map Coordinators Emily Green, David Pugh
Picture Research Brigitte Arora
DTP Designers Samantha Borland,
Sarah Martin, Pamela Shiels

Main Contributors Catherine Phillips,
Christopher and Melanie Rice

Photographers Demetrio Carrasco,
John Heseltine

Illustrators Stephen Conlin, Maltings
Partnership, Chris Orr & Associates,
Paul Weston

Printed and bound in China

First American Edition, 1998
18 19 20 21 10 9 8 7 6 5 4 3 2 1

Published in the United States by
DK Publishing, Inc., 345 Hudson Street,
New York, New York 10014

Reprinted with revisions 2000, 2001,
2004, 2007, 2010, 2013, 2015, 2018

Copyright 1998, 2018
© Dorling Kindersley Limited, London
A Penguin Random House Company

Published in Great Britain
by Dorling Kindersley Ltd.

A catalog record for this book is available
from the Library of Congress.

ISSN 1542-1554
ISBN 978-1-4654-6878-9

Throughout this book, floors are referred
to in accordance with European usage,
i.e. the "first floor" is one floor up.

The embellished Small Throne Hall of the
Winter Palace, Hermitage Museum

Introducing
St Petersburg

Breathtaking view of the Grand Cascade at Peterhof

◀ **Title page** Detail of the mosaics on the ornate vaulted ceiling of the Church on Spilled Blood. **Front cover main image** Burnished
onion domes of the Catherine Palace Chapel **Back cover image** Peterhof Palace, reflected in one of the grounds' many fountains

Contents

Colourful Russian handicrafts displayed in a store at Gostiny Dvor, Nevsky Prospekt

The Bronze Horseman of St Petersburg is a monument to Peter the Great

An illustration of St Isaac's Cathedral *(see pp82–3)*

HOW TO USE THIS GUIDE

This guide will help you to get the most from your visit to St Petersburg, providing expert recommendations as well as detailed practical information. *Introducing St Petersburg* maps the city and sets it in its geographical, historical and cultural context, with a quick-reference timeline on the history pages giving the dates of Russia's rulers and significant events. *St Petersburg at a Glance* is an overview of the city's main attractions. *St Petersburg Area by Area* starts on page 56 and describes all the important sights, using maps, photographs and illustrations. The sights are arranged in two groups: those in the central districts and those a little further afield. The guided walks reveal three characteristics of the city – the canals, the Neva and the islands. *Beyond St Petersburg* describes sights requiring one- or two-day excursions. Hotel, restaurant, shopping and entertainment recommendations can be found in *Travellers' Needs*, while the *Survival Guide* includes tips on everything from transport and telephones to personal safety.

Finding Your Way Around the Sightseeing Section

Each of the seven sightseeing areas is colour-coded for easy reference. Every chapter opens with an introduction to the area it covers, describing its history and character. For central districts, this is followed by a Street-by-Street map illustrating a particularly interesting part of the area; for sights beyond the city limits, by a regional map. A simple numbering system relates sights to the maps. Important sights are covered by several pages.

1 **Introduction to the area**
For easy reference, the sights are numbered and plotted on an area map, with metro stations shown where helpful. The key sights (great buildings, museums and open-air sights) are listed by category.

A locator map
shows where you are in relation to other areas of the city centre.

Each area has colour-coded thumb tabs.

The area shaded in pink
is shown in greater detail on the Street-by-Street map.

2 **Street-by-Street map**
This gives a bird's-eye view of interesting and important parts of each sightseeing area, with accurate drawings of all the buildings within them. The numbering of the sights ties in with the preceding area map and with the fuller descriptions on the pages that follow.

A suggested route for a walk is shown in red.

St Petersburg Area Map

The coloured areas shown on this map *(see pp16–17)* are the five main sightseeing areas into which central St Petersburg has been divided for this guide. Each is covered in a full chapter in the St Petersburg Area by Area section *(pp56–133)*. They are also shown on other maps throughout the book. In *St Petersburg at a Glance (pp34–51)*, for example, they help you locate the most interesting museums and palaces or where to see the city's many delightfully designed bridges. The maps' coloured borders match the coloured thumb tabs on each page of the section.

Practical information lists all the information you need to visit every sight, including a map reference to the Street Finder maps *(pp240–7)*.

Numbers refer to each sight's position on the area map and its place in the chapter.

3 Detailed information on each sight

All the important sights are described individually. They are listed to follow the numbering on the area map at the start of the section. The key to the symbols summarizing practical information is on the back flap.

Visitors' Checklist provides the practical information you will need to plan your visit.

Story boxes highlight unique aspects or historical connections of a particular sight.

4 St Petersburg's major sights

These are given two or more full pages in the sightseeing area in which they are found. Buildings of interesting architecture are dissected to reveal their interiors; museums and galleries have colour-coded floor plans to help you find important exhibits.

Stars indicate the best features or works of art.

INTRODUCING
ST PETERSBURG

GREAT DAYS IN ST PETERSBURG

In just over 300 years St Petersburg has had many faces. Peter the Great's folly, built on a swamp and intended to turn Russia's face towards the West, soon became a magnificent city reflecting the majesty of the Russian Empire. Then it was the "Cradle of the Revolution", where Lenin came to power. During World War II it was a symbol of national pride. Today it is Russia's cultural capital, with a wonderfully preserved heritage and an international arts programme. Taken together, the first three itineraries detailed below show the influences that shaped the city: imperial, Russian and Soviet. The others walk you through the city with a much more mixed offering. There is a day tour, a two-day tour, a three-day tour and a five-day tour. Follow the one that appeals to you, or simply dip in and out and be inspired.

Rastrelli's masterly main staircase at the Winter Palace

Imperial City

Two adults allow at least 6,000 roubles

- **Art and opulence**
- **Grand squares and views**
- **Remembering Rasputin**

Morning
The day starts at the centre of the city with the Baroque **Winter Palace** (see pp94–5), once the official residence of the imperial family and now the heart of the **Hermitage** museum (see pp86–93). Concentrate on the magnificent state rooms, where the Tsars received important guests. Do not miss the view over vast **Palace Square** (see p85), which incorporates the glorious sweep of the General Staff Building, formerly home to the state ministries and now part of the museum. Walk along the embankment to **Krokodil** (see p190) for lunch.

Afternoon
Head back along Galernaya ulitsa to **Senate Square** (see p80) – the **Bronze Horseman**, a statue of Peter the Great, rears up at its centre. There are fine views across the river to Vasilevskiy Island, lined with rich mansions and handsome institutions. Turn round, and take in **St Isaac's Cathedral** (see pp82–3), topped by a gilded dome. It took from 1818 to 1858 to construct this colossal structure, which, since the Soviet era, has been designated a museum. Under 1 km (half a mile) west, the **Yusupov Palace** (see p122) has an exhibition on Grigoriy Rasputin, the "holy man" murdered here by Prince Felix Yusupov. Dine at nearby **Romeo's Bar & Kitchen** (see p191), one of the city's best Italian restaurants, or for a more modest outlay, at **1913** (see p191) – the year the Romanovs celebrated 300 years on the throne.

Russian City

Two adults allow at least 4,800 roubles

- **Icons and incense**
- **A traditional lunch**
- **Shopping for souvenirs**

Morning
This itinerary takes in the best traditional Russian sights of a city where European influences can be more evident than Russian. Start at the **Russian Museum** (see pp106–9), the world's finest collection of Russian art. Marvel at the **Church on Spilled Blood**'s (see p102) interior, then enjoy a traditional Russian lunch at **Brasserie de Metropol** (see p189).

The Russian Revival-style Church on Spilled Blood

◄ St Petersburg – View of the Troitskiy Bridge, by 19th-century artist J Schroeder

Afternoon

Inspired by the morning's sights, nip across to the **Souvenir Market** *(see p201)*, which sells everything from icons to fur hats.

Then take the green metro line from Gostinyy Dvor to Ploshchad Aleksandra Nevskovo to **Alexander Nevsky Monastery** *(see pp132–3)*. Many notable Russians, including Tchaikovsky and Dostoevsky, are buried here. As the afternoon fades, you may like to attend a magical candlelit choral service at the Church of the Annunciation.

Round off the day with a visit to nearby **Russky Len** *(see p201)*, a shop selling wonderful Russian linen.

In the evening, visit the ballet *(see p204)* or dine at **Bellevue Brasserie** *(see p189)*, which overlooks the Hermitage and Palace Square. For both, book ahead.

The still-operational mint at Peter and Paul Fortress

Soviet City

Two adults allow at least 2,700 roubles

- **Revolutionary heritage sites**
- **Monuments to the People**
- **Soviet-themed dining**

Morning

To indulge a fascination for Leningrad, "Cradle of the Revolution", start at the city centre's edge at the **Smolnyy Institute** *(see pp130–31)*, home of the Revolution and later of the Communist Party. Opposite, catch bus No. 46 and ride past the monument to Dzerzhinsky, father of the Soviet secret police, past the **Field of Mars** *(see p96)* where the dead of the Revolution are buried, and across the river to the **Museum of Russian Political History** *(see p74)*. The Cruiser *Aurora* *(see p75)*, whose guns sounded the 1917 Revolution, is moored a short distance away. For lunch, try Georgian **Salkhino** *(see p187)*.

Afternoon

A little further north, the small **Kirov Museum** *(see p74)* is devoted to the head of the city's Communist Party, Sergey Kirov, whose assassination in 1934 prompted a wave of executions.

To appreciate the Soviet glorification of the People's achievements, take the metro to Moskovskaya and the **Victory Monument** *(see p133)*, whose awesome underground Memorial Hall shows life during the Siege of Leningrad. Then take the metro back to Tekhnologicheskiy Institute and ride the red line between Avtovo and Ploshchad Vosstaniya, where each station tells a part of the history of the city *(see p226)*. Finally, dine at **Kvartirka** *(see p188)* or **Restoran** *(see p186)*.

A Family Day Out

Family of 4 allow at least 4,500 roubles

- **Awesome views**
- **Gruesome specimens**
- **Food in a forest**
- **Skating or the circus**

Morning

The day starts with a stiff climb up to the colonnade of **St Isaac's Cathedral** *(see pp82–3)* for panoramic city views. Then cross the Neva to the **Strelka** *(see pp60–61)* of Vasilevskiy Island to take in one of the museums there *(see pp62–3)*: the **Zoological**, the **Institute of Russian Literature** or the **Kunstkammer**.

A pleasant walk across the river takes you to **Petrogradskaya** *(see pp66–75)*. Head to the inexpensive **Pelmeni Bar** for a filling lunch or, for somewhere cosier, try **Mesto Café** *(see p187)*.

Afternoon

The focus of Petrogradskaya is the **Peter and Paul Fortress** *(see pp68–9)*, with its opulent cathedral and grim history. Attractions include the tombs of the Romanovs, prison cells, displays on the history of the city, Peter the Great's rowing boat, and a rampart climb. In summer, the park surrounding the fortress has all kinds of family attractions.

Also in the park is **Gornyy Oryol** *(see p186)*, a restaurant designed as a fairy-tale castle, located near the entrance to the zoo.

After supper, take the metro to Krestovskiy Ostrov, then a short walk to the western spit of **Yelagin Island** *(see pp138–9)*, where there are fine sunsets and an ice rink in winter. Or, if it is too cold, make a visit to the **circus** *(see p203)*.

The Avtovo metro station celebrates post-war car production

Two Days in St Petersburg

- **Enjoy sweeping city views from Trinity Bridge**
- **Explore the unique art collections at the Hermitage**
- **Marvel at the sight of the Grand Cascade in Peterhof**

Day 1

Morning Stroll through the historic city of St Petersburg, from **Anichkov Bridge** *(p39)* to **Nevskiy prospekt** *(pp48–51)*. From here, visit the grand shopping arcade at **Gostinyy Dvor** *(pp110–11)*, and catch a glimpse of the Style-Moderne architecture of **Yeliseev's** *(p111)* on your way. Once you reach the **Admiralty Garden** *(p48)*, turn left towards the colossal **St Isaac's Cathedral** *(pp82–3)* to admire its lavish interiors and remarkable ceiling paintings.

Afternoon After lunch, head through **Palace Square** *(p85)* to the renowned **Hermitage** *(pp86–95)*, one of the largest museums in the world. Here you can explore the **Winter Palace State Rooms** *(p87)* and the **Pavilion Hall** *(p87)*.

Day 2

Morning Start by visiting **Trinity Bridge** *(p37)*, from where you can enjoy glorious views of the city. Next, head to the nearby **Peter and Paul Fortress** *(pp68–9)*.

Façade of the mosque at the Peter and Paul Fortress, St Petersburg

Enter the fortress through **Ivan Gate** *(p69)*, and spend the morning lost in this intriguing complex. Don't forget to visit the beautiful **Cathedral of SS Peter and Paul** *(pp70–71)*, where the Romanovs are entombed.

Afternoon Board a hydrofoil at the Hermitage Embankment for a scenic, 30-minute journey to **Peterhof** *(pp150–53)*. On arrival at Peterhof's Lower Gardens, take a walk along the delightful **Marine Canal** *(p150)*. Beyond the immaculate flower beds, view the **Grand Cascade** *(p153)*, a dazzling water structure that fronts the resplendent **Great Palace** *(p151)*. Afterwards, visit the **Upper Gardens** *(p150)*, which feature many magnificent fountains and ornamental ponds.

Three Days in St Petersburg

- **Visit one of the world's largest art collections at the Hermitage**
- **Admire the stunning Catherine Palace**
- **Enjoy a scenic boat trip from St Petersburg to Peterhof**

Day 1

Morning Begin your day at **Palace Square** *(p85)*, where you can admire the wonderful buildings and architecture. Then, devote the rest of your morning to the opulent **Hermitage** *(pp86–95)*. This former residence of the tsars now houses one of the world's largest art collections, and offers visitors a rich cultural experience. Stop by the splendid **Winter Palace State Rooms** *(p87)* and the **Pavilion Hall** *(p87)*.

Afternoon Take a walk along **Nevskiy prospekt** *(pp48–51)*, which runs through the heart of St Petersburg. Make a detour along the way, to visit the **Church on Spilled Blood** *(p102)*. The church was built as a memorial to Alexander II on the spot where he was assassinated.

Mosaic floor in the Pavilion Hall at the Hermitage, St Petersburg

Day 2

Morning Take a minibus *(marshrutka)* from Moskovskaya Metro Station to **Pavlovsk** *(pp160–63)*, an expansive park dotted with ornamental pavilions and statues. Look out for the **Apollo Colonnade** *(p160)* and the **Étoile** *(p161)*. Don't forget to visit the **Pavlovsk Palace** *(pp162–3)*, built in the 18th century.

Afternoon Take a taxi from Pavlovsk to nearby **Tsarskoe Selo** *(pp154–7)* to visit the magnificent **Catherine Palace** *(pp154–5)*, built for Tsarina Elizabeth. Of the many regal rooms within, the most striking are the **Great Hall** *(p154)*, the **Amber Room** *(p155)* and the **Green Dining Room** *(p155)*.

Day 3

Morning From the Hermitage Embankment, board a hydrofoil to **Peterhof** *(pp150–53)*, the magnificent palace of Peter the Great. The **Marine Canal** *(p150)* draws visitors towards Peterhof's centrepiece – the **Grand Cascade** *(p153)*, beyond which stands the spectacular **Great Palace** *(p151)*.

Afternoon Head across **Trinity Bridge** *(p37)*, towards the **Peter and Paul Fortress** *(pp68–9)*. Enjoy wonderful views of the city on your way. At the fortress, visit the Baroque **Cathedral of SS Peter and Paul** *(pp70–71)*. If the weather permits, join sunbathing locals on the beach.

Five Days in St Petersburg

- Look out from the bell tower at Smolnyy Convent
- Admire the bizarre displays at the Kunstkammer
- Wander through the imperial estate of Pavlosvsk

Day 1

Morning Cross the **River Neva** (*p86*) using the **Trinity Bridge** (*p37*), and head to the imposing **Peter and Paul Fortress** (*pp68–9*). Step into the elegant magnificence of the bright **Cathedral of SS Peter and Paul** (*pp70–71*), which houses the tombs of the Romanov family. Then, explore the grim history of this fortress, which was once a prison for political dissidents.

Afternoon Get a feel of historic and contemporary St Petersburg, with a stroll along the bustling **Nevskiy prospekt** (*pp48–51*). The city's most renowned street since the 18th century, it features an array of historic monuments, churches and fine buildings. Look out for the **Cathedral of Our Lady of Kazan** (*p113*), the statue of **Catherine the Great** (*p112*), and the **Gostinyy Dvor** (*pp110–11*). Stop for a meal at the shopping arcade.

Day 2

Morning The famous **Palace Square** (*p85*) provides an easy starting point, from which you can visit the grand buildings of the **Hermitage** (*pp86–95*). Spend the morning discovering

Exterior of the Cathedral of Our Lady of Kazan at Nevskiy prospekt, St Petersburg

the city's rich cultural heritage at this opulent museum.

Afternoon Take a hydrofoil from Heritage Embankment to **Peterhof** (*pp150–53*). Wander through the beautiful landscaped gardens, and catch a glimpse of the **Grand Cascade** (*p153*) and the stunning **Great Palace** (*p151*).

Day 3

Morning Start the day with a tour of the **Church on Spilled Blood** (*p102*), and admire its marvellous onion-shaped domes. Afterwards, walk to the nearby **Russian Museum** (*pp106–9*), housed in Mikhaylovskiy Palace. This splendid 19th-century complex has one of the greatest collections of Russian art on display.

Afternoon Catch the metro to Chernyshevskaya, from where you can walk to the **Smolnyy Convent** (*p130*). Explore the charming cathedral, and climb

the bell tower for a panoramic view of St Petersburg. Later, spend time at the adjoining **Smolnyy Institute** (*pp130–31*), an impressive Neo-Classical building that became Lenin's seat of power from 1917–18.

Day 4

Morning Travel to the vast estate of **Pavlovsk** (*pp160–63*) where you can meander through romantic ruins and pavilions.

Afternoon Hop into a taxi and head to **Tsarskoe Selo** (*pp154–7*). Tour the estate's fabulous **Catherine Palace** (*pp154–5*), and explore the **Amber Room** (*p155*), the **Great Hall** (*p154*), and the **Green Dining Room** (*p155*).

Day 5

Morning Begin with a trip to the **Admiralty** (*p80*), a former fortified shipyard. Then, head across **Palace Bridge** (*p38*) to **Vasilevskiy Island** (*pp58–65*). Enjoy a walk through the eastern end of this pleasant historic quarter, the **Strelka** (*pp60–61*). Visit the **Kunstkammer** (*pp62–3*), built to exhibit Peter the Great's infamous collection of oddities. The **Rostral Columns** (*p62*) are another distinct feature in this area.

Afternoon After lunch, head to the **Stieglitz Museum** (*p129*), a short walk east of the **Summer Garden** (*p97*). The museum's collection features art and craft displays from all over Europe. Further east is the 19-century Cathedral of the Transfiguration (*p129*), worth a visit for its ornate interiors.

The magnificent Grand Cascade in Peterhof, comprised of over 140 fountains and canals

Putting St Petersburg on the Map

The Russian Federation, or Russia as it is usually known, is the world's largest country, covering an area of 17.4 million sq km (6.7 million sq miles). Situated in its northwest corner, St Petersburg is Russia's second city, with a population of just under five million. Once Russia's capital and known as its "window on the West" *(see pp22–3)*, the city was built on the marshy lands where the Neva joins the Gulf of Finland. Of the 12 countries bordering Russia, Estonia and Finland are St Petersburg's closest neighbours.

White Sea

Arkhangelsk

NORWAY

Dalälven

Oslo

FINLAND

Lake Ladoga

See inset map, right

Vologda

Helsinki

ST PETERSBURG

Kristian-sand

SWEDEN

Stockholm

Tallinn

Veliky Novgorod

Frederikshavn

Gothenburg

Oskarshamn

ESTONIA

Pärnu

Tartu

Pskov

Lovat

Volga

DENMARK

Baltic Sea

Riga

LATVIA

Liepāja

Moscow

Copenhagen

Malmö

Klaipėda

LITHUANIA

Smolensk

Tula

Koszalin

Kaliningrad

Vilnius

Orsha

Orël

Hamburg

Szczecin

Olsztyn

Białystok

Minsk

BELARUS

Gomel

Berlin

POLAND

Warsaw

Odra

Pripyat

GERMANY

Wrocław

Radom

Lviv

UKRAINE

Kiev

Dnepr

Prague

Danube

CZECH REPUBLIC

Brno

Košice

Dnestr

Munich

Vienna

Bratislava

SLOVAKIA

AUSTRIA

Budapest

Oradea

Chisinau

MOLDOVA

Odessa

HUNGARY

Targu Mureș

ITALY

SLOVENIA

Osijek

Timișoara

ROMANIA

Venice

CROATIA

Pitești

Bucharest

Black Sea

Bologna

BOSNIA-HERZEGOVINA

Belgrade

Ruse

Varna

Florence

Sarajevo

SERBIA

Ancona

Split

Niš

BULGARIA

Burgas

Rome

Adriatic Sea

Dubrovnik

MONTENEGRO

KOSOVO

Skopje

Sofia

Tirana

MACEDONIA

Istanbul

Naples

Bari

ALBANIA

GREECE

Bursa

Ankara

TURKEY

For key to symbols *see back flap*

St Petersburg and Environs

Pechora

Pechora

Ukhta

Pinega

Vychegda

Syktyvkar

Kotlas

Kirov

Kazan

Yaroslavl

Ulyanovsk

Vladimir

Ryazan

RUSSIAN
FEDERATION

Samara

Orenburg

Uralsk

Saratov

Balashov

Mikhaylovka

Volgograd

Kharkov

Mariupol

Rostov-na-Don

Elista

Astrakhan

Sea of
Azov

Don

Donets

Volga

Caspian
Sea

Fort-
Shevchenko

Aktau

Beyneu

Makat

Atyrau

KAZAKHSTAN

Shubarkudyk

Aktobe

Orsk

Sibay

Magnitogorsk

Ufa

Ural

Zhem

Shalkar

Yrgyz

Ustyurt Plateau

Aral
Sea

St Petersburg and Environs

0 km   50
0 miles   50

Primorsk

M10

Vaskelovo

A129

Lake
Ladoga

A123

Sestroretsk

Novaya
Ladoga

Gulf of Finland

A18

ST PETERSBURG

M18

Sosnovyy
Bor

Kirovsk

A121

Pulkovo

Kolpino

M11

Gatchina

Tosno

Kirishi

Volosovo

M20

Vyritsa

M10

A115

Key

- Motorway
- Major road
- Minor road
- Railway
- International boundary
- Ferry route

0 km   180
0 miles   180

Putting Russia on the Map

Arctic
Ocean

St Petersburg

RUSSIAN FEDERATION

EUROPE

KAZAKHSTAN

CHINA

INDIA

AFRICA

Pacific
Ocean

Central St Petersburg

St Petersburg's five central areas as described in this book each have their own character, reflecting different sides of the city's past. The southern bank of the Neva, Palace Embankment, is lined with glorious, stately palaces. Gostinyy Dvor, to the east, has always been the commercial hub of the city with shops, bars and restaurants lining Nevskiy prospekt. To the west lies Sennaya Ploshchad, a mixture of romantic, tree-lined canals and reminders of the 19th-century low life of Dostoevsky's novels. Vasilevskiy Island, the city's largest, combines a naval heritage with scholarly institutions and museums. Petrogradskaya, to the north, is dominated by the Peter and Paul Fortress.

Vasilevskiy Island
Adorned with figures representing four great Russian rivers, the Rostral Columns (*see p62*) stand on the eastern tip of the island. From here there are sweeping views of the Neva and its embankments.

For keys to symbols *see back flap*

Petrogradskaya
Burial place of the Romanov tsars, the Cathedral of SS Peter and Paul *(see p70)* stands in the fortress where Peter the Great began building the city in 1703. Its gilded spire dominates the skyline of Petrogradskaya, an area otherwise characterized by many splendid Style-Moderne buildings.

Gostinyy Dvor
Nevskiy prospekt, the city's main artery, is crossed by waterways such as Moyka river *(see p38)*, shown here. These intersections are bustling in the summer, with cafés on river boats and by the water's edge.

Palace Embankment
Part of the Hermitage, the former imperial Winter Palace *(see pp94–5)*, dominates this grand waterfront with a burst of Baroque splendour. The embankment is lined with monuments from the famous Bronze Horseman *(see p80)* to Peter the Great's modest Summer Palace *(see p97)*.

0 metres   600

0 yards   600

Sennaya Ploshchad
Yusopov Palace *(see p122)* has ornate interiors and houses an exhibition on Gregory Rasputin. The surrounding area, with quiet streets lining its canals, is perfect for walks during the atmospheric White Nights.

THE HISTORY OF ST PETERSBURG

Founded in 1703, within ten years St Petersburg had become capital of the vast Russian Empire and quickly gained a reputation as one of Europe's most beautiful cities. In the 20th century it underwent three name changes, three revolutions and a 900-day siege. For a city less than 300 years old, it has an amazing history.

Long before St Petersburg was established as a city, the lands bordering the Neva River were inhabited by a population of various ethnic groups, including the Slavs and Finns. It was around 12,000 BC when the Finno-Ugric population, the Votes and Izhorians, migrated east from the Ural Mountains, to the Neva River basin. The area is rich with history and ancient sites dating back to 9,000 years have been discovered here.

The Neva opened up a route between the Baltic nations and the Byzantine Empire from the 8th to 13th century. By the 9th century, it was a part of the Veliky Novgorod Republic, and it was here that constant territorial wars with Sweden took place. A major battle broke out between the two powers in 1240, and the Russian army, led by the 20-year-old Prince Alexander Yaroslavich (later known as Alexander Nevsky), defeated the Swedes.

Painting by Mikhaylovich Vasnetsov depicting Viking ships at Vliky Novgorod

In the 16th century, Novgorod was suppressed by the nobility in Moscow, which resented the control the Republic had over access to the trade routes. Consequently, the lands along the Neva River were declared as part of the centralized Russian state. At the dawn of the 17th century, the demise of the last Riurik tsar – Fiodor Ioanovich, son of Ivan the Terrible – left the country in upheaval. Vasily Shuisky, the new ruler, asked the Swedes to support his government. The Swedes, realizing just how weak the divided country was, went on to occupy a significant portion of north-western Russia.

The First Romanovs

Following 15 years of unrest and power struggles among the ruling class, the nobility chose Mikhail Romanov as the tsar in 1613, thus initiating the 300-year Romanov rule. Under Mikhail, Russia recovered from her upheavals, but his greatest legacy was his son Aleksey. Intelligent and pious, Aleksey modernized the state, encouraging an influx of foreign architects, codifying laws and asserting the power of the state over the church.

800	1000	1200	1400	1600
	862 Rurik establishes Viking stronghold at Novgorod	**1147** Moscow is founded	**1480** Ivan III stops paying tribute to Mongols	
	863 Cyril and Methodius create early version of Cyrillic		**1462–1505** Reign of Ivan III	**1605–13** Time of Troubles
	1108 Town of Vladimir is founded	**1223** First Mongol raid	**1242** Alexander Nevsky defeats the Teutonic Knights	**1533–84** Reign of Ivan IV the Terrible	**1613** Mikhail Romanov becomes first tsar of the Romanov dynasty
988 Prince Vladimir converts to Orthodox Christianity		**1240** Mongol rule established in Rus		**1598** Boris Godunov claims title of tsar after 12 years as regent	

Boris Godunov

◄ Peter the Great instructing his workers during the building of St Petersburg (Alexander von Kotzebue, 1862)

Peter the Great

In the transition from a medieval to a more modern state, the future Peter the Great, founder of St Petersburg, was born. After his father Aleksey's death, Peter's childhood was overshadowed by severe rivalry between his mother's family, the Naryshkins, and that of his father's first wife, the Miloslavskiys. At the age of ten Peter ascended the throne, but the Streltsy Guards, influenced by the Miloslavskiys, started a bloody revolt. As a result Peter's sickly half-brother Ivan became his co-tsar, and Ivan's sister Sophia their regent. The memory of seeing his family brutally killed caused his hatred of Moscow and distrust of its conservative, scheming society.

Peter the Great (1682–1725)

When Ivan died in 1696, the 24-year-old Peter had grown into a giant of a man with a tempestuous combination of willpower and energy. Long hours spent drilling toy soldiers as a child developed into a full-scale reform of the Russian army. But Peter's dream was of a Russian navy. In 1697, he went on a European tour to study shipbuilding and other wondrous achievements. To everyone's dismay the young tsar spent more hours working at the docks than socializing at court. On his return to Russia he lost no time in bringing in westernizing reforms.

A New Capital

It was Peter's determination to found a northern port with an unrestricted passage to the Baltic that led to war with Sweden, at the time one of the strongest countries in Europe. By May 1703 Peter had secured the Neva river and began to build the Peter and Paul Fortress and a shipyard opposite (see pp22–3). Only an autocrat with Peter's drive could have succeeded in building a city on this fetid

Illustration in watercolours of the Naval Academy in St Petersburg, by artist Mochkot

| 1672 Birth of Peter the Great at Kolomenskoe Palace, Moscow | 1689 Peter banishes Sophia to Novodevichy Monastery, Moscow | 1697–8 Peter tours western Europe | 1698 Peter destroys the Streltsy Guards (see p22) | 1703 St Petersburg is founded |
| | | | | 1712 Seat of government moves to St Petersburg |

1680   **1690**   **1700**   **1710**

| 1682 The Streltsy rebellion. Peter becomes co-tsar with half-brother Ivan V, under regency of his half-sister Sophia | 1696 Ivan V dies; Peter becomes sole ruler | 1700 Start of Northern War against Sweden | 1714 Peter forbids the use of stone in buildings, except in St Petersburg |
| | | 1709 Victory over Charles XII of Sweden at Battle of Poltava | |

Sophia, regent 1682–9

Life at Elizabeth's Court

When Elizabeth was not busy looking over architectural plans, she would lie around on her bed, gossiping with a group of ladies whose chief task it was to tickle her feet. Her restless nature meant that her courtiers had to endure endless hunts and skating parties, and were required to keep her company at all hours. Her riotous cross-dressing masquerades were notorious, as was her vast wardrobe, allegedly containing over 15,000 dresses.

Tsarina Elizabeth going for a stroll at Tsarskoe Selo, surrounded by eager courtiers

bogland, where building materials were in short supply and disastrous floodings regular. More than 40,000 Swedish prisoners-of-war and peasants laboured and perished here, their bones contributing to the city's foundations.

Whether or not it was always Peter's intention to make this his new capital, it only became possible after his decisive victory at Poltava in 1709 put an end to the Swedish threat. St Petersburg was named capital of Russia in 1712 and, by Peter's death in 1725, there were 40,000 inhabitants in the city and many more in the surrounding labour encampments.

The Petticoat Period

For most of the rest of the 18th century Russia was ruled by women, whose taste did much to set the celebrated architectural tone of St Petersburg.

During the brief reigns of Peter's wife Catherine I (1725–27) and his grandson Peter II (1727–30), the court abandoned this frontier city for the more comfortable life in Moscow. But when the throne passed to Anna, daughter of Peter's co-tsar Ivan, she decided to create a recognizably European court in St Petersburg. Anna was 37 at the time, and had spent most of her life in Germany. This was obvious in her choice of ministers and favourites, of whom many were German. Fashion and style, however, were imported from France and opera from Italy. Though she herself was serious, plain and somewhat cruel, Anna did much to put the court on a footing with the most frivolous in Europe, as well as encouraging a flowering of culture.

Tsarina Elizabeth, daughter of Peter the Great, was the ideal successor to this

Elizabeth (1741–61)

twittering court. Elizabeth was attractive, energetic and cheerful, a combination that endeared her to almost everyone, especially the Guards who helped secure her place on the throne. She left the affairs of state to a series of well chosen advisors. The only element of seriousness lay in Elizabeth's perhaps surprising piety, which at times led her to retire temporarily into a convent. Her chief legacy is the splendid Baroque architecture she commissioned, mainly designed by her favourite architect Rastrelli *(see p95)*.

1720	1730	1740	1750

1721 Peace of Nystad ends war with Sweden

1733 Cathedral of SS Peter and Paul is finished after 12 years' work

1738 Russia's first ballet school is founded in St Petersburg

1745 Tsarevich Peter marries the future Catherine the Great

1757 St Petersburg Academy of Arts is founded

1717 Peter travels to Holland and France

1725 Catherine I is empress after death of Peter the Great

1727–30 Reign of Peter II

1730–40 Reign of Anna

1741 Anna's successor Ivan VI is deposed; Elizabeth takes power, supported by Guards' officers

Anna Ivanovna, daughter of Ivan V

1754 Rastrelli's Winter Palace is begun

Peter's New City

Determined to drag his country out of the medieval period, and inspired by the few Westerners he met in Moscow, Peter the Great was the first tsar to travel to Europe. He returned with many ideas for reforms and architectural novelties which he put into practice in his new city. In 1710, when the Swedish threat was over, the reluctant imperial family and government were moved to this chilly, damp outland. But Peter was adamant and soon a rational street plan, stone buildings and academies made St Petersburg a thriving capital in which fashions and discoveries from Europe were tried out before filtering through to the rest of Russia.

Extent of the City

 1712   ☐ Today

Plan of the New City

This map of 1712 shows Peter's original plan for his capital, with Vasilevskiy Island as centre. This was abandoned due to the hazards of crossing the Neva, and the city spread out around the Admiralty instead.

The Carpenter Tsar
During his 1697–8 tour of Europe, Peter (to the left in this picture) spent months at the Deptford Docks, labouring with his men to learn the basics of shipbuilding.

Based on Amsterdam, the original city grid was meant to follow a strict network of canals but this had to change (see p59).

Menshikov Palace

New Fashions
Peter's desire to westernize Russia led to a rule forcing his courtiers to have their bushy beards shaved off.

The Streltsy Rebellion

As a result of a malicious rumour that Peter's relatives planned the murder of his half-brother Ivan, in 1682 the Streltsy Guard regiments invaded the Kremlin. A horrifying massacre took place in front of the 10-year-old Peter who saw his advisor and members of his family murdered. This traumatic event is probably what caused Peter's facial tic and certainly his wish to build another capital city. In 1698 he took a terrible revenge by torturing over a thousand Streltsy Guards to death.

Brutal murders in the Kremlin, 1682

The Battle of Poltava
The struggle with Sweden for control over the Baltic led to the Great Northern War. Nine years after the embarrassing defeat at Narva, Peter the Great's army reforms bore fruit. In 1709 he won a decisive battle over Charles XII at Poltava, and thereby Russia's first victory over a major European power.

Where to see Peter the Great's City

Some of the buildings from the earliest days of St Petersburg still exist in the city centre, including the rustic Peter the Great's Cabin (*p75*), the Summer Palace (*p97*) and the Baroque Menshikov Palace (*p64*). Much of Peter and Paul Fortress (*pp68–9*) also dates from this time. It is also well worth visiting Monplaisir, Peter's first home at Peterhof (*pp150–53*).

Peter the Great's workshop, the Summer Palace

Kronwerk (outer defence walls)

Peter and Paul Fortress

The port was here until the 1880s.

Admiralty

Summer Palace

Marshy soil and a lack of local stone made construction difficult. Thousands of labourers died during the first stages.

Wine Goblet
The tsar, who could hold his drink, enjoyed pressing alcohol on his guests until they passed out. This elegant crystal goblet belonged to his close friend Alexander Menshikov and is engraved with his coat of arms.

Mice Bury the Cat
Coloured woodcuts, *lubki*, served as political cartoons in Peter's day. The tsar was always portrayed as a cat on account of his moustache.

Catherine I
After an unsuccessful first marriage, Peter was drawn to a Lithuanian girl who had followed the army back from the wars in 1704. Her healthy good looks were brought to the tsar's attention by Alexander Menshikov (*see p64*). Although only two daughters survived, their marriage was happy and Catherine succeeded Peter as the first woman on Russia's throne.

Catherine II

The future Catherine the Great, a German princess, was chosen by Elizabeth as a wife for her successor, the petty-minded Peter III.

Catherine the Great in 1762

When Peter ascended the throne in 1761 Catherine had resided in Russia for 18 years and was fully fluent in Russian. She had made it her duty to steep herself in the Russian culture which she later came to adore. Six months into Peter's reign, Catherine and her allies in the Imperial Guard deposed him; the tsar was assassinated within days and his wife was crowned Catherine II.

By Catherine's death at the age of 67, her reputation as an enlightened leader *(see p26)* had been overshadowed by her illiberal reaction to the news of the French Revolution in 1789 and by scandalous rumours concerning her later love affairs. She left a country vastly enlarged after successful campaigns against Turkey and Poland, however, in the hands of her short-lived son Paul.

War and Peace

During the Napoleonic Wars, under Catherine the Great's grandson Alexander I, Russia finally took its place alongside the other great European powers.

Much was expected of the new tsar who was in thrall to the ideals of enlightened government. Russia was by now desperately in need of reform. Of particular concern was the plight of the peasantry, who were tied to the land in serfdom. However, the necessities of war subsumed everything, and no inroads were made against the Russian autocracy during Alexander I's reign.

Determined to harness the wave of Russian patriotism, Alexander joined Britain and marched against Napoleon in Austria in 1805. After the crushing defeat at the battle of Austerlitz, however, the inexperienced tsar retreated, his army having lost 11,000 men.

At the Peace of Tilsit, signed in 1807, Napoleon divided Europe into French and Russian spheres, lulling Alexander into a false sense of security. In 1812 the French emperor invaded Russia, but was defeated by its size and climate. The Russian army followed his forces to Paris, taking part in the allied campaign which led Napoleon to abdicate in 1814. In celebration, Alexander commissioned a series of imposing public edifices in a fitting Empire style, including the General Staff Building with its imposing arch on Palace Square.

Murder of Paul I, 1801. Despite all his precautions, Catherine's unstable, paranoid son was murdered in a coup in his own fortified palace *(see p103)*

1760		1780		1800	
1762 Death of Elizabeth. Peter III becomes emperor but is murdered after six months. His wife takes the throne as Catherine II	**1783** Annexation of the Crimea	**1787–92** 2nd Russo-Turkish War	**1801** Paul I murdered. Alexander I becomes tsar	**1805–7** War with France ends with Treaty of Tilsit	
1767 Catherine II publishes her *Bolshoy Nakaz*	**1773–5** Pugachev Rebellion **1768–74** 1st Russo-Turkish War	**1782** Falconet's statue, the Bronze Horseman, is completed	**1796** Death of Catherine II; Paul I accedes *Alexander I (1801–25)*	**1812** Napoleon invades Russia **1816** Alexander I clamps down on reforms	

Decembrist rebels defeated by tsarist troops, 1825

The Decembrist Rebellion

Officers of the Russian army who had witnessed the freedoms of democratic Europe were frustrated by Alexander's failure to consider constitutional reform. When his stern brother Nicholas was declared tsar in 1825, these liberals rallied their soldiers to support the older brother Constantine, who had given up his rights to the throne, in the hope that he would be more open-minded. They made a stand on 14 December on what is now Senate Square *(see p80)*. Troops loyal to the tsar were instructed to fire on the rebels, killing hundreds before the leaders surrendered. The new tsar, Nicholas I, treated them with the severity which was to become the hallmark of his reign. Five leading figures were hanged, and over a hundred exiled to Siberia.

A City of Rich and Poor

For much of the 19th century, a walk along Nevskiy prospekt offered a microcosm of an increasingly divided society. Striding past drunks, beggars and prostitutes, the city's courtiers, cocky young officers and leading citizens headed for shops selling imported fashionable accessories, or to the distin-guished delicatessen Yeliseev's to buy caviar and champagne. They often lived beyond their means, mortgaging their serfs and lands to keep up with the astronomical costs of their luxurious lives. This was also a city in which the salary of a low-ranking government clerk was never sufficient to feed a family. In the countryside, tension was growing among the serfs tied to the large estates of the aristocracy. With such blatant inequality, pressure for political reform was inevitable.

After the unrelenting autocracy of Nicholas I, the "Iron Tsar", liberals welcomed the reign of his fair-minded son Alexander II. In 1861, the tsar passed the Edict of Emancipation, abolishing serfdom, but requiring peasants to buy their land at far from advantageous terms. Thus industriali-zation finally took off as peasants flocked to the big cities to work in factories, only to be met by even worse living conditions.

The Napoleonic Invasion

Napoleon's Grand Army of 600,000 men reached Moscow in September 1812, after the victory at Borodino, but was defeated by the tactics of non-engagement devised by the great Russian hero General Kutuzov. Finding himself in a city abandoned by its rulers and set on fire by its people, and with the Russian winter ahead, Napoleon was forced into a retreat over the frozen countryside. He eventually reached the border, with only 30,000 men left alive.

French army retreating from Moscow 1812

1822 Abolition of Masonic and secret societies

1833 Pushkin publishes *The Bronze Horseman*

1855 Death of Nicholas I; Alexander II succeeds him

1853–6 Crimean War

Leo Tolstoy

1865–9 Tolstoy writes *War and Peace*

1820

1840

1860

1825 The Decembrist Rebellion. Nicholas I becomes tsar

1851 The "Nicholas Railway" opens between Moscow and St Petersburg

1861 Emancipation of serfs

1864 Reforms in local government, law and education

1818 Construction of St Isaac's Cathedral starts

The Enlightened Empress

Born a minor German princess, Catherine II was a learned and energetic woman. She recognized the importance of the great Enlightenment philosophers Voltaire and Diderot, with whom she corresponded. She bought impressive collections of European art for the Hermitage *(see pp86–95)*, libraries for Russia's scholars and talked much about reducing the burden on Russia's serfs. However, a peasant uprising in the 1770s and news of the French Revolution in 1789 put paid to her liberal notions and, when she died, the majority of Russians were just as badly off as before.

Extent of the City

 1790   ☐ Today

Royal Guards Swear Allegiance
On 28 June 1762, Catherine usurped the throne of her unpopular husband Peter III in a palace coup. The guards regiments flocked to support her and the tsar was assassinated on 6 July.

The Temple alludes to Catherine's passion for Neo-Classical architecture.

A medal is presented to Count Orlov for his victory over the Turks at Chesma in 1770.

Catherine the Great

Catherine II "the Great" (1762–96) pursued an expansionist foreign policy. Russia's first naval victory, leading to the annexation of the Crimea, is commemorated allegorically on this fabric.

Count Alexey Orlov, brother of Catherine's one-time lover Grigoriy, played an important role in her takeover of the throne.

Catherine's Instructions
In 1767 the 36-year-old Catherine published her 22-chapter *Great Instruction (Bolshoy Nakaz)*. The book is a collection of ideas on which a reform of Russia's legal system was to be based.

Pretender Pugachev
The greatest threat to Catherine's reign was caused by the Cossack Pugachev who claimed to be Peter III. He was arrested, but escaped to lead a widespread peasant uprising which broke out in 1773 and only ended with his execution in 1775.

The New Academy of Sciences
Catherine, who founded over 25 major academic institutions in Russia, also commissioned new buildings for those already existing. Quarenghi built the Neo-Classical Academy of Sciences in 1783–5.

Where to see the Neo-Classical City

Catherine had the Marble Palace (see p96) and the Tauride Palace (see p130) erected for two of her lovers, and added the Small and Large Hermitage and the theatre (see p86) to the Winter Palace. Her architect Cameron designed the Cameron Gallery and the Agate Rooms at Tsarskoe Selo (see p154–7) and Pavlovsk Palace (see pp160–63).

Grecian Hall at Pavlovsk, created by Charles Cameron in 1782–6

Catherine is portrayed as Pallas Athena, goddess of wisdom and warfare, with her attributes of a shield and helmet.

Empire-Style Vase (1790)
Porcelain was much prized at court. In 1744 the first Russian producer, the Imperial Porcelain Factory, opened in St Petersburg.

The fabric, used for a screen, was made by the Pernons factory, Lyons, in 1770.

Mikhail Lomonosov
A philosopher, historian, linguist and scientist, Lomonosov (1711–65) personified the intellectual enlightenment of 18th-century Russia (see p63). This sculpture of him as a boy by the seashore refers to his fisherman origins.

Grigoriy Potemkin (1739–91)
Of all her lovers, Catherine respected and admired Prince Potemkin the most. He was a successful general and an influential counsellor. They remained friends until his death.

Alexander II was murdered by a revolutionary group in 1881. Tragically, he is said to have had the plans for a Russian parliament in his pocket

The Death of Tsarist Russia

Pressure for reform had built up such a head of steam that in 1881, when still no radical changes had taken place, a revolutionary group murdered Alexander II. The reign of Alexander III was one of fervent reaction. The press was under strict censorship and the secret police more active than ever. But workers began to get organized and opposition was growing. Nicholas II took over a country on the verge of breakdown, in spite of the rapid industrialization of the 1890s. The unsuccessful war with Japan (1904–5) was followed by "Bloody Sunday". On 9 January 1905 a peaceful demonstration carried a petition to the tsar only to be met by bullets. News of the massacre spread like wildfire and the 1905 Revolution broke out with strikes all over Russia. To avert further disaster, Nicholas II promised basic civil rights and an elected Duma (parliament) with the right to veto legislation. However, the tsar simply dissolved the parliament whenever it displeased him. This high-handed behaviour, along with the royal family's unpopular intimate friendship with Rasputin *(see p123)*, further damaged the Romanovs' reputation.

The outbreak of World War I brought a surge of patriotism which the tsar sought to ride. But, by late 1916, Russia had lost three and a half million men, morale at the front was low and food supplies at home scarce.

Red Army badge

World of Art Movement

The oppressive political climate at the turn of the century did not prevent art from flourishing. A small group of St Petersburg artists, including Bakst and Benois, grew into an influential creative movement under the inspired leadership of Sergey Diaghilev. Western art was introduced in their stylish *World of Art* magazine, while their stage designs and costumes for the Ballets Russes *(see p120)* brought Russian culture to the West.

Costume design by Leon Bakst, 1911

Revolution and Civil War

In February 1917 strikes broke out in the capital, now renamed Petrograd. The tsar was forced to abdicate, his family put under arrest and a Provisional Government set up. But revolutionaries returning from exile organized themselves and, in October, an armed revolution overthrew the government *(see pp30–31)*.

1902 Lenin publishes *What is to be Done?*

1881 Alexander II is assassinated by the "People's Will" group. Alexander III becomes tsar.

1898 Social-Democratic Workers' party is founded. Russian museum opens

The Romanov family in 1913

1913 300th anniversary of Romanov rule

1880

1900

1881–2 Anti-semitic pogroms

1894 Alexander III dies, Nicholas II accedes

1903 Pro-violence Bolsheviks (under Lenin) secede from Social-Democratic Workers' party

1905 The 1905 Revolution is followed by the inauguration of the first Duma in 1906

1887 Lenin's brother is hanged for attempt on the tsar's life

1904–5 Russo-Japanese War

1914 Outbreak of WWI; St Petersburg changes name to Petrograd

The leading Bolshevik party proved to be as careless of democracy as the tsar but, in March 1918, they kept their promise to take Russia out of the war. The army was desperately needed at home to fight the developing civil war. The Bolsheviks (Reds) found themselves threatened by a diverse coalition of anti-revolutionary groups which came to be known as the "Whites", initially supported by foreign intervention. It was the threat of the Whites rallying opposition around the royal family that led to their execution in July 1918. But the Whites were a disparate force and, by November 1920, the last troops had abandoned the struggle, leaving a devastated Soviet Russia to face two years of appalling famine. To manage, Lenin had to revise his aggressive "War Communism" nationalization project. His slightly milder New Economic Policy allowed for private enterprise.

The imperial palaces around St Petersburg were totally destroyed by the Germans in World War II. This photo shows Pavlovsk *(see pp160–63)* in 1944

The Stalin Years

In the five years after Lenin's death in 1924, Joseph Stalin used his position as General Secretary of the Communist Party to eliminate all rivals. He then established his long dictatorship.

The terror began in earnest with the collectivization of agriculture which forced the peasants to give up all livestock, machinery and land to collective farms. During this time, and in the ensuing famine of 1931–2, up to 10 million people are thought to have died.

A first major purge of intellectuals took place in urban areas in 1928–9. Then, in

Joseph Stalin on a propaganda poster from 1933

December 1934, Sergey Kirov, the party leader in Leningrad, was assassinated on the secret orders of Stalin *(see p74)*. Blamed on an anti-Stalinist cell, the assassination was used as the rationale for five years of purges throughout the country. By the time they were over, some 15 million people had been arrested, many sent to the Gulag (labour camps) and over a million executed.

Stalin's purge of the Red Army boded ill for World War II, for he had got rid of three-quarters of his officers. When the Germans invaded Russia in 1941 they cut off Leningrad in less than three months, subjecting the city to a 900-day siege *(see p133)* which left more than two million people dead, half of them civilians. Leningrad came to be known as a "Hero City".

The Germans were eventually defeated, but the Russian people, who lost 20 million souls to the war, were subjected to a renewed terror by Stalin, which lasted until his death in March 1953.

| **1917** The Russian Revolution *(see pp30–31)* | **1929** Collectivization of private land | **1934** Leningrad Party Secretary Kirov is killed; Stalin's purges intensify | **1939** Nazi-Soviet pact |
| **1918** Civil War starts. Capital moves to Moscow | **1924** Lenin dies; Petrograd is named Leningrad | | | **1941** Nazis attack Russia; Siege of Leningrad starts | **1947** The term "Cold War" is coined |

1920   **1940**

| **1921** Lenin bans all opposition after the Kronstadt mutiny | **1925** Trotsky is expelled from the Politburo | **1932** Socialist Realism is the only officially approved style in art | **1944** The Siege ends |
| | **1922** Stalin becomes General Secretary of the Party | | **1942** First performance of Shostakovich's *Seventh Symphony* in besieged Leningrad |

Sergey Kirov

The Russian Revolution

St Petersburg is known as the cradle of the Russian Revolution, a central event in the history of the 20th century. After the 1917 February Revolution which led to the abdication of Tsar Nicholas II, the Provisional Government declared a political amnesty. Exiled revolutionaries such as Lenin and Trotsky flooded into the city. By setting up a network of Workers' and Soldiers' Soviets, representative councils elected by the people, they established an alternative government. In October, when soldiers had deserted from the front in droves, the revolutionary leaders decided on an armed uprising which brought the Communists to power.

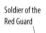

Extent of the City
▨ 1917   ☐ Today

The Ex-Tsar
Nicholas II, seen here clearing snow at Tsarskoe Selo during his house arrest in March 1917, was later taken with his family to Yekaterinburg where they were murdered.

Soldier of the Red Guard

Looting was tempting for the mob of sailors and soldiers, especially in the palace's well-stocked wine cellars.

Storming the Winter Palace

Late on the evening of 25 October 1917 the battleship Aurora *(see p75) fired some blank shots at the Winter Palace. The Red Guard, trained by Trotsky at the Smolnyy Institute, stormed the palace. Their aim was the arrest of the Provisional Government, unsuccessfully defended by 300 Cossacks.*

The Cossacks, who defended the palace with some cadets and members of the Women's Battalion, were too few to offer any serious resistance.

Lenin, Leader of the People
A charismatic speaker, as shown in this painting by Victor Ivanov, Lenin returned from exile in April to lead the Revolution. By 1918, his Bolshevik faction had shown their determination to rule.

Revolutionary Plate
Various ceramics with revolutionary themes, mixed with touches of Russian folklore, were produced to celebrate every occasion, in this case the Third International.

Leon Trotsky
The intellectual Trotsky played a leading military role in the Revolution. In 1927, during the power struggle after Lenin's death, he was exiled by Stalin. In 1940 he was murdered in Mexico by a Stalinist agent.

Propaganda
One hallmark of the Soviet regime was its propaganda. Artists were employed to design posters spreading its message through striking graphics. War Communism during the Civil War (1918–20) was encouraged by posters such as this one, extolling the "Workers' and Peasants' Defence".

Avant-Garde Art
Even before 1917, Russia's artists had been in a state of revolution, producing the world's first truly abstract paintings. A great example of this new movement is *Supremus No. 56*, painted in 1916 by Kazimir Malevich.

Ministers of the Provisional Government tried to keep order but were arrested.

New Values
Traditions were radically altered by the Revolution; instead of church weddings, couples exchanged vows under the red flag. Loudly trumpeted sexual equality meant that women had to work twice as hard – at home and in the factories.

1917 The February Revolution	**March** The tsar is persuaded to abdicate. Provisional Government is led by Prince Lvov	**October** Bolsheviks storm Winter Palace after signal from *Aurora* and expel Provisional Government	**March** Bolsheviks sign Brest-Litovsk peace treaty with Germany. Capital is moved to Moscow

1917

July Kerensky becomes Prime Minister of Provisional Government

Cruiser Aurora

1918

1918 January Trotsky becomes Commissar of War

December Lenin forms the CHEKA (secret police)

July Start of Civil War. Tsar and family are murdered in prison at Yekaterinburg

The Washington Dove of Peace, a Russian caricature (1953) from the days of the Cold War

Thaw and Stagnation

Three years after Stalin's death his successor Nikita Khrushchev denounced Stalin's crimes at the Twentieth Party Congress and the period known as "The Thaw" began. Political prisoners were released, and Solzhenitsyn's *One Day In the Life of Ivan Denisovich*, about life in the Gulag, was published.

In foreign affairs, things were not so liberal. Soviet tanks invaded Hungary in 1956 to prevent the country seceding from the

Warsaw Pact and, in 1962, Khrushchev's decision to put nuclear missiles on Cuba brought the world to the brink of nuclear war.

When Leonid Brezhnev took over in 1964, the intellectual climate froze once more and the persecution of political dissidents was stepped up. The first ten years of his regime were a time of relative plenty. But beneath the surface a vast black market and network of corruption was growing. The party apparatchiks, who benefited most from the corruption, had no interest in rocking the boat. When Brezhnev died in 1982, the politburo was determined to prevent the accession of a younger generation. Brezhnev was followed by 68-year-old Yuriy Andropov and, when he died, 72-year-old Chernenko.

Glasnost and Perestroika

When 53-year-old Mikhail Gorbachev announced his policies of *glasnost* (openness) and *perestroika* (restructuring), when he took over in 1985, he had no idea what would follow and that the end of the Soviet Union was in sight.

Mikhail Gorbachev and George Bush

For the first time since 1917 the elections to the Congress of People's Deputies in 1989 contained an element of genuine choice, with rebels such as Boris Yeltsin and human rights campaigner Andrey Sakharov winning seats. In 1991, local elections brought nationalist candidates to power in the

---

First in Space

It was under Krushchev that the Soviet Union achieved her greatest coup against the West, launching the first Sputnik into space in 1957. That same year the dog Laika was the first living creature in space, aboard Sputnik II. She never came down again, but four years later Yuriy Gagarin made spectacular history as the first man in space, returning to a hero's welcome. The Soviets lost the race to put a man on the moon, but their space programme worked as powerful propaganda, backing up the claims of politicians that Russia would soon catch up with and overtake the prosperity of the West.

Sputnik II and the space dog Laika, 1957

1950	1960	1970	1980

1950–1954 Korean War

1961 Stalin's body removed from its place alongside Lenin in Red Square. Yuriy Gagarin is first man in space

1962 Cuban missile crisis

1964 Brezhnev becomes General Secretary

1970 Solzhenitsyn wins Nobel Prize for Literature

1979 USSR invades Afghanistan

1982 Death of Brezhnev; replaced by Andropov

1953 Stalin dies

1955 Krushchev comes to power. Warsaw Pact is established

1957 Sputnik I is launched

1956 Stalin denounced by Khrushchev at 20th Party Congress. Hungarian uprising is crushed

1968 Soviet troops enter Czechoslovakia to suppress "Prague Spring"

1969 Strategic Arms Limitation Talks (SALT) with USA

Leonid Brezhnev (1906–82)

1984 Andropov is replaced by Chernenko

Demonstrations on Palace Square during the 1991 coup

work and travel, others cry out for a return to Communism and the albeit limited social protection it offered.

The social problems are still being resolved. Major international companies flooded in, and by early 1999 relative stability had been achieved. The elections of December 1999 dramatically reduced the power of the Communists, bringing in young liberal reformers and confirming optimism about Russia's future. The religious revival continues, and churches of all denominations have been restored to their original purpose.

republics, and democrats in the major Russian local councils. Russia and the Baltic Republics seceded from the Soviet Union, while the people of Leningrad, always in the vanguard of progressive movements and led by the reformist lecturer in law, Anatoly Sobchak, voted to restore the city's original name, St Petersburg.

With his momentous victory in the election for President of the Russian Republic, Yeltsin was able to deal the death blow to the Soviet Union. It came after the military coup against Gorbachev in August 1991, when Yeltsin's stand against tanks in Moscow made him a hero. In St Petersburg no tanks were on the street, but nonetheless Sobchak rallied supporters of democracy. By the end of the year, the Soviet Union no longer existed.

The new Russian State Emblem

In March 2000, Vladimir Putin was elected President of the Russian Federation, and re-elected in 2004. Dmitry Medvedev became President in 2008, with Putin as Prime Minister. In 2012, Putin and Medvedev switched roles, much to the dismay of many Russians who took to the streets in protest. The next elections are scheduled to be held in 2018.

St Petersburg Today

The economic reforms which Russia has undergone since 1991 have widened the gap between rich and poor and, while some revel in the new opportunities for

A church wedding, popular again since religion has gained new importance among the young

1991 Yeltsin becomes President of Russia. Dissolution of the USSR on 25 December

1998 Nicholas II is reburied with his family in SS Peter and Paul Cathedral on 17 July

2004 Putin is re-elected as President for a second term

2008 Georgian–South Ossetian Conflict; Russia recognizes the independence of Abkhazia and South Ossetia

2012 Putin becomes President again and Medvedev, Prime Minister

1990

2000

2010

2020

1990 Gorbachev is elected President of the USSR and awarded the Nobel Peace Prize

2000 Putin becomes President of Russia

2008 Medvedev becomes President of Russia; Putin becomes Prime Minister

2004 Beslan Siege; 300 people killed in a Beslan school by Chechen rebels

1989 USSR leaves Afganistan

ST PETERSBURG AT A GLANCE

A city built on water, St Petersburg offers beautiful scenery and a wide range of sights. The Peter and Paul Fortress *(see pp68–9)*, the city's first building, contrasts with Baroque monasteries and Neo-Classical palaces. The city's short but stormy history is reflected in many of its museums, which display everything from Catherine the Great's fine art collection in the Hermitage to memorabilia of the Revolution in the Kshesinskaya Mansion *(see p74)*.

To help you make the most of your stay, the following 12 pages are a time-saving guide to the best museums and palaces and the most interesting of the many bridges and waterways. The cultural figures that made St Petersburg a city of importance are also featured. Below is a selection of sights that should not be missed by any visitor.

St Petersburg's Top Ten Attractions

Russian Museum
See pp106–9

Mariinskiy Theatre
See p121

Nevskiy Prospekt
See pp48–51

Stieglitz Museum
See p129

Church on Spilled Blood
See p102

The Hermitage
See pp86–95

Cathedral of Our Lady of Kazan
See p113

St Isaac's Cathedral
See pp82–3

Cathedral of SS Peter and Paul
See p70

Alexander Nevsky Monastery
See pp132–3

◀ Statue of Mikhail Barclay de Tolly in front of the Kazan Cathedral

St Petersburg's Best: Bridges and Waterways

Like its waterbound sisters, Amsterdam and Venice, St Petersburg is built around a network of canals and rivers which are still the lifeblood of the city. They contribute to its unique atmosphere by creating eerie mists which rise from the ice-laden waters in winter and, in summer, form a glittering mirror of façades during the glowing sunsets and bright White Nights.

Bridges, necessary for communication between the islands, were also an excellent means to adorn the city with decorative sculptures, elaborate lampposts and wrought-iron work.

A walk or a boat trip *(see pp134–41, pp228–9)* is the best way to enjoy them.

Winter Canal
Laid out in 1718–20, this narrow canal is crossed by three bridges and Yuriy Velten's Hermitage Theatre foyer (1783–7).

PETROGRADSKAYA
(see pp66–75)

Malaya Neva

NABEREZHNAYA MAKAROVA

SREDNIY PR

VASILEVSKIY ISLAND
(see pp58–65)

BOLSHOY PR

UNIVERSITETSKAYA NAB

Bol Neva

DVORTSOVAYA NAB

PALACE EMBANKMENT
(see pp76–97)

ANGLIYSKAYA NAB

ISAAKIYEVSKAYA PLOSHCHAD

Moyka

SENNAYA PLOSHCHAD
(see pp116–125)

VOZNESENSKIY PROSPEKT

SENNAYA PLOSHCH...

Fontanka

Blagoveshchenskiy Bridge
Rebuilt in 1936–8, this bridge still retains its original cast-iron seahorse railings, designed by Bryullov.

Lion Bridge
One of the earliest of its kind, this pedestrian suspension bridge dates from 1825–6. Its cables are anchored inside four cast-iron lions, by sculptor Pavel Sokolov.

Egyptian Bridge
This bridge spanning the Fontanka was decorated in the Egyptian style fashionable at the time of its construction, in 1826.

| 0 metres | 500 |
| 0 yards | 500 |

Trinity Bridge
The ten-arched Trinity Bridge (1897–1903) is famous for its Style-Moderne lampposts and railing decorations, the work of the skilful French engineers Vincent Chabrol and René Patouillard.

Swan Canal
This tree-lined canal (1711–19) leading out to the Neva is named after the swans which were once drawn to its peaceful waters.

Bridge Passage
Cleverly designed to span the confluence of the Moyka and the Griboedov, the Theatre and Small Stable bridges were constructed by Traitteur and Adam in 1829–31.

Anichkov Bridge
This three-span bridge, carrying Nevskiy prospekt across the Fontanka, was built in 1839–41. At each corner are Pyotr Klodt's impressive sculptures of men taming wild horses.

Lomonosov Bridge
The distinctive domed granite towers, built in 1785–7, originally contained the bridge's opening mechanism. The bridge was rebuilt in 1912, but the towers were kept.

Bank Bridge
Dating from the same time as the Lion Bridge, and designed by the same team, this bridge is adorned by four magnificent cast-iron griffons. Its name derives from the nearby former Assignment Bank.

UL KUYBYSHEVA

TROITSKAYA PLOSHCHAD

Neva

SUVOROVSKAYA PLOSHCHAD

Moyka

GOSTINYY DVOR
(see pp98–115)

NEVSKIY PROSPEKT

SADOVAYA UL

NAB REKI FONTANKI

Exploring St Petersburg's Bridges and Waterways

A boat trip on St Petersburg's canals and waterways is one of the highlights of any visit to the city. From the Anichkov Bridge the river boats *(see p228)* loop along the Neva, Fontanka and Moyka rivers, taking in many impressive bridges and landmarks. Alternatively, you can choose your route to explore the city's rich architectural heritage by taking a water bus or taxi *(see p229)*. A pleasant wander along the embankments of the Griboedov Canal leads past imposing 19th-century apartment houses and fancifully decorated bridges. In winter it is sometimes possible (but not advisable) to walk on the frozen Neva.

The ice-laden Neva river in front of the Peter and Paul Fortress

The Neva and its Branches

Greatest of St Petersburg's numerous waterways, the Neva flows from Lake Ladoga in the east through the city to the Gulf of Finland, a distance of only 74 km (46 miles) in total. Vasilevskiy Island, one of more than 100 islands in the Neva Delta, divides the river into two separate branches, Bolshaya (Great) Neva and Malaya (Small) Neva.

Icebound for at least four months of the year, the Neva usually shows the first signs of cracking in March. The official opening of navigation is announced by the port authority in early spring. Before the Revolution the event was marked with great ceremony. The Commander of the Peter and Paul Fortress *(see pp68–9)*, at the head of a naval flotilla, would scoop some icy water into a silver goblet which he presented to the tsar in the Winter Palace *(see pp94–5)*.

Rivers and Canals

Inspired by Amsterdam, Peter the Great kept the many streams of the delta as canals, which also helped to drain the swampy ground. As the city grew, new ones were dug to improve the canal network.

The **Moyka** originally flowed from a swamp near the Field of Mars *(see p96)*. In the 19th century the aristocracy lined its quays with impressive Neo-Classical mansions which are still their main attraction. Canal boats and barges ply the 7-km (4-mile) long **Fontanka**, widest and busiest of the waterways, which was once the border of the city. These two rivers are linked by the **Kryukov Canal**, dug in the 18th century.

The **Griboedov Canal**, first known as the Catherine Canal in honour of Catherine the Great, was designed to move cargo from Sennaya Ploshchad. Today the atmosphere here is more tranquil. The stretch of water running south from the

Lion Bridge is particularly picturesque. The narrowest waterway is the **Winter Canal**, just to the east of the Winter Palace. Nearby is the delightful **Swan Canal** which runs along the Summer Garden *(p97)*.

Steady industrial growth in the 19th century prompted the construction of a new canal, the **Obvodnyy**, in 1834, to take the increasing number of heavy cargo barges and supply water to the city outskirts.

Neva Bridges

The most central of the Neva bridges is the **Palace Bridge** (Dvortsovyy most). The present structure, built early in the 20th century, replaced a seasonal pontoon bridge which linked the mainland to Vasilevskiy Island. The other bridge to this island, **Blagoveshchenskiy Bridge** (Blagoveshchenskiy

Finding the Bridges

Map references refer to the Street Finder on pp232–9.

Alexander Nevsky Bridge **8 F3**
Anichkov Bridge **7 A2**
Bank Bridge **6 E2**
Blagoveshchenskiy Bridge **5 B1**
Egyptian Bridge **5 B5**
Lantern Bridge **5 C2**
Lion Bridge **5 C3**
Liteynyy Bridge **3 A3**
Lomonosov Bridge **6 F3**
Palace Bridge **1 C5**
Peter the Great Bridge **4 F5**
Red Bridge **6 D2**
St Panteleymon's Bridge **2 F5**
Singer's Bridge **2 E5**
Small Stable Bridge **2 F5**
Theatre Bridge **2 F5**
Trinity Bridge **2 E4**

View of the Moyka and its south bank with a water taxi in foreground

Peter the Great Bridge, crossing the Neva near Smolnyy Institute

most, *see p65*) was the first permanent bridge over the Neva. Once known as Lieutenant Schmidt Bridge, it returned to its original name in 2007. The **Trinity Bridge** (Troitskiy most, *see p75*) was built in 1897–1903 by the French Batignolles company. At 582 m (1,910 ft), the Trinity Bridge was the Neva's longest, until the construction of the **Alexander Nevsky Bridge** (Most Aleksandra Nevskovo) in the 1960s, which is some 900 m (2,950 ft). Between these two is the **Liteynyy Bridge** (Liteynyy most) built in 1874–9. In 1917, the city authorities tried to prevent rebel workers crossing the Neva from the Vyborg Side by raising the central bridge span. The tactic failed since the revolutionaries decided to cross on foot over the frozen ice.

Near the Smolnyy Institute is the **Peter the Great Bridge** (Most PetraVelikovo), also known by its Soviet name Bolsheokhtinskiy most. It has a central drawbridge and distinctive steel twin arches, erected in 1909–11.

From April to November almost all Neva bridges are raised at night to give ships access to the Volga (*see pp228–9*).

Decorative Bridges

In the beginning, wooden bridges spanned the canals and rivers of St Petersburg. They were usually known by their colour – red, blue, green, and so on. The **Red Bridge** (Krasnyy most) which carries Gorokhovaya ulitsa over the Moyka, has preserved its original name. Built in 1808–14, this iron bridge is decorated with picturesque lamps on four granite obelisks. Lamps are also a feature of the **Lantern Bridge** (Fonarnyy most) which crosses the Moyka river near to the Yusupov Palace (*see p122*). Here the gilded lampposts are shaped to look like treble clefs. **Singer's Bridge** (Pevcheskiy most) at the other end of the Moyka takes its name from the choir of the nearby Academic Capella (*see p114*). Its engineer, Yegor Adam, also designed the lace-like patterning of the railings.

At the junction where the Griboedov meets the Moyka is an interesting ensemble, formed by the wide **Theatre Bridge** (Teatralnyy most) and **Small Stable Bridge** (Malo-

Konyushennyy most). The latter is cunningly designed to look like two bridges.

Among the more attractive bridges is Georg von Traitteur's pedestrian **Bank Bridge** (Bankovskiy most), crossing the Griboedov. Its cables are held up by two pairs of gold-winged griffons. The **Lion Bridge** (Lvinyy most), also by Traitteur, uses a similar device; in this case the suspension cables emerge from the open jaws of four proud lions.

St Panteleymon's Bridge (Panteleymonovskiy most, *see p101*) spans the Fontanka near the Summer Gardens. It was Russia's first chain bridge (1823–4). The Empire-style decoration has survived and includes gilded fasces and double-headed eagles perched on laurel wreaths. Next to the Nevskiy prospekt, the **Anichkov Bridge** (Anichkov most) is famous for its four vibrant bronze sculptures of wild horses and their powerful tamers, all of them in different poses. Further down the Fontanka, framed by a handsome Neo-Classical square by Carlo Rossi, is the **Lomonosov Bridge** (Most Lomonosova) with its unusual stone turrets.

The **Egyptian Bridge** (Egipetskiy most) spans the Fontanka close to the Kryukov Canal. It is ornamented with bronze sphinxes and bridge-heads resembling the entrance to an Egyptian temple. Originally constructed in 1826, the bridge collapsed under the weight of a passing cavalry squadron in 1905 but was rebuilt in 1955.

Lamppost, St Panteleymon's Bridge

A City Under Water

A 19th-century illustration of one of the many floods in St Petersburg

Peter the Great should have known it was a bad idea to found a city here. The first flood, just three months after he started the fortress in 1703, swept away his building materials. The water rises dangerously high on average once a year, but four floods, in 1777, 1824, 1924 and 1955, wrought massive damage. In 1824 the whole city went under water and 462 buildings were totally destroyed. This inspired Pushkin's poem *The Bronze Horseman* (*see p78*). Markers showing record water heights can be found by the Winter Canal and the Peter and Paul Fortress. In 1989 construction of a dam was begun to prevent future destruction.

St Petersburg's Best: Palaces and Museums

St Petersburg boasts more than 90 museums, many of them housed in palaces or other buildings of historical importance. Some are well known throughout the world, such as the Hermitage which began as Catherine the Great's private collection of European art. Others, including the Russian Museum and the Summer Palace, highlight local art, history and culture. Some of the most evocative museums are those commemorating the lives and work of famous artists, writers and musicians. This selection represents the most interesting in each category.

The Hermitage
Incorporating the breathtaking state rooms of the Winter Palace, the world-famous Hermitage holds nearly three million exhibits which range from Fine Arts to archaeological finds.

PETROGRADSKAY
(see pp66–75)

Malaya Neva

NAB MAKAROVA

SREDNIY PR

VASILEVSKIY ISLAND
(see pp58–65)

BOLSHOY PR

UNIVERSITETSKAYA NAB

Bol Neva

PALACE EMBANKME
(see pp76–97)

ANGLIYSKAYA NAB

ISAAKIYEV-
SKAYA
PLOSHCHAD   MOK

SENNAYA
PLOSHCHAD
(see pp116–125

Menshikov Palace
This grandiose Baroque palace on Vasilevskiy Island is testimony to the power of Peter the Great's friend and advisor, Prince Menshikov.

Imperial Country Palaces

To escape the pressures of the capital, successive Russian rulers built sumptuous retreats in the rural hinterland of St Petersburg. These offer a fascinating insight into the lifestyle of the Romanov dynasty.

Tsarskoe Selo's Catherine Palace was built by Rastrelli in a flamboyant Baroque style.

Peterhof's palace and pavilions are enhanced by the splendid cascades and fountains adorning the attractive grounds.

| 0 km | 15 |
| 0 miles | 15 |

Pavlovsk's Great Palace is set in an extensive naturalistic landscaped park, embellished with ponds, pavilions and monuments.

Kshesinskaya Mansion
Built for a prima ballerina of the Mariinskiy Theatre, this attractive Style-Moderne mansion now houses the Museum of Russian Political History containing souvenirs from the Revolution.

Summer Palace
Interiors and furniture, such as Peter the Great's original four-poster bed, give an idea of the tsar's relatively modest lifestyle.

Stieglitz Museum
A rich collection of applied art is displayed in Messmacher's magnificent building, which was inspired by palaces of the Italian Renaissance.

Russian Museum
Carlo Rossi's Mikhaylovskiy Palace is the splendid setting for an outstanding collection of Russian art, ranging from medieval icons to contemporary paintings and sculptures. This semi-abstract work, *Blue Crest* by Vasily Kandinsky, dates from 1917.

GOSTINYY DVOR
(see pp98–115)

Pushkin House-Museum
Period furnishings and personal belongings such as this inkstand recreate the atmosphere of Alexander Pushkin's last home.

| 0 metres | 500 |
| 0 yards | 500 |

Exploring St Petersburg's Palaces and Museums

The city's palaces range from imperial excess to the tasteful homes of the nobility, while art museums cover the fine and applied arts and folk crafts. The history of St Petersburg, from its foundation as Peter the Great's "window on the West" to its role as the "Cradle of the Revolution", is covered by a variety of museums while its culture is documented in the apartments of writers, composers and artists. More specialist interests, from railway engines and military paraphernalia to insects and whales, also find reflection in the wealth of museums.

Bedroom in the Chinese Palace (1760s), Oranienbaum

Peter the Great's Summer Palace overlooking the Fontanka

Palaces

The fabulous wealth of imperial St Petersburg is reflected in the magnificence of its palaces. No trip to the city is complete without a visit to at least one of the spectacular out-of-town imperial summer residences, **Peterhof** (see pp150–53), **Pavlovsk** (see pp160–63) or the Catherine Palace (see pp154–5) at **Tsarskoe Selo**. These palaces, built and added to in the last 200 years of Romanov rule, illustrate the extravagance of the imperial court and the wealth of the Empire's natural resources. An abundance of gold, lapis lazuli, malachite, marble and other precious minerals decorates many of the rich palace interiors. The palace parks and grounds are landscaped and filled with follies and monuments.

At the centre of the city, the **Winter Palace** (see pp94–5) is home to the Hermitage art museum and epitomizes the opulence of the court. Peter the Great's more intimate **Summer Palace** is nearby (see p97) and

makes a pleasing contrast. Peter's friend and counsellor, Prince Alexander Menshikov, also built two sumptuous residences, the **Menshikov Palace** (see p64) on Vasilevskiy Island, and his summer palace at **Oranienbaum** (see pp148–9), Lomonosov.

Overlooking the Moyka river is the **Yusupov Palace** (see p122) which is famed as the murder scene of Rasputin, the extraordinary peasant who exerted his malign influence over the Russian court.

For those in search of a tranquil setting, a pleasant day can be spent exploring the **Yelagin Palace** (see p128) and the island of the same name.

Art Museums

One of the world's greatest collections of Western art is housed in the **Hermitage** (see pp86–95) which is home to some 3 million pieces of art.

With its collections ranging from Egyptian mummies to Scythian gold, Greek vases, Colombian emeralds and a vast and dazzling array of Old Master, Impressionist and Post-Impressionist paintings, it is essential to be selective.

The **Russian Museum** (see pp106–9) is a showcase for Russian art, including the 20th-century avant-garde and the folk crafts which influenced it. Exhibitions from its holdings are also in the **Mikhaylovskiy Castle** (see p103), **Marble Palace** (see p96) and **Stroganov Palace** (see p114).

The **Academy of Arts** (see p65) exhibits work by past students as well as models of the city's notable buildings.

There are fascinating displays of applied arts from around the world in the **Stieglitz Museum** (see p129) which includes ceramics, woodcarving, ironwork and embroidery. Its interiors and the glass-roofed exhibition hall are equally impressive.

The Cyclist (1913) by Natalya Goncharova, Russian Museum

History Museums

St Petersburg's dramatic 300-year history is proudly recorded in a number of the city's museums. The **Cabin of Peter the Great** (see p75) was the earliest building to be constructed in the city and it offers an intriguing insight into the surprisingly humble lifestyle of this tsar.

A group of historic sights lies within the Peter and Paul Fortress. The **Cathedral of SS Peter and Paul** (see p70) houses the tombs of all but two of Russia's tsars since Peter the Great. The preserved cells of the grim **Trubetskoy Bastion** (see p71) act as a reminder of the hundreds of political prisoners to be confined within the fortress walls. In the **Commandant's House** (see p71), the courthouse where prisoners were once interrogated, an exhibition looks at medieval settlements in the area, while the **Engineer's House** (see p70) focuses on daily life in St Petersburg before the Revolution.

A wealth of revolutionary memorabilia, including Stalin-era posters and a huge propaganda stained-glass panel, can be found in the **Museum of Russian Political History**. The museum is located within the Kshesinskaya Mansion (see p74) which, in 1917, housed the Bolshevik headquarters. The **Cruiser Aurora** (see p75) also played a part in the Revolution, having fired a warning shot before the storming of the Winter Palace in October 1917.

For an impression of the prestigious pre-revolutionary school where poet Alexander Pushkin was a student, some of the classrooms of the **Lycée** at Tsarskoe Selo (see p157) have been restored to their 19th-century appearance.

On the southern outskirts of the city, in Victory Square (see p133), the **Monument to the Heroic Defenders of Leningrad** poignantly evokes the Siege of Leningrad (1941–4) and acts as an important reminder of the great hardships endured by St Petersburgers during World War II.

Office of Leningrad party secretary Sergey Kirov, Kirov Museum

Special Interest Museums

Remnants of Peter the Great's legendary "cabinet of curiosities" can be found in Russia's oldest museum, the **Kunstkammer** (see p62). Housed under the same roof is a **Museum of Anthropology and Ethnography**, displaying a large collection of artifacts from all over the world. For natural history, the **Zoological Museum** (see p62) encompasses most known life forms, including a unique collection of molluscs and blue corals.

The **Institute of Russian Literature** (see p62) houses manuscripts from Pushkin to Mayakovskiy. The **Artillery Museum** (see p72) covers military hardware, from pikes to ballistic missiles. Train enthusiasts will find plenty to enjoy in the **Railway Museum** (see p125), including an 1835 engine built for the Tsarskoe Selo railway.

The **Museum of Musical Life** in the Sheremetev Palace (see p131) displays period instruments and explains the role

of the Sheremetev family as leading music patrons in 19th-century St Petersburg. A stunning array of beautiful stage costumes are on display alongside photos, set designs and other theatrical ephemera in the **Theatre Museum** which is situated on Ostrovskiy Square (see p112).

House-Museums

A handful of evocative museums commemorates some of the city's most famous residents. The **Pushkin House-Museum** (see p115), the **Nabokov Museum** (see p124) and the **Dostoevsky House-Museum** (see p132) recapture something of the life and character of their former residents.

The **Anna Akhmatova Museum** in the former service quarters of the Sheremetev Palace (see p131) traces the dramatic life of the poet, who lived here for many years.

For an insight into the life of a powerful Communist official of the 1930s, visit the **Kirov Museum** (see p74). The museum is devoted to the popular leader whose assassination on Stalin's orders initiated the Great Terror (see p29).

Outside the city in **Repino** (see p148), the house of the painter Ilya Repin is set in beautiful woodland on the Gulf of Finland.

18th-century violin and score in Museum of Musical Life, Sheremetev Palace

Celebrated St Petersburgers

As the residence of the Russian imperial family and court from the early 18th century, St Petersburg was the focus of patronage and an almost boundless source of wealth. It was the perfect seedbed for creativity and the flowering of ideas. Institutions such as the Academy of Arts, the University, the Kunstkammer and the Imperial School of Ballet trained generations of cultural figures and scientists to the highest standards. So successful were they that, by the dawn of the 20th century, St Petersburg had become one of the most important cultural centres in Europe.

Grigoriy Kozintsev
Director Kozintsev confirmed his reputation in the West with his interpretation of Shakespeare's *Hamlet* (1964), made at Lenfilm *(see p72).*

Nikolai Gogol
A merciless satirist of St Petersburg society, Gogol lived on Malaya Morskaya ulitsa *(see p84)* for three years.

PETROGRADSKAY
(see pp66–75)

Malaya Neva

NAB MAKAROVA

SREDNIY PR

VASILEVSKIY ISLAND
(see pp58–65)

BOLSHOY PR.

UNIVERSITETSKAYA NAB

Bol Neva

PALACE EMBANKME
(see pp76–97

ANGLIYSKAYA NAB

ISAAKIYEV-SKAYA PLOSHCHAD

Mokya

Ilya Repin
This outstanding realist painter is seen here teaching life drawing at the Academy of Arts *(see p65)* where he was a professor.

SENNAYA PLOSHCHAD
(see pp176–125)

VOZNESENSKIY PROSPEKT

Fontanka

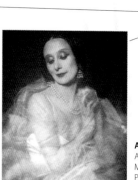

Pyotr Tchaikovsky
Tchaikovsky graduated from the Conservatory *(see p122)* in 1865 and went on to compose his world-famous operas and ballets.

Anna Pavlova
A prima ballerina at the Mariinskiy Theatre *(see p121),* Pavlova took Paris by storm in 1909 when she toured in *Les Sylphides* with the Ballets Russes.

Alexander Pushkin
The great poet, who sketched this self-portrait on a manuscript, died here in a flat that is now a memorial museum *(see p115)*.

Sergey Diaghilev
Driving force behind the Ballets Russes, Diaghilev also produced the influential *World of Art* magazine in his flat on 45 Liteynyy prospekt. He is shown here with Jean Cocteau *(left)*.

Anna Akhmatova
The poet's most famous poem, *Requiem*, is a powerful and moving indictment of the Stalinist regime. Akhmatova, seen here in a portrait by Nathan Altman, lived in the service quarters of the Sheremetev Palace *(see p131)*.

Dmitriy Shostakovich
Shostakovich's *Seventh Symphony* was broadcast live on the radio from the Great Hall of the Philharmonia *(see p100)* in August 1942, while the city was under siege. Many testified to its role in boosting the morale of the besieged citizens.

Fyodor Dostoevsky
The novelist Dostoevsky lived for many years among the slums of Sennaya Ploshchad *(see p124)* which provided the setting for his greatest work, *Crime and Punishment*.

0 metres   500
0 yards   500

Remarkable St Petersburgers

The streets of St Petersburg are redolent with literary and artistic associations. Fascinating art collections, house-museums, theatres and concert halls evoke the memory of famous St Petersburgers. The world of the 18th-century genius Lomonosov and 19th-century writers Pushkin and Dostoevsky can be imagined. So, too, can the spirit of Russian ballet when dancers such as Anna Pavlova and Vaslaw Nijinsky thrilled the Mariinskiy audiences. During these early years of the 20th century, writers, musicians, dancers and painters flocked to St Petersburg, bringing with them a wealth of creativity.

Symbolist "Silver Age" poet, Andrei Bely (1880–1934)

Writers

Considered the father of modern Russian literature, **Alexander Pushkin** (1799–1837) was simultaneously intoxicated by St Petersburg's beauty and sensitive to the underlying climate of political suspicion and intolerance which constrained writers in the wake of the Decembrist rebellion of 1825 *(see p25)*. **Nikolai Gogol** (1809–52) responded to these constraints by satirizing the status quo. In *The Nose*, he targeted the city's bureaucrats with their inflated sense of self worth and mind-numbing conformity.

Another aspect of the city altogether is revealed by **Fyodor Dostoevsky** (1821–81). His novel *Crime and Punishment*, one of more than 30 works set in the city, takes place against a backdrop of squalor in the notorious slums of Sennaya Ploshchad *(see p124)*. The story of the murder of an old moneylender was based on a real crime and the novel's publication in 1866 was blamed for a series of subsequent copy-cat killings.

Poetry, which flourished in the "Golden Age" of Pushkin, only regained its ascendancy over the novel in the "Silver Age" during the first decade of the 20th century. Some of the most exciting poets of the period, including **Aleksandr Blok** (1880–1921), **Andrei Bely** (1880–1934) and **Anna Akhmatova** (1889–1966), gathered at The Tower, a flat overlooking the Tauride Gardens *(see p130)*. Bely later wrote *Petersburg*, one of the earliest stream-of-consciousness novels. Akhmatova is honoured by a museum in the Sheremetev Palace *(see p131)* while one of her protégés, **Joseph Brodsky** (1940–96), went on to receive the Nobel Prize in literature in 1987. Brodsky became the bête-noire of the Leningrad literary establishment in the 1960s. The refusal of the authorities to publish his poetry, which they condemned as decadent, finally forced him to emigrate in 1972.

Musicians

The first important composer to emerge from the nationalist movement was **Mikhail Glinka** (1804–57), the earliest composer of Russian opera. In 1862, the Conservatory *(see p122)* was founded by **Anton Rubinstein** (1829–94) and this became the focus of musical life in St Petersburg. **Nikolai Rimsky-Korsakov** (1844–1908) taught here for 37 years and together with composers such as **Modest Mussorgsky** (1839–81), and **Aleksandr Borodin** (1834–87), he was part of "the mighty handful". They were a largely self-taught group aiming to develop a musical language based on Russian folk music and Slav traditions. Many of the operas premiered at the Mariinskiy *(see p121)*.

One of the musical geniuses of the 20th century was **Igor Stravinsky** (1882–1971). He spent much time abroad but, as works like *The Rite of Spring* testify, his cultural roots were firmly in his homeland.

The city's most important concert venue is the Great Hall of the Philharmonia *(see p204)* where **Pyotr Tchaikovsky**'s (1840–93) *Sixth Symphony* was premiered in 1893 and **Dmitriy Shostakovich**'s (1906–75) *Seventh Symphony*, his most famous work, was performed in 1942.

Portrait of composer Mikhail Glinka, painted by Ilya Repin in 1887

The Circus (1919) by avant-garde artist Marc Chagall

Artists

From the 18th century, the Academy of Arts *(see p65)* was the centre of artistic life in St Petersburg. **Dmitriy Levitskiy** (1735–1822), **Orest Kiprenskiy** (1782–1836), **Silvestr Shchedrin** (1791–1830), and Russia's first internationally recognized artist, **Karl Bryullov** (1799–1852), were all trained here.

In 1863, a group of students rebelled against the Academy and went on to establish the Wanderers movement *(see p108)*. To some extent the Academy and the Wanderers became reconciled when the most versatile of these artists, **Ilya Repin** (1844–1930), was appointed professor of painting at the Academy in 1893.

Five years later **Sergey Diaghilev** (1872–1929) and painter **Alexandre Benois** (1870–1960) launched the *World of Art* magazine *(see p109)*, proclaiming "Art for art's sake". Another collaborator, **Leon Bakst** (1866–1924), designed the most famous of the Ballets Russes costumes. Bakst also taught **Marc Chagall** (1889–1985) who later settled in France and had a profound impact on art in the West as well as in Russia. Other members of the Russian avant-garde include **Kazimir Malevich** (1878–1935) and **Pavel Filonov** (1883–1941).

Works by all of these artists can be seen at the Russian Museum *(see pp106–9)*.

Dancers and Choreographers

The skills of Russian dancers are legendary and the performances of the Mariinskiy (Kirov) Ballet Company continue to enthral audiences all over the world. Since 1836 the dancers have been trained at the former Imperial School of Ballet *(see p112)*. In 1869–1903 the outstanding choreographer at the Mariinskiy was **Marius Petipa**. He inspired a generation of dancers including **Matilda Kshesinskaya** *(see p74)*, **Vaslaw Nijinsky** (1890–1950) and the legendary **Anna Pavlova** (1885–1931).

Petipa's successor, **Mikhail Fokin** (1880–1942), is famous as the principal choreographer of the Ballets Russes *(see p121)*. The Mariinskiy tradition was revived after the Revolution by another graduate of the School of Ballet, **Agrippina Vaganova** (1879–1951). Her groundwork paved the way for a new generation of dancers including **Rudolf Nureyev** (1938–93) and modern dancers **Galina Mezentseva** and **Emil Faskhoutdinov**.

Film Directors

The Lenfilm Studios *(see p72)* were founded in 1918 on the site where the first Russian cine film had been shown in 1896. In its heyday Lenfilm produced 15 movies a year. Its two most remarkable directors, **Grigoriy**

Poster for *The Youth of Maxim* (1935) directed by Kozintsev

Kozintsev (1905–73) and **Leonid Trauberg** (1902–90), first joined forces in 1922 and began making short experimental films. The pair then went on to direct *The New Babylon* (1929), remarkable for its montage and lighting effects, and *The Maxim Trilogy* (1935–39). Kozintsev's versions of *Hamlet* (1964) and *King Lear* (1970), with music composed by Shostakovich for both films, mark the height of his success in the West.

The great polymath Mikhail Lomonosov

Scientists

The foundations of modern Russian science were laid in the 18th century by **Mikhail Lomonosov** (1711–65) *(see p63)* who worked for over 20 years in the Kunstkammer *(see p62)*. His treatise, *Elementa Chymiae Mathematica*, published in 1741, anticipates Dalton's theory of the atomic structure of matter.

In 1869, **Dmitriy Mendeleev** (1834–1907), a professor of chemistry, compiled the Periodic Table of Elements.

Many people believe that the world's first radio signal was sent by **Aleksandr Popov** (1859–1906) from the laboratories of St Petersburg University on 24 March 1896.

In 1904, the world-famous physiologist **Ivan Pavlov** (1849–1936) won the Nobel Prize in medicine for his theory of conditioned reflexes, which he demonstrated by experimenting on dogs and their hearing responses.

Nevskiy Prospekt
From the Admiralty to the Griboedov Canal

A pleasant stroll along this first stretch of St Petersburg's main artery reveals a wealth of attractive buildings. A profusion of architectural styles ranges from the Baroque Stroganov Palace to the magnificent Neo-Classical Cathedral of Our Lady of Kazan and the striking Style-Moderne Singer House. The stately avenue was once known as the "Street of Tolerance", referring to the clutch of churches of different denominations that were established here in the late 18th and early 19th centuries. *(See also p110)*

Literary Café Once called the Wolf and Beranger, this café was known for its fashionable clientele. Pushkin left from here for his fatal duel in 1837 *(see p85)*.

Admiralty *(p80)*

Palace Square *(p85)* and the Hermitage *(pp86–95)*

ADMIRALTEYSKIY PROSPEKT

NEVSKIY PROSPEKT

MALAYA MORSKAYA ULITSA

BOLSHAYA MORSKAYA ULITSA

BOLSHAYA MORSKAYA ULITSA

ZELENYY

The 1760s apartment blocks at Nos. 8 and 10 are an example of early St Petersburg Neo-Classicism.

St Isaac's Cathedral *(pp82–3)* and Angleterre Hotel *(p81)*

Admiralty Garden This garden was laid out in 1872–4. Near the fountain are busts of composer Mikhail Glinka, writer Nikolai Gogol and poet Mikhail Lermontov.

0 metres	100
0 yards	100

School No. 210 This school carries a sign, dating from the Siege, warning, "Citizens! This side of the street is more dangerous during artillery bombardment".

Vavelberg House Marian Peretyatkovich's severe granite building (1912) is uncharacteristic of the city's architecture. The upper storeys were inspired by the Palazzo Medici in Florence, the arcades by the Doge's Palace, Venice.

Dutch Church Building The Dutch church was housed behind the central Neo-Classical portico of Paul Jacot's seemingly secular building (1831–7). The elongated wings are still occupied by offices, flats and shops.

Locator Map

Stroganov Palace The façade of this splendid Baroque palace, one of the oldest buildings on the street (1753), is embellished with sculptural ornaments and the Stroganov coat of arms (see p114).

The Fashion House Marian Lyalevich designed this building for Mertens Furriers in 1911–12. The impact of the Neo-Classical arches is heightened by the beautiful plate glass.

Singer House was built for the Singer Sewing Machine Company in 1902–4 by Pavel Syuzor. The building is distinguished by a glass globe on a conical tower.

Continued (pp50–51)

The Lutheran Church (1833) was an important centre for the evangelical community. Converted into a swimming pool during the Soviet era, it is once again open as a church (see p114).

The Griboedov Canal, originally known as the Catherine Canal, was renamed in 1923 after the 19th-century Russian playwright Aleksandr Griboedov.

★ **Cathedral of Our Lady of Kazan** Ninety-six Corinthian columns, arranged in four rows, form an arc facing Nevskiy prospekt. Andrey Voronikhin's design was inspired by Bernini's colonnade for St Peter's in Rome (see p113).

Nevskiy Prospekt
From the Griboedov Canal to the Fontanka

Nevskiy prospekt has been the main focus for St Petersburg's shopping and entertainment since the mid-18th century. As the prospekt continues towards the handsome Anichkov Bridge on the Fontanka river, cafés, bars, restaurants and cinemas sit alongside three historic shopping arcades, the Silver Rows, Gostinyy Dvor and Passazh. Bustling with life, this stretch of the avenue also has many sights of historic and architectural interest, including the Anichkov Palace.

Passazh Arcade This popular shopping mall is covered by a glass canopy stretching 180 m (590 ft). The arcade opened in 1848 and was reconstructed in 1900.

Church on Spilled Blood *(p102)*

The Small Hall of the Philharmonia was the city's main concert hall in the early 19th century.

The Church of Saint Catherine (1762–82), by Vallin de la Mothe, is a mixture of Baroque and Neo-Classical styles. It is the oldest Roman Catholic church in Russia.

Belmond Grand Hotel Europe *(p103)*

Russian Museum *(pp106–9)*

The Armenian Church (1771–80) is a fine example of Yuriy Velten's decorative Neo-Classical style *(see p110)*.

KANAL GRIBOEDOVA

Nevskiy Prospekt 2 (Griboedova Canal)

MIKHAYLOVSKAYA ULITSA

NEVSKIY PROSPEKT

DUMSKAYA ULITSA

Nevskiy Prospekt 1

Gostinyy Dvor

Silver Rows Arcade (1784–7)

SADOVAYA ULITSA

PLOSH

The Duma Tower was built in 1804 as a watchtower for fires. The Duma building was the centre of local government from 1786–1918.

0 metres 100
0 yards 100

The Russian National Library houses over 33 million items, including the earliest surviving handwritten Russian book (1057).

Portik Rusca Perinnyie Ryadi Now standing alone, the six-columned portico by Luigi Rusca was originally the entrance to a long arcade of shops. The portico was dismantled during the construction of the metro and rebuilt in 1972.

★ Gostinyy Dvor This striking arcade has been St Petersburg's main bazaar since the mid-18th century *(see p110)*. It houses more than 300 outlets which sell everything from clothes and cosmetics to souvenirs and chocolates.

For key to symbols *see back flap*

Locator Map

★ **Yeliseev's** Famous for its beautiful Style-Moderne decor, this building is home to Yeliseev's delicatessen, and also houses the Akimov Comedy Theatre *(see p111)*.

Beloselskiy-Belozerskiy Palace Now a cultural centre and offices, this sumptuous palace was designed in Neo-Baroque style by Andrey Stakenschneider in 1847–8. The red façade is decorated with Corinthian pilasters and atlantes upholding balconies.

Quarenghi's Stalls were built in 1803–6 as trading rows. They were then handed over to the imperial chancellor and became known as the Cabinet.

Number 66 was occupied by the music publishers Bessel and Co in the 19th century. Tchaikovsky was one of many composers who frequented their offices.

Alexandrinskiy Theatre

A statue of Catherine the Great stands in Ostrovskiy Square *(see p112)*.

The Anichkov Palace was first built as a present from Tsarina Elizabeth to her lover, Aleksey Razumovskiy. It later became the winter residence of the heir to the throne *(see p111)*.

Moskovskiy railway station

Anichkov Bridge Four dynamic bronze statues of rearing horses and their tamers adorn this well-known landmark. They were designed in the 1840s by Pyotr Klodt *(see p37)*.

ST PETERSBURG THROUGH THE YEAR

Whatever the weather, Russians are always ready to celebrate and consequently take their public holidays very seriously. Flowers have great symbolic significance, from mimosa for International Women's Day, to lilac to mark the beginning of summer. Every official holiday, as well as some local festivals such as City Day, are celebrated both in the centre of town and in the many different districts, with regattas, parades and fireworks at night, when the torches on the Rostral Columns *(see p62)* are lit. Classical music is the central theme of a large number of festivals each year, attracting talented performers from all over the world. But even without an official holiday, Russian people love to get out and about, whether to ski or ice-skate in the winter months or gather mushrooms in late summer and autumn.

Spring

Spring has set in for good when the first sunbathers gather on the beaches outside the Peter and Paul Fortress *(see pp68–9)* and when, in early April after the waterways have thawed, the city's bridges open to allow ships through.

To warm themselves up after the months of cold, locals celebrate "maslennitsa", the making of pancakes *(blini)* prior to Lent. They then gather bunches of willow as a symbol of the approaching Palm Sunday. On the eve of Lent, "Forgiveness Sunday", it is common practice to ask forgiveness of those you might have offended during the year.

Once the snows have gone, the first trips to the *dacha*, or country house, are made to put the gardens in order.

Early sunbathers on the banks of the Peter and Paul Fortress

March

International Women's Day *(Mezhdunarodnyy zhenskiy den)*, 8 Mar. Men rush around the city buying flowers for their womenfolk. It is a tradition to

Candles lighting up Russian Orthodox church during Easter service

say *s prazdnikom* (congratulations on the holiday) to everyone. There are even special performances and concerts and, however sexist it may seem to non-Russians, it is a very popular day.

Dedication to Maestro *(Posvyashchenie Maestro)*, mid-Mar. An international music festival that celebrates the achievements of the world's greatest composers and musicians.

Easter Sunday *(Paskha)*. The dates on which Lent and Easter fall change every year. On Easter Sunday, St Petersburg churches are filled with worshippers, the evocative sound of ethereal music and chanting and the smell of incense. Russians traditionally greet each other with *Khristos voskres* (Christ is risen), to which the reply is *Voistine voskres* (He is truly risen).

April

Mariinsky Ballet Festival *(Festival Baleta Mariinskiy)*, early Apr.

As warm clothing and heavy boots are laid aside after winter, the public flock to the Mariinsky theatre where the world's most renowned dancers perform some of the popular ballets to celebrate the return of spring.

Cosmonauts' Day *(Den Kosmonavtiki)*, 12 Apr. Space exploration was one of the glories of the Soviet Union and this occasion is celebrated with fireworks at 10pm.

May

Day of Spring and Labour *(Den Vesny i Truda)*, 1 May. Public holiday. **Peterhof Fountains** *(Fontany v Petergofe)*, first weekend in May. Bands and orchestras accompany the switching on of the famous fountains at Peterhof *(see p150–53)*.

Victory Day *(Den Pobedy)*, 9 May. After a sombre ceremony at Piskarevskoe Cemetery *(see p128)*, smartly dressed veterans fill Nevskiy prospekt *(see pp48–51)* and Palace Square *(see p85)* in commemoration of the Nazi surrender in 1945.

City Day *(Den goroda)*, last week of May. A great variety of events, mainly taking place around the Peter and Paul Fortress *(see pp68–9)*, mark the founding of the city on 27 May 1703.

Musical Olympus International Festival, late May/ early Jun. Young musicians from all over the world are accompanied by St Petersburg's most famous orchestras.

Proud war veteran on Victory Day

Average Daily Hours of Sunshine

Sunshine Hours
St Petersburg's climate can vary dramatically from hot, sunny days and occasional heavy downpours during the summer months, to winters with sub-zero temperatures and snow. From mid-June to mid-July, it never gets dark. During the winter months the days are extremely short, but there can be days of bright sunshine.

Summer

A lilac in flower is the real symbol that warm weather has set in and there is an air of excitement once the Field of Mars (see p96) comes into bloom. Throughout the warm months, the city is deserted at weekends when people go off to their *dacha*, which is usually a summer house outside the city.

St Petersburg's main festive season is during the acclaimed White Nights in June, when the sun hardly sets and it never quite gets dark. Concerts, ballets and other performances take place all over the city, which fills with thousands of visitors (see p203). The most favoured place to be at nighttime is on the embankments of the Neva, which are crowded with revellers watching the bridges being raised around 2am.

June

International Protection of Children Day (Den Zatschity detey), 1 Jun. Performances and events for children are held throughout the city.

Russia Day (Den Rossii), 12 Jun. The day Russia became "independent" of the Soviet Union is marked with fireworks at 10pm.

Trinity Sunday (Troytsa), 50 days after Easter. Believers and atheists alike go to tidy the graves of their loved ones and raise a glass of vodka for their souls.

The White Nights Swing, Jazz Festival, mid-June. A large jam session supported by local and visiting musicians for anyone with an interest in jazz.

Stars of the White Nights, Classical Music Festival (Zvezdy Belykh nochey), Jun. This is the original White Nights festival, with first-class opera, classical music and ballet concerts performed at all major venues.

White Nights, Rock Music Festival (Belye nochi), late Jun. World-renowned rock bands perform at the Oktyabrskiy Bolshoy Kontzertnyy Zal (see p207).

Festival of Festivals (Festival-festivaley), last week in Jun. This is an international non-

Russian battleships moored on the Neva, Navy Day

competitive film festival showing the best international films released over the past year. The festival attracts film stars from all over the world.

Tsarskoe Selo Carnival (Tsarskoselskiy karnaval), last weekend in June. Funny costumes, music and mayhem fill the centre of Tsarskoe Selo (see pp154–7).

July

Sporting Competitions. St Petersburg is a popular sporting venue for numerous international events, offering everything from tennis to figure skating and yachting.

Navy Day (Den Voenno-morskovo Flota), first Sun after 22 July. The Neva resembles a shipyard, with submarines and torpedo boats adorned with flags and bunting.

August

With schools on holiday and temperatures at their highest, this is a quiet time, with most families escaping to their *dacha* outside the city.

Bridge opening in front of the Peter and Paul Fortress on a White Night

Average Monthly Rain and Snowfall

Rain and Snow-fall Chart
St Petersburg summers are humid and wet, but the downpours are a welcome relief from the summer heat. In winter frequent snowfalls build up to create metre-high drifts, usually not thawing until late March.

☐ Rainfall (from axis)
☐ Snowfall (from axis)

Autumn

City life begins to gain pace as people return from their *dacha* and families begin to prepare for the start of school.

In September, when theatres reopen after the summer break, the city's cultural life resumes. The Mariinskiy (Kirov) returns from touring, and new plays and operas are premiered. October marks the start of the festival season, with guest musicians and theatre groups from all over the world taking part.

The crisp autumn weather is ideal for gathering mushrooms.

Chanterelle mushrooms

Popular hunting spots can be found to the northwest of the city around Zelenogorsk and Repino *(see p148)*. Enthusiastic mushroom-gatherers rise early to hunt for chanterelles, oyster mushrooms, *podberyozoviki* (brown mushrooms) and *podosinoviki* (orange-cap bolens). The locals are skilled in identifying edible mushrooms while amateur pickers should be aware of the dangers of poisonous ones. An activity with fewer potential side effects might be a trip on the hydrofoil to Peterhof *(see pp150–53)* to see the magnificent fountains before they are switched off for the winter.

Children dressed up for the first day of school

September
Knowledge Day *(Den znaniy)*, 1 Sep. The city is full of children heading for their first day back at school, laden with flowers.

October
International Baltic House Theatre Festival *(Baltiyskiy dom)*, Oct. Actors, clowns and pantomime artists gather from around the world to perform in theatres and on the streets with two weeks of mayhem.

November
Day of National Unity, 4 Nov. A reminder that the Russian Federation is a multi-national country with various religions and political parties.
Sound Ways, Modern Music Festival *(Zvukovyye puti)*, mid-Nov. A chance to catch up with some of the most avant-garde trends in jazz and contemporary classical music from Russia and the rest of Europe. Musicians invited from abroad abound, and many of Russia's most renowned performers refuse international engagements in order to take part in this home-grown festival.
Christmas Fast, 28 Nov. During this time, vegetarians enjoy countless choices at many restaurants in the city.

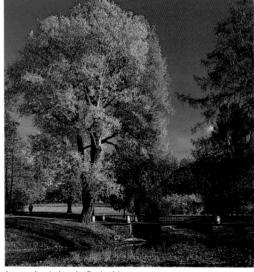

Autumn colours in the park at Tsarskoe Selo

Average Monthly Temperature

°C
30
20
15
10
0
-10
-20

☐ Maximum Temperature
☐ Minimum Temperature

°F
86
68
50
32
14
-4

Jan Feb Mar Apr May Jun Jul Aug Sep Oct Nov Dec

Temperature Chart
St Petersburg's climate is maritime and milder than might be expected. Summers are warm and often punctuated with hot days as early as May, though during the winter months temperatures often fall well below freezing. St Petersburg's average minimum and maximum temperatures throughout the year are shown in this chart.

Winter

As the ice thickens on the waters and the snow deepens, people head for the outdoors once more. Children's sledges are not expensive to buy, and all other equipment can be hired. Cross-country skiing needs no lessons to make it fun. Tsarskoe Selo *(see pp154–7)* and Pavlovsk *(see pp160–63)* parks provide ski and sledge hire at the ski bases *(lyzhnaya baza)*. Skates can be hired for use in the rink at Moskovskiy Park Pobedy, by Park Pobedy metro station in the south of the city, and also at the Central Park of Culture and Rest (Krestovskiy Ostrov metro station).

The truly hardened members of the local "walruses" swimming club break the ice by the Peter and Paul Fortress *(see pp68–9)* every day to take an early morning dip.

In the midst of winter activities come New Year and Christmas. New Year is the big holiday, while Christmas itself is celebrated according to the Orthodox calendar, on 7 January. Many people also still

Sledging on the frozen Neva outside the Hermitage *(see pp86–95)*

celebrate Old New Year, which falls on 14 January. A seasonal delight is the Christmas ballet, *The Nutcracker*, at the Mariinskiy Theatre *(see p121)*.

December
Christmas Markets
(Rozhdestvenskiy rynok), Dec. These markets appear throughout the city around the middle of the month, even though Russia doesn't celebrate Christmas until 7 January.
Art Square International Festival *(Festival Ploshchad Iskusstv)*, Dec/Jan. This classical music festival is the last one of the year and is made even more magical by the backdrop of snowy streets and frozen waterways outside.
New Year's Eve *(Novyy god)*, 31 Dec. Still the biggest holiday of the year, New Year's Eve is best celebrated with the local "champagne", Shampanskoe *(see p185)*. This is considered to be a family celebration, with people dressed as Grandfather Frost (the Russian equivalent of Santa Claus) and the Snow Maiden, the traditional bearers of gifts.

January
Russian Orthodox Christmas *(Rozhdestvo)*, 7 Jan. Christmas is celebrated in a quieter fashion than Easter, with a traditional visit to an evening service on Christmas Eve (6th), when the church bells ring out all over the city.

February
Defender of the Fatherland Day *(Den zashchitnika Otechestva)*, 23 Feb. The male equivalent of Women's Day. Men are congratulated and given flowers and presents.

Drilling a hole through the ice for winter-time fishing

Public Holidays

New Year's Day (1 Jan)
Russian Orthodox Christmas (7 Jan)
Defender of the Fatherland Day (23 Feb)
International Women's Day (8 Mar)
Easter Sunday (Mar/Apr)
Day of Spring and Labour (1 May)
Victory Day (9 May)
Russia Day (12 Jun)
Day of National Unity (4 Nov)

Aerial view of the Church on Spilled Blood in the morning light ▶

ST PETERSBURG AREA BY AREA

VASILEVSKIY ISLAND

It was Peter the Great's intention that Vasilevskiy Island (*Vasilevskiy ostrov*), the largest island in the Neva delta, was to be the administrative heart of his new capital. However, lack of access (the first permanent bridge was not built until 1842) and the hazards of floods and stormy crossings led to the abandonment of Peter's project, and the centre grew up across the river around the Admiralty (*see p80*) instead. The island's original street plan, based on canals that were never dug (*see p22*), survives in the numbered streets known as lines (*linii*), which run from north to south. The focal point of the island is at the east end with the fine ensemble of public buildings around the Strelka, or "spit". The rest of the island developed with the spread of industrialization in the 19th century and it became a middle-class haven. There was also a thriving German community here which is reflected in the Lutheran churches. Today much of the island has a sedate air, with tree-lined avenues, museums and some attractive 19th-century architecture. The northwest part of the island is covered with high-rise buildings.

Sights at a Glance

Museums
- **2** The Institute of Russian Literature
- **3** Zoological Museum
- **4** Kunstkammer
- **6** Menshikov Palace

Streets and Bridges
- **7** Bolshoy Prospekt
- **10** Blagoveshchenskiy Bridge

Historic Buildings and Monuments
- **1** Rostral Columns
- **5** Twelve Colleges
- **9** Academy of Arts

Churches
- **8** St Andrew's Cathedral

Restaurants *p186*
1. Casa del Myaso
2. Dans le Noir?
3. Grad Petrov
4. Ketino
5. Kneipe Jager Haus
6. Maria Karlotta
7. Marketplace
8. Repin
9. Restoran
10. Staraya Tamozhnya
11. Taverna Grolle

See also Street Finder map 1

◀ View of Vasilevskiy Island on an early summer morning

For keys to symbols *see back flap*

Street-by-Street: the Strelka

The eastern end of Vasilevskiy Island is known as the Strelka, or "spit". Once St Petersburg's main centre of commerce, it has become an area of learning. The Academy of Sciences and St Petersburg University are both situated here, as are various museums, institutes and libraries, housed in the former warehouses and customs buildings. The nautical theme is preserved in the two Rostral Columns. In front of these lighthouses is a lawn, a popular spot for newly-married couples to have their picture taken. From here there are views across the Neva towards the Peter and Paul Fortress (see pp68–9) and the Hermitage (see pp86–95).

The old Stock Exchange and Rostral Columns from across the Neva

The Lomonosov Monument
honours Mikhail Lomonosov (1711–65), who taught at the Academy of Sciences.

❺ Twelve Colleges
Originally erected to house the 12 ministries of Peter the Great's government, they now form the main building of St Petersburg University.

The Academy of Sciences was founded in 1724. The present building was constructed by Giacomo Quarenghi in 1783–5.

MENDELEEVSKAYA LINIYA

UNIVERSITETSKAYA NABEREZHNAYA

BIRZHEVOY PROEZD

❹ ★ Kunstkammer
The Kunstkammer houses Peter the Great's collection of biological curiosities. Its tower, crowned by a sundial, is a St Petersburg landmark.

DVORTSOVYY MOST

Palace Embankment

❸ Zoological Museum
With over 1.5 million specimens the museum is one of the finest of its kind in the world. The exhibits include a set of stuffed animals that belonged to Peter the Great and a world-famous collection of mammoths.

Academy of Sciences Library
was founded in 1714 with Peter the Great's personal book collection. It now has over 17 million volumes.

Sakharov
Monument

Locator Map
See Street Finder map 1

PETROGRADSKAYA

Malaya Neva

VASILEVSKIY ISLAND

Bolshaya Neva

The New Exchange Bazaar
was designed by Quarenghi in the early 19th century. At the time a busy market filled its Neo-Classical loggias. Today students have replaced the shoppers, as the building houses departments of the university.

NABEREZHNAYA MAKAROVA

BIRZHEVOY PROEZD

The former Stock Exchange was built in 1805–10 as the focal point of the Strelka. It was modelled on a Greek temple.

BIRZHEVOY
MOST

Peter and Paul Fortress

BIRZHEVAYA PLOSHCHAD

❷ The Institute of Russian Literature
Housed in a building erected in 1832, this literary museum, also known as Pushkin House, holds more than 70 books, prints and manuscripts.

❶ ★ Rostral Columns
Originally lighthouses guiding ships through the busy port of St Petersburg, these imposing 32-m-(105-ft-) high columns are a distinctive feature of St Petersburg's skyline. They are still lit for Navy Day (*see p53*) and other festivals.

Key

— Suggested route

| 0 metres | 100 |
| 0 yards | 100 |

❶ Rostral Columns
Ростральные колонны
Rostralnye kolonny

Birzhevaya ploshchad.
Map 1 C5. 🚌 7, 10, 24, 47, 191, K-209, K-252. 🚊 1, 7, 10, 11.

Situated on the Strelka before the former Stock Exchange, the impressive twin russet-coloured Rostral Columns were designed as lighthouses by Thomas de Thomon in 1810. During the 19th century the oil lamps were replaced by gas torches which are still lit on ceremonial occasions. The columns are decorated with protruding ships' prows in celebration of naval victories. The monumental figures around the base represent four of Russia's rivers: the Neva, Volga, Dnieper and Volkhov.

Rostral Column on the Strelka

❷ The Institute of Russian Literature (Pushkin House)
Институт русской литературы (Пушкинский Дом)
Institut Russkoy Literatury (Pushkinskiy Dom)

Naberezhnaya Makarova 4. **Map** 1 C5. **Tel** 328 0502. 🚌 7, 10, 47, 187, K-209, K-252. 🚊 1, 7, 10, 11. **Open** 11am–4pm Mon–Fri. 🚫 📷 English. 🌐 **pushkinskijdom.ru**

Founded at the beginning of the 20th century, this museum houses numerous manuscripts and exhibits connected to Russia's greatest poet, Alexander Pushkin. Known as Pushkin House, the museum focuses on preserving the legacy of Russian literary culture from the distant past to the present. The museum has grown into an unrivalled repository of rare and unusual artifacts connected with some of Russia's greatest writers, including Turgenev, Gogol, Dostoevsky, Tolstoy and Blok. A room is dedicated to the Silver Age poets, displaying work by Anna Akhmatova and Mikhail Bulgakov.

Today Pushkin House contains more than 3 million autographed manuscripts, including 12,000 pages from Pushkin alone. In addition to more than 700,000 books and print editions reflecting the history of Russian literature, the museum also preserves thousands of images, paintings, drawings and objects. Many of these are on view in the galleries, which are decorated with period furniture. In addition to the archives, the institute also publishes new scholarly editions, which are on sale at the museum.

Visitors who wish to take an English-language tour of the museum should be sure to phone ahead.

❸ Zoological Museum
Зоологический музей
Zoologicheskiy muzey

Universitetskaya naberezhnaya 1/3. **Map** 1 C5. **Tel** 328 0112. 🚌 7, 10, 24, 47, 191, K-209. K-252. 🚊 1, 7, 10, 11. **Open** 11am–6pm Wed–Mon. **Closed** second Wed of each month. 🚫 (free third Thu of each month). 📷 📹 English. 🌐 **zin.ru**

Housed in a former customs warehouse designed by Giovanni Lucchini in 1826, this museum has one of the world's largest natural history collections containing more than 1.5 million specimens. Some of the stuffed animals belonged to Peter the Great's Kunstkammer collection, including the horse he rode at the Battle of Poltava (*see p20*).

Dioramas recreate natural habitats for giant crabs, weasels, polar bears and blue whales. The museum is renowned for its collection of mammoths. One prized carcass was exhumed from the frozen wastes of Siberia in 1902 and is almost 44,000 years old.

Weasel in the Zoological Museum

❹ Kunstkammer
Кунсткамера
Kunstkamera

Universitetskaya naberezhnaya 3. **Map** 1 C5. **Tel** 328 0812. 🚌 7, 10, 24, 47, 191, K-209, K-252. 🚊 1, 7, 10, 11. **Open** 11am–6pm Tue–Sun. 🚫 📹 English. 🌐 **kunstkamera.ru**

The delicate, sea-green lantern tower of the Baroque Kunstkammer ("art chamber") is visible across this part of Vasilevskiy Island. The building, by Georg Mattarnoviy, was constructed in 1718–34 to exhibit Peter the Great's infamous Kunstkammer collection. While touring Holland in 1697 Peter attended

Manuscripts on display at the Institute of Russian Literature

The restrained Baroque façade of the Kunstkammer (1718–34), Russia's first museum

the lectures of Frederik Ruysch (1638–1731), the most celebrated anatomist of his day. He was so impressed with Ruysch's collection of rarities that on a return visit in 1717, he purchased the entire collection of over 2,000 anatomical preparations. He transported it to St Petersburg and exhibited it to a wide-eyed public, who were enticed by free glasses of vodka. At the time, Peter's collection also included bizarre, live exhibits of deformed or unusual people, including a hermaphrodite. This, Russia's first museum, also included a library, an anatomical theatre and an observatory.

Today the Kunstkammer houses the Museum of Anthropology and Ethnography, with the remnants of Peter's bizarre collection on display in the central rotunda. Included are the heart and skeleton of Peter's personal servant, "Bourgeois", a giant at 2.27 m (7.5 ft), and a cabinet of teeth extracted by the tsar who was an enthusiastic amateur dentist. Most gruesome of all is the collection of pickled oddities which include Siamese twins and a two-headed sheep.

The halls surrounding the Kunstkammer collection contain exhibitions on the peoples of the world. Often neglected by visitors, these marvellously old-fashioned displays present an informative range of artifacts, from an Inuit kayak to Javanese shadow puppets.

❺ Twelve Colleges

Двенадцать коллегий

Dvenadtsat kollegiy

Universitetskaya naberezhnaya 7. **Map** 1 C5. 🚊 7, 24, 47, 129, K-209. 🚋 1, 10, 11. **Closed** to public.

This distinguished Baroque building of red-and-white stuccoed brick is almost 400 m (1,300 ft) in length. It was intended for Peter the Great's newly streamlined administration of 12 colleges or ministries. The single, uninterrupted façade was designed to symbolize the government's unity of purpose, while the curious alignment, at right angles to the embankment, is explained by Peter's unrealized plan for a large square with an unbroken view across the

Mikhail Lomonosov
(1711–65)

Strelka. Another popular theory is that Prince Menshikov changed the plan in Peter's absence so that the building would not encroach on his grounds. Domenico Trezzini won the competition for the design in 1723, but subsequent bureaucratic wrangling delayed its completion for 20 years. The building's function gradually changed and in 1819 part of it was acquired by St Petersburg University. A string of revolutionaries, including Lenin in 1891, were educated here.

Among the famous Russian lecturers to teach here were the chemist Dmitriy Mendeleev (1834–1907) *(see p47)* and the physiologist Ivan Pavlov (1849–1936) *(see p47)*.

Overlooking the Neva, outside the Twelve Colleges, is an engaging bronze statue of the great 18th-century polymath Mikhail Lomonosov (unveiled in 1986). The son of a fisherman, Lomonosov was the first Russian-born member of the nearby Academy of Sciences. A "universal genius", he wrote poetry, systematized Russian grammar and was a pioneer in mathematics and the physical sciences. Thanks to his scientific discoveries, the art of porcelain, glass and mosaic production began in Russia.

A section of the west façade of Trezzini's Twelve Colleges

The southern façade of Prince Menshikov's 18th-century palace

❻ Menshikov Palace
Меншиковский дворец
Menshikovskiy dvorets

Universitetskaya naberezhnaya 15. **Map** 5 B1. **Tel** 323 1112. 🚌 7, 24, 47, 191, K-209. 🚎 1, 10, 11. 🚋 1, 10, 11. **Open** 10:30am–6pm Tue, Thu, Sat & Sun; 10:30am–9pm Wed & Fri. 🏷 (free first Thu every month)

The ochre-painted Baroque Menshikov Palace, with its beautifully carved pilasters, was one of the earliest stone buildings in St Petersburg. Designed by Giovanni Fontana and Gottfried Schädel for the infamous Prince Menshikov, the palace was completed in 1720. The palace estate originally extended as far as the Malaya Neva river to the north.

Prince Menshikov entertained here on a lavish scale, often on behalf of Peter the Great, who adopted the palace as a pied-à-terre. Guests would cross the Neva by boat and arrive to the grand welcome of a liveried orchestra.

The palace is now a branch of the Hermitage (*see pp86–95*) with exhibitions on early 18th-century Russian culture, revealing the extent to which Peter the Great's court was influenced by Western tastes.

The compulsory tour begins on the ground floor; besides the kitchen there are displays of Peter's cabinet-making tools, period costumes, sturdy oak chests and ships' compasses. Adorning the beautiful vaulted hallway are marble statues imported from Italy which include a Roman Apollo dating to the 2nd century AD.

Upstairs, the secretary's rooms are decorated with 17th-century Dutch engravings of Leyden, Utrecht and Kraków. A series of breathtaking rooms are lined with hand-painted blue and white 18th-century Dutch tiles. Tiles were not only fashionable, but also easy to keep clean. In the tiled bedroom of Varvara (Menshikov's sister-in-law and confidante) is a German-made four-poster bed, with a Turkish coverlet woven from cotton, silk and silver thread.

Hanging behind it is an exquisite 17th-century Flemish tapestry.

Menshikov and Peter often received guests in the aptly named Walnut Study which has Persian walnut panelling and commanding views of the Neva. Paintings hang from coloured ribbons, as was the fashion, including a late 17th-century portrait of Peter the Great by the Dutch painter Jan Weenix. The mirrors were a novelty at that time and such displays of vanity were anathema to the Orthodox Church.

The Great Hall, decorated in gold and stucco, is where balls and banquets were held. On one famous occasion, it was the setting for a "dwarfs' wedding" which Menshikov arranged for the amusement of his royal master.

Prince Menshikov

A leading advisor, comrade-in-arms and friend of Peter the Great, Aleksandr Menshikov (1673– 1729) rose from humble origins to his position as the first governor of St Petersburg. After Peter's death in 1725, Menshikov engineered the ascension of Catherine I (Peter's wife, and Menshikov's former mistress) to the throne, thus maintaining his power until her demise. His notorious extravagance and venality eventually caught up with him. Accused of treason, he died in exile in 1729.

The fine, Style-Moderne *apteka*, just off Bolshoy prospekt

❼ Bolshoy Prospekt
Большой проспект
Bolshoy prospekt

Map 1 A5. Ⓜ Vasileostrovskaya. 🚌 1, 6, 7, 10, 41, 42, 128, 151, 152, K-124, K183, K-346, K-350, K-690. 🚋 10, 11.

This imposing avenue was opened early in the 18th century to connect Menshikov's estate to the Gulf of Finland.

The mix of architectural styles ranges from the elegant Neo-Classicism of St Catherine's Lutheran Church (1768–71) at No. 1 to the simple Troyekurov House (No. 13, 6-ya liniya) in 17th-century Petrine Baroque.

Other buildings of note include St Andrew's food market (1789–90) and two Style-Moderne edifices. One is the former pharmacy, or *apteka*, (1907–10) around the corner on 7-ya liniya, and the other is Adolph Gaveman's Lutheran orphanage at No. 55 (1908).

The Academy of Arts (1764–88) on the Neva embankment, an example of early Russian Neo-Classicism

❽ St Andrew's Cathedral

Андреевский собор

Andreevskiy sobor

6-ya liniya 11. **Map** 1 A5. **Tel** 323 3418. 🚌 7, 24, 42, 100, 128, 151, K-62, K-154, K-183, K-200, K-349, K-690. 🚎 10, 11. ♿

First built on the initiative of Peter the Great's second wife, Catherine I *(see p23)*, who donated 3,000 roubles towards its construction, the original church was destroyed by fire.

The present Baroque church with its distinctive bell tower was constructed by Aleksandr Vist in 1764–80. The most stunning feature of the interior is the carved 18th-century iconostasis which incorporates icons from the original church. Next door is

The treasure of St Andrew's Cathedral, its beautiful Baroque iconostasis

Giuseppe Trezzini's small Church of the Three Saints (1740–60) which is dedicated to SS Basil the Great, John Chrysostom and Gregory of Nazianzus.

❾ Academy of Arts

Академия Художеств

Akademiya Khudozhestv

Universitetskaya naberezhnaya 17. **Map** 5 B1. **Tel** 323 3578. 🚌 7, 47, K-62, K-124, K-154, K-350. 🚎 10, 11. **Open** 11am–7pm Thu, Sat & Sun; noon–8pm Wed; 1–9pm Fri. 🎫 📷 🌐 **nimrah.ru**

Founded in 1757 to train home-grown artists in the preferred Western styles and techniques of art, the Academy spawned a galaxy of talent, including the great painter Ilya Repin *(see p44)* and architects Andrey Zakharov (1761–1811) and Andrey Voronikhin (1759–1814).

The innate conservatism of the Academy tended to discourage innovation and experiment and in 1863 a band of 14 students walked out of their graduation exams in protest. They went on to found a realist art movement and became known as the Wanderers or *Peredvizhniki* *(see pp108–9)*.

The imposing Academy, built between 1764–1880 by Aleksandr Kokorinov and Vallin de la Mothe, is an example of the

transition from Baroque to Neo-Classicism. Still an art school, it exhibits the work of students past and present, including canvases, architectural drawings and models of many of the city's notable buildings, such as the Smolnyy Convent *(see p130)*.

The splendid Neo-Classical halls and galleries, though faded, retain something of their original grandeur. Of note are the Conference Hall on the first floor, with its ceiling painting by Vasiliy Shebuev, and the adjoining Raphael and Titian galleries, adorned with copies of Vatican frescoes.

Flanking the river stairs outside the Academy are two sphinxes from the 14th century BC. Discovered among the ruins of Thebes in ancient Egypt, they were installed here in 1832. The faces are thought to bear a likeness of the pharaoh Amenhotep III.

❿ Blagovesh-chenskiy Bridge

Благовещенский Мост

Blagoveshchenskiy most

Map 5 B1. 🚌 6, K-154, K-350.

Opened in 1842 with this name, this was the first permanent crossing of the Neva. In 1855 it was renamed Nicholas Bridge but in 1918, after the Revolution, it was called Lieutenant Shmidt Bridge to commemorate a sailor who led an uprising of the Black Sea fleet in 1905. Reconstruction carried out in 1936–8 incorporated Aleksandr Bryullov's original railings, adorned with seahorses and tridents. In 2007 the bridge reverted to its original name.

PETROGRADSKAYA

The city was founded on the northern banks of the Neva river in 1703, at the height of the Great Northern War *(see p20)*. Building began with the construction of a wooden fortress and Petrogradskaya, or the Petrograd Side, soon became a marshy suburb of wooden cabins occupied by craftsmen working on Peter the Great's new city.

Nearby, the area around Trinity Square was originally a small merchants' quarter centred around a now demolished church and St Petersburg's first stock exchange.

Petrogradskaya was sparsely populated until the late 1890s when the construction of the Trinity Bridge (Troitskiy most) made the area accessible from the city centre. The bridge caused a housing boom at the height of a fashion for Style-Moderne architecture which is still in evidence today. The population quadrupled and the area became very popular with artists and professionals.

The highlight of Petrogradskaya, which is still largely residential, is the Peter and Paul Fortress.

Sights at a Glance

Museums
- ❷ Engineer's House
- ❹ Commandant's House
- ❻ Trubetskoy Bastion
- ❼ Artillery Museum
- ❿ Kirov Museum
- ⓫ Kshesinskaya Mansion
- ⓬ Cruiser *Aurora*
- ⓭ Cabin of Peter the Great

Gates
- ❶ St Peter's Gate
- ❺ Neva Gate

Cathedrals
- ❸ Cathedral of SS Peter and Paul

Streets, Squares and Parks
- ❽ Aleksandrovskiy Park
- ❾ Kamennoostrovskiy Prospekt
- ⓮ Trinity Square

See also Street Finder map 2

◀ Interior of the Baroque Cathedral of SS Peter and Paul in the Peter and Paul Fortress   For keys to symbols *see back flap*

Street-by-Street: Peter and Paul Fortress

The founding of the Peter and Paul Fortress on 27 May 1703, on the orders of Peter the Great, is considered to mark the founding of the city. It was first built in wood and was later replaced, section by section, in stone by Domenico Trezzini. Its history is a gruesome one, since hundreds of forced labourers died while building the fortress and its bastions were later used to guard and torture many political prisoners, including Peter's own son Aleksey.

The cells where prisoners were once kept are open to the public, alongside a couple of museums and the magnificent cathedral which houses the tombs of the Romanovs.

The Archives of the War Ministry occupy the site of the "Secret House", a prison for political criminals in the 18th and 19th centuries.

↑ Artillery Museum *(see p72)*

Kronverkskiy most

Zotov Bastion

❻ Trubetskoy Bastion
From 1872–1921 the dark, damp, solitary-confinement cells in the bastion served as a grim prison for enemies of the state. Today, the bastion is open to visitors.

The Mint, founded in 1724, still produces ceremonial coins, medals and badges.

The Naryshkin Bastion (1725) is where the noon cannon is fired. The tradition began in 1873, stopped after the Revolution and was resumed in 1957.

The beach is popular in summer and in winter, when members of the "walruses" swimming club break the ice for an invigorating dip.

❿ Neva Gate
This riverside entrance, also known as "Death Gateway", leads to the Commandant's pier from which prisoners embarked on their journey to execution or exile. The Neva river's flood levels *(see p39)* are recorded under the arch.

❹ Commandant's House
For 150 years this attractive Baroque house was the scene of interrogations and trials of political prisoners. It now houses a museum of local history.

❸ ★ Cathedral of SS Peter and Paul
Marbled columns, glittering chandeliers and painted decor combine with Ivan Zarudnyy's carved and gilded iconostasis to create a magnificent setting for the tombs of the Romanov monarchs.

Locator Map
See Street Finder map 2

The Boat House is now a ticket office and souvenir shop.

Golovkin Bastion

The Grand Ducal burial vault is the last resting place of several Grand Dukes shot by the Bolsheviks in 1919 and of Grand Duke Vladimir who died in exile in 1992.

❶ St Peter's Gate
The entrance to the fortress, by Domenico Trezzini, completed in 1718, features the Romanov double eagle with an emblem of St George and the dragon.

| 0 metres | 100 |
| 0 yards | 100 |

Ioannovskiy Ravelin contains a ticket office.

Ivan Gate, in the outer wall, was constructed from 1731–40.

Ioannovskiy most

Kamennoostrovskiy prospekt, Gorkovskaya Metro and Trinity Bridge

Statue of Peter the Great by Mikhail Chemiakin (1991).

Peter I Bastion

❷ Engineer's House
This building, dating from 1748–9, houses temporary exhibitions of artifacts used in everyday life in St Petersburg before the Revolution.

Key
— Suggested route

❶ St Peter's Gate

Петровские ворота

Petrovskie vorota

Petropavlovskaya krepost.
Map 2 E3. **M** Gorkovskaya.
🚌 46, 49, 76, 183, 223.

The main entrance to the Peter and Paul Fortress is through two contrasting arches. The plain Neo-Renaissance Ivan Gate (1730s) leads to the more imposing St Peter's Gate (1708–18), an ornate Baroque structure with scrolled wings and a rounded-gable pediment. Domenico Trezzini redesigned the Peter Gate, retaining Karl Osner's expressively carved bas-relief which allegorizes Peter the Great's victory over Charles XII of Sweden (*see p20*). It depicts St Peter casting down the winged sorcerer Simon Magus.

St Peter's Gate, entrance to fortress

❷ Engineer's House

Инженерный дом

Inzhenernyy dom

Petropavlovskaya krepost.
Map 2 D3. **Tel** 232 9454, 230 0329.
M Gorkovskaya. **Open** 11am–7pm Thu–Mon, 11am–6pm Tue. 🅿️
🇬🇧 English. **W** spbmuseum.ru

The Engineer's House, built in 1748–9, has a changing exhibition which gives a fascinating glimpse of daily life in St Petersburg before the Revolution. Architectural backdrops and historical paintings give way to an engaging miscellany of artifacts, ranging from model boats to duelling pistols and court costumes.

In 1915 there were more than 100 outlets selling musical instruments in the city and

An accordion and organ surrounded by Style-Moderne furniture, Engineer's House

the museum displays an excellent collection which includes phonographs, gramophones, symphoniums and piano accordions of the period.

A section on vintage technology features Singer sewing machines, typewriters, Bakelite telephones and box cameras.

❸ Cathedral of SS Peter and Paul

Петропавловский собор

Petropavlovskiy sobor

Petropavlovskaya krepost. **Map** 2 D4.
Tel 230 6431. **M** Gorkovskaya.
Open 10am–7pm Mon–Fri, 10am–5pm Sat, 11am–7pm Sun. 🅿️ 🇬🇧 English.
W spbmuseum.ru

Domenico Trezzini designed this magnificent church within the fortress in 1712. Employed by Peter the Great, who wished to turn his back on traditional Russian church architecture,

Trezzini produced a Baroque masterpiece of singular elegance. The bell tower was completed first in order to test the foundations and this served as an excellent viewpoint from which Peter could oversee the construction work of his new city. The cathedral was completed in 1733, but was badly damaged by fire in 1756 when the soaring 122-m (400-ft) spire was struck by lightning. The gilded needle spire, crowned by a weather-vane angel, remained the tallest structure in St Petersburg until the building of a TV transmitter in the 1960s.

The interior, with its glittering chandeliers, pink and green Corinthian columns and overarching vaults, is a far cry from the traditional Russian Orthodox church. Even the iconostasis is a Baroque flight of fancy. This masterpiece of gilded woodcarving was designed by Ivan Zarudnyy and executed in the 1720s by craftsmen from Moscow.

After Peter's death in 1725, the cathedral became the last resting place of the tsars. The sarcophagi are all of a uniform white Carrara marble, except the tombs of Alexander II and his wife Maria Alexandrovna,

Cathedral of SS Peter and Paul, with Dvortsovyy most in the foreground

which are carved from Altai jasper and Ural rhodonite. Peter the Great's tomb lies to the right of the iconostasis.

The only tsars who are not buried here are Peter II, Ivan VI and Nicholas II. In 1998 a controversial decision was taken to rebury the remains of the last Romanov tsar, his wife and children, and the servants that died together with them, in a chapel by the entrance to the cathedral.

The Grand Ducal Mausoleum, where relatives of the tsars are buried, was added to the northeast of the cathedral at the end of the 19th century.

Neva Gate leading from the river into the Peter and Paul Fortress

❹ Commandant's House

Комендантский дом
Komendantskiy dom

Petropavlovskaya krepost. **Map** 2 D4. **Tel** 230 6431. Ⓜ Gorkovskaya. **Open** 11am–7pm Thu–Mon, 11am–6pm Tue. 🖼 🗂 English.

Dating from the 1740s, the plain brick, two-storey Commandant's House served both as the residence of the fortress commander and as a courthouse. Over the years, political prisoners, including the Decembrist rebels *(see p25)*, were brought here for interrogation and sentencing.

The house is now a museum, with a ground-floor exhibition on medieval settlements in the St Petersburg region, and temporary exhibitions upstairs.

❺ Neva Gate

Невские ворота
Nevskie vorota

Petropavlovskaya krepost. **Map** 2 E4. Ⓜ Gorkovskaya.

This austere river entrance to the fortress was once known as the "Death Gate". Prisoners to be transported to the even more notorious Schlüsselburg Fortress (to the east of St Petersburg) for capital punishment, or to a "living death" in penal servitude, were led down the granite steps and taken away by boat. The appropriately dour, grey gateway dates from 1730–40

(reconstructed in 1784–7) and is unornamented apart from an anchor in the pediment. In the archway, brass plaques mark record flood levels. The catastrophic inundation of November 1824 is the one commemorated in Pushkin's poem, *The Bronze Horseman (see p80)*.

❻ Trubetskoy Bastion

трубецкой бастион
Trubetskoy bastion

Petropavlovskaya krepost. **Map** 2 D4. **Tel** 230 6431. Ⓜ Gorkovskaya. **Open** 10am–7pm daily. 🖼 🗂 English.

Peter the Great's son, the Tsarevich Aleksey, was the first political prisoner to be detained in the grim fortress prison. Unjustly accused of treason in 1718 by his overbearing father, Aleksey escaped abroad only to be lured back to Russia with the promise

of a pardon. Instead, he was tortured and beaten to death, almost certainly with Peter's consent and participation.

For the next 100 years prisoners were incarcerated in the much feared Secret House, since demolished. In 1872 a new prison block opened in the Trubetskoy Bastion which has existed as a museum since 1924. On the ground floor there is a small exhibition of period photographs, prison uniforms and a model of the guardroom. Upstairs are 69 isolation cells, restored to their original appearance, while downstairs there are two unheated, unlit punishment cells where the recalcitrant were locked up for 48 hours at a time. Once every two weeks, all detainees were taken to the Bath House in the exercise yard for de-lousing. Here prisoners were also put in irons before being carted off to penal servitude in Siberia.

Political Prisoners

The fortress' sinister role as a prison for political activists continued until after the Revolution. Generations of rebels and anarchists were

Leon Trotsky (1879–1940) in the Trubetskoy Bastion

interrogated and imprisoned here, including Leon Trotsky in the wake of the 1905 Revolution. Other prominent detainees were the leading Decembrists in 1825 *(see p25)*, Dostoevsky in 1849 *(see p125)* and, in 1874–6, the anarchist Prince Pyotr Kropotkin. In 1917 it was the turn first of the tsar's ministers, then of members of the Provisional Government. Then, in the Civil War *(see p29)*, the Bolsheviks held hostage four Romanov Grand Dukes who were subsequently executed in 1919.

Rocket launcher in the courtyard of the Artillery Museum

❼ Artillery Museum
Музей Артиллерии
Muzey Artillerii

Aleksandrovskiy Park 7, Kronverkskaya Embankment. **Map** 2 D3. **Tel** 232 0296. Ⓜ Gorkovskaya. **Open** 11am–5pm Wed–Sun. **Closed** last Thu each month. 📷

This vast, horseshoe-shaped building in red brick stands on the site of the Kronverk, the outer fortifications of the Peter and Paul Fortress (*see pp68–9*). Designed by Pyotr Tamanskiy and constructed in 1849–60, the building was originally used as the arsenal.

More than 600 pieces of artillery and military vehicles include tanks and the armoured car in which Lenin rode in triumph from Finland Station (*see p128*) to Kshesinskaya Mansion (*see p74*) on 3 April 1917. There are uniforms, regimental flags, muskets and small arms dating to medieval times, as well as several rooms devoted to World War II.

❽ Aleksandrovskiy Park
Александровский парк
Aleksandrovskiy park

Kronverkskiy prospekt. **Map** 2 D3. Ⓜ Gorkovskaya. ♿

The park's unique character as a centre of popular culture and entertainment was established in the year 1900 with the inauguration of the Nicholas II People's House. This was where pantomime artists, wild animal trainers, magicians and circus acts entertained the crowds, while the more serious-minded were drawn to the lecture halls, reading galleries and tea rooms. The *pièce de résistance* was the magnificent domed Opera House (1911), where the legendary bass singer, Fyodor Chalyapin, sometimes gave performances.

Today the Opera House offers less highbrow entertainment, as its change of name to Music Hall suggests. The adjoining 1930s buildings include the innovative Baltic House Theatre, the Planetarium and a waxworks museum.

The park still draws crowds on summer weekends and public holidays, although some of the attractions, especially the zoo, are rather tawdry.

❾ Kamennoostrovskiy Prospekt
Каменноостровский проспект
Kamennoostrovskiy prospekt

Map 2 D1. Ⓜ Gorkovskaya or Petrogradskaya. 🚌 46, K-30, K-76, K-223.

Developed during the construction boom of the late 1890s, this eye-catching avenue is noted for its Style-Moderne architecture. The first house, at No. 1–3 (1899–1904) was designed by Fyodor Lidval. The multi-textured façade, windows of contrasting shapes and sizes, ornate iron balconies and fanciful carvings are the most typical features of this Russian version of Art Nouveau. The neighbouring house (No. 5) was once occupied by Count Sergey Witte, a leading industrialist who negotiated the peace treaty with Japan in 1905 (*see p28*).

Situated just off the start of the avenue is the city's only mosque (1910–14). Designed by Russian architects, its minarets, majolica tiling and the rough granite surfaces of the walls are fully in keeping with the surrounding architecture. The mosque was, in fact, modelled on the Mausoleum of Tamerlane in Samarkand and involved Central Asian craftsmen.

At No. 10 is the tall portico of the Leningrad Film Studios (Lenfilm). It was on this site, in May 1896, that the Lumière brothers showed the first moving picture in Russia. Since its founding in 1918, some of the most innovative Soviet film directors, such as Leonid Trauberg and Grigoriy Kozintsev (*see p47*), have worked there.

Griffon, No. 1–3 Kamennoostrovskiy

At the intersection with ulitsa Mira, each house has individually designed turrets, spires, reliefs and iron balconies, forming a handsome Style-Moderne ensemble. Other buildings of interest include No. 24 (1896–1912), with its red-brick majolica and terracotta façade; No. 26–28, where Sergey Kirov lived (*see p74*); and on the corner of Bolshoy prospekt, the "Turreted House" with its Neo-Gothic portal.

Turreted House (1913–15), Kamennoostrovskiy prospekt

Style-Moderne in St Petersburg

In vogue throughout Europe from the 1890s to the 1900s, Art Nouveau marked a break with imitation of the past. The movement, known as Style-Moderne in Russia, began in the decorative arts and was then reflected in architecture, where it led to an abundance of ornamental details. Inspired by new industrial techniques, artists and architects made lavish use of natural stone and brick, wrought iron, stucco, coloured glass and ceramic tiles. Dominated by sinuous and undulating lines, with a predominance of floral- and vegetal-inspired elements, even traditional forms such as doors and windows are distorted or given unexpected curves.

In *fin-de-siècle* St Petersburg, the Style-Moderne flourished as the city underwent a building boom, particularly on Petrogradskaya. The city became a showcase for the talents of leading architects such as Fyodor Lidval and Aleksandr von Gogen.

Kshesinskaya Mansion reveals von Gogen's relatively severe version of Style-Moderne. Asymmetrical in composition, it is enlivened with wrought iron and glazed tiles *(see p74)*.

Yeliseev's is evidence of the skill of Gavriil Baranovskiy, who made excellent use of industrial techniques in the creation of large window spaces. The rich exterior detailing is matched by elegant shop-fittings and chandeliers inside *(see p111)*.

28 Bolshaya Zelenina ulitsa is one of the most outstanding examples of the use of stylized animal and fish motifs and a variety of surface decoration techniques. Fyodor von Postel's 1904–5 apartment block is reminiscent of the work of his contemporary, the Catalan architect Gaudí.

1–3 Kamennoostrovskiy pr is the work of St Petersburg's master of Style-Moderne, Fyodor Lidval. Delicate details such as floral and animal reliefs stand out against a background of discreetly elongated proportions and unusual window shapes.

Singer House (1910–14) reveals Pavel Syuzor's use of an unusually eclectic mix of architectural styles. Ornate Style-Moderne wrought-iron balconies and decorative wooden window frames combine with elements of Renaissance and Baroque revivals.

Portrait of Sergey Kirov (1930s), in the Kirov Museum

❿ Kirov Museum

Мyзей С. М. Кирова

Muzey S M Kirova

Kamennoostrovskiy prospekt 26–28, 4th floor. **Map** 2 D1. **Tel** 346 0217, 346 0289. Ⓜ Petrogradskaya. **Open** 11am–6pm Thu–Mon (5pm Tue). 🈂 English. 🆆 spbmuseum.ru

From 1926–36 this flat was home to one of Stalin's closest political associates, Sergey Kirov. As the charismatic first Secretary of the Leningrad Communist Party, Kirov soon gained national importance. His increasing popularity led Stalin to see in him a potential rival. On 1 December 1934, Kirov was gunned down at his office at the Smolnyy Institute *(see p130)* by Leonid Nikolaev, a party malcontent. Stalin used the assassination as an excuse to launch the Great Purges *(see p29)*, although most historians believe Stalin himself was behind Kirov's murder.

Kirov acquired the status of a martyr after his death, with countless buildings named in

his honour. His apartment, preserved as it was in his lifetime, is an example of the near cult status awarded Party leaders, with documents and photographs chronicling his political career, and a touching array of memorabilia including his clothing and favourite books.

⓫ Kshesinskaya Mansion

Особняк М. Кшесинской

Osobnyak M Kshesinskoy

Ulitsa Kuybysheva 4. **Map** 2 E3. **Tel** 233 7052. Ⓜ Gorkovskaya. **Open** 10am–6pm Mon, Tue, Sat & Sun (8pm Wed & Fri). **Closed** last Mon of month. 🈂 English. 🆆 polithistory.ru

This remarkable example of Style-Moderne architecture was commissioned for prima ballerina Matilda Kshesinskaya. Designed in 1904 by the court architect, Aleksandr von Gogen, the building is almost playfully asymmetric, with a single, octagonal tower. Most eye-catching of all are the many contrasting building materials with bands of pink and grey granite, cream-coloured bricks, delicately ornamented iron railings and majolica tiles.

The most impressive interior is the splendid recital hall with its pillared archway and palms. Nearby, the Kshesinskaya memorial room has some of the dancer's possessions, including sketches of Nicholas II.

In March 1917 the mansion was commandeered by the Bolsheviks and became their headquarters and, on Lenin's return to Russia *(see p128)*, he

addressed the crowds from the balcony facing the square. The mansion, previously home to a museum glorifying the October Revolution, now houses the Museum of Russian Political History. On the first floor the Bolshevik Party secretariat and Lenin's office have been faithfully restored. Upstairs is a fascinating collection of memorabilia from the revolutionary era, including Communist posters, Nicholas II coronation mugs and even a police file on Rasputin's murder *(see p123)*.

The museum holds an exhibition highlighting crucial events in Russian history. This permanent feature, with audio guides, is extremely popular among visitors.

Matilda Kshesinskaya

One of the finest prima ballerinas ever to grace the stage of the Mariinskiy Theatre *(see p121)*, Matilda Kshesinskaya (1872–1971) graduated from the Imperial School of Ballet *(see p120)* in 1890. She was equally famous for her celebrated affair with the tsarevich, later Tsar Nicholas II, which began soon after she graduated. Kshesinskaya emigrated to Paris in 1920 where she married the Grand Duke Andrey Vladimirovich, another member of the imperial family and the father of her 11-year-old son. It was in Paris that she wrote her controversial memoirs, *Dancing in St Petersburg*, which tells the tale of her affair with the last Russian tsar.

Aleksandr von Gogen's elegant recital hall in the Kshesinskaya Mansion

The historic cruiser *Aurora* (1900), moored in front of the Neo-Baroque Nakhimov Naval Academy (1912)

⑫ Cruiser Aurora

Крейсер Аврора

Kreyser Avrora

Petrogradskaya naberezhnaya 3.
Map 2 F3. **Tel** 607 4922. ▦ 49, K-30, K-183. ▦ 6, 40. **Open** 11am–6pm Wed–Sun. **W** navalmuseum.ru

According to the annals of the Revolution, at 9:40pm on 25 October 1917, the cruiser *Aurora* signalled the storming of the Winter Palace (*see p30*), by firing a single blank round from its bow gun.

The ship entered active service in 1903. It was later converted into a training ship and at the start of the Siege of Leningrad (*see p29*) it was sunk to protect it from German forces. The ship was raised in 1944 and has been a museum since 1956. When open, the famous gun, bell and the crew's quarters can be viewed, along with an exhibition on the ship's history.

⑬ Cabin of Peter the Great

Музей-домик Петра I

Muzey-domik Petra I

Petrovskaya naberezhnaya 6.
Map 2 F3. **Tel** 232 4576, 314 0374. Ⓜ Gorkovskaya. **Open** 10am–6pm Mon, Wed & Fri–Sun, 1–9pm Thu. **Closed** last Mon of month. ▦ ▦

This pine-log cabin was built for Peter the Great by his soldier-carpenters in just three days in 1703. Peter lived here for six years while overseeing the construction of his new city (*see pp22–3*). Catherine the Great, ever keen to glorify Peter, had a protective brick shell erected around the cabin.

There are only two rooms, both with period furnishings, and a hallway which doubled as a bedroom. Among Peter's personal possessions are a compass, a frock coat and his rowing boat.

Adorning the steps outside are two statues of the Shih Tze frog-lions, brought from Manchuria during the Russo-Japanese War (1904–5).

⑭ Trinity Square

Троицкая площадь

Troitskaya ploshchad

Map 2 E3. Ⓜ Gorkovskaya. ▦ 46. ▦ 6, 40.

Throughout the early 18th century, the whole of Petrogradskaya was known as Trinity Island. The name was derived from the Church of the Trinity (built in 1710; demolished 1930s) in Trinity Square, which formed the nucleus of the city's merchant quarter. In 2002–3 the Trinity Chapel was built here to honour the 300th anniversary of St Petersburg. Despite having no direct links to the mainland until the early 20th century, the area flourished with shops, a printing house and the city's first stock exchange.

In the 1905 Revolution (*see p28*) the square witnessed the massacre of 48 workers, killed by government troops. During the Communist era, the square became known as ploshchad Revolyutsii.

From the square, across the widest point of the Neva, the Style-Moderne Trinity Bridge (*see p37*) stretches nearly 600 m (1,970 ft). Its construction led to a building boom on Petrogradskaya (*see p67*) and its completion in 1903 coincided with the city's bicentenary.

The ornate Trinity Bridge, crossing the Neva from Trinity Square

PALACE EMBANKMENT

In terms of sheer scale and grandeur, St Petersburg's magnificent south waterfront has few equals. Its formidable granite quays stretch over 2 km (1 mile) from the Senate building in the west to Peter the Great's Summer Palace in the east, and the surrounding area of stately aristocratic palaces and ornamental canal bridges are justly famous worldwide.

Every aspect of the city's history is juxtaposed in this rich area. Falconet's statue of Peter the Great, the Bronze Horseman, is an eloquent testimony to imperial ambition while the square in

which it stands is where the Decembrist rebels rose up against the tsarist regime in 1825. In Palace Square, Rastrelli's Winter Palace (part of the Hermitage) evokes the opulence of Imperial Russia while the Eternal Flame, flickering in the Field of Mars, is a more sombre reminder of revolutionary sacrifice.

Dominating St Petersburg's skyline are the magnificent dome of St Isaac's Cathedral and the gilded spire of the Admiralty. Some of the best views can be appreciated by making a boat trip along the waterways (see pp228–9), or by strolling through the Summer Garden.

Sights at a Glance

Palaces and Gardens
⑭ Marble Palace
⑯ Summer Garden
⑰ Summer Palace

Museums
⑫ The Hermitage pp86–95

Historical Buildings and Monuments
❶ The Admiralty
❸ The Bronze Horseman
❹ Horseguards' Manège
❾ House of Fabergé

Churches
❺ St Isaac's Cathedral pp82–3

Streets and Squares
❻ St Isaac's Square
❷ Senate Square
❽ Malaya Morskaya Ulitsa
⑪ Palace Square
⑬ Millionaires' Street
⑮ Field of Mars

Hotels and Cafés
❼ Angleterre Hotel
⑩ Literary Café

Restaurants pp187–8
1 Borsalino
2 Bushe
3 Canvas
4 Clean Plates Society
5 Cococo
6 Da Albertone
7 Gastronom
8 Gogol
9 Gosti
10 King Pong
11 Literaturnoye Café
12 Percorso
13 La Russ
14 Tandoor
15 Teplo

0 metres 400
0 yards 400

See also Street Finder maps 2, 5 & 6

◀ The golden dome of St Isaac's Cathedral, visible from its gardens

For keys to symbols see back flap

Street-by-Street: St Isaac's Square

The highlight of St Isaac's Square is the imposing cathedral at its centre, which opened in 1858 and is the fourth church to stand on this site. The cathedral, and subsequently the square, were named after St Isaac of Dalmatia, because Peter the Great's birthday fell on this saint's day. The busy square, used as a market place in the first half of the 19th century, is now at the heart of an area teeming with buildings and statues of historical and architectural interest. Among them are the Admiralty, the Mariinskiy Palace and the Bronze Horseman.

❹ Horseguards' Manège
Built in 1804–7 by Giacomo Quarenghi, this building housed the Life Guards' Mounted Regiment.

❸ The Bronze Horseman
Etienne Falconet's magnificent statue of Peter the Great, his horse trampling the serpent of treason, captures the spirit of the city's uncompromising and wilful founder.

ADMIRALTEYSKAYA NABEREZHNAYA

PROEZD DEKABRISTOV

UL YAKUBOVICHA

ISAAKIEVSKA PLOSCH

❷ Senate Square
Dominating the western side of the square are Carlo Rossi's monumental Senate and Synod buildings, linked by a triumphal arch.

The Glory Columns, topped by bronze angels, were erected in 1845–6.

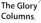

Myatlev House

❺ ★ St Isaac's Cathedral
The magnificent golden dome of the cathedral is visible all across the city. 100kg (220lb) of gold leaf was needed to cover the dome's surface.

The Former German Embassy was designed by Peter Behrens in 1911–12.

BOLSHAYA

MOY

| 0 metres | 100 |
| 0 yards | 100 |

The Hermitage
and Winter Palace

See Street Finder maps 2, 5 & 6

Locator Map

❶ The Admiralty
Sculptures and reliefs, celebrating the power of Russia's navy, decorate the Admiralty's façade. The archway of the main entrance is framed by nymphs carrying globes on their shoulders.

ADMIRALTEYSKIY PROSPEKT

GOROKHOVAYA UL

The Former Prince Lobanov-Rostovskiy Mansion is now a Four Seasons Hotel. The lions in front of the arcade are by Italian sculptor Paolo Triscorni.

VOZNESENSKIY PROSPEKT

MAL MORSKAYA UL

Nevskiy prospekt

The Former Ministry of State Property, designed by Nikolay Yefimov in 1844, is a fine example of Neo-Renaissance architecture.

❼ Angleterre Hotel
Originally built in the 1850s, the Angleterre Hotel (see p178) was the site of the first major public protest in the history of the Soviet Union. The hotel has been restored to its 19th-century splendour.

MORSKAYA UL

❻ St Isaac's Square
Overlooking the square is Pyotr Klodt's statue of Tsar Nicholas I. The reliefs on the pedestal depict episodes from his reign. Tellingly, two of them show the suppression of rebellions.

REKI MOYKI

Siniy most (see p81)

The Mariinskiy Palace, named in honour of Maria, daughter of Nicholas I, now houses the St Petersburg city hall.

Key

— Suggested route

❶ The Admiralty
Адмиралтейство
Admiralteystvo

Admiralteyskaya naberezhnaya 2.
Map 5 C1 🚃 7, 10, 24, 100, 191,
K-169, K-187, K-209, K-252. 🚊 1, 5,
7, 10, 11, 17, 22.

Having founded a city and built a fortress, Peter the Great's next priority was to create a Russian navy to guarantee access to the sea and dominance over Sweden.

The Admiralty began life as a fortified shipyard built on this site between 1704–11. Two years later, some 10,000 men were employed in building the first battleships.

One of Russia's most inspired architects, Andrey Zakharov, began to rebuild the Admiralty in 1806. The remarkable façade is 407 m (1,335 ft) in length and is adorned with an abundance of sculptures and reliefs which document the glory of the Russian fleet. Zakharov retained some of the original features, including the central gate tower and spire which he recast in Neo-Classical style with columned porticos and pavilions. The heightened spire was gilded and topped with a model frigate. This has become a symbol of the city, just like the trumpet-blowing pair of angels on the portals of the façade overlooking the Neva.

In the 1840s, shipbuilding was moved downstream and the Admiralty was handed over to the Russian navy. It has been occupied by the Naval Engineering School since 1925.

Tower and spire of the Admiralty (1806–23)

❷ Senate Square
Сенатская Площадь
Senatskaya ploshchad

Map 5 C1. 🚃 3, 10, 22, 27, 71, 100,
K-169, K-187, K-306. 🚊 5, 22.

The momentous Decembrist uprising took place here on 14 December 1825 *(see p25)*. During the inauguration of Nicholas I, Guards officers intent on imposing a constitutional monarchy attempted to stage a coup d'état in the square. After a confused stand-off which lasted several hours, the rebel forces were routed with grape-shot by the new tsar and loyalist troops. Five of the ringleaders were later executed and 121 others exiled to Siberia, thus effectively ending Russia's first revolution.

The imposing Neo-Classical buildings that command the western side of Senate Square were intended to harmonize with the Admiralty. Designed by Carlo Rossi between 1829–34, they were the headquarters of two important institutions which were originally created by Peter the Great: the Supreme Court, or Senate, and the Holy Synod which was responsible for the administration of the Orthodox Church. The two buildings, which now house historical archives, are linked to each other by a triumphal arch supported by Corinthian columns and decorated with a Neo-Classical frieze and a plethora of statuary.

The Bronze Horseman (1766–78)

❸ The Bronze Horseman
Медный Всадник
Mednyy Vsadnik

Senatskaya ploshchad. **Map** 5 C1.
🚃 3, 10, 22, 27, 71, 100, K-169, K-187,
K-306. 🚊 5, 22.

The magnificent equestrian statue of Peter the Great was unveiled in Senate Square in 1782, as a tribute from Catherine the Great. The statue is known as the Bronze Horseman after Pushkin's famous poem. A French sculptor, Etienne Falconet, spent more than 12 years overseeing this ambitious project. The pedestal alone weighs 1,625 tonnes and

The Bronze Horseman by Pushkin

The famous statue of Peter the Great is brought to life in Alexander Pushkin's epic poem *The Bronze Horseman* (1833). In this haunting

1956 stamp of Pushkin and the statue that inspired his poem

vision of the Great Flood of 1824 *(see p39)*, the hero is pursued through the mist-shrouded streets by the terrifying bronze statue. Pushkin's words evoke the domineering and implacable will for which the tsar was renowned: *"How terrible he was in the surrounding gloom! … what strength was in him! And in that steed, what fire!"*

was hewn from a single block of granite, which was hauled from the Gulf of Finland. It bears the simple inscription "To Peter I from Catherine II" in Latin and Russian. A serpent, symbolizing treason, is crushed beneath the horse's hooves.

❹ Horseguards' Manège

Конногвардейский манеж

Konnogvardeyskiy manezh

Isaakievskaya ploshchad 1. **Map** 5 C2. **Tel** 312 2243, 571 4157 (ticket office). **Open** variable. 🚌 3, 22, 27, 71, 100, K-169, K-187, K-306. 🚎 5, 22. ⚹ ▯

The enormous indoor riding school of the Life Guards' Mounted Regiment was built by Giacomo Quarenghi in 1804–7 to resemble a Roman basilica. Two clues to the building's original function are the dynamic frieze of a horse race beneath the pediment and the statues on either side of the portico. The statues of the unclad twin sons of Zeus reining in wild horses are copies from the Quirinale Palace in Rome. The Holy Synod, scandalized by this display of nakedness so near to St Isaac's Cathedral, ordered their removal. The statues were re-erected in 1954.

Next to the manège, which is now used as an exhibition hall, are two marble pillars surmounted by bronze angels cast in Berlin, which were sent over from Germany as a gift in 1840.

❺ St Isaac's Cathedral

See pp82–3.

❻ St Isaac's Square

Исаакиевская площадь

Issakievskaya ploshchad

Map 5 C2. 🚌 3, 10, 22, 27, 71, 100, K-169, K-187, K-306. 🚎 5, 22.

Dominated by Auguste de Montferrand's majestic St Isaac's Cathedral, this impressive square was created during the reign of Nicholas I, although a few of its earlier buildings date from the 18th century. The monument to Nicholas I at its centre was

St Isaac's Cathedral, statue of St Nicholas I and the Angleterre, St Isaac's Square

also designed by Montferrand. Erected in 1859 and sculpted by Pyotr Klodt, it depicts the tsar in the uniform of one of Russia's most prestigious regiments, the Kavalergardskiy guards. The pedestal is embellished with allegorical sculptures of his daughters and his wife, who represent Faith, Wisdom, Justice and Might.

On the western side of the square, at No. 9, is the Myatlev House, a Neo-Classical mansion dating from the 1760s, which belonged to one of Russia's most illustrious families. The French encyclopedist Denis Diderot stayed here in 1773–4 following an invitation from Catherine the Great. In the 1920s it became the premises of the State Institute of Artistic Culture where some of Russia's most influential avant-garde artists, including Kazimir Malevich and Vladimir Tatlin (*see p109*), worked.

The impressive granite-faced building alongside is the former German embassy, designed in 1911–12 by the German architect Peter Behrens.

Across the 100-m- (330-ft-) wide Blue Bridge (Siniy most), which was the site of a serf market until 1861, the Mariinskiy Palace (*see p79*) dominates the southern end of the square.

❼ Angleterre Hotel

Гостиница Астория

Gostinitsa Astoriya

Malaya Morskaya ulitsa 24. **Map** 6 D2. **Tel** 494 5666. 🚌 3, 10, 22, 27, K-169, K-306. 🚎 5, 22. See Where to Stay, p178.

Now one of St Petersburg's leading hotels, the seven-storey Angleterre was designed by Fyodor Lidval in the Style-Moderne (*see p73*) in 1910–12.

American writer John Reed, author of the famous eyewitness account of the Revolution *Ten Days that Shook the World*, was staying here when the Bolsheviks seized power.

In 1925, the poet Sergey Yesenin, husband of Isadora Duncan, hanged himself in the annexe, after daubing the walls of his room with a farewell verse in his blood "To die is not new – but neither is it new to be alive".

The hotel's banqueting hall was to be the venue for Hitler's prematurely planned victory celebration, so sure was he that he would conquer the city.

Restored Style-Moderne foyer in the Angleterre Hotel, on the eastern edge of St Isaac's Square

❺ St Isaac's Cathedral

Исаакиевский собор

Isaakievskiy sobor

St Isaac's, one of the world's largest cathedrals, was designed in 1818 by the then unknown architect Auguste de Montferrand. The construction of the colossal building was a major engineering feat. Thousands of wooden piles were sunk into the marshy ground to support its weight of 300,000 tonnes and 48 huge columns were hauled into place. The cathedral opened in 1858 but was deconsecrated and became a museum of atheism during the Soviet era. Officially still a museum today, the church is filled with hundreds of 19th-century works of art.

Angels with Torch
Ivan Vitali created many of the cathedral's sculptures, including the pairs of angels supporting gas torches which crown the four attic corners.

KEY

① **St Catherine's Chapel** has an exquisite white marble iconostasis, crowned by a sculpted Resurrection (1850–4) by Nikolay Pimenov.

② **Malachite** and lapis lazuli columns frame the iconostasis. About 16,000 kg (35,280 lbs) of malachite decorate the cathedral.

③ **The north pediment** is ornamented with a bronze relief (1842–4) of the Resurrection designed by François Lemaire.

④ **This chapel** honours Alexander Nevsky, who defeated the Swedes in 1240 *(see p19)*.

⑤ **The mosaic icons** on the iconostasis are by Bryullov, Neff and Zhivago.

⑥ **The silver dove** (1850) hanging in the cupola is a symbol of the Holy Spirit.

⑦ **Portraits of apostles and evangelists**

⑧ **Statue of St Matthew**

⑨ **The relief** of St Isaac blessing the Emperor Theodosius and his wife Flaccila is by Ivan Vitali. On the extreme left, Montferrand is depicted clutching a model of his cathedral.

⑩ **Red granite columns,** each weighing 114 tonnes, were transported from Finland by specially constructed ships.

⑪ **The vast interior** covers 4,000 sq m (43,000 sq ft).

⑫ **The walls** are adorned with 14 coloured marbles and 43 other types of semi-precious stones and minerals.

Exit

★ **Iconostasis**
Three rows of icons surround the royal doors through which a stained-glass window (1843) is visible. Above the doors is Pyotr Klodt's gilded sculpture, *Christ in Majesty* (1859).

VISITORS' CHECKLIST

Practical Information
Isaakievskaya ploshchad 1.
Map 5 C2. **Tel** 315 9732.
Open 10am–10:30pm Thu–Tue
(Oct–Apr: 11am–6pm). 🎟 📷
📆 ✝ religious festivals.

Transport
Ⓜ Admiralteyskaya, Sadovaya.
🚌 3, 10, 22, 27, 71, 100, K-169,
K-190, K-289. 🚋 5, 22.

The Dome
From the dome there are panoramic views
over the city which include the Admiralty
(see p80) and the Hermitage *(see pp86–95)*.
Adorning the gilded dome are angels
sculpted by Josef Hermann.

★ Ceiling Painting
The celestial *Virgin in
Majesty* by Karl Bryullov
(see p107), dating to 1847,
covers an area of 816 sq m
(8,780 sq ft). It is ringed
by exuberant gilded
stucco mouldings
and white marble.

The entrance is
through the side doors
on St Isaac's Square

South Doors
Three great doors of oak and bronze (1841–6),
weighing 20 tonnes, are decorated with carved
reliefs by Ivan Vitali. The exteriors of the doors
show scenes from the life of Christ and saints,
including Alexander Nevsky *(see p132)*.

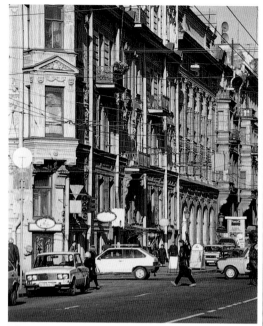

Malaya Morskaya ulitsa with No. 13 in the middle

❽ Malaya Morskaya Ulitsa

Малая Морская у лица

Malaya Morskaya ulitsa

Map 6 D1. ⬛ 3, 10, 22, 27, K-306. 🚎 5, 22.

Malaya Morskaya Ulitsa used to be referred to as ulitsa Gogolya after the great prose-writer, Nikolai Gogol (1809–52) who lived at No. 17 from 1833–6. It was here that Gogol wrote *The Diary of a Madman* and *The Nose*, two biting satires on the archetypal Petersburg bureaucrat "drowned by the trivial, meaningless labours at which he spends his useless life". Gogol's bitingly humorous, fantastical and grotesque tales reveal a nightmarish and deeply pessimistic view of modern urban life.

The composer Pyotr Tchaikovsky *(see p44)* died in the top-floor apartment of No. 13 shortly after the completion of his *Pathétique* symphony in November 1893. Officially he was supposed to have died of cholera, but it is commonly believed that he committed suicide, due to pressure from Conservatory colleagues wishing to avoid a scandal after Tchaikovsky's alleged homosexual affair.

The house at No. 23 was occupied by the novelist Fyodor Dostoevsky *(see p125)* from 1848–9. It was here that he was arrested and charged with political conspiracy for his participation in the socialist Petrashevsky Circle *(see p125)*. Today, the street manages to exude a 19th-century feel despite the many busy shops and businesses.

❾ House of Fabergé

Дом Фаберже

Dom Faberzhe

Bolshaya Morskaya ulitsa 24. **Map** 6 D1. **Closed** to public. ⬛ 3, 22, 27. 🚎 5, 22.

The world-famous Fabergé jeweller's was established in Bolshaya Morskaya ulitsa in 1842 by Gustav Fabergé, of French Huguenot origin. It was not until the 1880s that his sons Carl and Agathon abandoned conventional jewellery-making for intricate and exquisitely crafted *objets d'art* of a highly innovative design. Most famous of all their works are the imaginatively designed Easter eggs made for the tsars.

In 1900 Carl moved the business from No. 16–18 into purpose-built premises at No. 24, where it remained until the Revolution. The exterior, designed by his relative, Karl Schmidt, has striking triangular roof gables and multi-textured stonework. The original showroom, with its squat red granite pillars, was on the ground floor. It is still a jeweller's, but with no connection to Fabergé. In the workshops above, young apprentices were trained by master craftsmen in the arts of enamelling, engraving, stone cutting and jewelling.

In 1996, the 150th anniversary of Carl Fabergé's birth was marked by the unveiling of a memorial plaque at No. 24 and of a monument, designed by the sculptor Leonid Aristov and others, on the corner of Zanevskiy prospekt and prospekt Energetikov.

Fabergé Eggs

In 1885 Alexander III commissioned the Fabergé brothers to create an Easter egg for Tsarina Maria Fyodorovna. Inside the shell of gold and white enamel was a beautifully sculpted golden hen. A tradition was established and, by the Revolution, there were 54 Fabergé Easter eggs, no two of which were alike. The *pièce de résistance* is the Siberian Railway Egg, commissioned by Nicholas II in 1900. The Bonbonnière Egg was commissioned by Kelch, a wealthy industrialist, for his wife Varvara in 1903. A large private collection of Fabergé eggs and other jewellery is on view at the Fabergé Museum, housed in the spectacular Shuvalov Palace *(see p115)*.

A gilded Fabergé egg

Death of a Poet

In November 1836 Pushkin received an anonymous letter which awarded him the title of "Grand Master of the Most Serene Order of Cuckolds". It had been sent by Georges d'Anthès, a ne'er-do-well cavalry officer who for some time had been

Aleksey Naumov's painting of Pushkin, fatally wounded after his duel

making overtures towards Pushkin's wife, the beauty and socialite Natalya Goncharova. Pushkin challenged d'Anthès to a duel and, on the afternoon of 27 January 1837, he met his opponent in snow-bound woodland to the north of the city. D'Anthès fired first and Pushkin was mortally wounded. He died two days later, aged 38. D'Anthès was later reduced to the ranks and banished from Russia.

Sign outside the Literary Café

⑩ Literary Café
Литературное кафе
Literaturnoe kafe

Nevskiy prospekt 18. **Map** 6 E1. **Tel** 312 6057. **Open** 11am–11pm Sun–Thu, 11–1am Fri & Sat. Ⓜ Nevskiy Prospekt. ♿

Also known as the Café Wulf et Beranger after its original owners, this café is famous for its association with Alexander Pushkin, Russia's greatest poet *(see p45)*. It was here that Pushkin met his second, Konstantin Danzas, before setting out for his ill-fated duel with Baron d'Anthès. The café was a popular haunt for St Petersburg writers from its beginning, frequented by Fyodor Dostoevsky and the poet Mikhail Lermontov (1814–41), among others.

Despite its hallowed literary importance and elegant setting, in Vasiliy Stasov's handsome building of 1815, the café itself does not merit the high prices.

⑪ Palace Square
Дворцовая площадь
Dvortsovaya ploshchad

Map 6 D1. 🚌 7, 10, 24, 191. 🚎 1, 7, 10, 11.

Palace Square has played a unique role in Russian history. Before the Revolution the square was the setting for colourful military parades, often led by the tsar on horseback. In January 1905, it was the scene of the massacre of "Bloody Sunday" *(see p28)* when gathered troops fired on thousands of unarmed demonstrators. Then, on 7 November 1917, Lenin's Bolshevik supporters secured the Revolution by attacking the Winter Palace *(see pp30–31)* from the square, as well as its west side. It is still a favourite venue for political meetings and cultural events such as rock concerts *(see p53)*.

The resplendent square is the work of the inspired architect Carlo Rossi *(see p112)*. Facing the Winter Palace on its southern side is Rossi's magnificent General Staff Building (1819–29), the headquarters for the Russian army. Rossi demolished an entire row of houses to make room for it. The two graceful, curving wings (the eastern one now a branch of the Hermitage) are connected by a double arch leading to Bolshaya Morskaya ulitsa. The arch is crowned by a sculpture of Victory in her chariot (1829), by Stepan Pimenov and Vasiliy Demut-Malinovskiy. Forming the eastern side of this striking architectural ensemble is the Guards Headquarters, designed by Aleksandr Bryullov in 1837–43. To the west lies the Admiralty *(see p80)*.

The Alexander Column in the centre of the square is dedicated to Tsar Alexander I for his role in the triumph over Napoleon *(see pp24–5)*. On the pedestal are inscribed the words "To Alexander I, from a grateful Russia". The red granite pillar is balanced by its 600-tonne weight, making it the largest free-standing monument in the world. The column was designed by Auguste de Montferrand in 1829 and it took 2,400 soldiers and workmen two years to hew and transport the granite. It was erected in 1830–34. The column is topped by a bronze angel, and together they stand 47 m (154 ft) high.

The Alexander Column and General Staff Building in Palace Square

⓬ The Hermitage

Эрмитаж
Ermitazh

One of the largest museums in the world, the Hermitage occupies a grand ensemble of buildings. The most impressive is the Winter Palace *(see pp94–5)*, to which Catherine the Great added the more intimate Small Hermitage. In 1771–87, she built the Large Hermitage to house her growing collection of art. The Theatre was built in 1785–7, the New Hermitage in 1839–51. The New and Large Hermitages were opened by Nicholas I in 1852 as a public museum. From 1918 to 1939 the Winter Palace was slowly incorporated into the museum ensemble. In the late 1990s the majestic, Neo-Classical General Staff Building was added *(see p89)*. It houses the collections of 19th- and 20th-century art.

Atlantes
Ten 5-m- (16-ft-) tall granite Atlantes hold up what was the public entrance to the Hermitage museum from 1852 until after the Revolution.

★ Raphael Loggias
Catherine was so impressed by engravings of Raphael's frescoes in the Vatican that in 1787 she commissioned copies to be made on canvas. Small alterations were made, such as replacing the Pope's coat of arms with the Romanov two-headed eagle.

Theatre
During Catherine's reign, there were regular performances held in Quarenghi's theatre. Today it hosts conferences and concerts *(see p204)*.

KEY

① **The Winter Canal** *(see p38)*

② **A gallery** spanning the canal connects the theatre to the Large Hermitage and forms the theatre foyer.

③ **The Large Hermitage** was designed by Yuriy Velten to house Catherine's paintings.

④ **Court ministries** were located here until the 1880s.

⑤ **The New Hermitage** (1839–51) was designed by Leo von Klenze to form a coherent part of the Large

Hermitage. It is the only purpose-built museum within the whole complex.

⑥ **The Small Hermitage** (1764–75), by Vallin de la Mothe and Yuriy Velten, served as Catherine's retreat from the bustle of the court.

⑦ **Palace Square**

⑧ **River Neva**

⑨ **The Winter Palace** (1754–62) was the official residence of the imperial family until the Revolution.

Hanging Gardens
This unusual raised garden is decorated with statues and fountains. During the Siege of Leningrad (*see p29*) Hermitage curators grew vegetables here.

VISITORS' CHECKLIST

Practical Information
Dvortsovaya ploshchad 2 (Main building); 6/8 (General Staff Building). **Map** 2 D5. **Tel** 710 9079. **Open** 10:30am–6pm Tue, Thu, Sat & Sun; 10:30am–9pm Wed & Fri. (last adm: 1 hr before closing). 🅰 📞 English (571 8446 to book). 🅱 📷 💻
Ⓦ **hermitagemuseum.org**

Transport
Ⓜ Admiralteyskaya. 🚌 7, 10, 24, 191. 🚊 1, 7, 10, 11.

Winter Palace Façade
Rastrelli embellished the palace façades with 400 columns and 16 different window designs.

Main entrance via courtyard

General Staff Building ↑

⑦

⑥

⑨

⑧

★ Pavilion Hall
(1850–58) Andrey Stakenschneider's striking white marble and gold hall replaced Catherine's original interior. It houses Englishman James Cox's famous Peacock Clock (1772), which was once owned by Catherine's secret husband, Prince Grigory Potemkin.

★ Winter Palace State Rooms
The tsars spared no expense in decorating rooms such as the Hall of St George. These rooms were not intended for private life, but were used instead for state ceremonies.

The Hermitage Collections

Catherine the Great purchased some of Western Europe's best collections between 1764 and 1774, acquiring over 2,500 paintings, 10,000 carved gems, 10,000 drawings and a vast amount of silver and porcelain with which to adorn her palaces. None of her successors matched the quantity of her remarkable purchases. After the Revolution, the nationalization of both royal and private property brought more paintings and works of applied art, making the Hermitage one of the world's leading museums.

The Knights' Hall (1842–51) is used for displays of armour and weapons from the former imperial arsenal.

Entrance for tours and guided groups

First Floor

Stairs to ground floor

Raphael Loggias *(see p86)*

The Gallery of Ancient Painting (1842–51) is decorated with scenes from ancient literature. It houses a superb display of 19th-century European sculpture.

Skylight Rooms

Ground Floor

European Gold Collection

★ **Litta Madonna** (c.1491)
One of two works by Leonardo da Vinci in the museum, this masterpiece was admired by his contemporaries and was frequently copied.

The Hall of Twenty Columns (1842–51) is painted in Etruscan style.

Main Complex Gallery Guide

Enter via Palace Square, then cross the main courtyard; group tours use other entrances. Start with the interiors of the Winter Palace state rooms on the first floor to get an overview of the museum. For 19th- and 20th-century European Art use either of the staircases on the Palace Square side of the Winter Palace. Note that collections may move.

Main entrance

★ **Abraham's Sacrifice** (1635)
In the 1630s Rembrandt was painting religious scenes in a High Baroque style, using dramatic and striking gestures rather than detail to convey his message.

Second Floor

Stairs to first floor

Stairs to first floor

The Numismatic Collection consists of over 1 million objects. Only part of it is on display in temporary exhibitions.

Stairs to Numismatic Collection

Stairs to second floor

Stairs to second floor, Numismatic Collection only

Greek and Oriental Gold Collection

The Winter Palace state rooms *(see pp94–5)* contain magnificent Russian and European *objets d'art*.

★ **Portrait of Fath Ali Shah Standing** (1809-1810)
This royal portrait by court artist Mihr Ali, shows the second monarch of the Qajar dynasty. It was painted in the manner of European state portraiture, notable for its use of rich symbolism.

The General Staff Building
This spectacular, crescent-shaped building is directly across Palace Square from the main museum complex. The works on display here include Matisse's *La Danse* and masterpieces by Van Gogh.

Statue of Voltaire (1781)
Catherine the Great corresponded with Voltaire for over 15 years. She commissioned Jean-Antoine Houdon's marble statue, in which the French writer is dressed as a Greek philosopher.

Key to Floor Plan

- ☐ Prehistoric
- ☐ Classical
- ☐ Far East and Central Asia
- ☐ Russian
- ☐ Italian and Spanish
- ☐ Flemish, Dutch and German
- ☐ French and European
- ☐ Caucasus
- ☐ Temporary exhibition space
- ☐ Non-exhibition space
- ☐ No access

Exploring the Hermitage Collections

It is impossible to absorb the Hermitage's vast, encyclopedic collection in one or even two visits. Whether it be Scythian gold, antique vases and cameos, or Iranian silver, every room has something to capture the eye. The furniture, applied art, portraits and rich clothing of the imperial family went to make up the Russian section, which also includes the superb state rooms. The collection of European paintings was put together largely according to the personal taste of the imperial family, while most of the 19th- and 20th-century European art, notably the Impressionists, Matisse and Picasso, came from private collections after the Revolution.

Scythian gold stag dating from
7th–6th century BC

Prehistoric Art

Prehistoric artifacts found all over the former Russian Empire include pots, arrowheads and sculptures from Palaeolithic sites, which date back nearly 24,000 years, and rich gold items from the time of the Scythian nomads living in the 7th–3rd centuries BC.

Peter the Great's famous Siberian collection of delicate gold work includes Scythian animal-style brooches, sword handles and buckles. Objects continued to be discovered in Siberia and in 1897 a large stylized stag, which once decorated an iron shield, was found at Kostromskaya. This and other gold pieces are held in the European Gold Collection (for which a separate ticket is required). Copies are on display in the Scythian rooms.

Greek masters also worked for the Scythians, and from the Dnepr region came a late 5th-century comb decorated with amazingly naturalistic figures of Scythians fighting, as well as the late 4th-century Chertomlyk Vase with scenes

depicting animal taming. Excavations in the Altai, notably at Pazyryk in 1927–49, uncovered burials nearly 2,500 years old. Many perishable materials were preserved by the frozen land, including textiles, a burial cart and even a man's heavily tattooed skin.

Gonzaga Cameo (285–246 BC),
made in Alexandria

Classical Art

The large number of Graeco-Roman marble sculptures range from the famous Tauride Venus of the 3rd century BC, acquired by Peter the Great in 1720, to Roman portrait busts. The

smaller objects, however, are the real pride and joy of the Classical department.

The collection of red-figured Attic vases of the 6th–4th centuries BC is unequalled anywhere in the world. Exquisitely proportioned and with a lustrous shine, they are decorated with scenes of libation, episodes from the Trojan War, and, in one case, a famous image of the sighting of the first swallow (c.510 BC).

In the 4th and 3rd centuries BC, Tanagra was the centre for the production of small, elegant terracotta figurines. They were discovered in the 19th century and became so popular that fakes were produced on a grand scale. The Russian ambassador in Athens, Pyotr Saburov, put his collection together in the 1880s before the copies appeared, making it unusually valuable.

Catherine the Great's true passion was for carved gems, which she bought en masse. In just ten years, she purchased some 10,000 pieces. The largest and most stunning gem in the Classical collection, however, is the Gonzaga Cameo, which was presented by Napoleon's ex-wife Josephine Beauharnais to Tsar Alexander I in 1814.

The Greek and Oriental Gold Collection contains some items of 5th-century gold jewellery made by Athenian craftsmen. They used a filigree technique for working gold so finely that the detail can only be seen through a magnifying glass.

Far East and Central Asia

This selection of more than 180,000 artifacts covers a wide range of cultures, from ancient Egypt and Assyria, through Byzantium, India, Iran, China, Japan and the marvels of Uzbekistan and Tajikistan. The most complete sections are those where excavations were conducted by the Hermitage, mainly in China and Mongolia before the Revolution, and in Central Asia during the Soviet period.

Dating back to the 19th century BC, at the time of the Middle Kingdom, is a seated

8th-century fresco of a wounded warrior from Tajikistan

western oil painting, as in the *Portrait of Fatkh-Ali Shah* (1813–14). Uzbekistan and Tajikistan revealed marvellous frescoes in complexes of 8th-century buildings at Varaksha, Adjina-Tepe and Pendzhikent. Rare Mughal jewelled vessels, Iranian weapons and Chinese gold objects are displayed in the Greek and Oriental Gold Collection. These rooms are undergoing a three-year renovation.

Russian Art

Although major Russian works of art were transferred to the Russian Museum (*see pp106–9*) in 1898, everything else that belonged to the imperial family was nationalized after the Revolution. This included anything from official portraits and thrones to looking glasses and petticoats. Over 300 items of apparel belonging to Peter the Great alone survive. Later, the museum also began acquiring medieval Russian art, including icons and church utensils.

The tsars from Peter the Great onwards invited foreign craftsmen and artists to train locals. Peter studied with them and his

Universal sundial (1714–19) from Peter the Great's collection

fascination for practical things is reflected in his large collection of sundials, instruments and wood-turning lathes which includes the universal sundial by Master John Rowley. A bust by Bartolomeo Carlo Rastrelli (1723–30), however, portrays Peter as the mighty and cruel emperor.

Russian artists were soon combining traditional art forms with European skills to create such intricate marvels as the openwork walrus ivory vase by Nikolay Vereshchagin (1798), and the large silver sarcophagus and memorial to Alexander Nevsky, truly Russian in scale (1747–52).

The gunsmiths of Tula (south of Moscow) perfected their technique to such an extent that they began producing unique furniture in steel inlaid with gilded bronze, such as the decorative, Empire-style dressing table set (1801).

The state interiors (*see pp94–5*) are the pride of the Russian department, revealing the work of Russian and foreign craftsmen from the mid-18th to the early 20th century. The discovery of large deposits of coloured stones in the Urals inspired Russian artists to decorate whole rooms with malachite and to fill every corner of the Winter Palace with marble vases. It was through these rooms that the imperial family paraded on state occasions, greeting courtiers and ambassadors en route in the Field Marshals' Hall.

porphyry portrait of Pharaoh Amenemhet III. The star of the Egyptian collection is an extremely rare, small, wooden statue of a standing man from the 15th century BC.

From the Far East – Japan, India, Indonesia, China and Mongolia – comes an array of objects ranging from Buddhist sculptures and fabrics to a display of tiny netsukes (ivory toggles). Excavations at the cave temple of the Thousand Buddhas near Dun Huan in western China revealed 6th–10th-century icons, wall paintings and plaster sculptures, including the lions that once guarded the cave. During the 13th-century Mongol invasion, the town of Khara-Khoto was destroyed and taken over by the surrounding desert. The sand preserved many usually perishable objects, from 12th-century silks to woodcuts.

From Byzantium come early secular items, such as icons, religious utensils and a 5th-century ivory diptych with scenes from a Roman circus.

Iran produced a large number of silver and bronze vessels, many of which were taken by medieval traders to Siberia and the Urals where they were rediscovered by specialists in the 19th century. There is also a large collection of traditional Persian miniatures and a rich display of 19th-century Persian court portraits that mix traditional elements with those of

Steel dressing table set from Tula dating from 1801

Italian and Spanish Art

The display of Italian art contains some fine pieces. A few early works reveal the rise of the Renaissance in the 14th and 15th centuries and the styles then in vogue. Simone Martini's stiff *Madonna* (1340–44) contrasts with Fra Angelico's more humane fresco of the Virgin and Child (1424–30).

In the late 15th and early 16th century, artists disputed the merits of line, as practised by the Florentine school, and the merits of colour, virtue of the Venetians. The former can be seen in the *Litta Madonna* (c.1491) and the *Madonna Benois* (1478) by Leonardo da Vinci, a marble *Crouching Boy* by Michelangelo (c.1530) and two early portraits of the Virgin by Raphael (1502 and 1506). Venice is represented by *Judith* by Giorgione (1478–1510) and an array of works by Titian (c.1490–1576). The Skylight Rooms are packed with vast Baroque canvases, including works by Luca Giordano (1634–1704) and Guido Reni (1575–1642), and even larger 18th-century masterpieces by Tiepolo. The works of the Italian sculptor Antonio Canova (1757–1822) (*Cupid and Psyche, The Three Graces*) stand in the Gallery of Ancient Painting.

The Spanish collection is more modest, but Spain's greatest painters can all be

seen, from El Greco with *The Apostles Peter and Paul* (1587–92), through to Ribera, Murillo, and Zurbarán with *St Lawrence* (1636). The portrait of a courtier, *Count Olivares*, painted c.1640 by Velázquez, contrasts with a much earlier genre scene of a peasant's breakfast (1617–18).

Venus and Cupid (1509) by Lucas Cranach the Elder

Flemish, Dutch and German Art

The small collection of early paintings from the Netherlands includes a marvellous, jewel-like *Madonna and Child* (1430s) by

the Master of Flemalle. He is thought to have been the teacher of Rogier van der Weyden, who is represented by *St Luke Painting the Madonna* (c.1435).

Over 40 works by Rubens include religious subjects (*The Descent from the Cross*, 1617–18) and scenes from Classical mythology (*Perseus and Andromeda*, 1620–21), as well as landscapes and an immensely obese *Bacchus* (1636–40). His portraits, such as the *Infanta's Maid* (1625), reveal the link with his famous pupil Van Dyck, whose paintings include a series of formal, full-length portraits and a dashing and romantic self-portrait from the late 1620s.

The Dutch section is rich in Rembrandts. Within a short period of time he produced the dramatic *Abraham's Sacrifice* (1636), the gentle *Flora* (1634) and the brilliant effects of *The Descent from the Cross* (1634). One of his last works was the *Return of the Prodigal Son* (1668–9), which has an emotional depth unseen before.

Among the many small genre paintings is Gerard Terborch's *Glass of Lemonade* from the mid-17th century. All the usual elements of a genre scene are imbued with psychological tension and heavy symbolism.

In the German collection, it is the works of Lucas Cranach the Elder which captivate the viewer. His *Venus and Cupid* (1509), the stylish *Portrait of a Woman in a Hat* (1526) and the tender *Virgin and Child Beneath an Apple Tree* reveal the varied aspects of his talent.

French and English Art

French art was de rigueur for collectors in the 18th century. Major artists of the 17th century, including Louis Le Nain and the two brilliant and contrasting painters Claude Lorrain and Nicolas Poussin, are well represented. Antoine Watteau's elegant *Embarrassing Proposal* (c.1716), *Stolen Kiss* (1780s), by Jean-Honoré Fragonard, and François Boucher's fleshy and certainly far-from-virtuous heroines represent the more wicked side of

A Young Man Playing a Lute, by Michelangelo Caravaggio (1573–1610)

Still Life with the Attributes of the Arts (1766), by Jean-Baptiste Chardin

18th-century taste, but Catherine the Great preferred didactic or instructional works. She bought *Still Life with the Attributes of the Arts* (1766) by Chardin and, on the advice of Denis Diderot, Jean-Baptiste Greuze's moralizing *The Fruits of a Good Education* (1763). She also patronized sculptors, purchasing works by Etienne-Maurice Falconet (*Winter*, carved 1771) and Jean-Antoine Houdon (*Voltaire*, 1781).

Catherine also acquired English works, including a portrait of the philosopher John Locke (1697) by Sir Godfrey Kneller, who was also author of a portrait of Pyotr Potemkin (1682) in Russian 17th-century court dress. From Sir Joshua Reynolds Catherine commissioned *The Infant Hercules Strangling the Serpents* (1788). Her most daring purchase was of works by the still largely unknown Joseph Wright of Derby. *The Iron Forge* (1773) is a masterpiece of artificial lighting, but *Firework Display at the Castel Sant'Angelo* (1774–5) is a truly romantic fiery spectacle. She provided much work for English cabinet-makers and carvers of cameos. She became one of Josiah Wedgwood's most prestigious clients, ordering the famous Green Frog Service for her Chesma Palace (*see p132*).

The Green Frog Service, Wedgwood (1773–4)

19th- & 20th-Century European Art

Although the royal family did not patronize the new movements in art in the 19th century, there were far-sighted private individuals whose collections were nationalized and entered the Hermitage after the 1917 Revolution. Thanks to them, the Barbizon School is represented by works such as Camille Corot's charming silvery *Landscape with a Lake*, French Romanticism by two richly coloured Moroccan scenes of the 1850s by Delacroix. But Nicholas I himself did acquire works by the German Romantic painter Caspar David Friedrich, among them *On the Prow of the Ship* (1818–20).

Two collectors, Ivan Morozov and Sergey Shchukin, brought the Hermitage its superb array of Impressionist and Post-Impressionist paintings. Monet's art can be admired both in his early *Woman in a Garden* (1860s) and in the later, more exploratory, *Waterloo Bridge, Effect of Mist* (1903). Renoir and Degas perpetually returned to women as

subjects, as in Renoir's charming *Portrait of the Actress Jeanne Samary* (1878) and Degas' pastels of women washing (1880s–90s). Pissarro's *Boulevard Montmartre in Paris* (1897) is typical of his urban scenes.

A change in colour and technique appeared as artists investigated new possibilities. Van Gogh used deeper tones in his *Women of Arles* (1888) and stronger brushstrokes in *Cottages* (1890). Gauguin turned to a different culture for inspiration, and his Tahitian period is represented by enigmatic works, such as *Ea Haere la Oe* (1893). In *The Smoker* (c.1890–2) and *Mont Ste-Victoire* (1896–8), Cézanne introduced experiments with plane and surface which were to have a strong influence on the next generation.

Matisse played both with colour and surface, in the carpet-like effect of *The Red Room* (1908–9) and the flatness of the panels *La Musique* and *La Danse* (1909–10). His visit to Morocco introduced new light effects, as in *Arab Coffeehouse* (1913), but it was Picasso who took Cézanne's experiments one stage further. In early works such as *Visit* (1902) from his Blue Period, Picasso concentrates on mood, but the surface destruction of the Cubist period of 1907–12, including *L'Homme aux Bras Croisés*, fills a whole room.

L'Homme aux Bras Croisés, painted by Pablo Picasso in 1909

The Winter Palace

Preceded by three earlier versions on this site, the existing Winter Palace (1754–62) is a superb example of Russian Baroque. Built for Tsarina Elizabeth, this opulent winter residence was the finest achievement of Bartolomeo Rastrelli. Though the exterior has changed little, the interiors were altered by a number of architects and then largely restored after a fire gutted the palace in 1837. After the assassination of Alexander II in 1881, the imperial family rarely lived here. During World War I a field hospital was set up in the Nicholas Hall and other state rooms. Then, in July 1917, the Provisional Government took the palace as its headquarters, which led to its storming by the Bolsheviks (see pp30–31).

★ **Small Throne Room**
Dedicated in 1833 to the memory of Peter the Great, this room houses a silver-gilt English throne, made in 1731.

KEY

① **North façade overlooking the Neva**

② **The Nicholas Hall,** the largest room in the palace, was always used for the first ball of the season.

③ **The Field Marshals' Hall** (1833) was the reception room where the devastating fire of 1837 broke out.

④ **The Hall of St George** (1795) has monolithic columns and wall facings of Italian Carrara marble.

⑤ **The 1812 Gallery** (1826) has portraits of Russian military heroes of the Napoleonic War, most by English artist George Dawe.

⑥ **The Armorial Hall** (1839), with its vast gilded columns, covers over 800 sq m (8,600 sq ft). Hospital beds were set up here during World War I.

⑦ **The French Rooms,** designed by Bryullov in 1839, house a collection of 18th-century French art.

⑧ **South façade on Palace Square**

⑨ **The White Hall** was decorated for the wedding of the future Alexander II in 1841.

⑩ **West wing**

⑪ **The Gothic Library** and other rooms in the northwest part of the palace were adapted to suit Nicholas II's bourgeois lifestyle. This wood-panelled library was created by Meltzer in 1894.

⑫ **The Rotunda** (1830) connected the private apartments in the west with the state apartments on the palace's north side.

★ **Main Staircase**
This vast, sweeping staircase (1762) was Rastrelli's masterpiece. It was from here that the imperial family watched the Epiphany ceremony of baptism in the Neva, which celebrated Christ's baptism in the Jordan.

Alexander Hall
Architect Aleksandr Bryullov
employed a mixture of Gothic
vaulting and Neo-Classical stucco
bas-reliefs of military themes in
this reception room of 1837.

Bartolomeo Rastrelli

The Italian architect Rastrelli (1700–71)
came to Russia with his father in 1716 to
work for Peter the Great. His rich Baroque
style became highly fashionable and he
was appointed Chief Court Architect in
1738. During Elizabeth's reign, Rastrelli
designed several buildings, including the
Winter Palace, the Palace of Tsarkoe Selo *(see
pp154–9)* and Smolnyy Convent *(see p130)*. Unlike Elizabeth,
Catherine the Great preferred Classical simplicity and Rastrelli
retired in 1763, after she came to power.

Dark Corridor
The French and Flemish
tapestries here include
*The Marriage of Emperor
Constantine*, made in Paris
in the 17th century to
designs by Rubens.

★ Malachite Room
Over two tonnes of
ornamental stone were
used in this sumptuous
room (1839) which
is decorated with
malachite columns
and vases, gilded doors
and ceiling, and rich
parquet flooring.

The Gold Drawing Room
Created in the 1850s, this room was
extravagantly decorated in the 1870s
with all-over gilding of walls
and ceiling. It houses a display of
Western European carved gems.

⓭ Millionaires' Street
Миллионная у лица
Millionnaya ulitsa

Map 2 E5.

Millionaires' Street takes its name from the aristocrats and members of the imperial family who once inhabited its opulent residences. Since the main façades and entrances overlook the river, some house numbers correspond to the embankment side.

On the eve of the Revolution, No. 26 (on the embankment) was the home of Grand Duke Vladimir Aleksandrovich who was responsible for firing on peaceful demonstrators on Bloody Sunday *(see p28)*. His consort, Maria Pavlovna, was one of Russia's leading society hostesses who gave soirées and balls that eclipsed even those of the imperial court. The building (1867–72), which was designed by Aleksandr Rezanov in the style of the Florentine Renaissance, is now the House of Scholars.

Putyatin's house, at No. 12 Millionaires' Street, witnessed the end of the Romanov dynasty. It was here that Grand Duke Mikhail Aleksandrovich, Nicholas II's brother, signed the decree of abdication in March 1917. Next door, No. 10, was where French novelist Honoré de Balzac stayed in 1843, while courting his future wife, Countess Eveline Hanska. The mid-19th-century house was designed by Andrey Stakenschneider for his own use.

The delicately sculpted façade of No. 10 Millionaires' Street

Gala staircase of the Marble Palace, built of stone quarried in the Urals

⓮ Marble Palace
Мраморный дворец
Mramornyy dvorets

Millionnaya ulitsa 5 (entrance from the Field of Mars). **Map** 2 E4. **Tel** 595 4248. 🚌 46, 49. **Open** 10am–6pm Mon, Wed & Fri–Sun; 1–9pm Thu. ♿ 📷 English. 🌐 **rusmuseum.ru**

The Marble Palace was built as a present from Catherine the Great to her lover Grigoriy Orlov who had been instrumental in bringing her to power in 1762 *(see p24)*. An early example of Neo-Classical architecture, dating from 1768–85, the building is considered to be Antonio Rinaldi's masterpiece.

The palace takes its name from the marbles used in its construction. Most of the interiors were reconstructed in the 1840s by Aleksandr Bryullov, although the gala staircase and the Marble Hall are Rinaldi's work. The latter has marbled walls of grey, green, white, yellow, pink and lapis lazuli, and a ceiling painting, the *Triumph of Venus* (1780s) by Stefano Torelli.

The palace, which housed a Lenin museum for 55 years, is now a branch of the Russian Museum *(see pp106–9)*. On display are temporary exhibitions of work by foreign artists and modern art bequeathed by

Eternal Flame, Field of Mars

the German collectors Peter and Irene Ludwig. Their collection includes a Picasso, *Large Heads* (1969), and work by post-war artists Jean-Michel Basquiat, Andy Warhol, Ilya Kabakov and Roy Lichtenstein.

In front of the palace stands a curious equestrian statue of Alexander III by Prince Pavel Trubetskoy. Unveiled on Ploshchad Vosstaniya in 1911, the ridiculed statue was removed from its original site in 1937 and its vast pedestal was cut up to create statues of new heroes, such as Lenin.

⓯ Field of Mars
Марсово Поле
Marsovo Pole

Map 2 F5. 🚌 46, 49.

Once a vast marshland, this area was drained during the 19th century and utilized for military manoeuvres and parades, fairs and other festivities. It was appropriately named after Mars, the Roman god of war. Between 1917 and 1923 the area, by then a sandy expanse, was nicknamed the "Petersburg Sahara". It was landscaped and transformed into a war memorial. The granite *Monument to Revolutionary Fighters* (1917–19), by Lev Rudnev, and the Eternal Flame (1957) commemorate the victims of the Revolutions of 1917 and the Civil War *(see p29)*. The west of the square is dominated by an imposing Neo-Classical building erected by Vasiliy Stasov in 1817–19. This was formerly the barracks of the Pavlovskiy Guards which were founded by Tsar Paul I in 1796. The military-obsessed tsar is said to have only recruited guardsmen with snub noses like his own. The Pavlovskiy officers were among the first to turn against the tsarist government in the 1917 Revolution *(see pp30–31)*.

Today the huge square is a popular spot for locals in the summer evenings, when the flowers are in bloom.

⑯ Summer Garden

Летний сад

Letniy sad

Letniy Sad. **Map** 2 F4. 📷 46, 49, K-212.
Open May–Sep: 10am–10pm Wed–
Mon; Oct–Mar: 10am–8pm Wed–Mon.
♿ 🖥

In 1704 Peter the Great commissioned this beautiful formal garden which was among the first in the city. Designed by a Frenchman in the style of Versailles, the *allées* were planted with imported elms and oaks and adorned with fountains, pavilions and some 250 Italian statues dating from the 17th and 18th centuries. A flood in 1777 destroyed most of the Summer Garden and the English-style garden which exists today is largely the result of Catherine the Great's more sober tastes. A splendid feature is the fine filigree iron grille (1771–84) along the Neva embankment, created by Yuriy Velten and Pyotr Yegorov.

For a century the Summer Garden was an exclusive preserve of the nobility. When the garden was opened to "respectably dressed members of the public" by Nicholas I, two Neo-Classical pavilions, the Tea House and the Coffee House, were erected overlooking the Fontanka. These are now used for temporary exhibitions of art.

Nearby, the bronze statue of Ivan Krylov, Russia's most famous writer of fables, is a favourite with Russian children. It was sculpted by Pyotr Klodt in 1854 with charming bas-reliefs on the pedestal depicting animals from his fables.

Ivan Krylov's statue amid autumn foliage in the Summer Garden

⑰ Summer Palace

Летний дворец

Letniy dvorets

Naberezhnaya Kutuzova. **Map** 2 F4.
📷 46, 49, K-76, K-212. **Closed** for restoration until 2018.

Built for Peter the Great, the modest two-storey Summer Palace is the oldest stone building in the city. It was designed in the Dutch style by Domenico Trezzini and was completed in 1714. The Prussian sculptor Andreas Schlüter created the delightful maritime bas-reliefs (1713) as an allegorical commentary on Russia's naval triumphs under Peter the Great's stewardship.

Grander than his wooden cabin *(see p75)*, Peter's second St Petersburg residence is still by no means comparable to the magnificent palaces built by his successors. On the ground floor, the reception room is hung with portraits of the tsar and his ministers and contains Peter's oak Admiralty Chair. The tsar's bedroom has its original four-poster bed with a coverlet of Chinese silk, and an 18th-century ceiling painting showing the triumph of Morpheus, the god of sleep. Next door is the turnery which contains some original Russian lathes and an elaborately carved wooden meteorological instrument, designed in Dresden in 1714.

The palace boasted the city's first plumbing system with water piped directly into the kitchen. The original black marble sink can still be seen, along with the beautifully tiled kitchen stove and an array of early 18th-century cooking utensils. The kitchen opens onto the exquisite dining room, imaginatively refurbished to convey an atmosphere of domesticity. It was used only for small family gatherings since major banquets were held at the Menshikov Palace *(see p64)*.

An original staircase leads up to the first floor and the more lavish suite of Peter's second wife, Catherine. The throne in the aptly named Throne Room is ornamented with Nereides and other sea deities. The glass cupboards in the Green Room once displayed Peter's fascinating collection of curiosa before it was transferred to the Kunstkammer *(see p62)*. The palace is currently undergoing major reconstruction to restore the building as closely as possible to its original state.

The remarkable stove in the Summer Palace's tiled kitchen

GOSTINYY DVOR

The Great Bazaar, Gostinyy Dvor, was the commercial heart of St Petersburg at the beginning of the 18th century and today it still hums with activity. A profusion of smaller retail outlets soon appeared on and around Nevskiy prospekt. Thriving communities of foreign merchants and businessmen also took up residence in the neighbourhood.

Until the mid-19th century, shops in this area catered almost exclusively for the luxury end of the market, fulfilling the limitless demand, created by the royal and aristocratic households, for gold and silverware, jewellery and haute couture. Increasing commercial

and financial activity created a new middle class of business entrepreneurs. By the Revolution, banks proliferated around Nevskiy prospekt, their imposing new offices introducing diverse architectural styles to a largely Neo-Classical setting. Today the wheels of capitalism are turning again and Nevskiy prospekt still attracts a wealthy clientele. In contrast to the bustling commercial atmosphere of much of the area is the calm oasis of Arts Square, with the Russian Museum and other institutions which act as a reminder of the city's rich cultural life.

Sights at a Glance

Churches
1. Church on Spilled Blood p102
7. Armenian Church
15. Cathedral of Our Lady of Kazan
17. Lutheran Church

Museums
2. Mikhaylovskiy Castle
3. Russian Museum pp106–9
19. Pushkin House-Museum
20. Fabergé Museum

Streets and Squares
4. Arts Square
6. Nevskiy Prospekt
11. Ostrovskiy Square

12. Ulitsa Zodchego Rossi

Markets and Shops
8. Gostinyy Dvor
9. Yeliseev's
14. Apraksin Market

Palaces
10. Anichkov Palace
13. Vorontsov Palace
16. Stroganov Palace

Hotels
5. Belmond Grand Hotel Europe

Historic Buildings
18. Academic Capella

Restaurants pp188–90
1. Aragvi
2. Bellevue Brasserie
3. Brasserie de Metropol
4. Caviar Bar and Restaurant
5. City Grill
6. Erivan
7. Fartuk
8. Fiolet
9. Gras
10. Jack & Chan
11. Kavkaz-Bar
12. Kilikia
13. Kvartirka
14. L'Europe
15. Mama Roma
16. Meat Head
17. Park Giuseppe
18. Pelmeniya
19. Pirogovy Dvorik
20. Rada & K
21. Suliko
22. Tsar
23. Yat

See also Street Finder map 6

◀ Richly decorated façade on the southern portico of the 19th-century Church on Spilled Blood   **For keys to symbols** see back flap

Street-by-Street: Around Arts Square

The aptly named Arts Square, one of Carlo Rossi's finest creations, is surrounded by buildings revealing the city's impressive cultural heritage. The grand palace housing the Russian Museum is flanked by theatres and the Philharmonia concert hall. Behind it is the leafy Mikhaylovskiy Garden, a haunt of St Petersburg's intellectuals. The gardens stretch down to the beautiful Moyka river which together with two other waterways, the Griboedov and Fontanka, create a shimmering frame for this picturesque area.

❶ ★ **Church on Spilled Blood**
Colourful mosaics and elaborate stone carving are the main features of the church's exterior, which emulates traditional 17th-century Russian style.

Mikhaylovskiy Garden

NABEREZHNAYA REKI MOY

MOY

❸ ★ **Russian Museum**
Located in Rossi's Mikhaylovskiy Palace, this famous gallery boasts a fabulous collection of Russian painting, sculpture and applied art. The grand staircase and White Hall are original features.

KANAL GRIBOEDOVA

NAB KANALA GRIBOEDOVA

INZHENERNAYA ULITS

ITALYANSKAYA ULITSA

Statue of Pushkin (1957)

Nevskiy prospekt

❹ **Arts Square**
The square's present name derives from the number of cultural institutions situated here. On the western side, the Mikhailovsky Theatre opened in 1833 for opera performances.

The Great Hall of the Philharmonia is one of the major concert venues in St Petersburg (see p204).

❺ **Belmond Grand Hotel Europe**
This famous St Petersburg hotel was constructed by Ludwig Fontana in 1873–5. Mighty atlantes adorn its eclectic façade which stretches all the way down to Nevskiy prospekt.

Locator Map
See Street Finder map 6

The Panteleymon Bridge was rebuilt in 1907–8 to support a new tramway but it retains its original Empire-style decor by Lev Ilyin *(see p39).*

The bird statue, cast in 1995 by Rezo Gabriadze, refers to a popular rhyme about vodka drinking.

Statue of Peter the Great (1747)

❷ Mikhaylovskiy Castle
Originally built for Paul I in 1797–1801, this castle was acquired by the Guards Corps of Engineers in 1823. Today it forms part of the Russian Museum and displays historical portraits.

NAB REKI FONTANKA

ZAMKOVAYA ULITSA

FONTANKA

PLOSCHAD BELINSKOVO

SADOVAYA ULITSA

INZHENERNAYA ULITSA

KLENOVAYA ALLEY

KARAVANNAYA ULITSA

MANEZHNAYA PLOSCHAD

 Nevskiy prospekt

Key

— Suggested route

0 metres 100
0 yards 100

The Museum of Hygiene, with macabre displays of preserved human organs, was set up in 1919 to teach the public about health and hygiene.

The Circus or *"tsirk"* began performing in the 19th century when it was known as the Ciniselli Circus. It still offers traditional performances *(see p203)* in its historic venue by the Fontanka. Its original façade was reinstated in 2003.

❶ Church on Spilled Blood

Храм Спаса-на-Крови
Khram Spasa-na-Krovi

The Church on Spilled Blood, also known as the Resurrection Church of Our Saviour, was built on the spot where on 1 March 1881 Tsar Alexander II was assassinated *(see p28)*. In 1883 his successor, Alexander III, launched a competition for a permanent memorial. The winning design, in the Russian Revival style favoured by the tsar himself, was by Alfred Parland and Ignatiy Malyshev. The foundation stone was laid in October 1883.

A riot of colour, the overall effect of the church is created by the imaginative juxtaposition of materials. Inside, more than 20 types of minerals, including jasper, rhodonite , porphyry and Italian marble are lavished on the mosaics of the iconostasis, icon cases, canopy and floor. The interior reopened in 1998 after more than 20 years of restoration.

VISITORS' CHECKLIST

Practical Information
Nab kanala Griboedova 2b. **Map** 2
E5. **Tel** 315 1636. **Open** May–Sep:
10:30am–10:30pm (Oct–Apr:
10:30am–6pm) Thu–Tue. 🖂 📷 🖥 **cathedral.ru**

Transport
Ⓜ Gostinyy Dvor, Nevskiy Prospekt.

Mosaic Tympanum Mosaic panels showing scenes from the New Testament adorn the exterior. They were based on designs by artists such as Viktor Vasnetsov and Mikhail Nesterov.

The tent-roofed steeple is 81 m (265 ft) high.

Coat of Arms
The 144 mosaic coats of arms on the bell tower represent the regions, towns and provinces of the Russian Empire. They were intended to reflect the grief shared by all Russians in the wake of Alexander's assassination.

Intricate Detailing
The flamboyant Russian Revival style of the exterior provides a dramatic contrast to the Neo-Classical and Baroque architecture which dominates the centre of St Petersburg.

Jewellers' enamel was used to cover the 1,000 sq m (10,760 sq ft) surface of the five domes.

Glazed ceramic tiles enliven the façade.

Mosaic portraits of the saints are set in tiers of *kokoshniki* gables. Almost 7,000 sq m (75,300 sq ft) of mosaics embellish the church's extravagant exterior.

Twenty dark red plaques of Norwegian granite are engraved in gilt letters with the most outstanding events of Alexander II's reign (1855–81). Among the historic events recorded are the emancipation of the serfs in 1861 and the conquest of Central Asia (1860–81).

Window Frames
The windows are flanked by carved columns of ornate Estonian marble. The casings are in the form of double and triple *kokoshniki* (tiered decorative arches).

South façade of Mikhaylovskiy Castle and statue of Peter the Great

❷ Mikhaylovskiy Castle

Михайловский замок

Mikhaylovskiy zamok

Sadovaya ulitsa 2. **Map** 2 F5. **Tel** 570 5112. 🚌 46, K-212. **Open** 10am–6pm Mon, Wed & Fri–Sun; 1–9pm Thu. 🅿️ 🎦 book by phone. ♿

The imposing red-brick castle overlooking the Moyka and Fontanka rivers is also known as the Engineers' Castle. It was erected in 1797–1801 by Vasiliy Bazhenov and Vincenzo Brenna for Tsar Paul I. The tsar's obsessive fear of being assassinated led him to surround his new residence with moats and drawbridges, and to build a secret underground passage to the barracks on the Field of Mars (*see p96*). Unfortunately, all these precautions proved futile and, after living in his fortified castle for just 40 days, Paul fell victim to a military conspiracy which resulted in his murder (*see p24*).

In 1823 the fortress was acquired by the Guards Corps of Engineers. The school's most famous graduate was the writer Fyodor Dostoevsky (*see p125*). Today the castle serves as a branch of the nearby Russian Museum. It is used to house temporary exhibitions.

The Church of the Archangel Michael is accessed via the exhibition and is a good example of Brenna's Neo-Classical style.

In front of the castle stands a bronze statue of Peter the Great on horseback, designed by Bartolomeo Carlo Rastrelli and cast in 1747.

❸ Russian Museum

See pp106–9.

❹ Arts Square

Площадь Искусств

Ploshchad Iskusstv

Map 6 F1. Ⓜ Nevskiy Prospekt, Gostinyy Dvor.

Several of the city's leading cultural institutions are located on this leafy Neo-Classical square, hence its name. The attractive square was designed by Carlo Rossi in the early 19th century to harmonize with the magnificent Mikhaylovskiy Palace (now the Russian Museum) which stands on its northern side.

On the opposite side of the square is the Great Hall of the St Petersburg Philharmonia, also known as the Shostakovich Hall (*see p45*). This is where the Philharmonic Orchestra has been based since the 1920s (*see p204*). Constructed by Paul Jacot in 1834–9, it started as a Nobles' Club where concerts were held.

Among the works premiered here were Beethoven's *Missa Solemnis* in 1824 and Tchaikovsky's (*see p44*) *Pathétique* in 1893.

On the square's western side is the Mikhailovsky Theatre (*see p204*), rebuilt by Albert Kavos in the mid-19th century. In the centre of the square is a sculpture of one of Russia's greatest literary figures, Alexander Pushkin (*see p45*). The statue was executed by leading post-war sculptor, Mikhail Anikushin.

Belmond Grand Hotel Europe's elegant Style-Moderne restaurant (*see p190*)

❺ Belmond Grand Hotel Europe

Гранд Отель Европа

Grand Otel Evropa

Mikhaylovskaya ulitsa 1/7. **Map** 6 F1. **Tel** 329 6000. Ⓜ Nevskiy Prospekt, Gostinyy Dvor. ♿ See Where to Stay, p178.

One of Russia's most famous hotels, the ornate Grand Hotel Europe (1873–5) was designed by Ludwig Fontana. The building owes much of its character to alterations made in the 1910s by Style-Moderne architect Fyodor Lidval.

Before the Revolution, the hotel's magnificent restaurant was a favourite rendezvous for members of the diplomatic corps and secret police. In the 1970s, the hotel café became a popular meeting place for young intellectuals and artists.

Pushkin's statue in front of the Russian Museum, Arts Square

Majestic façade of the Mikhaylovskiy Castle, with a monument to Peter the Great at the entrance ▶

❸ Russian Museum

Русский Музей

Russkiy Muzey

The museum is housed in the Mikhaylovskiy Palace, one of Carlo Rossi's finest Neo-Classical creations, which was built in 1819–25 for Grand Duke Mikhail Pavlovich. Alexander III's plans to create a public museum were realized by his son, Nicholas II, when the Russian Museum opened here in 1898. Today, the museum holds one of the world's greatest collections of Russian art.

The Benois Wing, named after its main architect Leontiy Benois, was added in 1913–19.

Stairs to ground floor

★ Princess Olga Konstantinovna Orlova (1911) By the turn of the 20th century, Valentin Serov was the most successful portrait painter in Russia.

Temporary exhibitions of 20th-century art are often displayed.

Entrance

Stairs to first floor of Benois Wing

A Meal in the Monastery (1865–76) Vasiliy Perov's canvas exposes the hypocrisy of the Orthodox clergy, with the juxtaposition of good and evil, rich and poor, false piety and true faith.

Gallery Guide

The main entrance on Arts Square leads to the ticket office on the lower ground floor. The exhibition starts on the first floor. It is arranged chronologically, starting with icons in Room 1. It continues on the ground floor of the main building and Rossi Wing, then the first floor of the Benois Wing. Exhibitions are changed regularly.

Folk Art Toy (1930s) This clay toy from Dykomovo is part of the colourful selection of folk art which also includes lacquer boxes, painted ceramics and textiles.

★ **The Last Day of Pompeii** (1833)
Karl Bryullov's Classical subject
embodies the aesthetic principles of the
Academy of Arts. This vivid depiction of
the eruption of Vesuvius won him the
Grand Prix at the Paris Salon.

Stairs to
ground floor

14
15
12
16 17 13
11
10 9
8
1 2 3 7
The White Hall
contains original
Empire-style
furniture by
Carlo Rossi.
6
5
4

Rossi Wing   Start of exhibition

★ **Barge-Haulers on the Volga** (1870–73)
Ilya Repin was the most famous member
of the Wanderers, a group of artists
dedicated to social realism and
Russian themes. His powerful
indictment of forced labour imbues the
oppressed victims with sullen dignity.

44 43 42 41 40 39
49
54 36 35 34 33 32
37 31
38 30 29 28 27 26 25 24
18 19 23
20 22
21

Entrance points from
lower-ground-floor
ticket office

Phryne at the Festival of Poseidon in Eleusin
(1889) Henryk Siemiradzki's paintings are fine
examples of late European Neo-Classicism. He
is renowned for his academic scenes of life
in ancient Greece and Rome.

The portico of eight
Corinthian columns is
the central feature of
Rossi's façade. Behind
is a frieze of Classical
figures, designed by
Rossi and executed
by Demut-Malinovskiy.

Stairs to
first floor

The main entrance
is through a small
door leading to the
lower ground floor,
with a ticket office,
a cloakroom,
toilets and a café.

Key to Floor Plan
- Old Russian art
- 18th-century art
- Early 19th-century art
- Late 19th-century art
- 20th-century art
- 18th–20th-century sculpture
- Folk art
- Temporary exhibitions
- Non-exhibition space

Exploring the Russian Museum

Housing one of the world's greatest collections of Russian art, the museum originally comprised officially approved works from the Academy of Arts *(see p65)*. When the museum was nationalized after the Revolution, art was transferred from palaces, churches and private collections. By the 1930s, Socialist Realism had become state policy and avant-garde works were stored away, to re-emerge with the advent of *perestroika* in the 1980s.

Portrait of E I Nelidova (1773), by Dmitriy Levitskiy

The Angel with the Golden Hair, an icon from the early 12th century

Old Russian Art

The museum's fine collection begins with icons dating from the 12th–17th centuries. Russian icons derive from the Orthodox tradition and thus, just like Byzantine icons, tend to be sombre, marked by an absence of movement and a remote, mystic characterization of the saints. A superb example is one of the earliest icons, *The Angel with the Golden Hair*, in which the large, expressive eyes and delicate modelling of the Archangel Gabriel's face convey a sense of ethereal grace.

The Novgorod School *(see p167)* encouraged a much bolder and brighter style with a greater sense of drama and movement. And yet it is the poetically expressive and technically refined work of Andrey Rublev (c.1340 – c.1430) that is considered by many to mark the pinnacle of Russian icon painting.

18th–19th-Century Art

The first secular portraits (which owed much to the static quality of the icons) appeared in the second half of the 17th century. It was, however, under Peter the Great that Russian painting fully cast off from its Byzantine moorings. Peter the Great himself was the first patron to send young artists, often serfs, to study abroad. Secular art began to gain momentum in 1757 with the establishment of the Academy of Arts *(see p65)* which placed a heavy emphasis on classical and mythological subjects.

European influence permeates the work of Russia's first important portrait painters, Ivan Nikitin (1688–1741) and Andrey Matveev (1701–39). The art of portraiture matured with Dmitriy Levitskiy (1735–1822), among whose best-known works is a series of portraits of noble girls from the Smolnyy Institute.

Russian landscape painting was stimulated by the Romantic movement and in particular artists who sought inspiration abroad, including Silvestr Shchedrin (1791–1830) and Fyodor Matveev (1758–1826).

Ivan Aivazovskiy's (1817–1900) vast marine paintings, however, have something purely Russian in their scale and mood. Romanticism also influenced history painters such as Karl Bryullov (1799–1852), as in his depiction of *The Last Day of Pompeii*.

In 1863 a group of students, led by Ivan Kramskoy (1837–87), rebelled against the conservatism of the Academy of Arts. Seven years later they set up the Association of Travelling Art Exhibitions, and came to be known as the Wanderers *(Peredvizhniki)*, or the Itinerants. They demanded that painting should be more socially relevant, and were fundamentally committed to Russian subject matter.

The most versatile of the Wanderers was Ilya Repin *(see p44)* whose bold canvas *Barge-Haulers on the Volga* combines a visually powerful attack on forced

Knight at the Crossroads (1882), by Viktor Vasnetsov

The Six-Winged Seraph (1904), by Mikhail Vrubel

labour with a romantic view of the Russian people. Meanwhile, *A Meal in the Monastery* by Vasiliy Perov (1833–82) is a satirical and equally effective attack on social injustice.

The nationalist element led history painters such as Nikolay Ge (1831–94) and Vasiliy Surikov (1848–1916) to turn to Russian history for inspiration, treating their subjects with a new psychological understanding, as in Ge's canvas of 1871–2, in which Peter the Great interrogates his sullenly resistant son.

The general Slavic revival also breathed new life into landscape painting, concentrating on the beauties of the Russian countryside. The master of the genre was Isaak Levitan (1860–1900), whose *Golden Autumn Village*, dated 1889, is almost Impressionist in style, a sign perhaps that the ascendancy of the Wanderers was coming to an end.

Viktor Vasnetsov (1848–1926) turned to Russia's heroic, and often legendary, pre-European past, in realistically painted canvases such as *Knight at the Crossroads*. A haunting metaphor for Russia's uncertain future, the painting reveals that Vasnetsov was unable to avoid the *fin-de-siècle* melancholy and mysticism which was so potently expressed in the work of the next up-and-coming generation of artists, notably the Symbolists.

20th-Century Art

The dark, brooding canvases of Symbolist Mikhail Vrubel (1856–1910) combine Russian and religious themes with a more international outlook. Vrubel used colour and form to depict emotion and in *The Six-Winged Seraph* he employs a broken, vibrant, surface to express tension.

Another major contribution to 20th-century art was the "World of Art" movement, founded by Alexandre Benois and Sergey Diaghilev in the 1890s *(see p28)*. It rejected the notion of "socially useful art" in favour of a new tenet, "art pure and unfettered", and also opened up Russian painting to Western influences. Many members of the group, including Benois and Leon Bakst, designed stage sets

Portrait of the Director Vsevolod Meyerhold (1916), Boris Grigorev

and costumes for Diaghilev's Ballets Russes *(see p120)*.

The Russian avant-garde grew out of these local influences, plus the art of Cézanne, Picasso and Matisse. Mikhail Larionov (1881–1964) and Natalya Goncharova (1881–1962) both made brilliant use of Russian folk art as inspiration for primitivist works such as Goncharova's *Bleaching Canvas* (1908). They often altered their style in response to changing stimuli and later turned to Futurism's cult of the machine, as in Goncharova's *Cyclist* (1913) *(see p42)*.

The link between innovation in painting and the arts in general at this time is strikingly depicted in Boris Grigorev's angular portrait of Meyerhold, himself renowned for his radical approach to theatre.

Kazimir Malevich's (1878–1935) fascination with the juxtaposition of simple geometric shapes inspired the Suprematist movement. Vasily Kandinsky (1866–1944), a leading member of Munich's Blaue Reiter group, was also a key figure in the growth of Russian abstract art.

Marc Chagall (1887–1985), El Lissitskiy (1890–1941) and Alexander Rodchenko (1891–1956) are also represented.

Due to the high demand for the loan of avant-garde works abroad, the selection on view changes regularly.

Folk Art

Folk art became a strong influence on the development of modern Russian art in the 1860s when the wealthy industrialist and patron Savva Mamontov established an artists' colony at Abramtsevo, near Moscow. Vasiliy Polenov (1844–1927), Ilya Repin and Viktor Vasnetsov were among the painters encouraged to work alongside, and learn from, the serf craftsmen on the estate. The museum's collection of folk art is wonderfully diverse and includes exquisitely embroidered tapestries, traditional headdresses, painted tiles, porcelain toys, and lacquered spoons and dishes.

❻ Nevskiy Prospekt

Невский проспект

Nevskiy prospekt

Map 6 D1–8 D3. Ⓜ Nevskiy Prospekt, Gostinyy Dvor. See also pp46–9.

Russia's most famous street, Nevskiy prospekt, is also St Petersburg's main thoroughfare and artery. In the 1830s, the novelist Nikolai Gogol *(see p44)* declared with great pride: "There is nothing finer than Nevskiy Avenue…in St Petersburg it is everything…is there anything more gay, more brilliant, more resplendent than this beautiful street of our capital?". In this respect very little has actually changed, for Nevskiy prospekt's intrinsic importance still prevails today.

Laid out in the early days of the city, it was first known as the Great Perspective Road, running 4.5 km (3 miles) from the Admiralty *(see p80)* to the Alexander Nevsky Monastery *(see pp132–3)*. In spite of roaming wolves and uncontrollable flooding from the Neva *(see p39)* which made the avenue navigable in 1721, fine mansions, such as the Stroganov Palace *(see p114)* were built. Shops and bazaars, catering for the nobility, and inns for travelling merchants followed. A magnet attracting rich and poor alike, by the mid-18th century the avenue had become the place to see and be seen, to meet for gossip, business and pleasure.

Today, the street still teems with people until late into the night throughout the year. Many of the city's sights are close to the stretch between the Admiralty and Anichkov Bridge *(see pp48–9)*. Some of the best shops *(see pp196–7)* can be found along the stretch between the Fontanka and Vosstaniya. Nevskiy prospekt also offers a wealth of cultural interest: the Small Philharmonia concert hall *(see p204)*, the Russian national library, Beloselskiy-Belozerskiy Palace *(see p51)* and a wide variety of museums, theatres, churches, including the Church of St Catherine *(see p50)*, shops, cinemas and eateries.

The portico of the Armenian Church, built between 1771–9

❼ Armenian Church

Армянская церковь

Armyanskaya tserkov

Nevskiy prospekt 40–42. **Map** 6 F1. **Tel** 570 4108. Ⓜ Gostinyy Dvor. **Open** 9am–9pm.

Yuriy Velten designed the lovely blue-and-white Armenian Church of St Catherine, with its Neo-Classical portico and single cupola. The church, which opened in 1780, was financed by a wealthy Armenian businessman called Ioakim Lazarev, who acquired the money from the sale of a Persian diamond which Count Grigoriy Orlov purchased for Catherine the Great *(see p24)*.

Closed in 1930, the building has now been returned to the Armenian community and visitors are welcome to attend a service.

❽ Gostinyy Dvor

Гостиный двор

Gostinyy dvor

Nevskiy pr 35. **Map** 6 F2. **Tel** 630 5408. Ⓜ Gostinyy Dvor. **Open** 10am–10pm daily. Ⓦ **bgd.ru**

The term *gostinyy dvor* originally meant a coaching inn, but as trade developed around the inns, with travelling merchants setting up their stalls, it later came to mean "trading rows". The original wooden structure of this *gostinyy dvor* was destroyed by fire in 1736. Twenty years later, Bartolomeo

The historic Singer House located on the bustling Nevskiy prospekt

Rastrelli designed a new building but the project proved too costly and ambitious. Building recommenced in 1761 and continued until 1785. Vallin de la Mothe created the striking sequence of columned arcades and massive porticos. The prominent yellow building forms an irregular quadrangle which is bounded on one side by Nevskiy prospekt. The combined length of its façades is nearly 1 km (3,300 ft).

In the 19th century the gallery became a fashionable promenade where more than 5,000 people were employed. Serious damage during the Siege of Leningrad (see p29) led to major reconstruction, making it more like a modern department store. Even now, it has retained its layout of "stalls" of individual trading units. It offers a wide range of products, making it a central supplier of basic goods and souvenirs (see p197).

Style-Moderne stained-glass windows in Yeliseev's

Moderne building, designed by Gavriil Baranovskiy in 1901–3, it is adorned with bronzes, heroic sculptures and huge windows. A plaque by the main door honours the grandsons.

Today the second floor of the building is home to the Akimov Comedy Theatre, while the ground floor houses a shop that offers a range of expensive food delicacies.

⑩ Anichkov Palace
Аничков дворец
Anichkov dvorets

Nevskiy prospekt 39. **Map** 7 A2. Ⓜ Gostinyy Dvor. 🚌 3, 7, 22, 24, 27, 191. 🚎 1, 5, 7, 10, 11, 22. **Closed** to public except for special events.

In the early days, the broad Fontanka river was lined by palaces accessible mainly by boat. One of them was the Anichkov Palace (1741–50), remodelled in Baroque style in 1754. The palace was a gift from Tsarina Elizabeth to her lover Aleksey Razumovskiy. It was named after Lieutenant Colonel Mikhail Anichkov who set up camp on this site at the time of the founding of the city. Over the years the palace was rebuilt and altered many

times, according to the tastes of each successive owner. After Razumovskiy's death, Catherine the Great in turn gave the building to her lover, Prince Potemkin (see p27). In the early 19th century, Neo-Classical details were added by Carlo Rossi.

The palace then became the traditional winter residence of the heir to the throne. When Alexander III became tsar in 1881, he continued to live here, however, rather than move to the Winter Palace as was customary. After his death, his widow Maria Fyodorovna stayed on until the Revolution.

The palace originally had large gardens to the west but these were curtailed in 1816 when Ostrovskiy Square (see p112) was created and two Neo-Classical pavilions were added. The elegant colonnaded building overlooking the Fontanka to the east was commissioned by Giacomo Quarenghi in 1803–5. It was initially built as an arcade where goods from the imperial factories were stored before being allocated to the palaces. Later it was converted into government offices and now also houses the Cultural Centre of Children's Creative Work.

Columned arcades in the popular shopping centre, Gostinyy Dvor

⑨ Yeliseev's
Елисеевский гастроном
Yeliseevskiy gastronom

Nevskiy prospekt 56. **Map** 6 F1. **Tel** 456 6666. Ⓜ Gostinyy Dvor. **Open** 10am– 11pm daily. 🌐 kupetzeliseevs.ru

The successful Yeliseev dynasty was founded by Pyotr Yeliseev, an ambitious peasant who, in 1813, opened a wine shop on Nevskiy prospekt. By the turn of the century his grandsons owned a chocolate factory, numerous houses, inns and this famous former food store. The city's most opulent Style-

Quarenghi's addition to the Anichkov Palace from Nevskiy prospekt

Porticoed façade of Alexandrinskiy Theatre (1828–32), Ostrovskiy Square

⓫ Ostrovskiy Square

Площадь Островского

Ploshchad Ostrovskovo

Map 6 F2. Ⓜ Gostinyy Dvor. 🚌 3, 7, 22, 24, 27. 🚎 1, 5, 7, 10, 11, 22. **Russian National Library: Tel** 310 7137. **Open** 11am–7pm. **Theatre Museum: Tel** 571 2195. **Open** 11am–7pm Thu–Mon, 1–9pm Wed. **Closed** last Fri of each month and public hols. 🎭📷 Ⓦ **theatremuseum.ru**

One of Russia's most brilliant architects, Carlo Rossi, created this early 19th-century square, which is now named in honour of the dramatist Aleksandr Ostrovskiy (1823–86).

The focal point of the square is the elegant Alexandrinskiy Theatre *(see p204)*, designed in the Neo-Classical style which Rossi favoured. The portico of six Corinthian columns is crowned by a chariot of Apollo, sculpted by Stepan Pimenov.

The building was the new home to Russia's oldest theatre company, set up in 1756. Plays premiered here, and still performed today, include Nikolai Gogol's *The Inspector General* (1836) and Anton Chekhov's *The Seagull* (1901). In Soviet times the theatre was renamed the Pushkin Theatre.

In the garden was a monument to Catherine the Great, the only one in the city. It was designed principally by Mikhail Mikeshin and unveiled in 1873. The statue depicts Catherine surrounded by statesmen and other worthies, and includes the female president (1783–96) of the Academy of Sciences, Princess Yekaterina Dashkova.

The benches behind the monument are packed during the summer months with chess players and spectators. On the west side of the square, opposite the Anichkov Palace *(see p111)* is an elegant colonnade decorated with Classical sculptures. This is the extension of the Russian Library, made by Rossi in 1828–34. Founded in 1795, the library currently holds more than 28 million items. A prized possession is the personal library of the French philosopher Voltaire, which Catherine the Great purchased to show her appreciation of her sometime mentor and correspondent.

In the southeast corner of the square, at No. 6, is the Theatre Museum which traces the evolution of the Russian stage from its origins in mid-18th-century serf and imperial theatres. Amid the eclectic array of playbills, photographs, costumes, set designs and other artifacts, there are also some set designs by one of the great innovators of modern theatre, the director Vsevolod Meyerhold (1874–1940).

⓬ Ulitsa Zodchego Rossi

Улица Зодчего Росси

Ulitsa Zodchevo Rossi

Map 6 F2. Ⓜ Gostinyy Dvor.

There could be no better memorial to Carlo Rossi than the near perfect architectural ensemble of identical arcades and colonnades forming "Architect Rossi Street". The 22-m- (72-ft-) high buildings stand precisely 22 m (72 ft) apart and stretch for 220 m (720 ft). In 2008 the street had its 180-year anniversary. Seen from ploshchad Lomonosova, the perspective hypnotically coaxes the eye towards the Alexandrinskiy Theatre.

At No. 2 is the home of the former Imperial School of Ballet, now named after the teacher Agrippina Vaganova (1879–1951), one of the few dancers not to emigrate after the Revolution. The school began in 1738 when Jean-Baptiste Landé began training orphans and palace servants' children to take part in court entertainment. It has produced many of Russia's most celebrated dancers *(see p120)*, including Anna Pavlova and Rudolf Nureyev.

19th-century photograph of ulitsa Zodchego Rossi (1828–34)

Architect Carlo Rossi

Carlo Rossi (1775–1849) was one of the last great exponents of Neo-Classicism in St Petersburg. He found an ideal client in Alexander I, who shared his belief in the use of architecture to express the power of the ruling autocracy. By the time of his death, Rossi had created no fewer than 12 of St Petersburg's impressive streets and 13 of its squares, including Palace Square *(see p85)*. Rossi's status as Alexander I's favourite architect encouraged rumours that Rossi was the offspring of an affair between Tsar Paul I and Rossi's Italian ballerina mother.

Central corpus of Vorontsov Palace

⑬ Vorontsov Palace

Воронцовский дворец

Vorontsovskiy dvorets

Sadovaya ulitsa 26. **Map** 6 F2.
Closed to public. Ⓜ Gostinyy Dvor,
Sennaya Ploshchad.

The most exclusive military school
in the Russian Empire, the Corps
des Pages, occupied the Vorontsov
Palace from 1810–1918. Among
those privileged enough to
study here were a number of
the Decembrists *(see pp24–5)*
and Prince Felix Yusupov *(see
p123).* Today the palace houses
the Suvorov Military Academy.

Designed by Bartolomeo
Rastrelli *(see p95),* the handsome palace, which once stood
in its own extensive grounds,
was built in 1749–57 for Prince
Mikhail Vorontsov, one of
Tsarina Elizabeth's leading
ministers. Rastrelli's graceful
wrought-iron railings are
among the earliest examples
of their kind in Russia.

⑭ Apraksin Market

Апраксин двор

Apraksin dvor

Sadovaya ulitsa. **Map** 6 E2.
Ⓜ Gostinyy Dvor, Sennaya
Ploshchad, Sadovaya, Spasskaya.

Founded in the late 18th century, the market takes its name
from the Apraksin family who
owned the land it was built on.
When fire destroyed the original
wooden stalls in 1862, the
arcade was erected. By 1900
there were more than 600
outlets selling everything from
food, wine and spices to furs,
furniture and haberdashery.
The large street market has now

moved to Rustavelli Street, far
from the city centre. The historic
Apraksin Market is being
reconstructed; in the meantime
arcade shops continue to open.

⑮ Cathedral of Our Lady of Kazan

Собор Казанской Богоматери

Sobor Kazanskoy Bogomateri

Kazanskaya pl 2. **Map** 6 E1. **Tel** 314
4663. Ⓜ Nevskiy Prospekt. 🚌 3, 7,
22, 24, 27, 191. 🚊 1, 5, 7, 10, 11, 22.
Open 9am–7:30pm daily. 🎫 📷

One of St Petersburg's most
majestic churches, the
Cathedral of Our Lady of
Kazan was commissioned by
Paul I and took over a decade
to build (1801–11). The
impressive design by serf
architect Andrey Voronikhin
was inspired by St Peter's in
Rome. Its 111-m- (364-ft-) long,
curved colonnade disguises
the orientation of the building,
which runs parallel to Nevskiy
prospekt, conforming to a
religious stipulation that
the main altar face east. In
Voronikhin's original design
he intended to duplicate the
colonnade on the south side.

The cathedral is named after the
miracle-working icon of Our
Lady of Kazan. The icon is now
kept in the cathedral.

The interior decoration is
generally subdued. Its most
impressive features are the great
80-m- (262-ft-) high dome and
the massive pink Finnish granite
columns with bronze capitals
and bases. Occupied in the
Communist era by a Museum
of Atheism, the building was
returned to exclusive religious
use in 1999.

Completed in 1811, the
cathedral is intimately linked
with the wars against Napoleon
(see p24) fought during the
same period. In 1813 Field
Marshal Mikhail Kutuzov
(1745–1813), mastermind
of a successful retreat from
Moscow following the invasion
of Napoleon's Grand Army in
1812, was buried here with full
military honours. Kutuzov has
been immortalized in Tolstoy's
great novel *War and Peace*
(1865–9). His statue and that
of his comrade-in-arms, Mikhail
Barclay de Tolly (1761–1818),
both by Boris Orlovskiy, have
stood outside the cathedral
since 1837.

Pink granite columns and mosaic floor in main nave, Kazan Cathedral

⑯ Stroganov Palace
Строгановский дворец
Stroganovskiy dvorets

Nevskiy prospekt 17. **Map** 6 E1.
Tel 571 8238. Ⓜ Nevskiy Prospekt.
🚌 3, 7, 22, 24, 27, 191. 🚎 1, 5, 7, 10,
11, 17. **Open** 10am–6pm Mon, Wed &
Fri–Sun; 1–9pm Thu. 🅿

This Baroque masterpiece
was designed in 1752–4 by
Bartolomeo Rastrelli *(see
p95)*. Commissioned by the
enormously wealthy Count
Sergey Stroganov, the palace
was occupied by his descendants until the 1917 Revolution.
The vast Stroganov fortune was
amassed mainly through the
monopoly the family held on
salt, which they mined from
their territories in the north
of the Russian Empire.

The pink and white palace,
which overlooks both Nevskiy
prospekt and the Moyka river,
was one of the city's most
impressive private residences.
The magnificent river façade is
decorated with Doric columns,
cornices, pediments and inven-
tive window surrounds.

The Stroganovs were noted
collectors of everything from
Egyptian antiquities and Roman
coins to icons and Old Masters.
The palace was nationalized
after the Revolution and then
preserved for ten years as
a museum of the life of the

Neo-Romanesque portal of the Lutheran
Church (1832–8)

decadent aristocracy. When
it was closed, some of the
objects were auctioned in
the West, and the rest were
transferred to the Hermitage
(see pp86–95). The building now
belongs to the Russian Museum
(see pp106–9) and has temporary exhibitions and a collection
of waxwork figures.

⑰ Lutheran Church
Лютеранская церковь
Lyuteranskaya tserkov

Nevskiy prospekt 22–24. **Map** 6 E1.
Ⓜ Nevskiy Prospekt.

Set back a little from Nevskiy
prospekt, the attractive, twin-
towered Lutheran church is
dedicated to St Peter. Built in its

present form during the 1830s,
the church served St Petersburg's
ever-growing German community
(see p59). The prize-winning design
by Aleksandr Bryullov is in an
unusual, Neo-Romanesque style.

From 1936 the church was
used as a vegetable store
until, in the late 1950s, it was
converted into a swimming
pool. The basin was carved out
of the nave floor, the gallery
lined with spectator benches
and there was a high diving
board under the apse. The
building has now been handed
back to the German-Lutheran
Church of Russia. The church
has been fully restored and
now offers regular services.

The Academic Capella concert hall

⑱ Academic Capella
Академическая капелла
Akademicheskaya kapella

Naberezhnaya reki Moyki 20. **Map** 2
E5. **Tel** 314 1058. Ⓜ Nevskiy Prospekt.
Open for concerts only. 🅿 📧 See
Entertainment, p196.

Enclosed within a courtyard
off the Moyka river is this ochre-
coloured concert hall with a
façade in the French Classical
style of Louis XV. The Academic
Capella was designed by
Leontiy Benois in 1887–9 as
the residence of the Imperial
Court choir. Founded during
the reign of Peter the Great, the
choir is as old as the city itself.
Its former directors have included
the distinguished Russian composers Mikhail Glinka (1804–57)
and Nikolai Rimsky-Korsakov
(1844–1908).

With its excellent acoustics,
the Academic Capella can
claim to be one of the best
concert halls in the world.
Outside is the aptly named
Singers' Bridge (Pevcheskiy
most), which was designed
by Yegor Adam in 1837–40.

Elaborate west façade of the Stroganov Palace overlooking the Moyka river

Personal effects in Pushkin's study, Pushkin House-Museum

⑲ Pushkin House-Museum

Музей-квартира А. С. Пушкина

Muzey-kvartira AS Pushkina

Naberezhnaya reki Moyki 12. **Map** 2 E5. **Tel** 571 3531. **Open** 10:30am–6pm Wed–Mon. **Closed** last Fri of each month and public hols.

Every year on the anniversary of Alexander Pushkin's death (29 January 1837), loyal devotees of Russia's greatest poet come to lay floral tributes outside his apartment. Pushkin was born in Moscow in 1799, but spent many years of his life in St Petersburg and the museum is one of several places in the city with which the poet is associated.

From the autumn of 1836 until his death, Pushkin lived in this fairly opulent apartment overlooking the Moyka, with his wife Natalya, their four children and Natalya's two sisters. It was here on the couchette in the study that he bled to death after his fateful duel with d'Anthès *(see p85)*.

Some half-dozen rooms on the first floor have been refurbished in the Empire style of the period. By far the most evocative is Pushkin's study, which is arranged exactly as it was when he died. On the writing table is an ivory paper knife given to the poet by his sister, a bronze handbell and a treasured inkstand *(see p41)*. Embellished with the figure of an Ethiopian boy, the inkstand is a reminder of Pushkin's great grandfather, Abram Hannibal. Bought by the Russian ambassador in Constantinople as a slave in 1706, Hannibal served as a general under Peter the Great.

He was the inspiration for the unfinished novel *The Negro of Peter the Great* on which Pushkin was working at the time of his death.

On the wall in front of his desk is a Turkish sabre presented to Pushkin in the Caucasus, where he had been exiled in 1820 for his radical views. Ironically it was there that he spent some of his happiest years. It was there too that he began his most famous work, *Eugene Onegin*, a novel in verse written in 1823–30.

The most impressive feature of the apartment is the poet's library which contains more than 4,500 volumes in a staggering 14 European and Oriental languages. Among these are works by the authors whom Pushkin most admired, including Shakespeare, Byron, Heine, Dante and Voltaire.

⑳ Fabergé Museum

Музей Фаберже

Musey Faberzhe

Naberezhnaya reki Fontanki 21. **Map** 7 A1. **Tel** 333 2655. **Open** 10am–9pm Sat–Thu. **W** fabergemuseum.ru

Dedicated to the works of master jeweller Carl Fabergé, this museum was established in 2013 by billionaire philanthropist Viktor Vekselberg. More than 4,000 items are on display, including nine Imperial Easter Eggs created for the last two Russian emperors. The collection also includes masterpieces by famous contemporary Russian jewellers and silversmiths such as Ovchinnikov, Khlebnikov, Sazikov and Rückert.

The building housing the museum, Shuvalov Palace, is worth a visit in its own right. Built in the 18th-century, it has an impressive Grand Staircase and spectacular reception rooms. Severely damaged in the Soviet period, it was lovingly restored before the museum's opening.

The entrance to the Fabergé museum, housed in Shuvalov Palace

SENNAYA PLOSHCHAD

The western part of St Petersburg is an area of contrasts, home to some of the city's wealthiest residences and most poverty-stricken dwellings. The palatial architecture along the English Embankment is a world away from the decrepit living quarters around Sennaya ploshchad, which have changed little since Dostoevsky (see p125) described them. In between lies the old maritime quarter, once inhabited by Peter the Great's shipwrights, many of whom were English. This area extended all the way from the New Holland warehouses to St Nicholas'

Cathedral, which stands on the site of the naval parade ground. Theatre Square has been a hub of entertainment since the mid-18th century. It is dominated by the prestigious Mariinskiy Theatre and the Rimsky-Korsakov Conservatory, where many of Russia's greatest artists began their careers. Before 1917, the streets leading off the square were home to theatre directors, actors, ballerinas, artists and musicians. Today, performing artists are once more returning to live here, attracted by the peace of the tree-lined canals.

Sights at a Glance

Cathedrals
2 St Nicholas' Cathedral

Historic Buildings and Areas
1 Mariinskiy Theatre
3 Rimsky-Korsakov Conservatory
5 Choral Synagogue
6 New Holland
8 Main Post Office

Palaces
4 Yusupov Palace

Streets and Squares
7 The English Embankment
9 Bolshaya Morskaya Ulitsa
10 Sennaya Ploshchad

Museums
11 Railway Museum

Restaurants pp190–91
1 1913
2 Arcobaleno
3 Charlie
4 Conchita Bonita
5 Entree
6 Khochu Kharcho
7 Krokodil
8 Mindal Café
9 Romeo's Bar & Kitchen
10 Russian Vodka Room No. 1
11 Salhino
12 Senoval

See also Street Finder map 5

◀ The opulent Red Drawing Room in the Yusupov Palace

For keys to symbols see back flap

Street-by-Street: Theatre Square

Theatre Square was once known as Carousel Square and was frequently used as the site for fairs and festivals. During the 19th century when St Petersburg became the cultural capital of Russia, the Mariinskiy Theatre and Rimsky-Korsakov Conservatory were established, and the neighbourhood became home to many artists. Today, the tradition of entertainment is still thriving and Theatre Square remains a focal point for theatrical and musical life *(see p204)*. Nearby, the tree-lined canal embankments and the gardens surrounding the beautiful St Nicholas' Cathedral are enchanting places to stroll.

❹ Yusupov Palace
Historic site of the gruesome murder of Rasputin *(see p123)*, this grand palace belonged to the wealthy Yusupov family. Its opulent interiors include this Italian marble staircase and a tiny Rococo theatre.

The Monument to Rimsky-Korsakov, who taught at the Conservatory for 37 years, was designed by Veniamin Bogolyubov and Vladimir Ingal and erected in 1952.

Mariinskiy II theatre *(see p121)*

❸ Rimsky-Korsakov Conservatory
Tchaikovsky, Prokofiev and Shostakovich *(see p45)* were among the talents nurtured by Russia's first conservatory, founded in 1862 by pianist and composer Anton Rubinstein.

Monument to Mikhail Glinka *(see p46)*

❶ ★ Mariinskiy Theatre
This theatre has been home to the world-famous Mariinskiy (Kirov) Opera and Ballet Company since 1860. Hidden behind its imposing façade is the sumptuous auditorium where many of Russia's greatest dancers *(see p120–21)* have performed.

The Lion Bridge (Lvinyy most) is one of a number of quaint and curious suspension bridges on the narrow, tree-lined Griboedov Canal *(see p38)*. These bridges are well-known meeting places, notably for romantic trysts.

Locator Map
See Street Finder map 5

The House of Mikhail Fokin at No. 109 is where the renowned ballet-master and choreographer lived before the Revolution.

The Benois House belonged to an artistic dynasty which included the co-founder of the World of Art movement, Alexandre Benois *(see p109)*.

The Belfry, an elegant four-tiered structure with a gilded spire, was built to mark the main entrance to St Nicholas' Cathedral.

❷ **St Nicholas' Cathedral**
A fine example of 18th-century Russian Baroque, the lofty upper church is richly decorated with icons, gilding and this carved iconostasis. The lower church, beautifully lit with candles, is also open for worship.

Key

— Suggested route

NABKANALA GRIBOEDOVA

SKOVO-KORSAKOVA

NIKOLSKIY PEREULOK

KANAL GRIBOEDOVA

SADOVAYA ULITSA

0 metres 100
0 yards 100

The former Nicholas Market, characterized by its long arcade and steep roof, was constructed in 1788–9. In the 19th century it became an unofficial labour exchange as many unemployed workers gathered here.

Ballet in St Petersburg

Admired throughout the world, Russian ballet traces its origins back to 1738 when a French dancing master, Jean-Baptiste Landé, established a school in St Petersburg to train the children of palace employees. The Imperial School of Ballet, as it soon became known, flourished under a string of distinguished foreign teachers, culminating in Marius Petipa (1818–1910). Petipa first joined the school in 1847 as a principal dancer and later choreographed over 60 ballets, inspiring such famous dancers as Matilda Kshesinskaya *(see p74)*. Following the 1905 Revolution, a reaction against Classicism led to an increasing number of defections from the imperial theatres to the new private companies like Sergey Diaghilev's Ballets Russes. The dispersion of talent increased after the Bolsheviks seized power in 1917 and many artists went into exile abroad. Fortunately for Soviet Russia, the distinguished prima ballerina Agrippina Vaganova remained to train the next generation of dancers. St Petersburg's Russian Ballet Academy now bears her name *(see p112)*.

Anna Pavlova's (1885–1931) most famous role, The Dying Swan, was created especially for her by Mikhail Fokin. In 1912 Pavlova left Russia to form her own touring company, spreading her enthusiasm for ballet across Europe and beyond.

Vaslaw Nijinsky (1890–1950) had one of his greatest roles as the golden slave in Schéhérazade which took Paris by storm in 1910. A principal of the Ballets Russes before World War I, he revolutionized male roles. His incomparable technical skills and expressive qualities influenced future generations of dancers.

Rudolf Nureyev (1938–93), seen here in Sleeping Beauty at the Mariinskiy, defected to the West in 1961. As both choreographer and dancer, Nureyev continued to enthral audiences for over 30 years until his death in 1993.

The Mariinskiy Ballet, usually known abroad as the Kirov, is now reviving some of the original productions of the Ballets Russes, including their version of *Giselle*, previously not shown in Russia.

One of Russia's most important cultural institutions, the Mariinskiy Theatre

The Ballets Russes

The legendary touring company which revolutionized ballet between 1909 and 1929 was the brainchild of the impresario and art critic Sergey Diaghilev (see p45). Diaghilev found a kindred spirit in the choreographer Mikhail Fokin, who shared his vision of a spectacle that would fuse music, ballet and decor in a seamless artistic whole.

Diaghilev had the pick of dancers from the Mariinskiy and, in 1909, he brought his Ballets Russes to Paris. The company went from strength to strength with successful tours worldwide.

Diaghilev's new company had a remarkable impact on the contemporary art world. The ballets of Fokin, in particular, prepared audiences for greater innovation and experiment. Exciting contributions from costume and set designers Léon Bakst and Alexandre Benois, the composer Igor Stravinsky and the dancers Vaslaw Nijinsky, Anna Pavlova and Tamara Karsavina all played a part in expanding the artistic horizons. After Diaghilev's death in 1929, the Ballets Russes fragmented but its ethos and traditions have been preserved in many of today's leading companies.

Early 20th-century programme for the Ballets Russes

❶ Mariinskiy Theatre

Мариинский театр
Mariinskiy teatr

Teatralnaya ploshchad 1 and Dekabristov ulitsa 34 & 37. **Map** 5 B3. **Tel** 346 4141. 🚌 2, 3, 6, 22, 27, 71, K-1, K-2, K-62, K-124, K-154, K-169, K-186, K-350. 🚋 5, 22. **Open** For information on performances, see p204. 🅿 🖥 📷 ✉ 🆆 mariinsky.ru

Named in honour of Tsarina Maria Alexandrovna, wife of Alexander II, the theatre is known abroad by its Soviet title, the Kirov, while at home it has reverted to its original name, the Mariinskiy Theatre. In addition to the original building, there is also a concert hall nearby and a second stage, the Mariinskiy II.

The building was erected in 1860 by the architect Albert Kavos, who designed the Bolshoy Theatre in Moscow. It stands on the site of an earlier theatre which was destroyed by fire. In 1883–96, the Neo-Renaissance façade was remodelled by Viktor Schröter, who added most of the ornamental detail. The pale blue-and-gold auditorium, where so many illustrious dancers have made their debut, creates a dazzling impression. Its architectural decoration of twisted

Imperial eagle on the royal box

columns, atlantes, cherubs and cameo medallions has remained unchanged since the theatre's completion, and the imperial eagles have been restored to the royal box. The ceiling painting of dancing girls and cupids by Italian artist Enrico Franchioli dates from c.1856, while the superb stage curtain was added during Russian ballet's golden age in 1914. Equally remarkable is the glittering festive foyer, decorated with fluted pilasters, bas-reliefs of Russian composers and mirrored doors.

Although the Mariinskiy is better known abroad for its ballet company, it is also one of the country's leading opera houses. Most of the great 19th-century Russian operas were premiered here, including Mussorgsky's *Boris Godunov* (1874), Tchaikovsky's *Queen of Spades* (1890), and Shostakovich's controversial opera *Lady Macbeth of Mtsensk* (1934).

The Mariinskiy's luxuriant stage curtain, designed by Aleksandr Golovin in 1914

❷ St Nicholas' Cathedral

Никольский собор

Nikolskiy sobor

Nikolskaya ploshchad 1/3. **Map** 5 C4.
Tel 714 0862. 🚌 2, 3, 22, 27, 49, 71, 181, K-2, K-19, K-154, K-212.
Open 7am–7pm daily.

This stunning Baroque cathedral by Savva Chevakinskiy, one of Russia's great 18th-century architects, was built in 1753–62. Founded for sailors and Admiralty employees housed in the neighbourhood, and named after St Nicholas, the patron saint of sailors, the cathedral became known as the "Sailors' Church".

The striking exterior is decorated with white Corinthian pilasters and surmounted by five gilded cupolas. Nearby, within the cathedral's leafy grounds and overlooking the intersection of the Kryukov and Griboedov canals, is a slender four-tiered bell tower crowned by a spire.

Following the Russian tradition, there are two churches within the cathedral. The lower church, intended for daily use, is lit by icon lamps, candles and chandeliers, creating a magical effect. The icons (1755–7) are the work of the brothers Fedot and Menas Kolokolnikov. The upper church, used on Sundays and for weddings, is brighter and has a Baroque exuberance, with gilt and stucco ornamentation and Italianate paintings. The most impressive feature is the magnificent gilded iconostasis dating from 1755–60.

The pale blue-and-white Baroque façade of St Nicholas' Cathedral

Islamic arches and coffered ceiling in the Moorish Room, Yusupov Palace

❸ Rimsky-Korsakov Conservatory

Консерватория имени Римского-Корсакова

Konservatoriya imeni Rimskovo-Korsakova

Teatralnaya ploshchad 3. **Map** 5 B3.
Tel 571 8574. 🚌 2, 3, 6, 22, 27, 71, K-1, K-2, K-62, K-124, K-154, K-169, K-186, K-350. 🚊 5, 22. **Open** for performances only. 📷 📹 by appt (**Tel** 312 2507).

Russia's oldest music school, the conservatory was founded in 1862 by the piano virtuoso Anton Rubinstein (1829–94). The present building was designed in 1896 by Vladimir Nicolas.

Among those to graduate from the school before the Revolution were Tchaikovsky *(see p44)* and Sergey Prokofiev. In the Soviet years, the school continued to flourish, and the greatest musical figure to emerge from this era was composer Dmitriy Shostakovich (1906–75) *(see p45)*.

In the forecourt outside are two statues. On the left, a 1952 memorial honours the school's influential teacher, Nikolai Rimsky-Korsakov. On the right, the statue of Mikhail Glinka (1906) by Robert Bach is a reminder that the conservatory stands on the original site where Russia's first opera, Glinka's

A Life for the Tsar, was premiered in 1836 in the old Kamennyy (Stone) Theatre.

❹ Yusupov Palace

Юсуповский дворец

Yusupovskiy dvorets

Naberezhnaya reki Moyki 94. **Map** 5 B3.
Tel 314 9883. 🚌 3, 22, 27. **Open** 11am–5pm daily. 📷 English (audio tours only). 🆆 **yusupov-palace.ru**

Overlooking the Moyka, this yellow, colonnaded building (1760s) was designed by Vallin de la Mothe. The palace was acquired in 1830 by the aristocratic Yusupov family to house their superb collection of paintings. Major work was then carried out on the interior by Andrey Mikhaylov and Ippolito Monighetti.

The interiors, notable among them the exotic Moorish Room, with its fountain, mosaics and arches, can be viewed by guided or audio tour only. Separate tickets are needed for the tour of the cellars, which house an exhibition on Grigoriy Rasputin, the infamous "holy man" who was murdered here by Prince Felix Yusupov.

The elegant, Rococo-style family theatre seats just 180, and attending a concert *(see p204)* is an experience in itself.

The Grim Death of Rasputin

The Russian peasant and mystic Grigoriy Rasputin (1869–1916) exercised an extraordinarily powerful influence over the court and government of Russia (*see p28*). The mysterious circumstances of his dramatic death on 17 December 1916 are legendary. Lured to Yusupov's palace on the pretext of a party, Rasputin was poisoned, then shot by Prince Felix Yusupov and left for dead. Returning to the scene the prince found Rasputin still alive and a struggle ensued before Rasputin disappeared into the courtyard. Pursued by the conspirators he was shot another three times and brutally battered before being dumped in the river. When his corpse was found three days later, clinging to the supports of a bridge, water in his lungs indicated death by drowning.

❺ Choral Synagogue

Хоральная Синагога
Khoralnaya Sinagoga

Lermontovskiy prospekt 2.
Map 5 B3. **Tel** 713 8186.
3, 6, 22, 27, K-1, K-169.

In 1826 Tsar Nicholas I decreed that all Jews, save 29 employed on behalf of the Court, be exiled from the city. Further "purifications" took place in the 1830s. However, after Nicholas' death in 1855 the Jewish population grew rapidly and in 1879 a site was approved for a permanent house of prayer.

Designed in Moorish style by architects Ivan Shaposhnikov and Viktor Shreter, the Synagogue opened in 1893, by which time the Jewish community had reached 16,500, nearly 2 per cent of the city's population. Accommodating 1,200 or more, the Synagogue was the only Jewish place of prayer to survive the repressions of the 1930s.

Vallin de la Mothe's impressive arch on the Moyka, leading into New Holland

It continued to function during the Siege of 1941, the community remaining largely intact while other Jewish communities in Eastern Europe were decimated. Today, the Synagogue still has an active community.

❻ New Holland

Новая Голландия
Novaya Gollandiya

Naberezhnaya reki Moyki.
Map 5 B2. **Tel** 245 2035. 3, 6, 22, 27, 70, 100, K-169, K-350.
Open 9am–10pm Mon–Thu, 9am–11pm Fri–Sat.
W newhollandsp.ru

Created when the Kryukov canal was constructed between the Moyka and Neva rivers in 1719, this triangular island was originally used for storing ship timber. The name is in honour of the Dutch ship-builders who inspired Peter the Great's naval ambitions.

In 1765, the original wooden warehouses were rebuilt in red brick by Savva Chevakinskiy. At the same time Vallin de la Mothe designed the austere but romantic arch facing onto the Moyka

which creates an atmospheric entrance to the timber yard. Barges would pass through the arch and into a turning basin beyond, then return loaded with timber along the canals towards the Admiralty shipyards. Currently undergoing major renovation, parts of the site host art events and education programmes.

❼ The English Embankment

Английская набережная
Angliyskaya naberezhnaya

Map 5 A2. 6, 11, K-124, K-154, K-350.

English merchants settled here in the 1730s, and were soon followed by craftsmen, architects, artists, innkeepers and factory owners. By 1800 the area was one of the city's most fashionable addresses.

It still boasts impressive buildings. The Neo-Classical mansion at No. 10 was the fictional setting for the debutante ball of Natasha Rostova in Tolstoy's novel *War and Peace*. No. 28 was occupied by the lover of ballet dancer Matilda Kshesinskaya (*see p74*), and is the former headquarters of the Socialist-Revolutionary Party. On ploshchad Truda, the former palace of Grand Duke Nikolai Nikolaevich (son of Nicholas I) was given in 1917 to the trades unions.

Quarenghi's grand porticoed façade, at No. 32 on the English Embankment

❽ Main Post Office

Главпочтамт

Glavpochtamt

Pochtamtskaya ulitsa 9. **Map** 5 C2. **Tel** 315 8022. 🚌 3, 22, 27, 70, 100, K-169, K-187, K-306. 🚎 5, 22. **Open** 24 hours daily.

The building's main exterior feature is the arched gallery spanning Pochtamtskaya ulitsa. Built as an extension to Nikolay Lvov's main building, the gallery was added by Albert Kavos in 1859. Under the Pochtamt (Post Office) sign on the arch is a clock showing the time in major cities around the world.

Inside the post office, behind Lvov's porticoed Neo-Classical façade of 1782–9, is a splendid Style-Moderne hall character-ized by decorative ironwork and a glass ceiling. The hall was created in the early 20th century when a roof was constructed over what had originally been the courtyard stables.

Porticoed façade, Main Post Office

❾ Bolshaya Morskaya Ulitsa

Большая Морская улица

Bolshaya Morskaya ulitsa

Map 5 C2. 🚌 3, 22, 27, K-187, K-209. 🚎 5, 22.

Always one of St Petersburg's most fashionable streets, shady Bolshaya Morskaya ulitsa is the choice of the artistic elite to this day. It has some exceedingly handsome 19th-century mansions hidden away between St Isaac's Square *(see p81)* and Post Office Bridge (Pochtamtskiy most).

Stone atlas at No. 43 Bolshaya Morskaya ulitsa (1840)

The mansion at No. 61 was built by Albert Kavos in the 1840s for the St Petersburg Stage Coach Company. No. 52, nearby, was acquired by the Russian Union of Architects in 1932. Built by Aleksandr Pel in 1835–6, it was formerly the residence of the celebrated patron of the arts Aleksandr Polovtsov, who built up the impressive collection of the Stieglitz Museum *(see p129)*. The striking late 19th-century interiors with mahogany pan-elling, tapestries and carved ceilings were designed by Maximilian Messmacher and Nikolay Brullov and can be admired from the Osobnyak Polovtseva restaurant within.

Just across the street, No. 47 is a particularly fine example of Style-Moderne architecture with sculpted stone rosettes and

delicate iron tracery. This is the work of Mikhail Geisler and Boris Guslistiy, dating from 1901–2. It was in this mansion that the celebrated émigré novelist Vladimir Nabokov (1899–1977) grew up, and there is a small museum to him on the first floor. Admired for his linguistic ingenuity in both English and Russian, Nabokov hit the headlines across the world with the publication of *Lolita*, his *succès de scandale* of 1959.

Next door at No. 45 is the Union of Composers, the former home of socialite Princess Gagarina who lived here in the 1870s. The mansion was reconstructed in the 1840s by Auguste-Ricard de Montferrand, and it retains elements of the original 18th-century building.

Montferrand also built the former residence of millionaire industrialist Pyotr Demidov at No. 43. A mass of Renaissance and Baroque elements, the façade also bears the Demidov's coat of arms.

❿ Sennaya Ploshchad

Сенная площадь

Sennaya ploshchad

Map 6 D3. Ⓜ Sennaya Ploshchad, Sadovaya, Spasskaya.

This is one of the oldest squares in St Petersburg. The square's name, meaning Haymarket, derives from the original market where livestock, fodder and firewood were sold and which opened in the 1730s. A 10-minute stroll from Nevskiy, the area around the square was inhabited by the poor, and the market was the cheapest and live-liest in the city (the so-called "belly of St Petersburg"). The oldest building, at the centre

Style-Moderne mosaic frieze at No. 47 Bolshaya Morskaya ulitsa (1901–2)

Fyodor Dostoevsky

One of Russia's greatest writers, Fyodor Dostoevsky *(see pp45–6)* was born in 1821 in Moscow but spent most of his adult life in St Petersburg, where many of his novels and short stories are set. A defining moment in his life occurred in 1849 when he was arrested and charged with revolutionary conspiracy. After eight months of solitary confinement in the Peter and Paul Fortress *(see pp68–9)*, Dostoevsky and 21 other "conspirators" from the socialist Petrashevsky Circle were subjected to a macabre mock execution before being exiled to hard labour in Siberia until 1859. The sinister experience is recalled in his novel *The Idiot* (1868). He died in 1881.

The guardhouse on bustling Sennaya ploshchad

of the square, is the former guardhouse, a single-storey Neo-Classical building with a columned portico, which dates to 1818–20. The guardsmen's duties ranged from supervising the traders to flogging serfs, mostly for minor misdemeanours. By that time the neighbourhood had become synonymous with dirt, squalor, crime and vice. At No. 3 is the site of "Vyazemskiy's Monastery", the nickname for a notorious tenement overrun with pubs, gambling dens and brothels in the 1850s and 1860s.

This was the squalid world so vividly evoked in Fyodor Dostoevsky's masterpiece *Crime and Punishment*. As the contemptuous hero of the novel, Raskolnikov, wanders around the market, he absorbs the "heat in the street… the

airlessness, the bustle and the plaster, scaffolding, bricks and dust… that special St Petersburg stench… and the numerous drunken men" which "completed the revolting misery of the picture". The novel was finished in 1866 while Dostoevsky was living at Alonkin's House (No. 7 Przhevalskovo ulitsa), to the west of the square.

During the Soviet era the square was given a new image, stallholders were banished, trees were planted and it was optimistically renamed Peace Square (ploshchad Mira). The five-storey, yellow and white apartment blocks that surround the square today were also built then, in Stalin's version of Neo-Classicism. Sadly, in 1961, the square's most attractive monument, the Baroque Church of the Assumption, built in 1765, was pulled down to make way for one of the city's earliest metro stations.

⓫ Railway Museum
Музей железнодорожного транспорта *Muzey zheleznodorozhnovo transporta*

Sadovaya ulitsa 50. **Map** 6 D3. **Tel** 315 1476. Ⓜ Sennaya ploshchad, Sadovaya, Spasskaya. **Open** 10:30am–5:30pm daily. **Closed** last Thu of month. ☑ English.

More than 6,000 fascinating exhibits illustrate the history of the Russian railway system since 1813. The most interesting sections of the museum deal with the earliest railways, including Russia's first from Tsarskoe Selo to St Petersburg which began running in 1837, and the 650-km (404-mile) line from Moscow to St Petersburg (1851).

Exhibits include models of the first Russian steam engine, built by the Cherepanovs in 1834, and of an armoured train used by Trotsky to defend the city during the Civil War *(see p29)*. An insight into luxury travel in the late tsarist period can be gained from the walk-through section of a first-class sleeping compartment with Style-Moderne decoration.

Model of 1830s engine for the Tsarskoe Selo railway, Railway Museum

FURTHER AFIELD

While the majority of St Petersburg's sights are centrally located, the outlying areas of the city have a number of places of architectural, cultural and historical importance.

To the east is the Smolnyy district, taking its name from the tar yard which supplied the city's shipbuilding industry in the 18th century. The highlight of this area is Rastrelli's dazzling Baroque Smolnyy Convent. Nearby, the Smolnyy Institute is famed for its historic role as the Bolshevik headquarters during the October Revolution (see pp30–31). Southeast

of the centre lies the Alexander Nevsky Monastery where many of Russia's celebrated artists, architects and composers are buried.

The southern suburbs offer a strikingly different perspective of the city, with rows of grandiose 1930s–50s houses, a reminder that Stalin sought to destroy the city's historical heart by relocating the centre to the area around Moskovskaya ploshchad. The south also has the Chesma Church and the 1970s Victory Monument, a memorial to the suffering of St Petersburgers during the Siege of Leningrad.

Sights at a Glance

Palaces

- ❶ Yelagin Palace
- ❻ Tauride Palace
- ❾ Sheremetev Palace

Museums

- ❹ Stieglitz Museum
- ❿ Dostoevsky House-Museum

Churches

- ❺ Cathedral of the Transfiguration
- ❼ Smolnyy Convent
- ⓫ Alexander Nevsky Monastery
- ⓬ Chesma Church

Historic Buildings and Monuments

- ❷ Piskarevskoe Memorial Cemetery
- ❸ Finland Station
- ❽ Smolnyy Institute
- ⓭ Victory Monument

Key

- Central St Petersburg
- Motorway
- Major road
- Minor road
- Railway

0 kilometres 3
0 miles 3

East façade of Yelagin Palace with Srednaya Nevka river in foreground

❶ Yelagin Palace

Елагин дворец

Yelagin dvorets

Yelagin ostrov 1. **Tel** 430 1131.
Ⓜ Krestovskiy Ostrov. **Open** 10am–
6:30pm Tue, Thu–Sun; 1–9pm Wed.
Closed last Tue of month. 🎨
♿ to ground floor. 📷

One of the northernmost islands of St Petersburg, Yelagin Island is named after a court official who built a palace here at the end of the 18th century. Alexander I then bought the island in 1817 for his mother, Maria Fyodorovna, and commissioned Carlo Rossi to rebuild the palace. The magnificent Neo-Classical palace (1818–22), enlivened on the east façade by a half rotunda flanked by Corinthian porticoes, is part of an ensemble which includes an orangery, a horseshoe-shaped stable block and porticoed kitchens.

The palace interior was destroyed by fire during World War II but is now restored to its former glory. The Oval Hall is resplendent with statuary and trompe l'oeils while the rooms leading from it are exquisitely decorated with stucco, *faux marbre* and painted friezes, executed by gifted artists and craftsmen.

Statue of Mother Russia (1956–60),
Piskarevskoe Memorial Cemetery

In the Soviet period, the whole of the wooded island became the Central Park of Culture and Rest *(see pp138–9)*. Festivals and public entertainments are held here, and there is an exhibition of decorative art in the palace's former stables.

❷ Piskarevskoe Memorial Cemetery

Пискаревское
мемориальное кладбище

Piskarevskoe memorialnoe kladbishche

Prospekt Nepokorennykh 72–74.
Tel 247 5716. Ⓜ Akademicheskaya.
🚌 80, 123, 138, 178. **Open** 9am–6pm daily (May–Sep: 9am–9pm daily).
Memorial halls: 9am–6pm daily. 📷

This vast, bleak cemetery is a memorial to the two million people who died during the Siege of Leningrad, 1941–4 *(see p29)*. With little food and no electricity, water or heating, the citizens of Leningrad perished in vast numbers from starvation, cold and disease. Corpses were dragged on sledges to collection points from where they were taken for burial to mass cemeteries on the outskirts of town. Piskarevskoe was the largest, with 490,000 burials.

Today the cemetery is a place of pilgrimage for those who lost relatives and friends during those desperate times. The memorial complex, designed by Yevgeniy Levinson and Aleksandr Vasiliev, opened in 1960, on the 15th anniversary of the end of the war. Two memorial halls, one of which contains an exhibition on the Siege, flank the stairs down to a 300-m- (984-ft-) long avenue, which culminates in a towering,

heroic bronze statue of Mother Russia by Vera Isayeva and Robert Taurit. On the wall behind are verses composed by Olga Bergholts, herself a survivor of the Siege. The funereal music broadcast over the whole cemetery adds to the sombre atmosphere.

On either side of the avenue are 186 grassy mounds, each with a granite slab marking the year and indicating, with a red star or hammer and sickle, whether those interred were soldiers or civilians.

Locomotive 293, Finland Station

❸ Finland Station

Финляндский вокзал

Finlyandskiy vokzal

Ploshchad Lenina 6. **Map** 3 B3.
Ⓜ Ploshchad Lenina. See also p223.

On the night of 3 April 1917, the exiled Vladimir Lenin and his Bolshevik companions arrived at Finland Station after travelling from Switzerland on a sealed train. A triumphant reception awaited their return to Russia and, on leaving the station, Lenin spoke to cheering crowds of soldiers, sailors and workers. A statue erected outside the station in 1926 depicts Lenin delivering his speech.

The modern terminal was opened in the 1960s. On platform 5 there is a huge glass case containing Locomotive 293 which Lenin rode when fleeing the capital for a second time in July 1917. After spending the summer as a fugitive in Russian Finland, Lenin returned on the same train and spurred on the October Revolution *(see pp30–31)*.

❹ Stieglitz Museum
Музей Штиглица
Muzey Shtiglitsa

Solyanoy pereulok 13–15. **Map** 3 A5.
Tel 273 3258. 46, K-76, K-100,
K-217. **Open** Sep–Jul: 11am–4:30pm
Tue–Sat. **Closed** last Fri of month.

The millionaire industrialist
Baron Aleksandr Stieglitz
founded the Central
School of Industrial
Design in 1876.
His aim was to
provide a top-
quality collection
of original works for
the use of Russian
students of applied
arts and design.

19th-century crystal vase,
Stieglitz Museum

With a large budget
and the good taste of
Stieglitz's son-in-law, Aleksandr
Polovtsov (*see p124*), the collection, unusual in covering
both Western European and
Oriental art, soon outgrew the
school and in 1896 a Museum
of Applied Arts opened next
door. This magnificent building,
designed by Maximilian
Messmacher, was inspired
by Italian Renaissance palaces.
Inside, the halls and galleries
were decorated in an impressive variety of national and
period styles, echoing French
and German Baroque and,
above all, Italian Renaissance
monuments, such as St Mark's
Library in Venice, the Raphael
Loggias of the Vatican and the
Villa Madama, also in Rome.

After the Revolution the school
was closed and the museum
became a branch of the
Hermitage (*see pp86–95*).
Serious damage to the building
was inflicted during the Siege
of Leningrad (*see
p29*). At the end
of the war the
school was
revived to train
gilders and carvers
for the huge res-
toration programme
needed to repair
the damaged city.
Situated on
the ground floor, the
exhibition features opulent displays of glassware, ceramics
and majolica, as well as porcelain
from all the great European
manufacturers. One room,
decorated in the style of the
medieval Terem Palace in
the Kremlin, provides a superb
backdrop for a collection of
embroidered dresses and
headgear made by Russian
peasant women.

Some pieces of decorative
metalwork including locks, keys
and craft tools date back to the
Middle Ages. The workmanship

seen on the wooden furniture is
breathtaking. The Neo-Gothic cabinet is a beautiful example. Its
finely inlaid doors, depicting
church naves in perspective, open
to reveal sculpted biblical scenes.

One way to end your visit
is with a look at the stunning
Grand Exhibition Hall with its
curving staircase of Italian marble and magnificent glass roof.

❺ Cathedral of the Transfiguration
Спасо-Преображенский
собор
Spaso-Preobrazhenskiy sobor

Preobrazhenskaya ploshchad 1. **Map** 3
B5. **Tel** 272 3662. M Chernyshevskaya.
46, K-76, K-90, K-177, K-258. 3,
8, 15. **Open** 8am–8pm daily.

Despite its monumental Neo-
Classicism, and the surrounding
fence made of guns captured
during the Russo-Turkish wars
(*see p24*), Vasiliy Stasov's church
has an intimate air as it nestles
in its leafy square. The original
church on this site was built by
Tsarina Elizabeth to honour the
Preobrazhenskiy Life-Guards,
but it was rebuilt after a fire
in 1825. Today, the church is
famous for its excellent choir,
which is second only to that
in the Alexander Nevsky
Monastery (*see pp132–3*).

Dolls in 17th–19th-century Russian folk costumes, in front of the Terem Room, Stieglitz Museum

❻ Tauride Palace
Таврический дворец
Tavricheskiy dvorets

Shpalernaya ulitsa 47. **Map** 4 D4.
Ⓜ Chernyshevskaya. 🚌 46, 136.
Closed to public.

This finely proportioned palace
by Ivan Starov was built in 1783–
9 as a present from Catherine
the Great to her influential lover
Prince Grigoriy Potemkin *(see
p27)*. Potemkin had successfully
annexed the Crimea (Tauris)
to Russia in 1783 and was given
the title of Prince of Tauris,
hence the palace's name.

Uncompromising in its lack of
external ornamentation, the long,
yellow building with its distinctive
six-columned portico was one of
Russia's first Neo-Classical designs.
Sadly, the magnificent interiors
have been badly damaged
both by Catherine's son, Paul I,
who turned the palace into
a barracks, and by the many
reconstructions undertaken.

The palace played a vital
role in 20th-century cultural
and political life. In 1905, the
impresario Sergey Diaghilev
(see p45) organized the first
ever exhibition of Russian
18th-century portraiture here.
The following year the palace
hosted Russia's first parliament,
the State Duma. After the
February Revolution of 1917
it became the seat of the
Provisional Government, then
the Petrograd Soviet of Workers'
and Soldiers' Deputies. Today it
is still a government building.

The lovely gardens, with
winding streams, bridges and
an artificial lake, are among
the city's most popular parks.

The blue-and-white façade of the Smolnyy Cathedral and the adjacent convent buildings

❼ Smolnyy Convent
Смольный монастырь
Smolnyy monastyr

Ploshchad Rastrelli 3/1. **Map** 4 F4.
Tel 900 7015. 🚌 46, 136.
Open 7am–8pm daily.

The crowning glory of this
architectural ensemble is
the stunning blue-and-white
cathedral, with its dome and
four supporting cupolas topped
by golden orbs.

As a symbol of her majesty,
Tsarina Elizabeth founded the
convent where many young
noblewomen were to be
educated. It was designed in
1748 by Bartolomeo Rastrelli
(see p95), who conceived a
brilliant fusion of Russian and
Western Baroque styles. Work
advanced extremely slowly;
50,000 wooden piles were
used to secure the foundations
in the marshy soil and the
architect's model alone, now
in the Academy of Arts *(see p65)*,
took seven years to build.

Catherine the Great disliked
Rastrelli's work and had little
sympathy for the late Elizabeth.
When she came to power in
1762, funding for the project

stopped. It was only in 1835
that Nicholas I commissioned
the Neo-Classical architect
Vasiliy Stasov to complete the
cathedral. His austere white
interior contrasts dramatically
with the luxuriant exterior.

Following the revolution,
the cathedral was closed for
decades. It hosted various
cultural events from 1990–2016,
before being reconsecrated.

❽ Smolnyy Institute
Смольный Институт
Smolnyy institut

Smolnyy proezd 1. **Map** 4 F4. **Tel** 576
7461. 🚌 46, 54, 74, 136, K-15, K-76,
K-136. 🚎 5, 7, 11, 15, 16. Smolnyy
Museum: **Open** 10am–6pm Mon–Thu,
10am–3pm Fri, 10am–5pm Sat & Sun
by appt only. 🅿 ♿ 📷 English.

Built in 1806–8 to house a
school for young noblewomen,
the original having outgrown its
premises at the Smolnyy Convent,
this Neo-Classical building
was considered by Giacomo
Quarenghi to be his masterpiece.

It was from here, on 25 October
1917, that Lenin directed the
Bolshevik *coup d'état* while
the second All-Russian Congress
of Soviets was convening in the
Assembly Hall. The Congress
confirmed Lenin in power and
this was his seat of government
until March 1918. With the
Germans advancing and
with the outbreak of civil war
(see p29), the government left
for Moscow. The Institute was
taken over by the Leningrad
Communist Party. On
1 December 1934, the First
Secretary of the party, Sergey
Kirov *(see p74)*, was murdered
here, an event that was to

View of Tauride Gardens and the Tauride Palace beyond the lake

Isaak Brodskiy's 1927 painting of Lenin, Smolnyy Institute Assembly Hall

provide cover for the purges of the late 1930s *(see p29)*.

The rooms where Lenin lived and worked can be viewed by appointment. The rest of the institute is now the Mayor's Office. The imperial eagle has replaced the hammer and sickle, but the statue of Lenin has survived.

❾ Sheremetev Palace
Шереметевский дворец
Sheremetevskiy dvorets

Naberezhnaya reki Fontanki 34.
Map 7 A1. Ⓜ Mayakovskaya, Gostinyy
Dvor. 🚌 15, 22, 27, K-15, K-90, K-187,
K-258. 🚃 3, 8, 15. Anna Akhmatova
Museum: **Tel** 571 7239. **Open** 10:30am–
6:30pm Tue, Thu–Sun; noon–8pm Wed.
🖼 🎫 English. Museum of Musical Life:
Tel 272 4441. **Open** 11am–7pm Thu–
Mon, 1–9pm Wed. **Closed** last Wed of
each month. 🖼 🎫

The Sheremetev family lived here from 1712, when the palace was built by Field Marshal Boris Sheremetev, until the Revolution. The palace is also known as the Fountain House, or *Fontannyy dom*, because of the many fountains that once adorned its grounds. The Baroque building dates from the 1750s when it was designed by Savva Chevakinskiy and Fyodor Argunov, although numerous later alterations were made.

Field Marshal Sheremetev's descendants were fabulously wealthy, at one time owning some 200,000 serfs. They were among Russia's leading artistic patrons and the palace is now home to the Museum of Musical Life, which charts the family's contribution to the music of the city. In the 18th and 19th centuries, serf composers, musicians and actors from rural estates owned by the family performed in concerts and plays at the palace. Among those to praise the fine Sheremetev choir was the composer Franz Liszt. The museum's exhibits include a variety of period instruments and a number of scores, some of which are compositions by the Sheremetevs themselves.

One of Russia's greatest 20th-century poets, Anna Akhmatova, lived in one of the service blocks of the palace from 1933 to 1941 and then between 1944 and 1954. Her flat is open to the public as the Anna Akhmatova Museum *(Muzey Anny Akhmatovoy)* and is reached through the courtyard of No. 53 Liteynyy prospekt. By the time she moved into the palace, it had been divided into dingy communal apartments. The rooms where she lived and worked display some of her personal possessions, tracing her intriguing life. Recordings of the poet reading her own work can also be heard.

Anna Akhmatova

By 1914 Anna Akhmatova (1889–1966) was a leading light of Russia's "Silver Age" of poetry *(see p46)*. Tragedy gave her work a new dimension when first her husband was shot by the Bolsheviks, and later, her son and her lover were arrested in Stalin's purges. Anna herself was placed under police surveillance and officially silenced for more than 15 years. Her most famous poem, *Requiem* (1935–61), inspired by her son's arrest, was written in fragments and distributed to friends to memorize. Akhmatova's reputation was partially rehabilitated late in her life and she received honorary awards abroad.

Pilastered façade of Sheremetev Palace on the Fontanka embankment

❿ Dostoevsky House-Museum

Музей Достоевского
Muzey Dostoevskovo

Kuznechnyy pereulok 5/2. **Map** 7 B3.
Tel 571 4031. Ⓜ Vladimirskaya.
🚌 3, 8, 15. 🚎 49. **Open** 11am–6pm
Tue–Sun, 1–8pm Wed. 🅿 📷 English.
W md.spb.ru

This evocative museum was the
final home of the famous Russian
writer, Fyodor Dostoevsky *(see p46)*,
who lived here from 1878 until his
death in 1881. Dostoevsky was
then at the height of his fame, and
it was here that he completed
his last great novel, *The Brothers
Karamazov*, in 1880. Gambling
and debts, however, confined
him to a fairly modest lifestyle
in this five-roomed apartment.

Although Dostoevsky's public
persona was dour and humour-
less, he was a devoted and
affectionate husband and father.
The delightful nursery contains
a rocking horse, silhouettes of his
children and the book of fairy
tales which he read aloud to
them. In Dostoevsky's study are
his writing desk and a reproduction of his favourite painting,
Raphael's *Sistine Madonna*.

Chesma Church (1777–80), a very early example of
Neo-Gothic in Russia

⓬ Chesma Church

Чесменская церковь
Chesmenskaya tserkov

Ulitsa Lensoveta 12. Ⓜ Moskovskaya.
🚌 16. 🚎 29, 45. **Open** 10am–
7pm daily.

There is little Russian about the
highly unusual Chesma Church,
which was designed by Yuriy
Velten in 1777–80. Its fanciful
terracotta-coloured façade is
decorated with thin vertical stripes

of white moulding which
direct the eye upwards
to its zig-zagged crown
and Neo-Gothic cupolas.
The name commemorates
the great Russian naval
victory over the Turks
at Chesma in the Aegean
in 1770. During the
Communist era the church
became a museum to
the battle, but today
the building is once
again used as a church.
On the opposite side of
ulitsa Lensoveta is the Neo-
Gothic Chesma Palace
(1774–77), formerly
Kekerekeksinen, or
Frog Marsh Palace.
Also designed by Velten,
it served as a staging post
for Catherine the Great en route
to Tsarskoe Selo *(see pp154–7)*.
Wedgwood's famous dinner
service with its frog emblem,
now in the Hermitage *(see p93)*,
was designed specially for the
Chesma Palace.

The palace achieved
notoriety when Rasputin's
body lay in state here after his
murder in 1916 *(see p123)*. Now
substantially altered, it serves
as a home for the elderly.

⓫ Alexander Nevsky Monastery

александро-Невская лавра
Aleksandro-Nevskaya lavra

Ploshchad Aleksandra Nevskovo.
Map 8 E4. **Tel** 274 2635. Ⓜ Ploshchad
Aleksandra Nevskovo. 🚌 8, 24, 27,
46, 55, 58, 191, K-156, K-187, K-209.
🚎 1, 14, 16, 22. 🚎 7, 65. Holy Trinity
Cathedral: **Open** 6am–8pm daily.
Church of the Annunciation: **Tel** 274
2635. **Open** 11am– 5pm; closes 6pm
in summer. **Closed** Mon & Thu. 🅿
cemeteries & Church of the
Annunciation. 📷

Founded by Peter the Great
in 1710, this monastery is
named after Alexander Nevsky,
the prince of Novgorod,
who defeated the Swedes
in 1240. Peter defeated
them in 1709 *(see p20)*.

From the entrance, a path
runs between two large, walled
cemeteries, then across a stream
and into the main monastic

complex. The oldest building is
the Church of the Annunciation
(1717–22), designed by
Domenico Trezzini. The church
was the burial place for non-
ruling members of the Russian
royal family, politicians and
military leaders. A series of red
and white, mid-18th-century
monastic buildings, including
the Metropolitan's House
(1755–8), surround the
courtyard. Among the trees
in the courtyard lie the graves
of atheist Soviet scholars and
leading Communists.

Dominating the essentially
Baroque complex is the
twin-towered and domed
Neo-Classical Holy Trinity
Cathedral, constructed by
architect Ivan Starov in 1776–90.
The wide nave inside is flanked
by Corinthian columns with
statues by Fedot Shubin. This
leads to the impressive red
agate and white marble

iconostasis, which features
copies of works by Van Dyck,
Rubens and others. To the
right of the iconostasis is a
silver reliquary that contains
the remains of Alexander
Nevsky, transferred to the

Reliquary with Alexander Nevsky's remains,
Trinity Cathedral

⑬ Victory Monument

Монумент Защитникам
Ленинграда *Monument*
Zashchitnikam Leningrada

Ploshchad Pobedy. **Tel** 371 2951,
373 6563. Ⓜ Moskovskaya.
🚌 3, 11, 13, 39, 59, 90, 150, 187,
K-13, K-100, K-350. 🚎 27, 29, 45.
Memorial Hall: **Open** 11am–6pm
Thu & Sat–Mon, 11am–5pm Tue.
Closed last Tue of each month.
📷 book by phone.

Erected in 1975 to coincide with
the 30th anniversary of the end
of World War II, this is on the
site of a temporary triumphal
arch built to greet the returning
troops. Named the Monument
to the Heroic Defenders of
Leningrad, it commemorates
the victims of the Siege *(see
p29)*, and its survivors. It was
designed by Sergey Speranskiy
and Valentin Kamenskiy and
sculpted by Mikhail Anikushin.
A 48-m- (157-ft-) high obelisk of
red granite is near a vast, circular
enclosure which symbolizes
the vice-like grip of the siege.
Sculptures of soldiers, sailors
and grieving mothers surround
the monument.

An underpass on Moskovskiy
prospekt leads to the Memorial
Hall. Here solemn music gives
way to the persistent beat of a
metronome, the wartime radio
signal, intended to represent
the city's defiant heartbeat. The
subdued lighting comprises 900
dim, orange lamps, one for each
day of the Siege. Tablets are
inscribed with the names of the
650 Heroes of the Soviet Union
awarded the title after the war;
and a mosaic depicts the women
of the city greeting their men-
folk at the end of the conflict.

Around the hall a small
display of artifacts, including
Shostakovich's violin *(see p45)*,
records the contribution of
different sections of the community to the war effort, while an
illuminated relief map illustrates
the battle lines. Most disturbing
is the tiny piece of bread, which
was many people's daily ration.

Heroic partisans facing south towards the enemy during the Siege of Leningrad, detail of Victory Monument

previous church on this site
in 1724. Behind the reliquary
hangs a painting of Nevsky,
who has been venerated as
a saint in Russia since the
mid-16th century.

Many of the nation's leading
cultural figures are buried in the
two monastic cemeteries near
the main entrance. The city's
oldest graveyard, the Lazarus
Cemetery, to the east, contains
the graves of the polymath
Mikhail Lomonosov *(see p47)*
and a number of prominent
architects, including Andrey
Zakharov, Thomas de Thomon,
Giacomo Quarenghi, Carlo
Rossi *(see p112)* and Andrey
Voronikhin. Clustered together
along the northern wall of
the Tikhvin Cemetery (to the
west) are the tombs of some
of Russia's most famous composers. Fyodor Dostoevsky
(see p46) is also buried here,
to the right of the entrance.

Tombs of Interest at Tikhvin Cemetery

① Mikhail Glinka
(Composer, 1804–57)
② Ivan Krylov
(Poet, 1769–1844)
③ Marius Petipa
(Choreographer, 1818–1910)
④ Pyotr Klodt
(Sculptor, 1805–67)
⑤ Ivan Kramskoy
(Painter, 1837–87)
⑥ Pyotr Tchaikovsky
(Composer, 1840–93)
⑦ Modest Mussorgsky
(Composer, 1839–81)
⑧ Nikolai Rimsky-Korsakov
(Composer, 1844–1908)
⑨ Fyodor Dostoevsky
(Writer, 1821–81)

0 metres   50
0 yards   50

Main entrance

For keys to symbols *see back flap*

THREE GUIDED WALKS

Many of St Petersburg's sights are best appreciated on foot. The three walks chosen present different aspects of the city's character, though water plays a central part in each.

The first walk follows the Moyka river and the Griboedov Canal, which criss-cross the heart of the city, and reveals the magnificent scale of the buildings erected in the 18th and 19th centuries. It highlights the contrasts between rich palaces and overcrowded apartment blocks, gilded bridges and the dilapidation of the area around Sennaya ploshchad. An alternative way to appreciate the glorious old buildings set on the canals is to take a boat trip *(see pp228–9)*.

The second walk explores Yelagin and Kamennyy islands, where Petersburgers traditionally spend much of their free time. The islands to the north of the centre were once the preserve of the rich, who spent the hot summers in the cool of their *dachas*. Now locals come to walk and row boats in summer, to ski and skate in winter, and simply to breathe the fresh spring air.

The third walk follows the river Neva on the Petrograd side, from where there are awe-inspiring views of the city's grand south waterfront and of the river itself. The walk encompasses some significant historic sites including Trinity Square, the Cabin of Peter the Great and the cruiser *Aurora*.

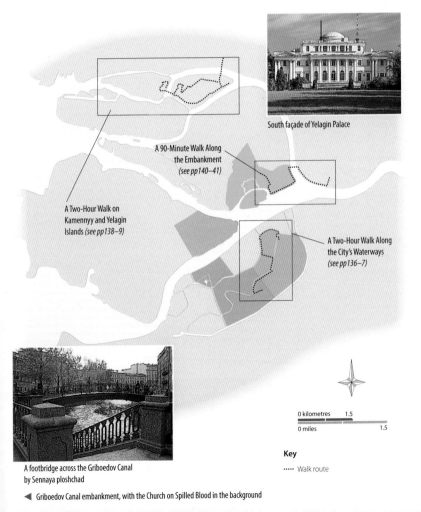

South façade of Yelagin Palace

A 90-Minute Walk Along the Embankment *(see pp140–41)*

A Two-Hour Walk on Kamennyy and Yelagin Islands *(see pp138–9)*

A Two-Hour Walk Along the City's Waterways *(see pp136–7)*

0 kilometres   1.5

0 miles   1.5

Key

••••• Walk route

A footbridge across the Griboedov Canal by Sennaya ploshchad

◄ Griboedov Canal embankment, with the Church on Spilled Blood in the background

A Two-Hour Walk Along the City's Waterways

A stroll along the embankments of the Moyka river and the Griboedov Canal is a chance to appreciate the history and splendid architecture of this beautiful city. The two waterways present interesting contrasts. The Moyka winds past the Imperial Summer and Winter Palaces and the lavish mansions of the aristocracy, while the Griboedov is lined with 19th-century apartments, once home to merchants, civil servants and, towards Sennaya Ploshchad (see p124), the working class. The walk also includes a short stretch of the majestic Nevskiy prospekt.

Tips for Walkers

Starting point: Church on Spilled Blood.
Length: 5.8 km (3 miles).
Getting there: Nevskiy Prospekt metro.
Stopping-off points: Bistro Layma, nab kanala Griboedova 16.

View of the Church on Spilled Blood ① and the Griboedov Canal

The Moyka River

Begin the walk at the magnificent Church on Spilled Blood ① (see p102), built over the spot where Alexander II was assassinated in 1881 (see p28). From here, walk around the church beside the park, crossing the canal bridge to Konyushennaya ploshchad. The square is embraced by the elongated façade of the former Imperial Stables ②. Straddling the junction of the Griboedov Canal and the Moyka river are two ingeniously linked bridges, the Malo-Konyushennyy most (Small Stable Bridge) and Teatralnyy most (Theatre Bridge) (see p39). Cross over these bridges to the north bank of the Moyka and the expansive façade of the Adamini House ③, designed by Domenico Adamini in 1823–7. Between 1916 and 1919 the basement was used by a artists' and writers' club known as "The Bivouac of the Comedians". Visitors included

the avant-garde theatre director Vsevolod Meyerhold and the poets Aleksandr Blok and Anna Akhmatova (see p46).

Turn left onto naberezhnaya reki Moyki and walk past the Round Market ④ built in 1790 by Giacomo Quarenghi, who had shopping arcades as one of his specialities. Continue along the embankment, passing Adam's Bolshoy Konyushennyy most (Great Stables Bridge) to Prince Abamelek-Lazarev's former mansion ⑤ built in 1913–15. The handsome façade, with Corinthian pilasters and graceful reliefs of dancing figures, is by Ivan Fomin. On the opposite bank is the 17th-century apartment block where Pushkin spent the last few months of his life. His flat is now a museum ⑥ (see p115).

At the intersection of Millionaya ulitsa and the beautiful Winter Canal (Zimnaya Kanavka) are the former barracks of the elite First Regiment of the Preobrazhenskiy Life-Guards. This prestigious corps was formed by Peter the Great in the 1690s.

Across the Winter Canal is the New Hermitage ⑦ (see p86). Ten granite atlantes bear the weight

Quarenghi's arcaded Round Market (1790) ④, overlooking the Moyka river

Key

• • • Walk route

View of the tree-lined Griboedov Canal

of the elaborate porch. Returning to the Moyka, the route passes a green, three-storey house ⑧, built by F Demertsov for Alexander I's military advisor and sometime chief minister, Count Aleksey Arakcheev.

The Moyka now makes a curve behind the majestic buildings of Palace Square *(see p85)* which includes the Staff of the Guards Corps ⑨ and the huge crescent of Carlo Rossi's imposing yellow General Staff Building ⑩. Cross the Pevcheskiy most (Singers' Bridge) *(see p39)* ⑪ and follow the Moyka down to the Zelenyy most (Green Bridge). The yellow building on the other side of the Moyka is the Literary Café ⑫, renowned as a meeting place for writers in Pushkin's day *(see p85)*.

Nevskiy Prospekt

Turn left onto St Petersburg's main street, where a range of architectural styles can be seen. On the left, the elegant façade of Paul Jacot's Dutch Church building ⑬ *(see p49)* hides a series of shops. Across the road, the superb façade of the

Baroque Stroganov Palace ⑭ *(see p114)* contrasts starkly with the triple-arched glass frontage of the Style-Moderne Fashion House ⑮ *(see p49)*. The colonnaded forecourt of the Cathedral of Our Lady of Kazan ⑯ *(see p113)* can be seen further along.

The Griboedov Canal

Cross Nevskiy prospekt by the attractive Singer Sewing Machine Building *(see p49)* and follow the Griboedov south. When you reach Georg von Traitteur's Bankovskiy most (Bank Bridge) *(see p37)* ⑰, decorated with golden griffons, cross the canal and continue past the wrought-iron railings to the rear of the former Assignment Bank ⑱ (now occupied by a finance and economics university). Further south the humped Kamennyy most (Stone Bridge) has survived since 1776 despite an attempt by a revolutionary group to blow it up, as Tsar Alexander II passed in his carriage in 1881. Across the Demidov most, on the corner of Kaznacheyskaya ulitsa ⑲ (No.1), is the apartment where Dostoevsky *(see p45)* wrote *Notes from the House of the Dead* (1861). Also with literary associations, the former Zverkov House ⑳ was where the novelist and dramatist Nikolai Gogol *(see p46)* lived in the 1830s.

The walk ends in Sennaya ploshchad *(see p124)*, where there are three metro stations.

Griffons on Bank Bridge (1826), Griboedov Canal

Apartment block where Dostoevsky lived ⑲, on the Griboedov Canal

A Two-Hour Walk on Kamennyy and Yelagin Islands

An area of rolling parkland, birch and lime groves and fine river views, the northern islands of the Neva delta offer a retreat from city life. The imperial family built palaces on Kamennyy and Yelagin islands at the end of the 18th century and were soon joined by wealthy aristocratic families. Before the Revolution, many government ministers, industrial magnates and celebrities built themselves a *dacha* here. Today these neglected houses, some intimate, some palatial, in styles ranging from Neo-Gothic to Neo-Classical and Style-Moderne, are being returned to their former glory by the business elite.

rather splendid Style-Moderne mansion in 1913–14. Continue west, and cross the canal bridge to reach the wooden Kamennoostrovskiy Theatre ⑤ which took only 40 days to erect in 1827. Its Neo-Classical portico, rebuilt by Albert Kavos in 1844, is still impressive. The banks of the Krestovka river, with views across to the boatyards of Krestovskiy Island, offer many ideal spots for a picnic (but bear in mind that admission is charged at weekends). To rejoin the walk, return to the path and cross 1-y Yelagin most to Yelagin Island.

Yelagin Island
This island is an oasis of calm, popular with those wishing to escape the city. A tollgate marks the entrance to the grounds of Carlo Rossi's graceful Yelagin Palace ⑥ *(see p128)*. The western

③ Wooden façade of Dolgorukov Mansion

South Kamennyy Island
Begin at Chernaya Rechka metro station and head south to Bolshaya Nevka river, then cross Ushakovskiy most (Ushikov Bridge) to Kamennyy Island, an area of recreation and relaxation. Just across the main road is the small red-brick Church of St John the Baptist ①, designed in Neo-Gothic style by Yuriy Velten in 1776–8. Nearby a yellow gateway leads to the grounds of Kamennoostrovskiy Palace ② (which is now a retirement home) from where Alexander I led the 1812 Russian campaign against Napoleon *(see p28)*.

Follow Kamennoostrovskiy prospekt to the Malaya Nevka river, then turn right on to naberezhnaya Maloy Nevki where there is an imposing wooden mansion ③ at No. 11 with a white-columned portico. The Dolgorukov

Mansion was built in 1831–2 by Smaragd Shustov for the Dolgorukovs, one of Russia's oldest aristocratic families.

From this point you can see across to Aptekarskiy or Apothecary's Island, named after the medicinal herb gardens founded by Peter the Great in 1714. St Petersburg's Botanical Gardens are still located there. Continue along the path, which turns into naberezhnaya reki Krestovki. The house on the left, towards the Malokrestovskiy most (Small Krestovskiy Bridge), is the former home of Sergey Chaev ④, who was the chief engineer of the Trans-Siberian railway. Chaev commissioned the fashionable architect, Vladimir Apyshkov, to build this

① The tower of the Church of St John the Baptist (1776–8)

⑤ Kamennoostrovskiy Theatre's impressive façade (1827)

spit of the island is ideal for viewing the spectacular sunsets over the Gulf of Finland, especially during the White Nights (see p53). If you want to venture further, head south across 2-y Yelagin most to Krestovskiy Island and the Kirov Stadium, Maritime Victory Park and Primorskiy Park Pobedy. Or, to the north, 3-y Yelagin most leads to Primorskiy prospekt and the Tibetan-inspired Buddhist Temple, erected by Gavriil Baranovskiy in 1909–15.

North Kamennyy Island

Return to Kamennyy Island across 1-y Yelagin most, taking the left fork on to Teatralnaya alleya from where you can see the former mansion of Aleksandr Polovtsov ⑦, minister of foreign affairs under Nicholas II. This splendid Neo-Classical mansion with Style-Moderne touches was built by Ivan Fomin in 1911–13. Leave Teatralnaya alleya and cut through the quiet and restful park, passing between the ponds and the canal. Near the junction with Bolshaya alleya are two more early 20th-century mansions. Follenveider's mansion ⑧ on the left, with its

⑦ Early 20th-century Polovtsov Mansion

distinctive tented tower, was designed by Roman Meltzer in 1904 and now belongs to the Danish consulate. Yevgeniya Gausvald's dacha ⑨ dates from 1898 and stands as one of the earliest Style-Moderne buildings in St Petersburg. It was designed by Vasiliy Schöne and Vladimir Chagin. Finally, the last stage of the walk leads along the 2-ya Berezovaya alleya, back to the starting point at Ushakovskiy most and Chernaya Rechka metro.

Key

• • • Walk route

Tips for Walkers

Starting point: Chernaya Rechka metro station (see p227).
Length: 6 km (3.5 miles).
Stopping-off points: Café in former stables of Yelagin Palace (summer only) and plenty of places to picnic.

The tree-shrouded grassy banks of the Krestovka river

A 90-Minute Walk Along the Embankment

Muscovites envy St Petersburgers their dramatic and open skyline, and this stroll along the northern banks of the Neva offers grand views, not only of the magnificent south waterfront, but also of the Petrogradskaya Side, as seen from Trinity Bridge where it crosses the river at its widest point. In winter the Neva lies frozen, an expanse of whiteness. In warmer months the water pulses hypnotically through the city. The walk encompasses the best of the city's Style-Moderne architecture, the Cabin of Peter the Great, the cruiser *Aurora*, whose guns began the 1917 Revolution, and the train that brought Lenin to Russia.

Look out for the needle-sharp steeple of the Baroque Cathedral of SS Peter and Paul ⑤. The bridge was completed in time for the city's bicentenary in 1903 by the French firm Batignol, which also constructed the Eiffel Tower.

Return to the shore, and stroll east along Petrovskaya Embankment, passing the Cabin of Peter the Great ⑥ *(see p75)*. The tiny cabin was built from pine logs in 3 days in

⑤ View of Peter and Paul Fortress with the Cathedral of SS Peter and Paul

Kamennoostrovskiy Prospekt

From Gorkovskaya metro station, cross the road via the underpass and walk south along Konverskiy prospekt, an avenue noted for its Style-Moderne architecture. Almost immediately, the minarets of the city's only mosque jut up ahead. Sobornaya Mosque ① *(see p72)*, one of Europe's largest, was built in 1913.

Slightly further on, at the junction with ulitsa Kuybysheva, is the Kshesinskaya Mansion ② *(see p74)*, a delicate, asymmetrical Style-Moderne building commissioned in 1906 for the ballerina Matilda Kshesinskaya (Nicholas II's former lover). Once the Bolshevik Party HQ, from whose balcony Lenin addressed the crowds, it now houses the Museum of Russian Political History with exhibits from the revolutionary era.

Take a right down ulitsa Kuybysheva then bear left onto Kamennoostrovskiy prospekt *(see p72)*. To your left is Trinity Square ③ *(see p75)*, the heart of the old city's merchant quarter, and site of the "Bloody Sunday" massacre during the 1905 Revolution, and of the relatively new Trinity Chapel.

Trinity Square

Until the fall of the USSR, the square was known as Revolution Square in memory of the 48 workers who were mown down here by government troops. Walk onto Style-Moderne Trinity Bridge ④ *(see p37)*, which spans the Neva at its widest point and affords fine views of the river and the Peter and Paul Fortress *(see pp68–9)*.

⑥ Interior of the tiny Cabin of Peter the Great

⑨ The cruiser *Aurora* (1900) moored in front of the Nakhimov Naval Academy

View across the frozen River Neva featuring the golden dome of St Isaac's Cathedral on the south embankment

May 1703, and Peter lived here for 6 years, supervising the building of his city. The brick shell was added later by Catherine the Great. On the steps outside the cabin are the Manchurian Lions ⑦, two odd statues brought from Manchuria during the disastrous (for Russia) Russo-Japanese War of 1904–5.

Palace. This event brought the Bolsheviks to power in 1917. The battleship also contains a museum.

Further along the embankment, the Neo-Baroque building on the left is the Nakhimov Naval Academy ⑨, built in 1910–11.

Now cross Sampsonievskiy most onto Pirogovskaya naberezhnaya. From here you can catch tram No. 6 to the end of the walk if you wish.

Key

••• Walk route

The Cruiser Aurora

Follow the embankment to Petrogradskaya naberezhnaya and the historic old cruiser *Aurora* ⑧ (see p75), famous for firing the shots that signalled the storming of the Winter

Continuing on foot, the embankment leads down to Arsenalnaya naberezhnaya, past the Military Medical Academy ⑩ – built in the time of Tsar Paul I in a High-Classical style. Turn left onto Ploshchad Lenina ⑪. In the square is one of the city's few remaining statues of Lenin.

Statue of Lenin in Ploshchad Lenina ⑪, near Finland Station

Tips for Walkers

Starting point: Sobornaya Mosque.
Getting there: Gorkovskaya metro station (see p227).
Length: 3.5 km (2 miles).
Stopping-off points: There are places selling snacks along the north embankment, especially around the cruiser *Aurora* and the Cabin of Peter the Great.

Ploshchad Lenina

The majority of statues of Lenin were torn down after the collapse of the USSR. This one was erected in 1926. Note the famous '"taxi-hailing" pose that was so popular among architects of monuments to "Grandfather Lenin", as Soviet children were taught to refer to him. Directly opposite the square, on the other side of the river, looms the "Bolshoy Dom", the gloomy former headquarters of the KGB. Here, death sentences were passed on an estimated 47,000 citizens of St Petersburg, who were then executed by firing squad. It is now the FSB's (the KGB's successors) HQ and a prison. Finally, walk across Ploshchad Lenina to Finland Station ⑫ (see p128), home to the train that brought Lenin to Russia to lead the 1917 October Revolution – and to alter the destiny of the largest country on earth. Finland Station also houses the Ploshchad Lenina metro station.

BEYOND ST PETERSBURG

BEYOND ST PETERSBURG

The countryside around St Petersburg is typical of northwest Russia. Among its flat sweeps of land, pine forests and lakes there are sights of cultural interest, including the imperial palaces and the walled medieval city of Veliky Novgorod. Venturing away from St Petersburg allows a richer and deeper insight into this splendid land.

Before St Petersburg was founded in 1703, the surrounding landscape was a marshy and inhospitable wilderness, inhabited by wolves. Nevertheless, the area from the Gulf of Finland to Lake Ladoga was of strategic importance for trading and thus one of the reasons for continuous wars between Sweden and Russia. At the time the only city of importance here was Novgorod, an independent and quite wealthy principality *(see p19)*. It has retained its medieval atmosphere, so different from the imperial palaces adorning the countryside south of St Petersburg, each of which reflect the tastes of their owners. Peter the Great's fine residence, Peterhof, is dominated by water; the nearby Gulf and the numerous fountains mirror his maritime interest. Elizabeth wanted vibrant colour and

excess to accommodate her extravagant balls, hence the grand Baroque palace at Tsarskoe Selo. Catherine the Great's love of intimacy led her to add private apartments to Tsarskoe Selo, and the exquisite Chinese Palace at Oranienbaum. Paul I's military mania had him turn Gatchina into a castle, while his wife Maria Fyodorovna created a feminine, elegant residence at Pavlovsk. All the palaces except Oranienbaum suffered devastating damage during World War II *(see p29)*. A great deal of effort has been made to restore them over the last 60 years.

While the aristocracy indulged in their extravagances, the middle classes had more modest country houses. The *dacha* of the artist Repin gives a feel of his more bohemian lifestyle.

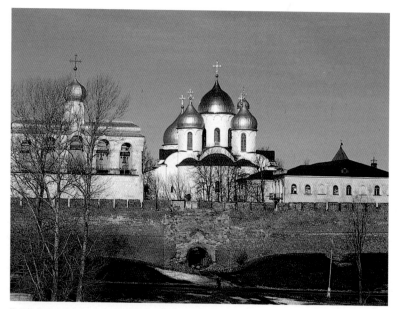

The Veliky Novgorod Kremlin with the Cathedral of St Sophia and its belfry

◀ The impressive Grand Cascade in front of the Great Palace, depicting the biblical tale of Samson and the lion

Exploring St Petersburg's Surroundings

Many St Petersburgers leave the city to spend time at their *dacha* or country house for weekends and holidays. But there are several ways of experiencing the countryside around St Petersburg. There are many stunning imperial palaces, spread out like pearls in a necklace south of the city. Each one of them offers splendid interiors as well as beautifully laid out parks and gardens with lakes. Around the artist's studio at Repino is a more typical Baltic landscape, with pine and fir trees stretching down to the pebbly beaches of the Gulf of Finland.

Further away to the south, the medieval town of Veliky Novgorod is a great representative of an old Russian city, complete with a walled kremlin and onion-domed churches.

Façade of the Chinese Palace at Oranienbaum

Getting Around

It is relatively easy to get to all of the imperial palaces, and to Repino, by suburban train or by coach *(see p231)*. Driving is less convenient, often taking longer than the train, and driving standards are variable. In summer, a hydrofoil service from the centre offers an alternative way to get to Peterhof *(see pp230–31)*. Each of these sights can easily be visited in a day. Veliky Novgorod is situated further away, however, and so it makes sense to spend longer there. Mainline trains depart from Moscow railway station *(see p231)* for Veliky Novgorod.

Coastal landscape along the Gulf of Finland

For keys to symbols *see back flap*

Sights at a Glance

1. Repino
2. Oranienbaum
3. Peterhof
4. Gatchina
5. Tsarskoe Selo
6. Pavlovsk
7. Veliky Novgorod

Key

Area of main map

Key

- ▬▬ Motorway
- ▬▬ Major road
- ▭▭▭ Minor road
- ▬▬ Scenic route
- ▬▭▬ Main railway
- ▬▬ Minor railway

Gilded cupolas of the chapel of
Catherine Palace at Tsarskoe Selo

❶ Repino

Репино

Repino

47 km (29 miles) NW of St Petersburg. 🚃 from Finland Station. 🚌 211 from Chernaya Rechka metro. Penaty: Primorskoe shosse 411. **Tel** 432 0828. **Open** 10:30am–4pm Wed–Sun. 🅿️ 🎫 English. ♿ ground floor.

Studio of the eminent artist Ilya Repin at his home in Repino

Only about an hour's drive from St Petersburg on Primorskoe shosse, the northern coastal road, is a region of lakes, pine-scented forests and sandy beaches. Among the green-painted *dachas* and sanatoria is Repino, a resort named after one of Russia's greatest artists, Ilya Repin *(see p108–9)*, who lived here for over 30 years until his death in 1930 at the age of 86. His extraordinary *dacha*, with its steeply pitched glass roof and angled windows, was restored after damage in World War II and is now open as a museum.

Named Penaty in honour of the Roman household gods, *penates*, the house was redesigned by Repin himself to accommodate all that an artist might need, including a glass-panelled veranda downstairs, which was used as a winter studio. On display in the first-floor studio are the artist's brushes and a number of his works, including an unfinished portrait of Pushkin *(see p46)* and Repin's last self-portrait.

Works by the artist adorn the dining room, including portraits of the singer Fyodor Chalyapin and writer Maxim Gorky who were among Repin's many visitors. A revolving dining table enabled guests to serve themselves and to store away their used dishes, since there were no servants. Anyone failing to obey this household rule had to give an impromptu speech from the lectern in the corner.

In the garden, two small wooden follies are hidden among the trees, and Repin's grave is marked by a simple cross on the top of a hillock.

❷ Oranienbaum

Ораниенбаум

Oranienbaum

Oranienbaum, 40 km (25 miles) W of St Petersburg. **Tel** 422 3753, 423 1627 or 422 8016 (excursions). 🚃 from Baltic Station. Grounds: **Open** 9am–8pm (free after 5pm). 🎫 Chinese Palace: and Palace of St Peter III: **Open** Jun–Sep: 10:30am–6pm Wed–Mon. Sliding Hill Pavilion: **Closed** temporarily. 🅿️ 🎫

As the extravagant project of Peter the Great's closest friend and main political advisor, Aleksandr Menshikov *(see p64)*, Oranienbaum was far more ambitious in conception than Peter's palace at Peterhof *(see pp150–53)*, which lies just 12 km (7 miles) to the west. The grandiose plan bankrupted Menshikov and, when he fell from grace in 1727, the estate entered the state treasury.

The Baroque appearance of Oranienbaum's Great Palace has changed little since it was constructed in 1710–25. Built by Gottfried Schädel and Giovanni-Maria Fontana, its sweeping wings culminate in two remarkable pavilions. Parts of the palace and the east (Japanese) pavilion are open to the public.

From 1743 to 1761 the estate became the residence of the heir to the throne, the future Peter III, who built himself a miniature fortress with a small lake for his "navy" and a parade ground where he was fond of playing war games with soldiers. Peter also commissioned Antonio Rinaldi to build him a modest palace.

Peter's wife, Catherine (later Catherine the Great), abhorred her isolated existence here, but after Peter's murder *(see p24)* she recovered her spirits and created what she described as her "personal *dacha*". Built by Rinaldi in the 1760s and known as the Chinese Palace, it is famous for its Rococo interiors and chinoiserie.

The most unusual building at Oranienbaum is Rinaldi's Sliding Hill Pavilion, built in 1762 on Catherine's initiative. Wooden sledging hills were a common source of amusement among the Russian nobility. Catherine's visitors would climb the blue and white pavilion before descending at top speed by sledge or toboggan along a roller-coaster run. The track,

Façade of Menshikov's Great Palace (1710–25), Oranienbaum

500 m (1,640 ft) long, was originally flanked by a colonnade. Sadly, this structure collapsed in 1813 but there is a model in the pavilion.

A pleasant few hours can be spent in the grounds, with their secluded paths, pine woods, ponds and bridges.

Oranienbaum was the only local palace to escape German occupation during World War II *(see p29)*. In 1948, the estate was renamed Lomonosov after the famous 18th-century physicist *(see p47)* who laid many of the foundations of modern Russian science. The complex has now reverted to its original name, an allusion to the exotic orange trees planted here by Menshikov.

Chinoiserie decorations in Catherine the Great's Chinese Palace, Oranienbaum

❸ Peterhof

See pp150–53.

❹ Gatchina

Гатчина
Gatchina

45 km (28 miles) SW of St Petersburg.
🚇 from Baltic Station. 🚌 431, K-18, K-18a from Moskovskaya metro station.
Tel +8 813 719 3492. **Open** 10am–6pm Tue–Sun. **Closed** first Tue of month.
📷 🎫 English (phone to book). 💻
🌐 gatchinapalace.ru

In 1765, Catherine the Great presented the village of Gatchina to her lover, Prince Grigoriy Orlov. He then

Austere central section of Gatchina Palace

commissioned Antonio Rinaldi to build a Neo-Classical palace which was completed in 1781. When Orlov died, two years later, Catherine transferred the estate to her son and heir Paul (later Paul I). Paul asked his favourite architect Vincenzo Brenna to re-fashion the palace. Brenna's large-scale alterations included the construction of an additional storey and a moat with a drawbridge.

The next Romanov to spend any time here was Alexander III who made it his permanent family residence in the late 19th century. The estate provided a safe and remote haven from the sporadic social unrest which was threatening the capital *(see p28)*. The imperial family led a simple and secluded existence here. In keeping with the increasingly bourgeois tastes of the nobility in the whole of Europe, they scorned the state rooms, confining themselves instead to the cosy and more intimate servants' quarters. In 1917, immediately after the Bolshevik party had seized power, the proclaimed leader of the Provisional Government, Aleksandr Kerensky, fled to Gatchina where he made a last ditch attempt to rally his supporters. After a week, he deserted his troops and slipped away into exile.

After World War II, in which the palace was badly damaged, Gatchina was used for many years as a military academy. The lengthy and thorough restoration process is ongoing. Of the restored rooms, the three most impressive are the Marble Dining Room, Paul I's gloomy bedroom at the top of one of Brenna's towers and the magnificent White Ballroom. There is also a display of weaponry on the ground floor.

The delightful grounds are the wildest of all the palace parks. Among the attractions are the circular Temple of Venus (1792–3) on the secluded Island of Love and the Birch House (1790s). The latter appears to be a pile of logs, but it actually conceals a suite of exquisite rooms.

The lake has boats for hire and its clean water makes it an ideal spot for swimming.

❺ Tsarskoe Selo

See pp154–7.

Gatchina's sumptuous White Ballroom with its pseudo-Egyptian statues

❾ Peterhof

Петергоф

Petergof

With its commanding views of the Baltic, Peterhof is a perfect expression of triumphalism. Originally designed by Jean-Baptiste Le Blond, the Great Palace (1714–21) was transformed during the reign of Tsarina Elizabeth when Bartolomeo Rastrelli added a third storey and wings with pavilions at either end. He tried to preserve Le Blond's early Baroque exterior, but redesigned the interiors, indulging his love for gilded Baroque decoration. Peterhof stands at the centre of a magnificent landscaped park, with both French and English gardens.

View from palace of Grand Cascade leading down to the Gulf of Finland

The Imperial Suite

The imperial suite lies in the palace's east wing. Peter's Oak Study is one of the few rooms to have survived unaltered from Le Blond's design. Some of the oak panel designs are originals (1718–21) by Nicholas Pineau.

Cottage Palace ←

Orangery ←

Roman Fountain ←

Pyramid Fountain ←

KEY

① **The Upper Gardens** are framed by borders and hedges and punctuated with ornamental ponds.

② **Mezheumnyy Fountain**

③ **Neptune Fountain**

④ **Oak Fountain**

⑤ **Eve Fountain**

⑥ **Samson Fountain**

⑦ **The Marine Canal** enabled the tsars to sail from the Gulf of Finland up to the Great Palace.

⑧ **Adam Fountain**

★ **The Grand Cascade**

The dazzling cascade (1715–24) is a sequence of 37 gilded bronze sculptures, 64 fountains and 142 water jets (see p153), descending from the terraces of the Great Palace to the Marine Canal and the sea.

Peter the Great's Palace

After his victory over the Swedes at Poltava in 1709, Peter the Great decided to build a palace "befitting to the very highest of monarchs". A visit to Versailles in 1717 furthered Peter's ambitions and he employed more than 5,000 labourers, serfs and soldiers, supported by architects, water-engineers, landscape gardeners and sculptors. Work proceeded at a frenetic pace from 1714 until

Jean-Baptiste Le Blond's original two-storey Great Palace

Peterhof was officially opened in 1723. Le Blond's Great Palace was completed in 1721 and has changed considerably over the decades. Catherine the Great commissioned Yuriy Velten to redecorate some of Rastrelli's interiors in the 1770s, including the Throne Room and the Chesma Room.

VISITORS' CHECKLIST

Practical Information
Petrodvorets, 30 km (19 miles) W of St Petersburg. **Tel** 420 0073. Great Palace: **Open** 10:30am–6pm Tue–Sun. **Closed** last Tue of each month. Other pavilions: **Open** May–Sep: 11am–5pm Tue–Sun; Oct–Apr: 11am–5pm Sat & Sun. Fountains: **Open** May–early Oct: 10:30am–5pm.

Transport
🚇 from Baltic Station *(see p231)* to Novyy Petergof. 🚢 Hermitage (May–Oct) *(see p222)*.

★ **Main Staircase**
Caryatids and gilded carvings adorn Rastrelli's glittering staircase. The ceiling fresco depicts Aurora and Genius chasing away the night.

0 metres 25
0 yards 25

Golden Hill Cascade

Marly and Hermitage

⑤

⑥

⑦

Hydrofoil and Gulf of Finland

⑧

nplaisir

★ **The State Rooms**
The highlight of the State Rooms is the opulent Throne Room, redesigned by Yuriy Velten in 1770. The relatively restrained stucco ornamentation, red velvet hangings and parquet floor provide an exquisite setting for portraits of Russia's imperial family.

Exploring Peterhof Park

The grounds at Peterhof include the Upper, Lower and Alexandria parks, covering an area of around 607 hectares (1,500 acres). As well as the numerous palaces and fountains, there are tree-lined avenues, wooded paths and the Baltic shore. Le Blond designed the grounds next to the Great Palace to be laid out in the formal French style with geometrically arranged flower beds, sculptures, summer houses and pergolas. The trees and shrubs, including limes, elms, maples and roses, were imported from all over Russia and abroad.

Cottage Palace in Alexandria Park

Monplaisir Palace (1714–22), overlooking the Gulf of Finland

Monplaisir

This delightfully unpretentious palace was designed in 1714 by Johann Braunstein. Even after the Great Palace was built, Peter continued to live and entertain at Monplaisir where his guests were usually subjected to a punishing regime of heavy drinking. At breakfast the coffee cups were filled with brandy and by nightfall guests were often discovered wandering drunk in the park.

While not as lavish as those of the Great Palace the interiors are still impressive, in particular the wood-panelled Ceremonial Hall. A painting on its vaulted ceiling depicts Apollo surrounded by characters from a masque. Russian icon painters skilfully carried out the decoration of the exquisite Lacquered Study in the Chinese style, then in vogue. Peter's collection of canvases by Dutch and Flemish artists hang in the rooms and there are wonderful views of the gulf from the tsar's Naval Study.

Adjoining Monplaisir is the Catherine Wing, which was built for Tsarina Elizabeth by Rastrelli in 1747–54. Catherine the Great was staying here in 1762 when her lover, Count Orlov, arrived with news of the coup which was to bring her to the throne (see p26).

Marly Palace

Named after Marly-le-Rois, the king of France's hunting lodge which Peter the Great visited on a tour of Europe in 1717, this beautifully proportioned country residence was built for the tsar's guests. The rooms open to the public include the Oak and Plane Tree studies, Peter's bedroom and the Dining Room. The palace is set in its

Elaborate tiled kitchen in the Marly Palace (1720–3)

own formal garden with sculptures, fountains, a large pond and Niccolò Michetti's Golden Hill Cascade, which was added in 1731–7.

The Hermitage

Standing in splendid isolation on the shores of the gulf, this elegant pavilion (1721–5), by Braunstein, was conceived as a private dining venue for the tsar and his friends. To highlight the need for solitude, the building was raised on a plinth and surrounded by a moat that was crossed by a small drawbridge. The stuccoed façade is decorated with Corinthian pilasters, elaborate wrought-iron balconies and enlarged windows. All the servants were confined to the ground floor and a mechanical device took meals up from the kitchen.

Cottage Palace

The romantic landscaped grounds of Alexandria Park, named after Alexandra, wife of Nicholas I, provide a perfect setting for the Cottage Palace. The Neo-Gothic house is more imposing than the term cottage suggests. The Scottish architect, Adam Menelaws, designed it in 1826–9 for Nicholas I and his wife, who wanted a domestic environment in keeping with their bourgeois tastes.

The Gothic theme is pursued throughout, most effectively in the Great Drawing Room with the rose-window motif in the carpet and the lace-like tracery of the stuccoed ceiling. The exquisite 5,200-piece crystal and porcelain dinner service in the Dining Room was made for the royal couple at the Imperial Porcelain factory.

The Fountains at Peterhof

Jean-Baptiste Le Blond submitted his "water plan" to Peter the Great in 1717, by which time the tsar had begun sketching his own ideas. The centrepiece is the Grand Cascade, fed by the underground springs of the Ropsha Hills about 22 km (14 miles) away. The cascade is a celebration of the triumph of Russia over Sweden *(see p21)*, symbolized by Mikhail Kozlovskiy's glorious sculpture of Samson rending the jaws of a lion. An imaginative variety of fountains, mostly concentrated in the Lower Park, includes triton and lion fountains, dragon fountains with chequerboard steps, and smaller fountains with fish-tailed boys blowing sprays of water through conches. Most playful are trick fountains such as the Umbrella which "rains" on those who come too close.

The Adam Fountain, sculpted by Giovanni Bonazza, was commissioned by Peter in 1718, along with a similar statue of Eve. The two fountains suggest the earthly paradise the tsar had recreated at Peterhof.

The Roman Fountains were designed by Ivan Blank and Ivan Davydov in 1738–9. The two-tiered marble fountains were inspired by one in St Peter's Square in Rome.

The Neptune Fountain predates Peterhof by more than 50 years. The Baroque sculpture was erected in 1658 in Nuremberg to mark the end of the Thirty Years War and was sold to Tsar Paul I in 1782 because there was not enough water to make it work.

The Grand Cascade was originally adorned with lead statues which weathered badly and were recast in bronze and gilded after 1799. Shubin, Martos and other noted sculptors worked to create this stunning cascade.

The Pyramid Fountain (1720s) is one of a number of fountains whose jets create a special shape. Over 500 jets of water rise in seven tiers to create an "obelisk" commemorating the Russian victory over Sweden.

❺ Tsarskoe Selo

Царское Село

Tsarskoe Selo

The lavish imperial palace at Tsarskoe Selo was designed by Rastrelli *(see p95)* in 1752 for Tsarina Elizabeth. She named it the Catherine Palace in honour of her mother, Catherine I, who originally owned the estate. The next ruler to leave a mark on the palace was Catherine the Great, and during her reign she commissioned the Scotsman Charles Cameron to redesign the Baroque interiors according to her more Neo-Classical taste. Cameron also built an ensemble of buildings for taking traditional Russian cold and warm baths, containing the Agate Rooms, and the Cameron Gallery. Post-war restoration continues and 35 state rooms are now open, as well as the beautiful park.

★ **The Great Hall**
Light streams into Rastrelli's glittering hall illuminating the mirrors, gilded carvings and the vast ceiling painting, *The Triumph of Russia* (c.1755), by Giuseppe Valeriani.

Atlantes
The stunning 300-m- (980-ft-) long Baroque façade is adorned with a profusion of Atlantes, columns, pilasters and ornamented window framings.

Entrance

0 metres 25
0 yards 25

The Cavaliers' Dining Room
The table is laid for Tsarina Elizabeth's gentlemen-in-waiting, in the refined gold and white room created by Rastrelli.

★ Amber Room
The original amber panels (1709) by Andreas Schlüter were a gift from Friedrich Wilhelm I of Prussia to Peter the Great. The room has been recreated from photos, complete with carved reliefs and panels in Florentine mosaic.

VISITORS' CHECKLIST

Practical Information
Tsarskoe Selo, 25 km (16 miles) S of St Petersburg. Palace: **Tel** 465 2024. **Open** May–Sep: noon–5:45pm Wed–Mon; Oct–Apr: 10am–4:45pm Wed–Mon. **Closed** last Mon of month. 🎫 📷 🏛 💺 Agate Rooms: **Open** 11am–6pm Fri–Wed (weather dependent). Cameron Gallery: **Open** 11am–5pm Fri–Wed. Park: **Open** daily. 🎫 mid-May–Sep. 🌐 **tzar.ru**

Transport
🚉 from Vitebskiy Station to Detskoe Selo, then 🚌 371 or 382.

To the Lycée and the Church of the Sign *(see p157)*

★ Green Dining Room
Cameron's restrained Neo-Classical style contrasts with the Baroque flamboyance of Rastrelli's work. The exquisite stucco bas-reliefs, sculpted by Ivan Martos, were based on motifs from frescoes discovered in Pompeii.

KEY

① **The Cameron Gallery** *(see p156)*.

② **The Agate Rooms** *(see p156)* are part of the imperial baths and faced with semi-precious stones from the Urals.

③ **The Great Staircase (1860)**, by Ippolito Monighetti, ascends to the state rooms on the first floor.

④ **The Royal Chapel** is richly decorated in dark blue and gold. Built by Chevakinskiy in the 1740s, it contains an elaborate six-tiered iconostasis.

⑤ **The Blue Drawing Room** is characterized by blue floral motifs painted on silk. Among the royal portraits hanging here is a painting of Peter the Great by Ivan Nikitin, dating from around 1720.

⑥ **The Picture Gallery** displays canvases by Italian, French, Dutch and Flemish masters of the 17th and 18th centuries.

⑦ **The French-style formal gardens** were laid out in the 1740s. Their formality and symmetry contrasts with the naturalistic English-style landscaping of the park *(see p156)*, created in 1768.

Exploring Tsarskoe Selo

The magnificent parks and gardens of Tsarskoe Selo (the Tsar's Village) were created out of dense forest by thousands of soldiers and labourers. Work began on the formal gardens in 1744 but later, in 1768, Catherine the Great commissioned one of Russia's first landscaped parks. The 567 hectares (1,400 acres) of grounds are dotted with captivating pavilions set around the central lake. The grounds and the town of Tsarskoe Selo, to the northeast of the palace, are also a delight to explore.

Formal gardens in front of Catherine Palace, Catherine Park

Catherine Park

The formal gardens to the southeast of the palace are laid out geometrically with radiating avenues, parterres and terraces, decorative ponds, hedges, elegant pavilions and Classical statuary. Nearest to the palace are Cameron's **Agate Rooms** (1780–87), which were restored in 2013. Their heavily rusticated lower storey contrasts with the upper tier, modelled on a Renaissance villa. The building takes its name from the agate, jasper and malachite covering the interior.

Girl with a Pitcher by Pavel Sokolov (1816)

The impressive **Cameron Gallery**, built in 1783–7, has a rusticated stone ground floor, surmounted by a Neo-Classical peristyle of 44 Ionic columns. Ranged along the colonnade are bronze busts of ancient philosophers, poets and rulers. In 1792–4 Cameron added a long stone ramp to facilitate access to the gardens for the ageing Catherine the Great. The Neo-Classical **Lower and Upper Baths** were built by Ilya Neyelov in 1777–80. The domed Lower Baths were for the use of courtiers while the exquisite Upper Baths were reserved for members of the imperial family. Construction work on Rastrelli's **Grotto** began in 1749, but the original decoration of the interior with more than 250,000 shells continued well into the 1770s.

The gardens' main avenue leads to the **Hermitage** (1756), a Baroque pavilion built by Rastrelli, where Elizabeth would entertain small groups of guests for dinner.

The romantic landscaped area of the lower park was begun in 1768 by master gardeners such as John Bush, who worked under the overall supervision of the architect, Vasiliy Neyelov. A 16-km (10-mile) waterway was built to feed the numerous canals, cascades and man-made lakes, including the *pièce de résistance,* the **Great Pond**. From Giacomo Quarenghi's pavilion (1786) on the island, musicians would serenade Catherine and her courtiers as they floated by in gilded gondolas.

A naval theme links Vasiliy Neyelov's Dutch, Neo-Gothic **Admiralty** (1773–7) with the 25-m- (82-ft-) high **Chesma Column** which is decorated with ships' prows. The column, designed by Antonio Rinaldi in 1771, commemorates the Russian victory over the Turks in the Aegean.

The reflection of the pink dome and minaret of the **Turkish Bath** shimmers in the placid waters on the far side of the lake. Nearby is Neyelov's colonnaded **Marble Bridge** (1770–76). Perched on a rock overlooking the pond is the **Girl with a Pitcher**, a statue by Pavel Sokolov. The figure inspired Pushkin to write his memorable poem, *Fountain at Tsarskoe Selo*, in which he muses on the girl who has broken her urn and now "sits timelessly sad over the timeless stream".

Evidence of the 18th-century craze for chinoiserie can be found on the border with the wilder Alexander Park where Cameron built his **Chinese Village** in 1782–96. Other examples are Yuriy Velten's **Creaking Pavilion**, designed to creak when visitors entered, and Neyelov's **Great Caprice** (1770s), a hump-backed bridge surmounted by a pagoda-like columned structure.

The Moorish-style Turkish Baths (1852) by Ippolito Monighetti

Creaking Pavilion (1778–86)

The Town of Tsarskoe Selo
This town of 106,000 inhabitants was developed in the 19th century as a summer resort for the aristocracy. In 1937, it was renamed after the poet Alexander Pushkin *(see p45)*, who was educated at the local **Lycée** in 1811–17, and is also referred to as Pushkin town. The school, one of Russia's most prestigious, founded by Alexander I in 1811 to educate members of the nobility.

The attractive **Church of the Sign** (1734) is one of the town's oldest buildings. In a garden next door a statue by Roman Bach depicts Pushkin dressed in the Lycée uniform.

Pushkin and his new bride, Natalya, spent the summer of 1831 in the delightful wooden house, now named **Pushkin's Dacha**. The writer Nikolai Gogol was among the many friends they entertained here.

On the town's western edge is the **Alexander Palace**, commissioned by Catherine for her grandson, the future Alexander I. Designed in 1792 by Giacomo Quarenghi, the austere, Neo-Classical building has a colonnaded façade and protruding wings. It was the residence of Russia's last tsar, Nicholas II and his family from 1904 until their arrest in 1917 *(see p30)*. It is currently closed for renovation.

✚ Church of the Sign
Sobornaya Ploshchad 1. **Tel** 476 7777.
Open 9am–6pm daily.

▥ Lycée
Sadovaya 2. **Tel** 476 6411.
Open 10:30am–5pm Wed–Mon.
Closed last Fri of month.

▥ Pushkin's Dacha
Pushkinskaya 2/19. **Tel** 476 6990.
Open 10:30am–5pm Wed–Sun.
Closed last Fri of month.

Alexander Pushkin's statue (1900),
by Roman Bach

Tsarskoe Selo Park

① *Catherine Palace pp154–5*
② Agate Rooms
③ Cameron Gallery
④ Lower and Upper Baths
⑤ Hermitage
⑥ Grotto
⑦ Admiralty
⑧ Chesma Column
⑨ Turkish Bath
⑩ Marble Bridge
⑪ Girl with a Pitcher
⑫ Creaking Pavilion
⑬ Great Caprice
⑭ Lycée
⑮ Church of the Sign
⑯ Pushkin's Dacha
⑰ Alexander Palace

0 metres   500
0 yards   500

For keys to symbols *see back flap*

View of a bridge across a waterway in the beautiful Pavlovsk Park ▶

⑥ Pavlovsk

Павловск

Pavlovsk

To celebrate the birth of her grandson, Catherine the Great presented her son, the Grand Duke Paul, with these lands in 1777. She also "gave" him her favourite architect, Charles Cameron, to design both palace and park. Work at Pavlovsk (from "Pavel" or Paul) began in 1780 and was continued by Paul's grieving widow, Maria Fyodorovna, long after his death. "English gardens" were at the height of fashion and inspired Cameron's design of a seemingly natural landscape dotted with pavilions (used for informal parties), romantic ruins and attractive vistas around the Slavyanka river.

Cold Baths

This austere pavilion was built by Cameron in 1799 as a summer swimming pool, complete with elegant vestibule, paintings, furniture and rich wall upholstery.

The Apollo Colonnade

Cameron's colonnade (1782–83) encircles a copy of the Apollo Belvedere, above a romantically dilapidated cascade.

★ Pavlovsk Palace

Cameron's elegant Palladian mansion (1782–6) forms the central block of today's palace *(see pp162–3)*, with wings added in 1789 by Paul's favoured architect, Vincenzo Brenna.

★ Temple of Friendship

This Doric temple (1780) was the first use of Greek forms in Russia.

Pavlovsk Railway
Station

Visconti Bridge
One of the most famous
bridges which cross the
winding Slavyanka,
it was designed
by Andrey
Voronikhin
in 1807.

VISITORS' CHECKLIST

Practical Information
Pavlovsk. **Tel** 452 1536. Grounds:
Open daily. 🌳 May–Nov 10am–
5pm. Palace: **Open** 10am–5pm
Wed, Thu, Sat–Mon. **Closed** first
Mon of month. 🎟 🚻 🏪 🎧 📷
English. 🌐 **pavlovskmuseum.ru**

Transport
🚌 from Vitebskiy and Kupchino
railway stations, then bus 370,
383, 493, K-286, K-299, K-513 *(see
p230)* or from Moskovskaya metro
station, then bus K-299, K-505.

The Étoile
The Étoile, the earliest
landscaped area in the park,
was laid out by Cameron
in 1780. The circle of statues
represents the nine Muses,
protectresses of the arts
and sciences.

KEY

① **Cameron's Dairy** (1782)
housed both a milking shed
and a stylish salon.

② **Aviary**

③ **Three Graces Pavilion**

④ **The Centaur Bridge** by
Voronikhin (1805) nestles on
a bend of the Slavyanka river.

⑤ **Green Woman Alley**

⑥ **The Beautiful Valley** was
the favourite spot of Elizabeth,
wife of Alexander I.

⑦ **Paul's Mausoleum** (1808–9)
bears the inscription "To my
beneficent consort".

⑧ **The Rose Pavilion** was the
favourite haunt of Maria Fyodorovna
from 1812. She held many concerts
and literary evenings in this cottage.

0 metres   200
0 yards   200

**Pil Tower
and Bridge**
Brenna's tower
(1795–7) contained
a spiral staircase,
lounge and library.
The bridge was
a later addition
made in 1808.

Exploring Pavlovsk Palace

Catherine commissioned Charles Cameron to build the Great Palace (1782–6) while Paul and his wife Maria Fyodorovna travelled around Europe incognito as the Comte and Comtesse du Nord. They, meanwhile, bought up everything they saw to fill their new home, including French clocks, Sèvres porcelain, tapestries and furniture. Once back in Russia, they brought in Brenna to add taller, more elaborate wings to Cameron's elegant Palladian mansion, turning it into a true palace.

West façade of the Palladian mansion

Plan of Pavlovsk Palace, First Floor

Key

▨ Southern wing

☐ State rooms

Stairs to private apartments and Egyptian Vestibule on the ground floor

1 Italian Hall	8 Boudoir
2 Paul's Study	9 State Bedroom
3 Tapestry Room	10 Dressing Room
4 Hall of War	11 Picture Gallery
5 Grecian Hall	12 Throne Room
6 Hall of Peace	13 Hall of Knights
7 Maria Fyodorovna's Library	14 Chapel

State Rooms

Nearly all of the palace apartments at Pavlovsk, including the official ones, are relatively modest in scale. They reflect Maria Fyodorovna's intensely feminine tastes which have given Pavlovsk a distinct charm rather than grandeur.

A fire in 1803 necessitated some remodelling of the palace interiors by Andrey Voronikhin. The entrance hall, or Egyptian Vestibule, gained its present appearance after he added the painted bronze figures and zodiac medallions. At the top of the stairs is Brenna's State Vestibule, where the bas-reliefs reflected Paul's passion for all things military. It leads onto the Italian Hall, situated beneath the central cupola, with lantern windows and heavy doors of rosewood and mahogany.

The northern row of rooms on this floor were for Paul, the southern ones for Maria. Paul's Study is dominated by Johann Lampi's fine portrait of Maria (1794), who holds a drawing

of six of their children. Beneath it is a model temple of amber, ivory and gilded bronze, made by Maria herself. Next door, the Tapestry Room is named after the Don Quixote tapestries made by Gobelin and presented to Paul by Louis XVI. The mahogany writing table was actually made for Mikhaylovskiy Castle (see p103) but, after Paul's murder there in 1801 (see p24), Maria moved much of the specially designed furniture to Pavlovsk Palace.

The corner rooms are a Hall of War for Paul and Maria's contrasting Hall of Peace, both richly adorned with bas-reliefs and heavy gilding. Between the two lies the magnificent Grecian Hall, Cameron's Neo-Classical masterpiece.

Maria Fyodorovna's rooms commence with a small, comfortable library. The chair at the desk was designed for her by Voronikhin; note the pots built into the spine for flowers. Her Boudoir has pilasters painted with motifs copied from the Raphael Loggias in the Vatican, and a porphyry fireplace.

The Italian Hall, originally by Cameron and Brenna, 1789

Maria Fyodorovna's Boudoir, designed by Brenna, 1789

Brenna's Picture Gallery (1789), with chandeliers by Johann Zeck

The State Bedroom was reputedly never slept in, but was part of court ceremony. Opposite the bed is a 64-piece Sèvres toilet set, complete with a coffee cup and an eye bath, which was a gift from Marie Antoinette.

Another present dominates the Dressing Room, a superb set of steel furniture including dressing table, chair, vases and inkstand made by the renowned gun-makers of Tula (1789). This was presented to Maria by Catherine the Great.

Southern Wing

From the elegantly curved picture gallery, built in 1798, there are excellent views. Only a few of the paintings, mostly purchased during the young couple's trip to France, are worthy of special notice, as their taste was for applied art.

The largest room in the palace is the Throne Room, designed by Brenna (1797) after Paul became tsar. Despite its name it was generally used for balls and state dinners. The tables are now laid with part of a 606-piece gilded dinner service. Vast blue Sèvres vases stand on plinths, bought directly from the factory (Paul and Maria spent huge sums on porcelain there alone). The ceiling was painted during restoration after World War II (see p29), and is taken from an original design which was never used.

The Knights of St John chose Paul as Grand Master when they fled Napoleon's occupation of Malta in 1798. This suited Paul's military taste and he commissioned vast lamps, thrones and decorative items (now in the Hermitage), as well as the Hall of Knights, for ceremonies of the Order. The pale-green room is adorned with Classical statues, saved from the Germans in World War II by being buried in the grounds.

The suite of rooms ends with the Imperial Chapel of SS Peter and Paul, a very un-Orthodox church by Brenna (1797–8), decorated with copies of European paintings.

Private Apartments

Located on the ground floor are the private apartments. The Pilaster Room (1800), with its golden pilasters, is furnished with a dark mahogany suite. The Lantern Study, designed a few years later by Voronikhin, is named after its apsed bay window forming the "lantern".

Maria Fyodorovna's Dressing Room leads into the Bedroom (1805) she actually used (as opposed to the State Bedroom upstairs). Pieces of the original silk were saved in the war and used to edge the new curtains.

The small pink and blue Ballroom was for private parties and hung with paintings by the most fashionable artist of the day, Hubert Robert. The General Study, used as a family sitting room, is decorated with portraits of the family. The Raspberry Room, Paul's private study, contains paintings with views of Gatchina Palace, made for Mikhaylovskiy Castle.

The Lantern Study, one of Voronikhin's most successfully designed interiors, 1804

Maria Fyodorovna (1759–1828)

Paul's wife, Maria Fyodorovna, bore 10 children, and Pavlovsk was considered her 11th child. Paul himself preferred Gatchina (see p149) and in 1788 Maria was given Pavlovsk entirely. She devoted all her energy to adorning both palace and park, giving precise directions to designers and architects, who bemoaned their lack of independence. Born Sophia of Württemberg-Stuttgart, Maria had a practical German upbringing which she put to good use. Pieces of her own work, from furniture to family portraits, are throughout the palace.

Inkstand (1795) created from an initial design by Maria Fyodorovna

❼ Veliky Novgorod

The ancient town of Veliky Novgorod (New Town) was founded in 859 by the Varangian (Viking) Prince Rurik *(see p19)*. The city's proud tradition of self-government began in the 11th century and lasted until 1478, when Ivan III subjugated the city. Favourably sited on the River Volkhov with convenient connections from Scandinavia to the Aegean, the city of Veliky Novgorod became a powerful trading community during this period. In 1570, Ivan the Terrible put Veliky Novgorod to the sword, torturing and massacring thousands of its inhabitants when the city plotted against him. It was, however, the rise of St Petersburg which finally set the seal on Veliky Novgorod's decline. Much of the city's splendid cultural heritage, damaged in World War II, has been restored and can be appreciated in the many medieval churches and picturesque streets of the old town.

Bejewelled metal icon cover on display in the Chamber of Facets

The Kremlin

Situated on the left bank, or Sofiskaya Storona (Sophia side), of the River Volkhov, the formidable red-brick walls and cone-topped towers of the oval-shaped Detinets, or Kremlin, date from the 11th to the 17th centuries. According to the prevailing practice at the time, the first stone of the original walls was laid on the body of a living child.

Of the many towers, the 17th-century Kukui is the most remarkable, and also the tallest at 32 m (105 ft). The lower floors once contained a wine cellar and treasury chamber, while the octagonal room beneath the cupola was used, according to chronicles, "for surveying the whole town". At the heart of the fortress is Veliky Novgorod's oldest and largest church, the

Kremlin walls, with the silver dome of St Sophia's Belfry (15th century)

strongly Byzantine **Cathedral of St Sophia** (1045–62). It was modelled on the cathedral of the same name in Kiev, but the tendencies of the Veliky Novgorod school already appear in the lack of ornament and the scarcity of windows, necessary because of the cold. On the north wall a section of whitewash has been removed to reveal the original mosaic effect of the grey-yellow stone and brick façade.

The exquisitely sculpted and extremely rare bronze doors adorning the west side were seized as booty in 1187 from the Swedish town of Sigtuna. In the lower left-hand corner there are portraits of the craftsmen, named in the Latin inscription as Riquin and Weissmut. The interior is divided by piers into five aisles, three ending in altar apses. Fragments of early frescoes survive, but the iconostasis is one of the oldest in Russia and contains icons from the 11th–17th centuries.

East of the cathedral is **St Sophia's Belfry**, much altered since it was first built in 1439. The bells, now displayed below, were cast in the late 16th and early 17th centuries.

The northwest corner of the Kremlin is occupied by the **Archbishops' Court**, in its heyday a powerful body with its own treasury, police force and military guard. Beneath the 15th-century clock tower an attractive staircase leads to the **Library**, which houses magnificent medieval religious manuscripts. Backing onto the cathedral, the **Chamber of Facets** is the most famous part of this ensemble. A superb reception hall with star-shaped vaulting dates from 1433 and displays treasures from the cathedral, including jewelled mitres and icon covers in precious metals. Within the Kremlin

The 11th-century Cathedral of St Sophia, the landmark of Veliky Novgorod

is the **Museum of History, Architecture and Art**, which houses a magnificent collection of 12th–17th-century icons of the Veliky Novgorod school. One of the most remarkable is the 12th-century portable icon of the Virgin of the Sign, whose miraculous image is said to have saved Novgorod from the armies of Prince Andrey Bogolyubskiy of Suzdal in 1169. Scenes from the battle are depicted on a vibrant 15th-century icon *(see p167)*. There are also works by leading 18th- and 19th-century artists, including Dmitriy Levitskiy, Karl Bryullov and Vasiliy Serov *(see p108)*. The museum has a number of precious public documents and private letters written on birch bark, some of which date from the 11th century. These give details of ordinary, everyday life and are evidence of the unusually widespread literacy among the city's inhabitants.

In the Kremlin's central square, the huge, bell-shaped **Millennium Monument** was sculpted by Mikhail Mikeshin. The monument was unveiled in 1862, a thousand years after Rurik's arrival in Novgorod. The figure kneeling before the Orthodox cross personifies Mother Russia while, below, the decorative frieze depicts Rurik, Ivan III, Mikhail (the first Romanov tsar), Peter the Great and many others. The frieze around the base shows over 100 figures: heroes, statesmen, artists, composers, princes and chroniclers.

🔲 Cathedral of St Sophia
Tel (8162) 773556. **Open** 10am–6pm daily.

🏛 Chamber of Facets:
Tel (8162) 773608. **Open** 10am–6pm Thu–Tue. 🎨 📷 English by appt.

🏛 Museum of History, Architecture and Art
Tel (8162) 773770. **Open** 10am–6pm Wed–Mon. 🎨 📷 English by appt.

The carved Royal Gates of an iconostasis in the Museum of History, Architecture and Art

Yaroslav's Court

Across the River Volkhov was the official seat of the princes, known as Yaroslav's Court. The palace of Yaroslav the Wise (1019–54) has since disappeared but several churches have survived. The area adjacent is Veliky Novgorod's commercial centre, once the site of the medieval market, part of whose wall still stands.

VISITORS' CHECKLIST

Practical Information
190 km (118 miles) S of St Petersburg. 🚇 220,000. *i* Red Izba, Sennaya Ploshchad 5, (8162) 773074. 🌐 visitnovgorod.com

Transport
🚆 from Moscow Station.
🚌 from Coach Station *(see p231)*.

The oldest church on this side of the river, **St Nicholas' Cathedral** (1113–36), was built by Prince Mstislav. It dominates the area and once symbolized the prince's power.

Novgorod's merchants were keen to show their recognition of God's hand in their prosperity, and so funded many of the city's churches. **St Paraskeva Pyatnitsa**, erected in 1207 and then rebuilt in 1345, was dedicated to the patron saint of commerce. The more decorative **Church of the Holy Women** and **Church of St Procopius**, both 16th century, were financed by wealthy Moscow merchants. The fanciful tastes of the Muscovite patrons mark a departure from Veliky Novgorod's austere style.

Millennium Monument, celebrating Veliky Novgorod's 1,000 years of history

Yuriev Monastery walls and bell tower with the silvery domes of the Cathedral of St George in the background

Beyond Yaroslav's Court

In the 12th century, Veliky Novgorod boasted over 200 churches, while there are only 30 today. Many of these are hidden away in the quiet hinterland of 19th-century streets to the east of Yaroslav's Court. On Ilyina ulitsa, the arrangement of windows, niches and inset crosses on the **Church of the Saviour of the Transfiguration** façade (1374) is almost whimsical. Inside, there are original frescoes by one of Russia's greatest medieval artists, Theophanes the Greek (1335–c.1410), who came from Constantinople and decorated 40 Russian churches. Andrey Rublev (1360–1430), Russia's most famous icon painter, worked under Theophanes at the beginning of his career.

On the same street, the five-domed **Znamenskiy Cathedral**, or Cathedral of the Sign (1682–8), has an attractive gateway and faded frescoes on the outer walls. The beautiful interior was decorated in 1702 by Ivan Bakhmatov.

The **Church of Theodore Stratilates** on Mstinskaya ulitsa to the north was built in 1360–61 by the widow of a wealthy Novgorod merchant. The delicate purple and pink frescoes contrast with the harsher colours found in most 14th-century Novgorod frescoes. *The Annunciation*, for example, combines sensitivity and charm with religious intensity.

Fresco inside Znamenskiy Cathedral

Further Afield

A pleasant stroll 3 km (2 miles) south along the riverbank leads to the **Yuriev Monastery**. This is the area's largest and most important monastery, founded in 1030 and built on the orders of Prince Vsevolod. Its imposing Cathedral of St George was built in 1119–30 by "Master Peter", the first named architect in Russian chronicles. This beautifully proportioned church, with its three asymmetrical cupolas, was restored in the 19th century, and unfortunately most of the interior murals were lost. There were once 20 monastic buildings in the complex, dating mainly from the 19th century.

In the woods across the road lies the fascinating open-air **Museum of Wooden Architecture**, which displays churches and peasant huts moved from local villages. Of particular interest are the 17th-century two-tiered Kuritsko Church of the Dormition and the tiny wooden church of St Nicholas from Tukhel village.

🕇 **Yuriev Monastery**
Yurevskaya nab. **Tel** (8162) 773020.
Open 10am–6pm daily.

🏛 **Museum of Wooden Architecture (*Vitoslavlitsi*)**
Yurevo. **Tel** (8162) 773770. **Open** May–Sep: 10am–8pm daily; Oct–Apr: 10am–6pm daily.

A 19th-century peasant hut (*izba*), Museum of Wooden Architecture

Russian Icon Painting

The Russian Orthodox Church uses icons for both worship and teaching, but never for mere ornament, and there are strict rules for the creation of each image. Icons were believed to be imbued with the force of the saint depicted, and were therefore invoked for protection during wars. Because the content was considered more important than the style, old, revered icons were often repainted again and again. The first icons were brought to Russia from Byzantium. Greek masters came too, to train local painters. The northern schools which developed during the 13th–15th centuries were less restricted by Byzantine canons and have an earthy style linked to Russian peasant life. Novgorod, never under the Mongol yoke and with a thriving economy, was the source of many of the finest icons made for the northern monasteries.

Battle of Novgorod and Suzdal
This mid-15th-century work of the Novgorod School is thought to be Russia's earliest historical painting. Icons could have a political purpose – in this case to use Novgorod's great past as a justification for its independence from Moscow. Note the multiple touches of red – a colour central to everyday Russian life and typical for icons of the Novgorod School.

Virgin of Vladimir
The most venerated icon in Russia, this 12th-century work was made in Constantinople. Its huge influence on Russian icon painting cannot be overstated.

The Iconostasis

The iconostasis screens off the sanctuary from the main part of the church, as if it were a boundary between heaven and earth. In Russian practice it is covered with icons strictly arranged in up to six tiers, each with its own dogmatic purpose.

Old Testament Trinity by Rublev
Andrey Rublev was one of the greatest artists of the Moscow School. He was strongly influenced by recent developments in Byzantine painting, brought to Russia by Greek masters in the late 14th century. His Trinity icon dates from the early 15th century.

The Festival Tier shows the 12 major church festivals, such as the Entry into Jerusalem and the Crucifixion. Such pictorial representation aided the faith of the illiterate.

Christ Enthroned

The Deesis Tier, above the Royal Gates, contains Christ Enthroned, flanked by the Virgin and St John interceding on behalf of mortal sinners.

The Royal Gates represent the entrance from the temporal world to the spiritual, between which the priests pass during the service.

The Local Tier is for local saints, those the church is dedicated to and patron saints of major donors.

TRAVELLERS' NEEDS

WHERE TO STAY

Space in the historic centre of the city may be at a premium, but new hotels continue to open. A number of "mini-hotels" – privately-run establishments with anywhere between 4 to 15 rooms – continue to sprout in or near the centre, and investors have opened large, luxury hotels in outstanding locations. The quality of service in the larger hotels is as good as that on offer in Western Europe. Many tourists visiting in the summer with a package tour, however, are still housed in large, somewhat anonymous hotels outside the centre. These provide reasonable service and full amenities such as restaurants, bars and fitness facilities. Travelling outside the White Nights period cuts costs and opens up the opportunity for booking one of the many excellent deals available at more central hotels. Bookings can be made independently or via an agency. For the summer months, particularly during the White Nights, reservations should be made well in advance for accommodation of all price levels.

Helvetia Hotel, located in a charming early 19th-century building *(see p177)*

Where to Look

There are few large, inexpensive hotels in central St Petersburg. Many of those listed in this section are scattered around the city.

Visitors on a package tour usually find themselves staying in a former Intourist hotel such as the Park Inn by Radisson Pribaltiyskaya or Pulkovskaya, which are situated in modern high-rise areas on the city's outskirts. Mini-hotels and bed-and-breakfast establishments, by contrast, are frequently found in quiet streets near the centre. Independent travellers should consider their priorities from the start, be it location, price or the amenities.

How to Book

Hotel reservations for the White Nights *(see p53)* should be made several months in advance, and as early as possible for the more popular establishments. All the hotels listed here can be booked through online reservation sites such as **Booking.com**. All hotels and agencies recommended can provide visa support *(see p210)*, unless stated otherwise.

Facilities

Rooms in all the hotels listed include at least a shower, television, telephone and Wi-Fi Internet. Most have air conditioning. Large hotels have a luggage room for storing baggage after the midday check-out time. Bars frequently open at night, and extensive fitness and sauna facilities are more or less standard features in bigger establishments.

Price

The most important thing to remember in St Petersburg is that prices in big hotels more than double for the six weeks or so of the White Nights and for the St Petersburg International Economic Forum in early June. These higher prices are quoted throughout the hotel listings *(see pp174–9)*. Normal prices return during the "mid-season", usually April–May and late July–late September. Outside that period, particularly during the "White Days" of winter, there are frequently excellent deals to be had.

Nearly all large central hotels, it should be noted, fall into the luxury category, and offer everything from exclusive single rooms to imperial suites priced at several thousand dollars a night. By opting for a smaller hotel with fewer facilities or a bed and breakfast (usually a small,

Fitness centre at the Belmond Grand Hotel Europe *(see p176)*

◀ Visitors browsing through the charming Yeliseyevsky store

basic hotel rather than a family home), you can be just as central for much less money. Many smaller hotels have only shower cabins, not full baths.

Note that prices are not displayed in hotels, and that only some small hotels and hostels take credit cards. It is important to be prepared to pay in cash.

Entrance to the luxurious, modern Corinthia Hotel *(see p177)*

Hidden Extras

Large hotels, which provide visa support and obligatory passport registration *(see p210)* for free, often do not include local taxes or breakfast in the prices they quote. Both of these can be a significant addition to the final bill. (The price categories used in the hotel listings on pages 176–9 include both breakfast and taxes.) Be warned that the cost of making international or even local phone calls from your room in the larger hotels is likely to be prohibitive. On the other hand, phones which use the local network are relatively cheap. Phonecards can be purchased to make international calls from street booths or fixed phones; and Russian pay-as-you-go SIM cards can be bought at most mobile phone shops *(see p218)*.

In smaller hotels, breakfast tends to be included in the price, but you should expect to pay extra for the initial visa support. Calls from phones in small hotels and hostels may be free or very cheap if they use the local telephone system. Phonecards can be used to make international calls from such phones.

Security

Some top-range establishments have metal detectors and selective bag searches at entrances. Smaller hotels have a doorman, who may ask to see a visitor's card or identification. Since this is simply a precaution for guests' protection, there is no reason to object.

Most hotels have safes in the rooms and/or security deposit boxes at the front desk. Large sums of money and valuables should always be left in one of these places.

Travellers with Specific Needs

Due to the thick snow in winter, most buildings in St Petersburg have steps leading up to their entrances, making access very difficult for disabled visitors. Most of the elite hotels are fully wheelchair accessible, with staff trained to provide assistance, and other hotels are increasingly adding ramps, widening doors and trying to adapt to meet the needs of disabled travellers.

Room in the Belmond Grand Hotel Europe *(see p176)*

Those with special requirements should contact their preferred hotel before booking.

Children

St Petersburg has never been vaunted as a great children's destination, and few hotels cater specifically for families. However, it is possible to arrange babysitters in all the larger hotels, and, increasingly, in some of the smaller ones. Visitors are advised to check the situation before booking.

The stylish Lounge Bar at the Vedensky Hotel *(see p174)*

Mini-Hotels

Not necessarily budget options because some are very luxurious, St Petersburg's extensive range of mini-hotels, with anything from 4 to 15 or 20 rooms, offer some of the most comfortable and pleasant accommodation. The personalized service is often hard to beat. **Filippov Hotels**, **Hotels on Nevsky** and **Rinaldi Bed & Breakfast** are some of the city's better-known mini-hotels.

The antique grand piano in the Pavarotti Suite of the Belmond Grand Hotel Europe *(see p176)*

The elegant interior of the Petro Palace Hotel *(see p174)*

Budget Accommodation

Truly cheap accommodation is hard to find in St Petersburg. Visitors on a tight budget can choose from the more modest mini-hotels, which usually describe themselves as B&Bs. This usually means they offer a small number of rooms in a converted flat in an ordinary building, with a housekeeper who makes breakfast in the apartment's kitchen. There may be a shared toilet rather than a separate one.

Accommodation agencies such as **Ostwest**, **STN**, **Hamlet Property Management** and **Pulford Real Estate** also offer short-term apartment rental, which can be cheap for a group of friends who are sharing. Another budget option is **Airbnb**, which offers private accommodations owned by locals.

In many cases, although the apartment has been refurbished, the communal staircase to the building may be a little grubby. This grittiness can be off-putting at first, but it does offer the feel of living in the true St Petersburg.

The best way to cut costs is to travel in the off season instead of during the White Nights. Mini-hotels and short-let apartments can be extremely cheap at this time of the year, and even the big hotels offer excellent deals. April can be dry and sunny, if still cold, and October can be beautiful, particularly if you catch the brief northern autumn. Travelling in February more or less guarantees the vision of a Russia covered in snow.

Hostels

For the budget traveller seeking comfortable accommodation in a reasonably central location, there are now several hostels to choose from. All offer visa support and registration and are friendly. **Hostel Life** is a popular option for its central location and friendly staff who help organize tours around St Petersburg and beyond. The inexpensive but clean and comfortable **Nord Hostel** is unmatched for location. You could also try **CubaHostel Backpackers**, **Hostel All Seasons**, **Graffiti Hostel** and **Wonder Hostel**.

None of these are "youth" hostels, although young people do tend to dominate in the summer months. In the off season, however, 50 per cent of the guests tend to be over forty.

Staying with Families

For a really good insight into Russian lifestyle, staying with a family can be an interesting and cheap option. The system works very much like any B&B in Europe, with prices including breakfast but no other meals. Extra meals can usually be provided at a small cost. **HOFA (Host Families Association)** and **Ostwest** have a wide range of families on their books and a particularly good reputation in this area. Your hosts are likely to be extremely hospitable and will tend to overfeed you rather than otherwise. Many of HOFA's hosts are academics, well educated and speak several languages. Generally, hosts will be keen to talk to you about their life in Russia and Western perceptions of their country.

Many Russian apartments are reached through scruffy entrance halls or decrepit courtyards, but do not let this put you off, as it gives little indication of the quality of the accommodation.

Camping and Outdoor Living

Russians love getting out of town for walks, swimming and mushroom gathering. All are possible on day trips from the city, but staying out of town is more complicated. St Petersburg's cold winter weather does not make it ideal for camping, though

Park Inn by Radisson Veliky Novgorod *(see p176)*

the forests along the north side of the Gulf of Finland are excellent in milder seasons.

Renting a *dacha* or small house in the country might turn out to be difficult. Most people with modest *dachas* let them to people they know. None of the firms specializing in *dachas* lets them to foreigners, and demand within 100 km (62 miles) of the city far outstrips the properties available. As a result, rental costs can be exorbitant (about US$5,000 per week). In order to find anything at all, book as early as February. The best range of *dachas* (from around US$500 per week) is available through **Alexander**, but you will need to speak Russian, or use a travel company that does, to make a booking. The best option for cheaper living with modern facilities is to rent a chalet attached to a hotel. **Retour Hotel** offers chalets, a small zoo, a swimming pool, sauna, tennis courts and riding.

Extended Stays

Visitors who intend to stay in St Petersburg for a month or more will find the cost of renting apartments much cheaper. While hostels do not offer long-term reductions, companies such as **Pulford Real Estate** have plenty of flats that are available at more modest rates than those advertised for short lets. Be aware, however, that tourist visas cannot usually be registered *(see p210)* for more than three months, and a longer stay will require a non-tourist visa

Dacha in a pine forest near Repino on the Gulf of Finland *(see p148)*

arranged through a company that can legally register you for the period you will be in the country.

Recommended Hotels

The hotels featured in this guide have been selected across a wide price range for their excellent facilities, outstanding location and, often, good value. They are arranged by type of accommodation, and then alphabetically within each price range. Historic hotels are often centuries-old buildings or restored mansions. Luxury options abound, offering the very best in service and amenities. The style-conscious and trendy may prefer hip boutique hotels. Modern lodgings and chain hotels are generally comfortable and have the standard amenities.

DK Choice hotels have been highlighted in recognition of an exceptional feature – a stunning location, notable history, inviting atmosphere or great value.

DIRECTORY

Accommodation Agencies

Airbnb
W airbnb.com

Alexander
Potemkinskaya ul 13.
Map 3 C4.
Tel 327 1616.
W anspb.ru

Express To Russia
Muchnoi per 2.
Map 6 E2.
Tel 570 6342.
W expresstorussia.com

Hamlet Property Management
Naberezhnaya kanala Griboedova 5.
Map 6 E1.
Tel 309 0509.
W hamletspb.com

HOFA Host Families Association
Tavricheskaya ul 5, Apartment 25.
Map 4 D5.
Tel 7911 7665464.
W hofa.ru

MIR Travel Company
Nevskiy pr 11/2.
Map 6 D1.
Tel 455 2595.
W mir-travel.com

Ostwest
Ul Vosstaniya 7.
Map 7 C2.
Tel 327 3416.
W ostwest.com

Pulford Real Estate
Naberezhnaya reki Moyki 6.
Map 2 E5.
Tel 331 5877.
W pulford.com

STN
Karavannaya 7.
Map 7 A1.
Tel 600 2080.
W 2piter.com

Mini-Hotel Networks

Anabel
Tel 400 2211.
W anabel.ru

Filippov Hotels
Tel 939 2463.
W filippovhotel.ru

Hotels on Nevsky
Tel 703 3860.
W hon.ru

Rinaldi Bed & Breakfast
Tel 325 4188.
W rinaldi.ru

Hostels

CubaHostel Backpackers
Kazanskaya ul 5.
Map 6 E2.
Tel +7 911 921 7115.
W cubahostel.ru

Graffiti Hostel
Ligovskiy pr 33-35.
Map 7 C2.
Tel 326 3805.
W graffitihostel.ru

Hostel All Seasons
Yakovlevskiy per 11.
Tel 327 1070.
W hostel.ru

Hostel Life
Nevisky pr 47 (entrance from Vladimirskiy prospekt 41).
Map 7 A2.
Tel 243 4666.
W hostel-life.ru

Nord Hostel
Bolshaya Morskaya ul 10.
Map 6 D1.
Tel 571 0342.
W nordhostel.com

Useful Website
W russia-hostelling.ru

Wonder Hostel
Nevskiy pr 23.
Map 6 E1.
Tel +7 952 203 6648.
W wonderhostels.ru

Camping

Retour Hotel
Bolshaya Kupalnaya str. 28, Sestroretsk. 26 km (16 miles) NW of St Petersburg.
Tel 409 3599.
W hotelretur.ru

Where to Stay

Boutique

Vasilevskiy Island

Trezzini Art Hotel $$
Bolshoy prospekt 21, 199004
Tel *332 1035* **Map** 1 A5
W trezzini-hotel.com
Delightful small hotel with classic styling. Rooms are well-furnished and overlook a quiet square. Close to many museums and palaces.

Petrogradskaya

Sharf Hotel $
Malyy prospekt 16, 197110
Tel *644 7774* **Map** 1 A4
W sharfhotel.ru
Accommodation in huge, modern apartments with neat rooms and kitchen facilities. It is available for short and long-term letting.

Tradition Hotel $$
Dobrolubova prospekt 2, 197198
Tel *405 8855* **Map** 1 C4
W traditionhotel.ru
Centrally located hotel with large rooms featuring exposed brick walls, underfloor heating and antique-style furniture.

Vedensky Hotel $$
Bolshoy prospekt 37, 197198
Tel *332 4222* **Map** 1 C2
W vedenskyhotel.com
Plush hotel with elegant rooms. Great location with views of the old town. It has a rooftop restaurant.

Palace Embankment

3 Mosta $
Naberezhnaya reki Moyki 3, 191186
Tel *611 1188* **Map** 2 E5
W 3mosta.com
Family-owned, this homely 18th-century building fuses historical

The entrance to the magnificent Vedensky Hotel

charm with modern styles. It's mere steps from the Hermitage and Palace Embankment.

Casa Leto Private Hotel $$
Bolshaya Morskaya ulitsa 34, 190000
Tel *600 1096* **Map** 6 D2
W casaleto.com
Tiny establishment that boasts light-filled rooms and many complimentary extras. It has a superb central location and attentive staff.

DK Choice

Petro Palace Hotel $$
Malaya Morskaya ulitsa 14, 190000
Tel *571 2880* **Map** 6 D1
W petropalacehotel.com
Housed in a tastefully renovated and extended 19th-century building, this stylish hotel attracts wealthy Russians as well as tourists. The extensive facilities it offers include a fitness suite, pool and massage services. There are good views of the city from the seventh floor.

Gostinyy Dvor

Mesto Hotel $
Naberezhnaya reki Fontanki 11, 191011
Tel *941 0286* **Map** 7 A1
W mesto-hotel.ru
Outstanding hotel featuring contemporary furnishings and exposed brick walls. Some rooms have kitchenettes. It is walking distance from Nevsky Prospekt.

A Boutique Hotel $$
Sadovaya ulitsa 7-11, 191023
Tel *571 2913* **Map** 6 F1
W ahotelspb.ru
This small, cosy hotel offers rooms with carefully designed interiors, comprising hardwood floors and wood-panelled ceilings. The walls feature works by contemporary local artists. The staff are friendly and efficient.

The Brothers Karamazov $$
Sotsialisticheskaya ul. 11A
Tel *335 1186* **Map** 7 A4
W karamazovhotel.com
Named after Dostoevsky's final novel, this hotel is located down a quiet lane just a short walk from his old apartment (now a museum).

Price Guide

Prices are based on one night's stay in high season for a standard double room, inclusive of service charges and taxes.

$	under 7,000R
$$	7,000 to 14,000R
$$$	over 14,000R

It offers comfortable rooms and the staff is attentive.

Dom Boutique Hotel $$
Gangutskaya ulitsa 4, 191187
Tel *245 1040* **Map** 2 F4
W domboutiquehotel.com
Housed in a 19th-century mansion, this hotel overlooks the Summer Garden and Fontanka river. It has beautiful interiors with antique furniture. Free walking tours available.

Sennaya Ploshchad

Hotel 1913 $$
Voznesenskiy prospekt 13, 190000
Tel *418 3013* **Map** 5 C2
W hotel-1913.ru
Atmospheric place with old-fashioned decor. It offers a variety of rooms, including small apartments and studios and also serves substantial breakfasts.

Domina Prestige Hotel St Petersburg $$$
Naberezhnaya reki Moyki 99, 190000
Tel *385 9900* **Map** 5 C2
W dominarussia.com
Located near St Isaac's Cathedral, this hotel has a lavish interior with Classical sculptures in the foyer and bright colour schemes throughout.

Chain

Vasilevskiy Island

Courtyard St Petersburg Vasilevskiy $$$
2-ya liniya 61/30, 199178
Tel *380 4011* **Map** 1 A4
W marriott.com
Riverside hotel in an imposing 19th-century building with lovely views and a central location. The rooms feature modern Scandinavian designs.

Solo Sokos Hotel Palace Bridge $$$
Birzhevoy pereulok 2-4, 199044
Tel *335 2200* **Map** 1 B4
W sokoshotels.fi
Smart place offering spacious rooms and great spa facilties. Helpful and attentive staff.

Palace Embankment

Herzen House $$
Bolshaya Morskaya ulitsa 25, 190000
Tel 315 5550   **Map** 6 D2
🅦 herzen-hotel.ru
Modern rooms and free beverages and pastries round the clock. Easy access to the metro and main sights. It also offers a special Russian tea service on Wednesdays.

Gostinyy Dvor

Atlantic Hotel $$
Kazanskaya ulitsa 14, 191186
Tel 314 4030   **Map** 6 E2
🅦 hotel-atlantic.ru
This unpretentious hotel is conveniently located for sightseeing and nightlife. It offers modest rooms and a good breakfast.

Sennaya Ploshchad

Gogol Hotel $
Nab kanala Griboedova 69, 190001
Tel 571 1841   **Map** 6 D3
🅦 gogolhotel.com
Chic hotel with tasteful decor and parquet floors. Some rooms overlook the Griboyedov Canal.

Arkadia Hotel $$
Naberezhnaya reki Moyki 58a, 190000
Tel 571 6173   **Map** 6 D2
🅦 arkadiahotel.ru
Attractive place in the historic centre. It boasts Classical interiors, pretty gardens and a tiny pool.

Further Afield

Andersen Hotel $
Chapygina ulitsa 4a, 197022
Tel 740 5140
🅦 andersenhotel.ru
Located on the Petrogradskaya Side, with good access to the city's sights. Well-furnished rooms.

Bristol Hotel $
Rasstannaya ulitsa 2a, 192007
Tel 242 9900
🅦 bristol-hotel.spb.ru
Comfortably furnished hotel near transport links. Offers an excellent breakfast.

Okhtinskaya Hotel $
Bolsheokhtinskiy prospekt 4, 195027
Tel 318 0040
🅦 okhtinskaya.com
Modern building with airy rooms that have great views over the Neva.

Stony Island Hotel $
Kamennoostrovskiy prospekt 45, 197022
Tel 337 2434
🅦 stonyisland.ru
Minimalist-style hotel in a historic building on the elegant main

Elegant interior of a room in the Park Inn by Radisson Veliky Novgorod

street of the Petrogradskaya Side. Smoking is prohibited on the premises.

Aparthotel Kronverk $$
Ulitsa Blokhina 9, 197198
Tel 703 3663
🅦 kronverk.com
Modern hotel in a scenic location on Petrogradskaya, right by the Peter and Paul Fortress and a short stroll from the Leningrad Zoo.

Azimut Hotel St Petersburg $$
Lermontovskiy prospekt 43/1, 190103
Tel 740 2640
🅦 azimuthotels.com
Refurbished Soviet-era monolith that towers over the historic quarter. Offers great views of the city. Complimentary refreshments are available in the lobby.

Crown Plaza Ligovsky $$
Ligovskiy prospekt 61, 191040
Tel 244 0001
🅦 ihg.com
Located steps from the Moskovskiy railway station and Nevskiy prospekt, this hotel offers spacious rooms with floor-to-ceiling windows. It also has a fully equipped gym and a restaurant that serves Mediterranean cuisine.

Holiday Inn St Petersburg Moskovskye Vorota $$
Moskovskiy prospekt 97a, 196084
Tel 448 7171
🅦 hi-spb.com
Stylish high-rise hotel with good transport links all over the city. There is an on-site supermarket and a spacious conference hall.

Hotel Dostoevsky $$
Vladimirskiy prospekt 19, 191002
Tel 331 3200
🅦 dostoevsky-hotel.com
Elite hotel with most of its rooms overlooking courtyards. Located near Nevskiy prospekt. Guests have access to a gym and sauna.

Neptun Hotel $$
Naberezhnaya Obvodnovo kanala 93a, 191119
Tel 324 4600
🅦 neptun.spb.ru
Reliable, no-frills hotel with smart rooms. Their excellent fitness complex includes a gym, pool, spa, bowling, tennis and squash courts, as well as a children's club.

Original Sokos Hotel Olympia Garden $$
Batayskiy pereulok 3a, 190013
Tel 335 2270
🅦 sokoshotels.fi
Run by a reputable Finnish chain, a large characterful place defined by its hardwood floors. There is a sauna and a gym on-site.

DK Choice

Park Inn by Radisson Pribaltiyskaya $$
Ulitsa Korablestroiteley 14, 199226
Tel 329 2626
🅦 parkinn.com
The Park Inn Pribaltiyskaya is a huge, 1980s package-tour hotel, set right on the Gulf of Finland. It boasts splendid views, and a water park with pool and sports facilities. There is also a wellness and spa centre. The hotel provides free shuttle bus service to the city centre.

Park Inn by Radisson Pulkovskaya $$
Pobedy ploshchad 1, 196240
Tel 740 3900
🅦 parkinn.com
Modern rooms, some of which give views of Victory Monument. Good base for trips to Tsarskoe Selo and Pavlovsk. Complimentary shuttle buses to and from the airport are available.

For more information on types of hotels *see page 173*

**Staybridge Suites
St. Petersburg** $$
*Moskovskiy prospekt 97V,
196084*
Tel *448 2050*
W sbs-spb.com
Located a short 5-minute walk
from the metro, this modern
hotel offers apartment-style
accommodation with fully
equipped kitchens. It features
an on-site gym, covered
courtyard and a library, as
well as several small shops
and a self-service laundry.

DK Choice

**Novotel
St Petersburg Centre** $$$
*Ulitsa Mayakovskovo 3a,
191025*
Tel *335 1188*
W novotel.com
This ultra-chic block is situated
in the heart of St Petersburg,
just a stone's throw from Nevskiy
prospekt. The ninth-floor
executive suites offer superb
views, and a number of rooms
have been fully customized for
disabled access. The Côte Jardin
restaurant offers a Russian take
on Mediterranean cooking.

Beyond St Petersburg

Hotel Novgorodskaya $
*Desyatinnaya ulitsa 6a, Veliky
Novgorod, 173007*
Tel *(8162) 772260*
W novgorodskaya.nov.ru
Conveniently close to the
historic centre, this hotel
offers comfortably furnished
rooms. Free Wi-Fi.

Hotel Volkhov $
*Predtechenskaya ulitsa 24,
Veliky Novgorod, 173007*
Tel *(8162) 225500*
W hotel-volkhov.ru
The Volkhov boasts one
of the best locations in
the historical centre. Buffet
breakfast on offer. The hotel
also features a free sauna,
a plunge pool and a small
art gallery. Wi-Fi included.

Aquamarine Spa Hotel $$
*Primorskoye shosse 593-H,
Zelenogorsk, 197720*
Tel *702 2619*
W hotel-aquamarin.ru
This refurbished Soviet-era
hotel has lovely spa facilities.
The grounds include tennis
courts and children's
playgrounds, and there
are also areas for picnics
and barbecue.

DK Choice

**Park Inn by Radisson
Veliky Novgorod** $$
*Studencheskaya ulitsa 2, Veliky
Novgorod, 173020*
Tel *(8162) 940910*
W parkinn.com
This well-equipped hotel
comprises a large, modern
complex with conference halls,
tennis courts and a stylish pool.
Rooms are pleasantly furnished
and many have charming views
over the river Volkhov. The spa
centre provides sauna and
massage treatments. The hotel
also offers accommodation in
semi-luxurious apartments.

Historic

Vasilevskiy Island

Hotel Shelfort $
3-ya liniya 26, 199004
Tel *328 0555*   **Map** 1 A5
W shelfort.ru
Characterful interiors with
beautifully restored traditional
tiled stoves. Friendly staff,
efficient service, and the hotel
is within walking distance of
the Hermitage Museum.

Palace Embankment

**Four Seasons Hotel Lion
Palace St Petersburg** $$$
Voznesenskiy prospekt 1, 190000
Tel *339 8000*   **Map** 5 C1
W fourseasons.com
Home to one of the city's
best restaurants, Percorso
(see p188), this opulent hotel
is set in a historic building
with lavish Russian Empire-
style interiors. Spacious and
welcoming rooms.

Opulent interior of the Belmond Grand
Hotel Europe

Rocco Forte Hotel Astoria $$$
*Bolshaya Morskaya ulitsa 39,
190000*
Tel *494 5757*   **Map** 6 D2
W roccofortehotels.com
The hotel's graceful interior
boasts historic charm. Front-
facing rooms offer superb
views over St Isaac's Cathedral
and the square.

Taleon Imperial Hotel $$$
Nevskiy prospekt 15, 191186
Tel *324 9911*   **Map** 6 D1
W taleonimperialhotel.com
Stunning hotel with rooms
that overlook the river Moyka.
Located in a restored former
palace, writers such as Dostoevsky
would read their works in what
is today the Grand Ballroom.

Gostinyy Dvor

Golden Triangle Hotel $$
*Bolshaya Konyushennaya ulitsa12,
191186*
Tel *490 7710*   **Map** 6 E1
W goldtriangle.ru
Elegant hotel set in a 19th-
century building that mixes
modern and traditional styles.
There are working fireplaces
in some rooms and a hearty
breakfast is served.

Rossi Boutique Hotel $$
*Naberezhnaya reki Fontanki 55,
191023*
Tel *635 6333*   **Map** 6 F2
W rossihotels.com
Charming place with Classical
decor and antique-style
furnishing within a restored
landmark building. River views
from most rooms, and guests
can enjoy an on-site spa and
fitness center.

**Belmond Grand
Hotel Europe** $$$
Mikhaylovskaya ulitsa 1/7, 191186
Tel *329 6000*   **Map** 6 F1
W grandhoteleurope.com
Luxury hotel with historic
interiors, brilliant service
and six restaurants – one of
which, L'Europe, was the first
interior space in Russia to be
lit with electric lighting.

Further Afield

Agni Club Hotel $$
Nevskiy prospekt 94/2, 191025
Tel *457 0225*
W agnihotel.ru
Set in an18th-century building,
this hotel is centrally located
and has airy rooms. It offers
complimentary tea and coffee
all day in its café that overlooks
the Nevskiy prospekt.

Akyan Hotel $$

Ulitsa Vosstaniya 19, 191036
Tel *426 4000*   **Map** 7 C1
W akyanhotel.com
Located within the historic
Badayev House, this hotel is a
paragon of Russian Art Nouveau
architecture. Family-friendly, it
offers cosy rooms and luxury suites.

Helvetia Hotel $$$

Ulitsa Marata 11, 191025
Tel *326 5353*
W helvetiahotel.ru
This 19th-century mansion boasts
a pleasant courtyard for summer
dining. The well-appointed interiors
are a harmonious blend of old
and new motifs.

Beyond St Petersburg

Hotel Ekaterina

Sadovaya ulitsa 5a, Pushkin, 196601
Tel *466 8042*
W hotelekaterina.ru
Simple rooms with old-fashioned
furniture in an atmospheric
location within the grounds
of the Catherine Palace. The
surrounding parkland offers
the perfect setting for leisurely
strolls during the summer months.

Bip Castle $$

*Mariinskaya ulitsa 4, Pavlovsk,
196105*
Tel *244 2828*
W bip-hotel.ru
Housed in an 18th-century castle
built on the order of Emperor
Paul I, this unique hotel offers
stylish rooms, including one
tower duplex with an open-air
terrace. Its restaurant specializes
in seasonal fare.

Luxury

Palace Embankment

Angleterre Hotel $$$

Malaya Morskaya ulitsa 24, 190000
Tel *494 5666*   **Map** 6 D2
W hotelangleterre.ru
Stylishly refurbished hotel
situated adjacent to St Isaac's
Cathedral. It features a charming
cinema that screens first-run
films in their original language –
often English movies with
Russian subtitles.

Renaissance St Petersburg Baltic Hotel $$$

Pochtamtskaya ulitsa 4, 190000
Tel *380 4000*   **Map** 5 C2
W marriott.com
A sumptuous hotel with an
intimate feel, which has been
elegantly styled in a subtle
combination of old and new.

The beautiful Pushka Inn Hotel, Gostinyy Dvor

W St. Petersburg $$$

*Voznesenskiy prospekt 6,
190000*
Tel *610 6161*   **Map** 5 C1
W wstpetersburg.com
Walking distance from St Isaac's
Cathedral and the Admiralty,
this hotel has hip, modern
and spacious rooms. It offers
great views over the city from
its exclusive rooftop terrace.
The hotel also houses one of
the most well-regarded spas
in town.

Gostinyy Dvor

DK Choice

Kempinski Hotel Moika 22 $$$

*Naberezhnaya reki Moyki 22,
191186*
Tel *335 9111*   **Map** 2 E5
W kempinski.com
Located right opposite the
Palace Square and close to all
majoy sights, the Kempinski
offers great views of the
Hermitage from some rooms.
Guests can pamper themselves
with a relaxing Turkish bath or
indulge in international cuisine
at the brasserie restaurant,
which offers panoramic views
from the top of the hotel.

The State Hermitage Museum Official Hotel $$$

Ulitsa Pravdy 10, 191119
Tel *777 9810*   **Map** 7 A3
W thehermitagehotel.ru
Set inside a 19th-century
mansion, this hotel is historically
associated with Dostoevsky
and the composer Rimsky-
Korsakov. It offers an elaborate
experience of dining with
imperial porcelain, and
includes luxurious bathing
with Hermes amenities.

Sennaya Ploshchad

DK Choice

Alexander House $$$

*Naberezhnaya Kryukova kanala
27, 190068*
Tel *334 3540*   **Map** 5 C4
W a-house.ru
Wonderful family guesthouse
run as a boutique hotel, with
each room named after and
decorated in the style of a
capital city. All rooms are
comfortably furnished and
most have lovely views. The
common areas have working
fireplaces. Breakfast can be
enjoyed in the rooms.

Ambassador Hotel $$$

*Rimskovo-Korsakova prospekt 5-7,
190068*
Tel *331 6633*   **Map** 6 D3
W ambassador-hotel.ru
Splendid hotel with opulent
interiors. The top-floor restaurant
affords fine city views. Facilities
include an indoor pool, sauna,
gym as well as a beauty salon.

Further Afield

Corinthia Hotel $$$

Nevskiy prospekt 57, 191025
Tel *380 2001*
W corinthia.com
Swanky place with three bars
that proves popular with visiting
celebrities. This is an excellent
location for exploring the city
centre on foot.

Grand Hotel Emerald $$$

Suvorovskiy prospekt 18, 191036
Tel *740 5000*
W grandhotelemerald.com
Located in the old part of the city,
the Post-Modern exterior of this
hotel hides a Classical interior.
Superb fitness centre with a
sauna, pool and Turkish bath.

For more information on types of hotels *see page 173*

Radisson Royal Hotel $$$
Nevskiy prospekt 49/2, 191025
Tel *322 5000*
Ⓦ radissonblu.com
Modern hotel in a historic building.
The rooms as well as the bar and
café overlook the busy main street.

Beyond St Petersburg

DK Choice

Baltic Star Hotel $$
Berezovaya alleya 3, Strelna, 198515
Tel *438 5700*
Ⓦ balticstar-hotel.ru
Set in the country between
St Petersburg and Peterhof,
the Baltic Star is popular with
official delegations. The interiors
of this modern building are
styled historically. There are 20
cottages for guests who prefer
privacy, as well as a pool, gym
and beauty salon.

Grand Peterhof Spa Hotel $$
Gofmeysterskaya ulitsa 2, Peterhof,
198510
Tel *334 8690*
Ⓦ grandpeterhof.ru
Fantastic spa hotel close to
the historic sights. Rooms are
decorated in Classical style, all
with air-conditioning and 24-
hour room service.

President Hotel $$
Primorskoye shosse 572, Zelenogorsk,
197720
Tel *433 8682*
Ⓦ hotel-president.spb.ru
Wonderful place in the woods
with tastefully furnished rooms
and superb spa facilities. A number
of cottages are available within
the grounds.

Modern
Vasilevskiy Island

Nashotel $$
11-ya liniya 50, 199178
Tel *323 2231*
Ⓦ nashotel.ru
Floral themes run through
this brightly decorated hotel.
Exceptionally good service.

Trezzini Art-hotel $$
Bolshoy prospekt V.O. 21, 199004
Tel *332 1035* **Map** 1 A5
Ⓦ trezzini-hotel.com
This cosy, family hotel is located
next to one of the oldest churches,
and is close to the Neva river.
The lobby hosts an art gallery
displaying works by local artists.
Friendly and helpful staff.

Radisson Royal Hotel, St. Petersburg

Petrogradskaya

Mark Inn $
Ulitsa Markina 1, 197198
Tel *438 7667* **Map** 1 C2
Ⓦ markinn.ru
Simple yet comfortable, this
hotel offers an inexpensive way
to stay in close proximity to most
of the city's main attractions; the
Peter and Paul Fortress is just a
15-minutes stroll away. The staff
is attentive and helpful.

Posadskiy Dvor $
Bolshaya Posadskaya ulitsa 9/5,
197046
Tel *658 0490* **Map** 2 E2
Located close to top tourist
destinations and a short walk from
where the Aurora Cruiser is moored,
this hotel offers rooms with basic
comforts and hydro-massage showers. Entrance from the courtyard.

Palace Embankment

Admiral Hotel $
Bolshaya Morskaya ulitsa 13, 191186
Tel *315 4502* **Map** 6 D1
Ⓦ admiralhotels.ru
Pleasant budget hotel in a central
location, offering basic, modern
rooms with en-suite bathrooms.
It is located within easy reach
from all major attractions.

Amulet Hotel $
Malaya Morskaya ulitsa 7, 191186
Tel *570 1732* **Map** 6 D1
Ⓦ amulet-hotels.ru
Quiet hotel within walking
distance of the main sights.
Simple rooms with old-style
furniture. Guests can access
hotel computers. Wi-Fi available.

The Bridge Hotel $$
Adiralteyskaya nab. 12, 190000
Tel *702 5553* **Map** 5 C1
Ⓦ bridge-spb.com
Mere steps away from the
Hermitage and Dvortsovyy
Bridge, this hotel offers spacious
and comfortable rooms. Some
rooms also overlook the Neva,

with an unparalleled view of
the Kunstkammer museum.

Comfort Hotel $$
Bolshaya Morskaya ulitsa 25, 190000
Tel *570 6700* **Map** 6 D2
Ⓦ comfort-hotel.ru
Wonderfully located at the heart
of the historic centre. Modest rooms
and cheerful service. It also provides free transfers to any train
station when booked directly.

Petr Hotel $$
Admiralteyskiy prospekt 8, 190000
Tel *315 2401* **Map** 6 D1
Ⓦ petr-hotel.com
This hotel offers a comfortable
stay right in the heart of the
city's historic centre, within easy
reach of the major attractions.
A 24-hour concierge service
is available.

Gostinyy Dvor

Dynasty $
Ulitsa Rubinshteina 28/29, 191002
Tel *644 5343* **Map** 7 A3
Ⓦ eurasia-hotel.ru
This small, budget hotel is
situated on the city's de facto
Restaurant Row, and is within
walking distance from Nevskiy
prospekt and the Fontanka River.
It offers simple yet stylish rooms,
with a lounge and bar right next
to the lobby.

Mini-Hotel Polikoff $
Nevskiy prospekt 64/11, 191023
Tel *995 3488* **Map** 7 A2
Ⓦ polikoff.ru
Simple interiors with rooms
overlooking a quiet courtyard,
close to the Fontanka River. Situ-
ated on the second floor, visitors
should note that there is no lift.

Asteria $$
Nab. reki Fontanki 71, 191023
Tel *335 6888* **Map** 6 E3
Ⓦ asteria.ru
Set in a superb location with
a view of the Fontanka River,

this hotel is close to most of the central attractions. Its restaurant serves Russian as well as international fare.

Korona Guest Centre $$
Malaya Konyushennaya ulitsa 7, 191186
Tel *571 0086* **Map** 6 E2
W korona-spb.com
Lovely family-run hotel with spacious rooms, located on one of the only pedestrian streets in the city centre.

M-Hotel $$
Sadovaya ulitsa 2, 191023
Tel *448 8383* **Map** 6 F2
W mhotelspb.ru
Nice, large rooms at this simple hotel. Decent buffet breakfast. Tours can be booked directly with the hotel.

Pushka Inn Hotel $$$
Naberezhnaya reki Moyki 14, 191186
Tel *644 7120* **Map** 2 E5
W pushkainn.ru
Housed in a 19th-century mansion, this delightfully cosy establishment has immaculate rooms. Efficient staff and a café that is popular with locals.

Sennaya Ploshchad

DK Choice

Grand Mark Hotel $
Galernaya ulitsa 12, 190000
Tel *570 0536,*
7 921 905 2377 **Map** 5 C1
W grandmarkhotels.com
Situated in the historic city centre within walking distance of the main sights, the Grand Mark is run by an enthusiastic team that ensures their guests enjoy a comfortable stay. Rooms are small but spotless, and include a flat-screen TV. Guests are served hearty continental breakfasts. Free Wi-Fi.

Happy Pushkin Hotel $
Galernaya ulitsa 53, 190000
Tel *777 1799* **Map** 5 B2
W happypushkin.com
Compact rooms decorated in quirky Classical style, within a restored mansion that was once home to the poet Alexander Pushkin. Good breakfast and attentive staff.

Hotel Garrah $
Gorokhovaya ulitsa 23, 190000
Tel *+7 981 707 3234* **Map** 6 D2
Centrally located hotel with big, cheerfully decorated rooms. It has good transport links and a

small playground for children in the courtyard.

Veles Hotel $
Zastavskaya ulitsa 19, 196084
Tel *334 2525*
Basic mini-hotel offering rooms with bathtubs as well as family rooms that include a kitchen. Friendly and helpful staff. Offers bike rentals. On-site spa.

Further Afield

Atrium Hotel $
Nevskiy prospekt 170, 191024
Tel *777 1950*
W hotel-atrium.ru
Close to the Alexander Nevsky Monastery, this hotel is set in a restored 19th-century building. It is a perfect blend between Classic interior and modern facilities, and boasts one of the city's most well-regarded gastropubs.

Domotelli $
Nevskiy prospekt 32, 191011
Tel *917 5777*
W domotelli.ru
Well-equipped apartments in various locations, all close to the Pionerskaya metro.

Hotel Adeliya $
Nevskiy prospekt 82, 191025
Tel *579 9287*
W nevskiy82.ru
This small hotel, located on the city's main thoroughfare, has smartly decorated, air-conditioned rooms. Facilities include free Wi-Fi and private parking.

Hotel Park Krestovskiy $
Severnaya Doroga 12, 197110
Tel *406 9777*
W otelpark.ru
Set near a large public park, this hotel is perfect for those who

wish to combine a city stay with some green space. A free shuttle bus is provided by the hotel to the Krestovkiy Ostrov metro station. There are two restaurants and an airy lobby bar.

Cronwell Inn Stremyannaya $$
Stremyannaya ulitsa 18, 191025
Tel *406 0450*
W stremyannaya-hotel.ru
Pristine rooms, fresh bread from the hotel's bakery and helpful staff make for a pleasant stay at this hotel.

Vesta Hotel $$
Nevskiy prospekt 92, 191025
Tel *272 1322*
W vesta-hotel.com
Peaceful central option tucked away on a quiet street, with cosy, cheerful interiors. Great breakfast and service.

Beyond St Petersburg

Friedental $
Moskovskoe shosse 10, Pushkin, 196601
Tel *476 0041*
Small, cosy hotel located in a residential building close to the sights. Tempting breakfast. Parking available.

Home Hostel $
Zoi Kruglovoy ulitsa 23, Veliky Novgorod, 173007
Tel *+7 952 485 6750*
Modest hostel in a local family home. Characterful dormitory-styled accommodation with shared bathrooms.

Rachmaninov Hotel $
Bolshaya Moskovskaya ulitsa 10, Veliky Novgorod, 173000
Tel *(8162) 780280*
W rachmaninoff-hotel.ru
A short walk from the city's ancient Kremlin, this hotel is housed in a 19th-century mansion. It offers spacious rooms with comfortable new furnishings and modern amenities.

New Peterhof Hotel $$
Sank-Peterburgskiy prospekt 34, Peterhof, 198510
Tel *319 1010*
W new-peterhof.ru
Located right next to the park and the palace, this hotel incorporates a contemporary design using eco-friendly technologies. The rooms offer spectacular views of the Peter and Paul Cathedral, and there is also features a spa with a large swimming pool, Turkish hammam and a Finnish sauna.

Terrace and bar of the Renaissance St Petersburg Baltic Hotel

For more information on types of hotels see page 173

WHERE TO EAT AND DRINK

A huge variety of restaurants serving international cuisine line almost every block in the centre of St Petersburg. Most have simple, set menus at lunch and dinner, offering visitors a risk-free opportunity to try out more expensive places. Russian cuisine is still popular, and is available at numerous traditional-style restaurants. Ethnic food from the former Soviet republics and abroad provides an array of vegetarian dishes. Small cafés offer a chance to escape the more garish tourist traps found near some sights. Although getting a plain green salad may still pose a problem, other fresh salads are offered by most restaurants as well as good-quality cafés. For a list of recommended restaurants and cafés, *see pp186–93*.

The exquisite Art Nouveau interiors of the L'Europe restaurant *(see p190)*

Where to Eat

Restaurants on Nevskiy prospekt tend to be more expensive than those on other streets. A few steps off Nevskiy, however, a variety of eateries line the streets – Bolshaya Konyushennaya, Rubinshteyna, Vladimirskiy prospekt and Ulitsa Vosstaniya – offering something to suit most pockets and tastes. Venture out a little further and the short Ulitsa Belinskogo, for instance, offers at least five highly recommended options.

Types of Restaurant

All large hotels offer good eating opportunities, but hotel restaurants are included in this guide only if they are outstanding or found in places that are short on other options.

Style and fashion can dominate in some restaurants, so the food often suffers and prices can be unreasonably high. Other establishments, however, manage to combine food, decor and service in fine Russian style. Dining

trends include "Imperial Russian" amid opulent interiors (Staraya Tamozhnya, *see p186*), and exotic Caucasian restaurants (Kavkaz-Bar, *see p189*). Top restaurants serve a mix of European and Russian dishes, with some Asian elements.

The former Soviet republics Georgia and Armenia have left their mark on Russian cuisine. Try Salkhino *(see p187)* or Lagidze *(see p191)* for Georgian

Outdoor café in the arcade of Gostinyy Dvor *(see p110)*

food, and Erivan *(see p189)* for Armenian fare. Asian restaurants are numerous, if usually uninspiring; the sushi restaurant Yakitoriya *(see p186)* is a rare exception.

Reading the Menu

Large restaurants and some cafés have menus in English. Any restaurant that accepts credit cards will usually have English-speaking waiters, and, in those places that do not, most waiters try to overcome language difficulties.

Payment and Tipping

All restaurants and cafés show meal prices in roubles. The listings in the guide give an indication of price ranges in roubles as restaurants cannot accept foreign currency by law *(see pp216–17)*. Guests must pay with either cash or a credit card.

Major restaurants accept most credit cards, but it is advisable to check beforehand. Amex and Diners Club cards are almost never accepted. Credit card payment is still limited in Russia, especially in smaller establishments, so it is advisable to carry some cash with you at all times.

Tips are usually 10–15 per cent unless service is already included in the bill. To ensure the waiter receives the tip, it is best to give it in cash, rather than as part of a credit card payment.

Opening Times

Most restaurants in St Petersburg open at noon and stay open until around 11pm or midnight. Increasingly, the more expensive restaurants, and particularly those that are attached to a nightclub *(see pp206–7)*, may stay open well into the early morning hours. Cafés close early, usually around 10pm.

For those who wish to eat after an evening event, many restaurants stay open until the last customer leaves. Some small bars offer food into the small hours. In addition, if all else fails, the lights of many fast-food outlets, such as Stolovaya #1 Kopeika *(see p195)*, are often to be found burning after midnight. The city's two 24-hour restaurants are Khochu Kharcho for Georgian cuisine *(see p190)* and Du Nord 1834 for French *(see p191)*.

Elegant interior of the historic Literaturnoye Café *(see p188)*

Street sign for Pirosmani*(see p192)*, located in Petrogradskaya

Making a Reservation

It is always advisable to book ahead, especially during the White Nights *(see p53)* when upmarket restaurants may take bookings weeks in advance. Your hotel concierge can help. Smaller restaurants and cafés do not require reservations, but as they rely on special events such as weddings and birthdays they sometimes close unexpectedly.

Children

Russians are acquiring the habit of taking their children out to dine with them. On the whole, Russians love children; few restaurants will refuse them entry, and staff will often adjust dishes to meet their needs. A number of city eateries, such as Tres Amigos *(see p193)* and Il Patio *(see p195)*, have children's parties and even nannies at weekends.

A cosy room at Botanica is equipped with a play area, books and a TV. Some places advertised to foreigners – but none in this guide – have "entertainment" that is not suitable for children.

Live Music

Most restaurants and cafés have some kind of music on Fridays or Saturdays – DJs or live acts. The listings that follow on pages 186 to 193 note those which have live music on other days as well.

Vegetarians

Traditional Russian food is meat-oriented, but an increasing number of eateries aimed at a more Westernized crowd, such as Krokodil *(see p190)*, include vegetarian options, and Georgian and Armenian cuisines offer a wide range of vegetable and bean dishes. There are several vegetarian dining options in St Petersburg – Rada & K *(see p189)* and Ukrop *(see p191)* are the best.

Smoking

As in the rest of Europe, Russian law forbids smoking in any public space, including bars and restaurants. Even open-air terraces fall under this regulation, though some establishments continue to provide outdoor smoking areas. In Russia, patrons, as well as business owners, can be fined by the police for breaking the law.

Dress Code

Formal dress is de rigueur only in large and fashionable restaurants, but guests should always be neatly and cleanly dressed. Trainers and tracksuits are acceptable in the less expensive cafés.

Disabled Access

Only a few restaurants have ramps or no stairs at all, but waiters and doormen are used to visitors in wheelchairs and are usually very helpful.

Cafés and bars prove more problematic, with stairs and narrow doors, and certainly no toilets for the disabled. Disabled travellers may find themselves confined to hotel dining or the more expensive eateries and bars.

Recommended Restaurants

The restaurants listed in this guide have been selected for their atmosphere, quality and good value. Establishments range from simple to lavish and cater to different tastes, from traditional, home-cooked recipes to gourmet cuisine. They are listed by area and then by price, with map references and an indication of the main type of cuisine offered.

DK Choice restaurants stand out from the crowd, whether it is for outstanding service, stunning views, intimate atmosphere or renowned chefs. These special places are highly recommended by both local and visiting diners.

WEBSITES

W **tripadvisor.com** is a great source of regularly updated restaurant reviews. Most restaurants have websites, but many are in Russian only, or are poorly maintained. Many places appear on the St Petersburg restaurant site, which has an English-language version at: W **restoran.ru**

For Russian-speakers, there are now many listings and reviews online. Try: W **allcafe.ru** and W **menu.ru**

The Flavours of St Petersburg

Russia's culinary reputation centres on warming stews, full of wintry vegetables such as cabbage, beetroot and potatoes. Yet St Petersburg was once the capital of a vast empire stretching from Poland to the Pacific and this is reflected in the variety of food on offer there. Aubergine (eggplant) and tomatoes, from the Caucasus in the south, bring in the flavours of the Mediterranean, while spices from Central Asia lend an exotic touch. On the stalls of the city's Kuznechniy Market, caviar and crayfish sit alongside honey from Siberia and melons and peaches from Georgia.

Wild Mushrooms

Caviar, the roe of sturgeon from Russia's warm southern waters

Russian Countryside

Many St Petersburgers have small country houses within easy reach of the city, and spend weekends from spring to early winter tending their immaculate vegetable gardens, or combing the countryside for wild berries and mushrooms. Much of this bountiful harvest is made into preserves and pickles. There is a refreshing soup, *solianka*, in which pickled cucumbers impart an unusual salty taste. Pickled mushrooms in sour cream make a regular appearance on restaurant menus, as do a variety of fresh berry juices.

In a country where food shortages are a fairly recent memory, very little is wasted. *Kvas*, a popular, mildly alcoholic drink is frequently made at home by fermenting stale bread with sugar and a scattering of fruit. Summer visitors should make a point of trying the seasonal cold soup *okroshka*, which is based on *kvas*.

Russia is also a land with hundreds of rivers and lakes, and has a long tradition of fish cookery. Dishes range from simple soups, such as *ukha*, to caviar and sturgeon, and salmon cooked in a bewildering variety of ways.

Pickled mushrooms · Spiced cheese · Rye bread

Blinis · Gherkins

Salted fish · Soured cream · Pickled herring

A typical spread of *zakuski* (cold appertizers)

Local Dishes and Specialities

Borsch (beetroot soup) and *blinis* (buttery pancakes) with caviar are perhaps two of the most famous Russian dishes – one peasant dish which varies with the availability of ingredients and the other a staple for the week leading up to Lent, when rich food would be eaten to fatten up before the fast. Much of Russia's cuisine is designed to make use of what is readily to hand or is warming and filling. A popular main course is *kulebiaka*, a hearty fish pie, larded with eggs, rice, dill and onion and encased in a buttery crust. Another is beef stroganoff with its creamy mushroom sauce, created in 18th-century St Petersburg by the chef of the wealthy Stroganoff family.

Beetroot

Borsch Made with meat or vegetable stock, this beetroot soup is usually served with dill and soured cream.

Market vegetable stall in St Petersburg

The Caucasus

The former Soviet states of the Caucasus – Georgia, Azerbaijan and Armenia – are renowned for their legendary banquets, where the tables are laden with an enormous quantity and variety of food and drink. They still supply Russia's cities with a tempting range of fine subtropical produce. Limes, lemons, oranges, walnuts, figs, pomegranates, peaches, beans, salty cheeses and herbs are all shipped in season to St Petersburg's markets and its many Georgian restaurants. The cuisine of Georgia, with its focus on freshly grilled meats, pulses, vegetables, yogurt, herbs and nut sauces – including the hallmark walnut sauce, *satsivi* – is famously healthy and makes a delicious, unusual-tasting treat.

Central Asia

From the Central Asian republics of the old Soviet Union come a range of culinary traditions based on the nomadic lifestyles of Russia's one-time overlords, the

Freshly picked lingonberries from Russia's bumper autumn harvest

Mongol or Tartar Hordes. The meat of fat-tailed sheep, which thrive in the dry desert air, is used to make communal piles of *plov* (pilaf) around which guests sit, eating in the traditional manner with their hands.

Served in St Petersburg's Uzbek restaurants, it shares the menu with warm flat breads, spicy noodle soups, *manti* (tasty dumplings reminiscent of Chinese cuisine) and a variety of melons and grapes, which proliferate in the desert oases, and apricots and nuts, grown in the mountains.

ZAKUSKI

A traditional Russian meal generally begins with *zakuski*, a selection of cold appetizers. These may include pickled mushrooms (*gribi*), gherkins (*ogurtsi*), salted herrings (*seliodka*), an assortment of smoked fish, *blinis* topped with caviar, various vegetable pâtés (sometimes known as vegetable caviars), stuffed eggs (*yaitsa farshirovanniye*), spiced cheese (*brinza*), beetroot salad (*salat iz svyokly*) and small meat pies (*pirozhki*), accompanied by fried rye bread and washed down with shots of vodka. A bowl of steaming soup often follows, before the main course reaches the table.

Kulebiaka Rich, buttery puff pastry is wrapped around a mix of fish, hard-boiled eggs, rice, onion and chopped dill.

Pelmeni These meat-stuffed dumplings may be served in a clear broth, or with tomato sauce or soured cream.

Kissel A mix of red berries is used to make this soft, fruity jelly, which is served topped with a swirl of fresh cream.

What to Drink in St Petersburg

Russian vodka is famous throughout the world and the Russian Standard distillery in St Petersburg is Russia's second largest distillery, the largest being in Moscow. Vodka first appeared in Russia sometime in the 14th or 15th century. Peter the Great *(see p20)* was particularly fond of anise- or pepper-flavoured vodkas and devised modifications to the distillation process which greatly improved the quality of the finished drink.

Tea is Russia's other national drink. Traditionally made using a samovar and served black, tea has been popular in Russia since the end of the 18th century, when it was first imported from China.

A 19th-century Russian peasant family drinking vodka and tea

Clear Vodka

Kubanskaya

Vodka is produced from grain, usually wheat, although some rye is also used in Russia. Local vodkas dominate in St Petersburg, the best of which are Diplomat, Five Star and Russian Standard. Moscow's Kristall company, which produces Kristall and Gzhelka vodka, is increasingly popular, while Flagman distillery proudly proclaims that it is the official purveyor of vodka to the Kremlin. The range of vodkas available these days is over-whelming. There is one golden rule: if it is under $7 or $8 for half a litre, do not drink it.

Vodka is always served with food, often with a range of richly flavoured accompaniments called *zakuski (see p183)*, particularly black bread, pickled cucumbers and herring. Vodka is not always served ice cold, but it should be chilled.

| Putinka | Russian Standard | Stolichnaya |

Flavoured Vodka

The practice of flavouring vodka has entirely practical origins. When vodka was first produced commercially in the Middle Ages, the techniques and equipment were so primitive that it was impossible to remove all the impurities. This left unpleasant aromas and flavours, which were disguised by adding honey together with aromatic oils and spices. As distillation techniques improved, flavoured vodkas became a speciality in their own right. Limonnaya, its taste deriving from lemon zest, is one of the most traditional, as is Pertsovka, flavoured with red chilli pepper pods. Klukvennaya (cranberry) and Oblepikha (sea buckthorn, an orange Siberian berry) are also favourites. Some of the best flavoured vodkas are made at home by soaking peach stones or whole berries in alcohol for months.

Pepper vodka

| Limonnaya | Klukvennaya | Oblepikha |

Major Wine Regions

- Wine-growing region
- Moldova
- Ukraine
- Russia
- Georgia
- Armenia
- Azerbaijan
- — International boundaries

Wine

The Soviet Union was one of the world's largest producers of wine (*vino*), but many of the major wine regions are now republics in their own right. Several indigenous types of grape are cultivated in the different regions, along with many of the more familiar international varieties.

Georgia is considered the best wine-making area. Its wines include those made from the Rkatsiteli grape, characterized by a floral aroma and subtle, fruity flavour, and the Gurdzhaani, which gives a unique, slightly bitter touch. Among its best red wines is the smooth Mukuzani. Moldova produces white, sparkling wines in the south and central regions, while the south is also known for its red wines. Since 1799, Moldova also produces a sweet, champagne-like wine called Shampanskoe.

White and red Georgian wine   Shampanskoe

Other Alcoholic Drinks

Brandy (*konyak*) was originally a by-product of wine-making and commercial production only began in Russia in the 19th century. Armenian brandy is one of the finest, with a distinctive vanilla fragrance resulting from its ageing in 70–100-year-old oak barrels. Georgia and Daghestan also produce good brandies. St Petersburg beer (*pivo*) is among the best in Russia. Baltika, Vena and Stepan Razin make a full range of beers in bottles and on draught. In addition, Tver beers such as Afanasy are well worth trying. Various imported beers are also available.

Baltika Beer   Armenian brandy

Other Drinks

Kvas is a lightly fermented drink made from rye and barley, consumed by adults and children alike. Russia's vast range of mineral waters (*mineralnaya voda*) includes many with unusually high mineral contents. Mineral waters from the Caucasus are particularly prized. Also widely available are fruit juices (*sok*, *mors* or *kompot*), including cranberry (*klyukva*). Look out for traditional Russian *sbiten*, made from honey and herbs.

Mineral water   Kvas   Cranberry juice

Tea

Russian tea is served black with a slice of lemon and may be drunk from tall glasses or cups. Sweetened with jam or sugar, tea (*chay*) is an ideal accompaniment to rich cakes and pastries. The boiling water for tea traditionally comes from a samovar. The water is used to brew a pot of tea, from which a little is poured into a cup and is then diluted with more hot water.

A glass of tea, with jam (*varenye*) to sweeten it

The Samovar

Made from brass or copper and heated by coals in the central chimney, samovars traditionally provided boiling water for a wide variety of domestic purposes and were an essential wedding gift. Modern electric ones are made of stainless steel and are used mainly for boiling water to make tea. The word samovar comes from *samo* meaning "itself" and *varit* meaning "to boil".

Where to Eat and Drink

Vasilevskiy Island

Marketplace $
Russian   **Map** 1 A5
7-ya liniya 34/2, Vasilevskiy ostrov, 199004
Tel +7 981 784 9814
This relaxed self-service café offers Russian, Asian and European favourites in a cosy, country-chic setting. A popular spot for casual meals and snacks. Free Wi-Fi.

Casa del Myaso $$
International   **Map** 1 C5
Birzhevoy proezd 6, 199034
Tel 320 9746
Literally translated as the "House of Meat", this atmospheric basement restaurant, with vaulted brick ceilings, has a variety of meat dishes on offer. There is also a salad bar with cold snacks.

Grad Petrov $$
German   **Map** 1 C5
Universitetskaya naberezhnaya 5, 199034
Tel 326 0137
Cheerful German *kneipe* (pub) that serves beer brewed in the classic style and hearty German dishes. Try the *Ein Meter Thüringer* (one-metre sausage with red cabbage).

Ketino $$
Georgian   **Map** 1 A5
8-ya liniya 23, 199004
Tel 326 0196
Guests can sample well-prepared authentic Georgian delicacies in this friendly place. Vegetarian options are available. Wine can be costly.

Kneipe Jager Haus $$
German
Sredniy pr 64, Vasilevskiy ostrov
Tel 321 3376
Modelled after a traditional German *kneipe*, this establishment has the atmosphere of a beer restaurant in Munich. There is a great choice of sausages and international beer.

Maria Karlotta $$
International   **Map** 5 B1
Universitetskaya naberezhnaya 21, 199034
Tel 320 2120
Located in a restored palace that is now a hotel, this elegant restaurant is named after the wife of the first architect of St Petersburg. It boasts an extensive wine list and excellent service. The kitchen specializes in European and Russian cuisine.

DK Choice

Restoran $$
Russian   **Map** 1 C4
Tamozhennyy pereulok 2, 199034
Tel 327 8979
Buff-coloured walls and wooden tables serve as the perfect setting for a selection of flavoured home-made vodkas and superb game dishes. The menu features a variety of reliable Russian classics as well.

Taverna Grolle $$
Russian   **Map** 5 A1
Bolshoy prospect 20, Vasilevskiy ostrov, 199034
Tel 323 6258
This 24/7 upscale tavern serves grilled meat and fish alongside Russian specialities such as *pelmeni* and *borscht*. Situated in a historic neighbourhood, it is close to various museums and palaces, and offers charming views.

Dans le Noir? $$$
International   **Map** 1 B4
Birzhevoy pereulok 4, 199034
Tel 335 2212   **Closed** *Mon*
Intriguing concept-restaurant where diners eat in total darkness. They are guided and served by blind waiters. After the meal they can see pictures of the menu and find out what they ate.

DK Choice

Repin $$$
International   **Map** 5 A1
8-ya liniya 11-13, Vasilevskiy ostrov, 199034
Tel 335-2290
Located within the Sokos Hotel, this elegant dining room offers a mix of Russian and international cuisine, with a particular emphasis on presentation and service. Standards are uniformly high and the widely spaced tables and seating areas give it a club-like atmosphere.

Staraya Tamozhnya $$$
Russian   **Map** 1 C5
Tamozhennyy pereulok 1, 199034
Tel 327 8980
St Petersburg's oldest restaurant, Staraya Tamozhnya offers a range of seafood, plus classic delicacies such as black and red caviar.

Petrogradskaya

Gornyy Oryol $
International   **Map** 1 C3
Aleksandrovskiy Park 1A
Tel 323 0505
This eatery resembles a fairy-tale castle with columns, narrow windows, sculptures and fountains. Specializing in Georgian cuisine, the menu also boasts Russian and European dishes. Popular with wedding parties. Book ahead.

Yakitoriya $
Japanese   **Map** 2 F3
Petrovskaya naberezhnaya 4, 197046
Tel 970 4858
Favourably located near the Peter and Paul Fortress, Yakitoriya is part of a vast Russian chain of Japanese restaurants in the city. Serves a consistently high standard of sushi.

Zhelaniya $
Russian   **Map** 1 B3
Prospekt Dobrolubova 23, 197198
Tel 232 9883
Designed to resemble the interior of a *dacha*, this homely restaurant prepares lovely standard Russian dishes such as sweet and savoury dumplings.

A table piled high with traditional Russian specialities

Splendid views of the Neva from the Flying Dutchman restaurant

DK Choice

Salkhino $$
Georgian **Map** 2 D2
Kronverkskiy prospekt 25, 197101
Tel *232 7891*
This sister restaurant to Ketino on Vasilevskiy Island offers generous home cooking by two Georgian women who know how to tempt. Their *khachapuri* (cheese-filled bread) is the best in town. Try the aubergine (eggplant) stuffed with walnuts. They also prepare various meat dishes and mouthwatering home-made desserts.

ChiliPizza $$
Pizzeria **Map** 1 C4
Dobrolubova prospekt 8, 197198
Tel *244 3290*
Upbeat and reliable restaurant with a modern interior. Offers an extensive selection of appetizing pizza varieties. Quick and efficient service.

Demyanova Ukha $$
Seafood **Map** 1 C3
Kronverkskiy prospekt 53, 197198
Tel *232 8090*
The city's first specialist fish restaurant retains its premier position over the competition by dint of sheer hard work along with unpretentious, traditional cooking.

Dozari Bar $$
International **Map** 1 C4
Prospekt Dobrolyubova 14a, 197198
Tel *928 6070*
This barge with panoramic vistas serves classically inspired Russian and continental cuisine. It is also a venue for late-night revelry with live music, karaoke, an extensive cocktail menu and bar snacks.

Flying Dutchman $$
International **Map** 1 C4
Mytninskaya naberezhnaya 6, 197198
Tel *313 8866*
The three restaurants on board this atmospheric replica of the *Flying Dutchman* ship have splendid views across the Neva to the Winter Palace. Japanese, Italian and Russian cuisine.

Italy Café $$
Italian **Map** 1 C2
Bolshoy prospekt 58, 197136
Tel *900 6333*
Located in an upscale shopping centre this two-story restaurant specializes in Italian classics such as pizzas, pastas and risottos. Its floor-to-ceiling windows provide a bird's-eye view of the surrounding neighbourhood.

Korushka $$
International **Map** 2 E3
Zayachij Ostrov, Petropavlovskaya Krepost 3, 197046
Tel *917 9010*
Exquisite dishes served in tranquil surroundings with great views across the Neva. Russian and international fare, along with grilled fish.

Mesto Café $$
Russian **Map** 1 C3
Kronverkskiy prospekt 59, 197198
Tel *405 8799*
Designed to resemble a turn-of-the-century Parisian boudoir, at Mesto Café the experimental elements extend into the kitchen as well. Modern takes on Russian classics are served in an eclectic manner by a friendly staff.

Mozzarella Bar $$
Fusion **Map** 1 B3
Bolshoy prospekt 13/4, 196128
Tel *955 1097*
Attracts the hip, young and casual crowd for its unusual fusion of Italian and Japanese food that has something for everyone. Friendly and efficient staff.

Nevesomos't $$
International **Map** 1 C1
Bolshoy prospekt 37, 197198
Tel *332 4222*
Hotel Vedensky's seasonal rooftop oasis, Nevesomos't, offers stunning views of the city. The menu concentrates on grilled meats and seafood paired with signature cocktails. Cooking classes are offered here throughout the summer.

Pryanosti & Radosti $$
International **Map** 2 E2
Malaya Posadskaya ulitsa 3
Tel *333 4633*
One of the only places in the city that serves breakfast 24 hours a day, this chic eatery is appropriate for a romantic evening or a family meal. Also popular for its European and Georgian cuisine.

Tbiliso $$
Georgian **Map** 2 D2
Sytninskaya ulitsa 10, 197101
Tel *232 9391*
Highly rated Georgian restaurant with an authentic menu that includes such dishes as chicken seasoned with the delectable walnut sauce, *satsivi*, and *mamalyga* (ground corn with salted cheese). Waiters are traditionally dressed.

Volna $$
Fusion **Map** 2 F3
Petrovskaya naberezhnaya 4, 197046
Tel *322 5383*
Focusing on seasonal cooking, this popular place near the Cruiser Aurora has minimal interiors and large windows, offering river-side views. Excellent international wines.

Palace Embankment

Bushe $
Café **Map** 6 D1
Malaya Morskaya ulitsa 7, 191186
Tel *315 5371*
Tremendously popular café chain serving delicious freshly baked breads and pastries as well as light meals, sandwiches and desserts.

Clean Plates Society $
International **Map** 6 D2
Gorokhovaya ulitsa 13, 190000
Tel *934 9764*
Cosy eatery popular for its eclectic menu. The burgers stand out, as do the home-made Russian favourites and Central Asian dishes. Don't miss the unique hot and cold, non-alcoholic berry drinks.

Da Albertone $
Italian **Map** 2 E5
Millionnaya ulitsa 23, 191186
Tel *915 5501*
Conveniently close to the Hermitage, this simple Italian restaurant has some lovely pizzas and consistently good service. Well-equipped children's room.

For more information on types of restaurants *see pages 180–81*

The beautiful dining area in Gosti restaurant, located on the Fontanka River

Teplo
Italian $
Map 5 C2
Bolshaya Morskaya ulitsa 45, 190000
Tel *570 1974*
This popular place serves faultless Italian dishes and some Russian favourites. Book in advance.

Canvas
International $$
Map 5 C2
Renaissance St Petersburg Baltic Hotel, Pochtamtskaya ulitsa 4, 190000
Tel *380 4000*
Withcity views from the sixth-floor, Canvas offers fine Russian and European cuisine. Excellent service.

Cococo
Russian $$
Map 5 C2
Voznesensky prospekt, 6, 190000
Tel *418 2060*
Offering à la carte and a variety of tasting menus, Cococo is ideal for diners seeking cutting-edge gastronomy.

Gastronom
International $$
Map 2 F5
Naberezhnaya reki Moyki 1/7, 191186
Tel *314 3849*
Stylish eatery serving Italian, Russian and Japanese cuisine. It features outdoor seating and a chic interior with comfortable sofas.

Gogol
International $$
Map 6 D1
Malaya Morskaya ulitsa 8, 191186
Tel *312 6097*
With 19th-century Russian-style decor, Gogol serves homemade bread and vodka alongside dishes such as rabbit stew and venison with apple sauce.

Gosti
Fusion $$
Map 6 D1
Malaya Morskaya ulitsa 13, 191186
Tel *312 5820*
Casual and cosy place offering Italian classics alongside Serbian specialities. Spread over several floors, it has a separate play area for children.

King Pong
Asian $$
Map 5 D1
Bolshaya Morskaya ulitsa 16, 191186
Tel *315 8256*
Spacious spot with a variety of flavourful and well-prepared dishes from all across southeast Asia. Has a separate children's menu.

Literaturnoye Café
Russian $$
Map 6 E1
Nevskiy prospekt 18, 191186
Tel *312 6057*
Historic restaurant from where the Russian poet Alexander Pushkin set off for his fatal duel. Serves traditional, rather heavy recipes.

La Russ
Russian $$
Map 2 E5
Naberezhnaya reki Moyki 37, 191186
Tel *571 7591*
Worth visiting for the nightly cabaret show alone, La Russ offers delicious Russian fare. The decor and the food reflect the classic charm of 1920s Russia.

Tandoor
Indian $$
Map 6 D1
Admiralteyskiy prospekt 10, 190000
Tel *312 3886*
Well-known Indian restaurant with atmospheric interior. Offers generous portions of signature Indian recipes and high standards of service. Vegetarian options available.

Borsalino
Italian $$$
Map 6 D2
Angleterre Hotel, Malaya Morskaya ulitsa 24, 190000
Tel *494 5666*
This restaurant is housed inside the historic Angleterre Hotel that overlooks St Isaac's Cathedral. Authentic and high-quality food.

DK Choice

Percorso
Italian $$$
Map 5 C1
Voznesenskiy prospekt, 1 (Four Season Lion Palace), 190000
Tel *339 8044*
This elegant temple to Italian gastronomy is one of the finest restaurants in the city. Fresh produce is flown in from Italy weekly, and the sleek bar is the perfect place for a pre-dinner drink or discreet rendezvous.

Gostinyy Dvor

Aragvi
Georgian $
Map 2 F5
Nab reki Fontanki 9, 191011
Tel *570 5643*
Aragvi features light, elegant interiors and large windows overlooking the Fontanka river. Serves authentic Georgian cuisine, which includes *satsivi* and *khachapuri*.

City Grill
International $
Map 7 A2
ulitsa Rubinshteyna 4, 191025
Tel *+7 921 938 2708*
Along St Petersburg's de facto Restaurant Row, this understated burger place charms with its bare brick walls, friendly young staff and top-quality burgers and sides.

Fartuk
International $
Map 7 A2
Ulitsa Rubinshteyna 15–17, 191025
Tel *764 5256*
Popular with locals and tourists for its relaxed outdoor dining, European-influenced food and home-made lemonade. Book in advance.

Jack & Chan
Fusion $
Map 6 F1
Inzhenernaya ulitsa 7, 191011
Tel *982 0535*
This relaxed eatery with mismatched furniture and a shipping container entrance offers casual dining. Try the prawn and avocado salad with glass noodles.

Kilikia
Armenian $
Map 6 E2
Naberezhnaya kanala Griboedova 40, 191023
Tel *327 2208*
Welcoming Armenian restaurant with vaulted brick ceilings and a handy picture menu to guide diners. Pleasing Armenian recipes and attentive service.

Key to Price Guide *see page 186*

Kvartirka
Russian $ **Map** 7 A2
Nevskiy prospekt 51, 191025
Tel 315 5561
Fun, Soviet-era themed café with hearty portions of traditional Russian food. Even the service is mock Soviet style, carrying the theme throughout.

Mama Roma
Italian $ **Map** 7 A1
Karavannaya ulitsa 3/35, 191011
Tel 314 0347
Part of a well-run chain of authentic Italian restaurants offering consistently high standards of food. The interior is light and airy. Features a salad bar and business lunch options.

Pelmeniya
International $ **Map** 7 A1
Nab reki Fontanki 25, 191011
Tel 415 4185
Named after Russia's ubiquitous dumpling dish, this fun buffet-style eatery serves dumplings from around the world. Polish, Chinese, Japanese, Georgian and Mongolian versions on the menu.

Pirogovy Dvorik
Café $ **Map** 6 E2
Naberezhnaya kanala Griboedova 22/5, 191011
Tel 310 0160
Bustling café-bakery chain with a wonderful selection of freshly made Russian pastries as well as soups, sandwiches, light meals and desserts.

Rada & K
Vegetarian $ **Map** 6 F3
Gorokhovaya ulitsa 36, 191023
Tel +7 953 373 9759
Intimate vegetarian restaurant that attracts a hip young crowd. Serves healthy Indian dishes along with meatless versions of Russian staples such beef stroganoff and *borsch*.

Brasserie de Metropol
International $$ **Map** 6 F2
Sadovaya ulitsa 22/2, 191911
Tel 571 8888
Elegant place with a spacious classic interior and snug rooms perfect for sampling the home-brewed beer. Broad selection of Russian and international cuisine.

Erivan
Armenian $$ **Map** 6 F2
Naberezhnaya reki Fontanki 51, 191011
Tel 703 3820
Welcoming place, comfortably furnished in Armenian style. Traditional recipes with lots of mutton and veal, but there are also rarities such as brains in olive oil served. Vegetarian options available.

Fiolet
Fusion $$ **Map** 6 F2
Rossi Boutique Hotel, Naberezhnaya reki Fontanki 55, 191023
Tel 407 5207
Smart hotel-restaurant that serves an impressive range of remarkably good Asian fusion dishes. The interior blends Classical and contemporary designs. Outdoor terrace for summer dining.

Gras
Russian $$ **Map** 6 F1
Inzhenernaya ulitsa 7, 191011
Tel 209 0443
The young chef at this farm-to-table restaurant experiments with unusual yet delightful pairings. The rare Russian ingredients offer a unique experience that is as memorable as it is affordable.

Kavkaz-Bar
Caucasian $$ **Map** 7 A1
Karavannaya ulitsa 18, 191011
Tel 312 1665
Georgian and Armenian cuisine accompanied by excellent wines and brandies. Some of the best vegetarian kebabs in town can be had here. Superb location and intimate atmosphere.

Meat Head
International $$ **Map** 2 E5
Konyushennaya ploshchad 2, 191186
Tel 923 0044
Plenty of meat on the menu, including the superb New Zealand lamb steak. The exposed-brick ceiling adds character to the place.

Park Giuseppe
Italian $$ **Map** 2 F5
Naberezhnaya kanala Griboedova 2b, 191011
Tel 571 7309
Delightful spot with summer terrace and lovely views across the Moyka. Serves savoury pizzas baked in a wood-burning oven.

Suliko
Georgian $$ **Map** 6 E2
Kazanskaya ulitsa 6, 191186
Tel 314 7373
Central Georgian restaurant tucked away behind the Kazan Cathedral. Frequented by local Georgians, who come to enjoy the hearty traditional fare.

DK Choice

Tsar
Russian $$ **Map** 2 F1
Sadovaya ulitsa 12, 191011
Tel 640 1900
Housed within a former palace, Tsar occupies a suite of pains-takingly restored rooms that offer a sumptuous setting for the enjoyment of first-rate Russian classics. Every detail, down to the cut-crystal glassware and portraits of Russian nobility, exudes opulent indulgence. The service is suitably subdued.

The stylish Caviar Bar, located in the Belmond Grand Hotel Europe

For more information on types of restaurants *see pages 180–81*

Yat
International $$
Map 2 E5
*Naberezhnaya reki Moyki 16,
191186*
Tel *957 0023*
Homely eatery with friendly staff,
kids' play area and a limited menu
of wholesome food options to
choose from – their assorted
homemade pickles are excellent.

Bellevue Brasserie $$$
International   Map 2 E5
*Kempinski Hotel Moika 22,
Naberezhnaya reki Moyki 22, 191186*
Tel *335 9111*
On the ninth floor of the hotel,
offers fantastic views of Palace
Square and the Winter Palace.
Excellent modern European menu.

Caviar Bar and Restaurant $$$
Russian   Map 6 F1
*Belmond Grand Hotel Europe,
Mikhaylovskaya ulitsa 1/7, 191186*
Tel *329 6000*
The city's only caviar restaurant
is tiny and showcases the most
elegant and varied ways of
serving caviar and fish. Try caviar
on a delicate *blini* or one of the
special Russian regional dishes.

DK Choice

L'Europe $$$
International   Map 6 F1
*Belmond Grand Hotel Europe,
Mikhaylovskaya ulitsa 1/7, 191186*
Tel *329 6000*
This Art-Nouveau hall with
elegant stained-glass ceiling is
not a re-creation of the city's
glorious past, but the real thing,
beautifully restored. The food is
first-class European. Regular
celebrations of Russian cuisine
and culture include Tchaikovsky
ballet shows on Friday evenings
and vodka tastings.

Sennaya Ploshchad

Senoval
Café $
Map 5 C3
Ulitsa Dekabristov 13, 190000
Tel *314 6932*
This underground café-restaurant
is always buzzing with a lively
young crowd attracted to its low
prices and generous servings.
Standard Russian fare on the
platter. Friendly and cheerful staff.

1913 $$
Russian   Map 5 C2
Voznesenskiy prospekt 13/2, 190000
Tel *315 5148*
The intriguingly named 1913 is
the place for generous portions
of outstanding regional dishes

The impressive dining hall at L'Europe restaurant

such as *draniki* with bacon
and sorrel soup, as well as
lobster fricassee.

Arcobaleno $$
Fusion   Map 5 C2
*Domina Prestige Hotel St Petersburg,
Bolshaya Morskaya ulitsa 54, 190000*
Tel *385 1292*
This vibrant, modern hotel-
restaurant offers excellent Italian
fusion cuisine. The bright-hued
interior justifies the name, which
means rainbow in Italian.

Charlie $$
International   Map 6 D3
*Naberezhnaya kanala Griboedova
54, 190000*
Tel *+7 911 926 0012*
Steps away from the bustle of
Sennaya Ploshchad, this calm eatery
features an eclectic mix of inter-
national favourites. The seafood
and desserts are delicious.

Conchita Bonita $$
Mexican   Map 6 E2
Gorokhovaya ulitsa 39, 190031
Tel *570 6050*
High-energy Mexican bar and
restaurant with phenomenal
cocktails and a reasonable range
of spicy Latin American speci-
alities such as *taquitos* and *fajitas*.
Decent service.

The elegant Tsar restaurant, located in
a former palace

Entree $$
French   Map 5 C4
Nikolskaya ploshchad 6, 190068
Tel *572 5201*
This bistro serves beef, duck
and salmon *carpaccio* as well
as a variety of traditional
dishes. Visit the separate café/
patisserie to sample their
delicious pastries.

Khochu Kharcho $$
Georgian   Map 6 D3
Sadovaya ulitsa 39/41, 190031
Tel *310 3236*
One of the city's few 24-hour
restaurants, serves a great range
of delectable Georgian favourites
including *kharcho* – the traditional Georgian meat soup.

DK Choice

Krokodil $$
International   Map 5 B2
Galernaya ulitsa 18, 190000
Tel *314 9437*
Small and intimate, this
enduringly popular bar and
restaurant has a broad selection
of tempting international dishes
and excellent fish options that
include fried halibut and
salmon steak. There is an
excellent children's menu.

DK Choice

Mindal Café $$
Georgian   Map 5 B2
*Angliyskaya naberezhnaya 26,
190000*
Tel *312 3238*
Housed in a stunning historic
mansion with a summer terrace
and glorious views over the
Neva, Mindal Café is the perfect
place to sample Georgia's
exemplary cuisine. Diners can
expect personal attention and
cooking demonstrations from
the well-known head chef
Marina Naumova.

Romeo's Bar & Kitchen $$
Italian   **Map** 5 B4
Prospekt Rimskovo-Korsakova 43, 190068
Tel *572 5448*
One of the top Italian restaurants, conveniently close to the Mariinskiy Theatre. The many tempting choices include squid ink ravioli and asparagus with fried eggs.

Russian Vodka Room No. 1 $$
Russian   **Map** 5 B2
Konnogvardeyskiy bulvar 4, 190000
Tel *570 6420*
Old-world style dining room with modern interpretations of Russian classics. More than 100 different varieties of vodkas feature in the menu. The restaurant also houses a museum of Russian vodka.

Salhino $$
Georgian   **Map** 5 C4
Voznesenskiy prospekt 55, 190068
Tel *314 8682*
Lovely place that is very popular with locals. It is renowned for its *chebureks* – deep-fried meat pastries with a thin, crispy crust. Children's menu available.

Further Afield

Du Nord 1834 $
French
Ligovskiy prospekt 41/83, 191040
Tel *578 1245*
This charming French café is one of the few 24-hour eateries in St Petersburg. It has an appetizing selection of pastries and also serves classic French dishes.

Lagidze $
Georgian
Ulitsa Belinskovo 3, 191014
Tel *579 1104*
Located on one of the city's shortest and best restaurant-lined streets, Lagidze provides Georgian food and wine in a modest but modern interior.

ObedBufet $
International
Nevskiy prospekt 114, 191025
Tel *961 6311*
Upscale café that boasts salad bars, steam tables, live-cooking stations and a dessert bar. The focus is on freshly prepared, hearty food. Both dine-in and takeaway options available.

Pelmennaya Dyuzhina $
Russian
Ligovskiy prospekt 30a, 191040
Tel *318 0017*
Part of a successful chain of *pelmini* eateries in town, offering a mind-boggling array of one of

Russia's best-known dishes – stuffed dumplings. The wooden furniture adds to the warm ambience.

Puri $
Uzbek/Caucasian
Industrialnyy prospekt 17/1a, 195426
Tel *240 2030*
Serves faultless Uzbek and Caucasian delights, many of which are cooked in a traditional *tandoor* oven. The comfortable Eastern-style interior adds character to the place.

Schelkunchik $
International
Ligovskiy prospekt 10/118, 191036
Tel *717 6868*
Simple canteen-style eatery with its own micro-brewery. Serves a reliable choice of delectable Russian and international dishes.

Tony's Kitchen $$
International
Malyy prospekt 88, Vasilevskiy ostrov, 199406
Tel *988 8020*
Spacious, welcoming place spread over two floors with an open summer terrace. Good range of meaty Russian and European dishes, plus hookah options.

Ukrop $
Vegetarian
Ulitsa Marata 23, 191025
Tel *946 3036*
Superb café-restaurant with bright raw-wood interior and an imaginative range of artfully presented vegetarian and vegan fare.

Baklazhan $$
Asian
Ligovskiy prospekt 30a, 191040
Tel *677 7372*
Relaxed, Georgian-inspired restaurant with expertly prepared renditions of Asian classics at reasonable prices. Home-made noodles and baked goods come highly recommended.

DK Choice

Cafe Abajour $$
Steakhouse
9-ya liniya 20 Vasilevskiy ostrov, 199004
Tel *325 2236*
A steak-lover's paradise, Abajour is second to none when it comes to serving big juicy steaks cooked to absolute perfection and accompanied by an excellent choice of wines. Homely modern interior attracts a smart young crowd. Book ahead.

Caffe Italia $$
Italian
Prospekt Bakunina 5, 191024
Tel *905 6474*
Expect bona fide Italian cuisine at this popular spot, served by its Italian staff for added authenticity. Spacious, with a cheerful ambience.

Cat Café $$
Caucasian
Stremyannaya ulitsa 22/3, 191025
Tel *571 3377*
Intimate place adorned with cat-related paraphernalia that serves lovely Armenian and Georgian cuisine. Off the beaten track, but well worth a visit.

Claret Café $$
Russian
Helvetia Hotel, Ulitsa Marata 11, 191025
Tel *710 6546*
Small restaurant with chic styling, an open fire and excellent service. Classic Russian fare complemented by a good range of wines.

Dickens $$
English
Naberezhnaya reki Fontanki 108, 2nd floor, 1-90013
Tel *702 6263*
Inviting English pub specializing in steaks and game dishes. It offers a small but respectable wine list, old-world-style decor and lovely views onto the Fontanka.

The brightly decorated and popular Baklazhan restaurant

For more information on types of restaurants *see pages 180–81*

Ferma $$
International
Finlyandskiy prospekt 1, 194044
Tel *643 0430*
Very upmarket, featuring concrete walls adorned with a quirky collection of farming paraphernalia. Serves a high standard of Russian and European cuisine.

Karl and Friedrich $$
International
Yuzhnaya doroga 15, Krestovskiy ostrov, 197110
Tel *633 0303*
Fun restaurant-brewery in the woods with outdoor seating. Aimed at families – has a children's entertainer every evening and weekend. Meat-dominated menu and great beer.

Mamalyga $$
Caucasian
Leninskiy prospekt 84/1, 198332
Tel *646 7571*
This cavernous yet cosy, restaurant offers a variety of Georgian food, from mouth-watering cheese-filled bread (*khachapuri*) to kebabs grilled on an open fire. There is a spacious playroom for kids with a babysitter on duty.

Marcelli's $$
Italian
Ulitsa Vosstaniya 15, 191036
Tel *986 9111*
Italian restaurant/café and deli with casual, spacious interior. Founded on a philosophy of serving the best possible food at the most reasonable price.

Geografia $$
Fusion
Ulitsa Rubinshteina 5
Tel *340 0074*
This eatery has become popular for its eclectic menu of dishes made using fresh local produce and served in an upscale setting. Extensive wine and cocktail list.

Moskva $$
International
Nevskiy prospekt 114, 191025
Tel *937 6497*
Stunning sixth-floor location with panoramic city views from the summer terrace. The vast menu covers recipes from around the world prepared to exacting standards by specialist chefs.

Palermo $$
Italian
Naberezhnaya reki Fontanki 50, 191002
Tel *764 3764*
Good Italian family restaurant, offering classic Sicilian recipes

with the addition of a few European favourites. Decorated in Italian style with frescoes, it has a great atmosphere, too.

DK Choice

Pirosmani $$
Georgian
Bolshoy prospekt 14 Petrogradskaya, 197110
Tel *235 4666*
This colourful Georgian restaurant is set out like a Georgian hill village, with wattle-and-daub houses, a stained-glass window and ponds. Walls are hung with works by Pirosmani, arguably the best Georgian painter of the 20th century. Try the *lobio* (beans in spicy sauce) washed down with Old Tbilisi wine.

Russian Fishing $$
Russian
Yuzhnaya doroga 11, Krestovskiy ostrov, 197110
Tel *633 0200*
Stylized fisherman's hut with a pond. Guests can catch their own fish – trout, sturgeon, beluga, sterlet – and watch it being cooked. Attracts families during the day.

Ryba $$
International
Ulitsa Akademika Pavlova 5, 197022
Tel *918 6969*
Choice of traditional Italian food including a wide variety of pastas and pizzas or Asian wok-based dishes at one of the highest restaurants in the city. Breathtaking views over rooftops.

Schengen $$
International
Kirochnaya ulitsa 5
Tel *922 1197*
One of the few restaurants in town that offer traditional Western breakfast every day. The superb chef cooks up delicious, wholesome dishes popular with tourists and locals alike. Great service.

Serbish $$
Serbian **Map** 3 A5
Ulitsa Pestelya 8/36, 191028
Tel *904 3844*
The city's only Balkan restaurant lays on the charm with its minimal, homely decor and an extensive list of Serbian wines. The restaurant's speciality is *cevapi*, a grilled dish made from minced meat that is typical of the region.

Shinok $$
Ukrainian
Zagorodnyy prospekt 13, 191002
Tel *571 8262*
Decent Ukrainian food served in large portions accompanied by Ukrainian vodka. There is a Ukrainian folk show every evening at 8pm, and lots of jollity. The interior is rustic; the staff, friendly.

Staraya Derevnya $$
Russian
Ulitsa Savushkina 72, 197183
Tel *431 0000*
With an informal interior styled as an old-fashioned apartment, this is one of the friendliest restaurants in town. Enjoy traditional Russian fare with Russian and Gypsy song performances most evenings.

The charming rustic interior of Shinok

Key to Price Guide *see page 186*

Sunduk $$
Café
Furshtatskaya ulitsa 42, 191123
Tel 272 3100
Offbeat art café that boasts an extensive wine list and a filling Russian and European menu. Good live jazz performances keep the atmosphere lively.

Tres Amigos $$
Mexican
Ulitsa Rubinshteyna 25, 191002
Tel 572 2685
The restaurant has a bizarre mix of decor inspired by Aztecs and beer halls. Good selection of Latin American fare and cocktails. Excellent children's room.

Troika $$
Russian
Zagorodnyy prospekt 27, 191180
Tel 407 5343
Lots of glitz and glamour; good food; but Troika focuses more on entertainment; think elaborate floor shows with circus acrobatics, folk songs and Russian dancing.

Xren $$
International
Zagorodnyy prospekt 13, 191002
Tel 347 8850
Four uniquely styled rooms, well prepared and stylishly presented food and a good selection of wines. Marbled beef steaks are a house speciality. DJs every weekend.

DK Choice

Birreria $$$
Italian
Vladimirskiy prospekt 19, 191002
Tel 943 6004
Magnificent views of Vladimirskiy Cathedral, a superb selection of Italian beers, as well as the chance to watch football matches in style make Birreria a popular place for a meal, drinks or even a sedate lunch. The menu features classic Italian fare, with thin-crust pizzas topping the list, and delectable Neapolitan street food.

Beyond St Petersburg

Bake'n'Bards $
Russian
Litseiskiy pereulok 1/4, Pushkin, 196601
Tel 996 0235
In a historical 19th-century house with preserved interiors that give the feeling of being in Tsarskoe Selo during the time of the tsars. Serves exemplary renditions of traditional Russian fare.

The splendid decor at the Dom Berga restaurant

Dom Berga $
Russian
Bolshaya Moskovskaya ulitsa 24, Veliky Novgorod, 173000
Tel (8162) 948838
Traditional Russian cuisine in an atmospheric 19th-century mansion. A good venue to sample *Medovukha* – an old Russian alcoholic drink made with honey.

Mechta $
Russian
Konyushennaya ulitsa, 38/37, Pushkin, 196601
Tel 451 7280
After exploring the palace and grounds at Tsarskoe Tselo, this cosy spot offers hearty Russian fare in a country cottage setting.

La Chatte Café $$
Café
Bolshaya Moskovskaya ulitsa 86, Veliky Novgorod, 173014
Tel (8162) 998753
Modern café serving cakes and pastries as well as soups, pizzas, sandwiches. There are cocktails and draft beer to accompany the food.

Daniel $$
International
Srednyaya ulitsa 2/3, Pushkin, 196601
Tel 466 9116
Set in wooded grounds with covered outdoor seating amid flower beds, Daniel provides a fine choice of Russian and European cuisine. Excellent service.

Napoli $$
Italian
Ulitsa Studencheskaya 21/43, Veliky Novgorod, 173014
Tel (8162) 603095
Laid-back Italian restaurant offering authentic dishes from various regions of Italy and a good selection of home-made pasta. Intimate ambience.

Oldham $$
English
Bolshaya Moskovskaya ulitsa 55, Veliky Novgorod, 173023
Tel (8162) 900560
Popular English pub and steak house serving ale on tap and plenty of delicious pub food. Convivial atmosphere.

Shalyapin $$
Russian
Ulitsa Nagornaya 1, Repino, 197738
Tel 432 0775
Charming spot with a classic 19th-century interior, serving irresistible *shashlik* (kebabs). Vast fireplace in winter and roof terrace in summer.

Stroganoff Bar & Grill $$
Russian
Primorskoye shosse 418, Repino, 197738
Tel 432 0575
Designed to resemble a country mansion, this is a great place to relax and enjoy some fine Russian cuisine. It has a children's playroom and a separate menu that caters to young taste buds.

XIX Vek $$
Russian
Srednyaya ulitsa 2a, Pushkin, 196600
Tel 465 2685
Classy restaurant popular with wedding parties. Just a short walk from Catherine's Palace, the place serves superb Russian food in palatial surroundings.

For more information on types of restaurants *see pages 180–81*

Light Meals and Snacks

Despite their plastic chairs and metal tables, Russian and ethnic cafés often serve very tasty food – from simple sandwiches to hefty meat dishes. Look out for the word кафе (café) and try one. Cautious travellers can experiment in one of the restaurants listed opposite, which frequently offer moderately priced meals between noon and 4pm. A number of bars and "art cafés" with live music (see p207) also have excellent kitchens. (In the evening these may be filled with people and noise, but at lunchtime they are calmer.) During the summer many cafés add tables outside – which is great for people-watching. In colder weather, the ground-floor cafés of the Moika or Radisson SAS hotels, Jili-bili or Il Patio are almost as good.

Russian

Traditional Russian dishes such as borsch and draniki (potato pancakes) are widely offered. Pelmeni (dumplings filled with meat) and vareniki (dumplings filled with fruit or vegetables) are in a class of their own. Specialist pelmeni establishments are truly "local", with no flashy decor or tourists. Try the **Pelmeni Bar** behind the Peter and Paul Fortress. Russian bliny and blinchiki (flat pancakes) come in both sweet and savoury varieties at the outstandingly cheap **Cherdak**.

Some places listed are notable mainly for their location: **Holst Maslo** is near the Hermitage (see pp86–95); **Sadko** is next to the Mariinskiy Theatre; **Café de Clie** is next to the Peter and Paul Fortress. Near St Isaac's Square (see p81) is **Idiot**, a vegetarian café popular with ex-pats. **Dachniki** is cheap and cheerful. **Botanica** is known for its vegetarian dishes and generous portions.

Ethnic Food

Georgian and Armenian foods are popular in St Petersburg. The **Kavkaz-Bar** restaurant (see p189) also has an informal café, and other small cafés offer Caucasian dishes. **Namaste** is a highly-rated Indian café, while **Wong Kar Wine** serves Asian food alongside splendid views of the Mikhailovskiy Castle and the Summer Garden. Filling Uzbek food is on offer at **Chaikhana Alo Halol**, a bustling and cheap café located near all the major tourist attractions in the city centre.

Fast Food, Pizza and Pasta

The first Russian fast food was pirozhki, small shaped pies filled with potato, cabbage or meat. The best pirozhki come from **Stolle**. Pyshki, tiny deep-fried donuts usually covered in powdered sugar, are also extremely popular. The oldest pyshki shop is **Pyshechnaya,** which opened in 1958 on Bolshaya Konyushennaya ulitsa.

In addition to the well-known fast-food chains, local options include **Tarelka** and **Stolovaya #1 Kopeika**, where customers can choose by pointing. **Teremok** specializes in pancakes. **Troitskiy Most** is a popular and inexpensive vegetarian option. Pizza and pasta houses are popular. (**Il Patio** caters for children.)

Pastries and Sweets

Russians are sweet-toothed, and in private homes tea is never offered without biscuits or cakes. Ice cream – best bought from one of the many street sellers – is enjoyed all year round. **Sladkoezhka** sells a wide range of fresh cream desserts and pastries, and is probably the city's favourite spot for a hit of sugar. Coffee shops, such as **Bushe** and the **Shokoladnitsa** chain, also offer a variety of cheese-cakes and cakes. At **Stirka 40°** customers drink tea while doing their washing (it doubles as the city's only launderette).

Pubs and Bars

Most bars serve a good range of food. In addition to the standard English and Irish pubs, where food is unadventurous, expensive and the clientele is composed mostly of ex-pats, there are now a number of Russian "pubs", such as **Barslona** and **Tolsty Fraer**, that offer a range of excellent local beers. **The Office Pub** offers a rest from the bustle of Nevskiy prospekt, just behind Kazan Cathedral.

One of the joys of summer is to drink beer sitting on one of the pontoons that appear with the warm weather on the canals and rivers, particularly around Nevskiy prospekt. While such places do not usually offer food, they do allow customers to linger and watch the sunset.

Sushi

An enduring craze for sushi bars – which tend to be quite good – means that there are plenty of good alternatives for quick, healthy lunches in St Petersburg. Menus are easy to understand because they include pictures of each dish. Try **Dve Palochki** or **Planet Sushi**.

Eating Out on Day Trips

More effort is required when seeking a place for a modest lunch outside the city. Pavlovsk (see pp160–63) and Peterhof (see pp150–53) have reasonable cafés in the palaces, although space is limited in summer. Peterhof's tiny **Trapeza** is always a favourite. At Tsarskoe Selo (see pp154–7), there are several cafés along and around Oranzhereynaya ulitsa, leading off the park. Gatchina Palace (see p149) has cafés in the grounds and even Oranienbaum (see p148) has a tiny café, too. In general, however, the best option is to take a picnic to Gatchina or Oranienbaum. (Delicious takeaway pies can be bought from **Stolle**.) In Veliky Novgorod (see pp164–7), the **Golden Ladle** serves many kinds of beer and snacks.

DIRECTORY

Russian

Antrakt
Антракт
Pereulok Krylova 2.
Map 6 F2.
Tel 310 4267.

Botanica
Ботаника
Ulitsa Pestelya 7.
Map 3 A5.
Tel 272 7091.

Brynza
Брынза
Kamennoostrovskiy 10A.
Map 2 E2.
Tel 944 4490.

Café de Clie
Kronverkskiy prospekt 27.
Map 2 D2.
Tel 232 3606.

Cherdak
Чердак
Ligovskiy prospekt 17.
Map 7 C1.
Tel 272 5564.

Dachniki
Дачники
Nevskiy prospekt 20.
Map 6 E1.
Tel 905 4445.

Holst Maslo
Холст Масло
Bolshaya Morskaya
ulitsa 7.
Map 6 D1.
Tel 570 4069.

Idiot
Идиот
Naberezhnaya reki
Moyki 82.
Map 5 C2.
Tel 946 5173.

Pelmeni Bar
Пельмени-бар
Kronverkskiy prospekt 53a
(entry from ulitsa Markina).
Map 1 C3.
Tel 498 0977.

Sadko
Садко
Ulitsa Glinki 2.
Map 5 B3.
Tel 903 2373.

Soiree
Суаре
Ulitsa Zhukovskovo 28.
Map 7 B1.
Tel 272 3512.

Troitskiy Most
Naberezhnaya reki
Moyki 30.
Map 6 E1.
Tel 921 5978.

Tryn-Trava
Трын-Трава
Nevskiy prospekt 22–24.
Map 6 E1.
Tel 571 0385.

Wolkonsky
Волконский
Bolshaya Konyushennaya
21/23 (second floor).
Map 6 E1.
Tel +7 911 024 5607.

Ethnic Food

Chaikhana Alo Halol
Чайхана Аъло Халол
Naberezhnaya kanala
Griboedova 52.
Map 6 D2.
Tel +8 952 353 5012.

Namaste
Malaya Konyushennaya
ul 5.
Map 6 E1.
Tel 570 6886.

Wong Kar Wine
Naberezhnaya reki
Fontanki 14.
Map 7 A1.
Tel 943 1930.

Fast Food, Pizza and Pasta

Il Patio
Nevskiy prospekt 30.
Map 6 E1. **Tel** 314 3215.
Nevskiy prospekt 182.
Map 8 E3. **Tel** 71 3177.

Pelmenia
Пельмения
Tel 415 4185.

Pyshechnaya
Пышечная
Bolshaya
Konyushennaya 25.
Map 2 E5.
Tel 314 0868.

Stolle
Штолле
Nevskiy prospekt 11.
Map 6 D1. **Tel** 314 7021.
Vladimirskiy prospekt 15.
Map 7 A2. **Tel** 499 4866.

Stolovaya #1 Kopeika
Столовая № 1
Копейка
Nevskiy prospekt 54.
Map 6 F1.
Tel 571 2400.

Tarelka
Тарелка
Nevskiy prospekt 53.
Map 7 B2.
Tel 383 5501.

Teremok (pancakes)
Теремок
Nevskiy prospekt 60.
Map 7 A2.
Tel 363 2332.

Troitskiy Most
Троицкий мост
Kamennoostrovskiy
prospekt 9/2.
Map 2 E2.
Tel 942 2397.

Coffee, Pastries and Sweets

Bushe
Буше
Ulitsa Vosstaniya 10.
Map 7 B1.
Tel 640 5151 (ext. 41).

Café Singer
Кафе Зингер
Nevskiy 28.
Map 6 E1.
Tel 571 8223.

FermA
Sadovaya ulitsa 42.
Map 6 D3.
Tel 643 0400.

Shokoladnitsa
Шоколадница
Nevskiy prospekt 18.
Map 6 D1.
Tel 677 1300.

Sladkoezhka
Сладкоежка
Marata ulitsa 2.
Map 7 B2. **Tel** 571 1420.
Sadovaya ulitsa 60.
Map 5 C4. **Tel** 310 8144.
Gorokhovaya 44.
Map 6 E3. **Tel** 310 8005.

Stirka 40°
Стирка 40°
Kazanskaya ulitsa 26.
Map 6 D2.
Tel 314 5371.

Pubs and Bars

Barslona
Барслона
Dumskaya ulitsa 1.
Map 6 E2.
Tel 900 2271.

The Office Pub
Офис Паб
Kazanskaya ulitsa 5.
Map 6 E2.
Tel 571 5428.

Tolsty Fraer
Толстый Фраер
Dumskaya ul 3.
Map 6 E2.
Tel 570 0102.

Sushi

Dve Palochki
Две палочки
Ulitsa Vosstaniya 15.
Map 7 C1.
Tel 335 0222.

Eurasia
Евразия
Nevskiy prospekt 13.
Map 6 D1.
Tel 315 1858.

Planet Sushi
Планета Суши
Nevskiy prospekt 30.
Map 6 E1.
Tel 314 8215.

Day Trips

Golden Ladle
Золотой Ковш
Novo-Luchanskaya ulitsa
14, Veliky Novgorod.
Tel (8162) 730599.

Linea
Sankt-Peterburgskiy
prospekt 46, Petrodvorets
(Peterhof).
Tel 450 7878.

Podvorie
Подворье
Filtrovskoye 16,
Pavlovsk.
Tel 454 5464.

Trapeza
Трапеза
Kalinskaya ulitsa 9,
Petrodvorets (Peterhof).
Tel 450 6393.

SHOPS AND MARKETS

A trip round St Petersburg's shops and markets provides an insight into local life. Even today, shopping in the city requires flexibility and even a sense of adventure: you can never depend on finding what you set out to find, but may confidently expect to end up buying something you never guessed you needed. Imported goods have pushed out many local products. Even so, Russian linen, the city's celebrated Krupsksaya chocolates, vodka, caviar, and Russian crafts and toys all make wonderful gifts. Larger shops are concentrated around main streets such as Nevskiy and Bolshoy prospekts, and metro stations, notably Sennaya Ploshchad and Vasilevskiy Ostrov. However, most buildings are occupied by shops or restaurants at ground level. Do venture in.

Ladies' fashion at one of the numerous upscale boutiques along Nevskiy prospekt

Opening Hours

Hours vary, but shops usually open from 10am until at least 7pm, though "fashionable" outlets may stay open later. A few, mainly cheap food shops, close for lunch. On Sundays department stores remain open, as do other large shops. During the summer, smaller places may reduce their hours and close at weekends. There are 24-hour food shops all over town.

How to Pay

Accepting payment in non-Russian currency is a criminal offence. The only place you might be able to pay in foreign currency is at a tourist market.

There are numerous, reliable exchange offices and ATMs inside metro stations and outside banks (see p216). Moreover, many stores now accept credit cards. However, cash is still the predominant way to pay in Russia, even in large cities. Despite the many signs advertising the option to pay by card, don't be surprised if you are told that the machine is "out of order." In some shops, customers are forced to peer at goods stacked behind the counter. If you would like a closer look, point to what you want and say "mozhno" ("may I?"). To purchase something, pay for it at the cash desk and then return to collect the item from the counter with your receipt. Shop assistants will usually realize if you do not speak Russian, and will write down the prices for you to hand to the cashier. Defective goods can generally be returned provided they are accompanied by a receipt.

Bargaining Etiquette

If a set price is displayed at markets, this indicates no bargaining. In all other cases you can usually get some reduction if you haggle, especially since visitors (and prosperous-looking Russians) are likely to be quoted a higher price. Haggling in Russia, however, is a serious matter, so do not bother unless you genuinely intend to buy.

Buying Art and Antiques

Under Russian law, all objects made before 1956, and all objects made from valuable materials such as gold, silver, precious stones and fur, are subject to strict export controls. Works of art, including contemporary watercolours, also fall under this ruling, likewise books published before 1946. Be aware that, although there are green and red channels at the airport customs, and not all suitcases are X-rayed, there are random checks. In practice, customs officials may turn a blind eye to prints and watercolours without frames, and unless a book is extremely rare you are likely to be able to export it without authorization. In all other cases, strict rules are applied. Permission to export both books and art objects can be obtained from a department of the **Ministry of Culture**. This process is relatively speedy. The gallery from which or the artist from whom the item is purchased should always assist with the paperwork.

If you have not obviously tried to cheat customs, any objects not allowed through can simply be handed over to someone who is remaining in St Petersburg. If, however, there is any hint of foul play, the item will be placed in storage at

Second-hand bookshop sign

Russian box-camera (1920s)

Export Permissions

Ministry of Culture
Министерство культуры
Ministerstvo kultury
Malaya Morskaya ulitsa 17.
Map 6 D1. **Tel** 571 0302.
Open 11am–5pm Mon–Fri.

Tertia *(see p201)* has exportable antiques to suit all budgets

the airport, for which, if you wish to reclaim it later, there will be a charge. Any objects that remain unclaimed after a year will be confiscated, as will objects which have obviously been hidden to avoid detection. Valuable pieces may be donated to a museum.

Department Stores

Known as a "univermag" or universal shop, Russian department stores evolved from the old trading rows, which were literally rows of kiosks owned by different traders. Present-day department stores have altered a great deal and now operate as a complex of boutiques and distinct sections. Even though the goods on sale do not differ much from those that are available in European shops, every visitor to St Petersburg should explore **Gostinyy Dvor** *(see p110)*, the oldest shopping centre in the city, and **Passazh** *(see p50)*, a smaller department store. Despite the glitzy goods, however, the narrow passages and layout speak of a different age.

The newer shopping centre such as the **Nevsky Centre** *(see p201)* and **Galeria** are more like Western European and American shopping malls, with upmarket boutiques and food outlets. **DLT** (Dom Leningradskoy Torgovli) *(see p201)* on Bolshaya Konyushennaya is the city's top luxury department store, with a wide selection of designer clothing and fragrance.

Markets and Bazaars

Food can be bought in one of the 11 markets (*rynoks*) dotted around the city. The most centrally located is **Kuznechnyy** *(see p201)*, just off Nevskiy prospekt, which sells flowers, fruit, vegetables, delicious home-made cream cheese and wonderful natural honey which you can sample. Note that prices at markets tend to be higher than at the supermarkets, but buyers do have the option of haggling.

Apraksin Dvor has been the site of a thriving market since the mid-18th century. Today it sells everything from cigars to CDs. While the market is undergoing reconstruction, only the shops that have a roof over them remain open.

Flea markets are perpetually being moved on, though some sellers continue to pop up at the city's main markets. The true seeker of unusual finds amid the trash will set off on a Friday or Saturday morning for Udelnaya metro, where a vast unofficial market sprawls along the railway line.

Souvenir watercolours and prints of varying quality are sold throughout the year at the open-air market, **Vernisazh** *(see p201)*, outside the Church of St Catherine *(see p50)* on Nevskiy prospekt. The small **Souvenir Market** *(see p201)* near the Church on Spilled Blood *(see p102)*, sells a wide selection of *matryoshka* dolls *(see p198)*. You are also likely to find handmade chess sets, watches, fur hats, old cameras and military paraphernalia.

Visitors browse the shelves at the Hermitage museum Shop

Museum Shops

The best museum shop is found inside the **Hermitage** *(see pp86–95)* and sells reproduction prints and objects, books on the city and its art, jewellery and silk scarves, both inside the museum and online: www.hermitagemuseum.org.

The **Russian Museum** *(see pp106–9)* has several outlets, though these are not run by the museum itself. The best is in the Stroganov Palace *(see p114)*.

Of the other shops attached to museums, the best are found in the **Peter and Paul Fortress** *(see pp68–9)* and in the palaces at **Pavlovsk** *(see pp160–63)*, **Peterhof** *(see pp150–53)* and **Tsarskoe Selo** *(see pp154–7)*. These tend to sell souvenirs (rather than reproductions of exhibits and other related objects): amber and semi-precious-stone jewellery, dolls, lacquered boxes and books on the city. The prices are not fixed, so check how much something is worth before starting to haggle.

Souvenirs sold at the tourist market opposite the Church on Spilled Blood

What to Buy in St Petersburg

It is easy to find interesting and beautiful souvenirs in St Petersburg. They range in price from small, enamelled badges, which sell for very little, through to hand-painted Palekh boxes and samovars which can be very expensive. Traditional crafts were encouraged by the state in the old Soviet Union and many items, such as lacquered boxes and bowls, matryoshka dolls, wooden toys and chess sets, are still made by craftsmen and women using age-old methods. Memorabilia from the Soviet era also make good souvenirs and Russia is definitely the best place to buy the national specialities, vodka and caviar.

Samovar
Used to boil water to make tea, samovars come in all shapes and sizes (see p185). A permit is needed to export a pre-1945 samovar.

Vodka and Caviar
An enormous variety of both clear and flavoured vodkas (such as lemon and pepper) is available (see p184). They make excellent accompaniments to black and red caviar (ikra), which are often served with blini (see p182).

Red caviar

Clear vodka

Flavoured vodka

Black caviar

Malachite egg   Amber ring

Semi-Precious Stones
Malachite, amber, jasper and a variety of marbles from the Ural Mountains are used to make a wide range of items – everything from jewellery and chess sets to inlaid table tops.

Wooden Toy
These crudely carved wooden toys often have moving parts. They are known as Bogorodskiye toys and make charming gifts.

Matryoshka Dolls
These dolls fit one inside the other and come in a huge variety of styles. The traditional dolls are the prettiest, but those painted as Russian, Soviet and world leaders are also very popular.

Chess Sets
Attractive chess sets made from all kinds of beautiful materials, including malachite, are widely available. This wooden chess set is painted in the same style as the matryoshka dolls.

Lacquered Artifacts

Painted wooden or papier-mâché artifacts make popular souvenirs and are sold all over the city. The exquisite hand-painted, lacquered Palekh boxes can be very costly, but the eggs decorated with icons and the typical red, black and gold bowls are more affordable.

Palekh Box

The art of miniature painting on papier-mâché items originated in the late 18th century. Artists in the four villages of Palekh, Fedoskino, Mstera and Kholui still produce these hand-painted marvels. The images are based on Russian fairy tales and legends.

Painted wooden egg

Bowl with Spoon

The brightly painted bowls and spoons, usually known as "Khokhloma", have a lacquer coating, forming a surface which is durable, but not resistant to boiling liquids.

Russian hand-painted tray

Tuners

Strings

Musical Instruments

Russian folk music uses a wide range of musical instruments. This *gusli* is similar to the Western psaltery and is played by plucking the strings with both hands. Also available are the brightly painted balalaika and the *bayan* (accordion).

Russian Scarf

These brilliantly coloured traditional woollen shawls are good for keeping out the cold of a Russian winter. Mass-produced polyester versions are also available, mostly in big department stores, but these are not as warm.

Gzhel Vase

Ceramics with a distinctive blue-and-white pattern are produced in Gzhel, an area near Moscow. Ranging from figurines to household crockery, they are popular with Russians and visitors alike.

Soviet Memorabilia

An eclectic array of memorabilia from the Soviet era is on sale. Old banknotes, coins, pocket watches and Red Army kits, including belt buckles, badges and other items of uniform, can be found alongside watches with cartoons of KGB agents on their faces.

Pocket watch

Badge with
Soviet symbols

Red Army
leather belt

Where to Shop in St Petersburg

The main department stores in the city centre stock everything from souvenirs to vodka and furs, all of a high quality. For some local products, however, it is best to visit specialist shops, most of which are conveniently located in or near the centre. In a city which prides itself on its intellectuals, books and art are, appropriately, St Petersburg's other main exports. Soviet memorabilia has also become very popular for souvenirs.

Food and Drink

Good vodka is to be had everywhere. Avoid cheaper brands in "amusing" packaging: they are invariably of poor quality. Diplomat and Gzhelka are good, standard brands.

Caviar should be bought only from a food shop or department store. **Gostinyy Dvor** and the **Land** supermarket store on Vladimirskiy prospekt are the most central, reliable places for both vodka and caviar. The many **Gastronom 811** outlets also stock a wide range of alcoholic drinks. All kinds of food shopping can be done at **Kuznechnyy**, which is stacked high with Russian specialities. All kinds of meats and cheeses are on sale at the **Stockmann Delicatessan**.

St Petersburg's **Krupskaya Fabrika** chocolate factory has long been famous in the Soviet Union. The **Chocolate Museum** sells novelties such as famous buildings crafted in chocolate.

Souvenirs and Crafts

In summer, when traders set up stalls by tourist spots, the city is flooded with *matryoshka* dolls, music boxes shaped like a church, painted lacquerware and chess sets. In winter, it can be quiet on the retail front. The **Souvenir Market** and **Vernisazh** market, however, operate all year, and there are good gifts to be found in Gostinyy Dvor and Passazh department stores. Shops in or near museums also stock souvenirs – notably those in the Stroganov Palace (see p114) and Tsarskoe Selo (see pp154–7). The shop inside the Hermitage (see pp86–95) sells higher range goods and excellent art books. Local porcelain from the

Imperial Porcelain Factory is much prized. The factory makes everything from gaily painted rustic cups to reproduction revolutionary-era porcelain.

Soviet Memorabilia

Artifacts from the Soviet era are now produced specifically for the tourist market. Be careful when buying on the street: many apparently genuine articles are modern reproductions. Original pieces can be picked up at the **Souvenir Market**, though the **Komissionnyy Magazin** shop is more reliable. The flea market at **Udelnaya** is a must for all lovers of Soviet-era memorabilia. Soviet badges are easily transportable. A selection of actual Soviet military surplus is available from **Voennyy Kollektsioner**.

Antiques and Art

Although older antiques and many works of art need to be cleared with customs, some pieces, such as small watercolours, may be exempt. Many shops are extortionately expensive, but **Tertia** is an exception, with readily export-able items to suit all pockets, and **Russkie Sezony** is a veritable treasure trove. Only buy an expensive object if you are sure the relevant paper-work and export applications can be obtained (see p196). **Antikvariat** should be able to provide the paperwork for purchases made in the centre.

Paintings all require export licences, but as galleries can provide these themselves is it worth dropping in to **Anna Nova**, **S.P.A.S.** or **Borey** to see what they have. The **Union of**

Artists has exhibitions by traditional local artists. The **Pushkinskaya 10** art centre stages shows at weekends, some with works for sale.

Books, Film and Music

St Petersburgers perceive their city as an intellectual focal point, with a great literary and artistic past. The centre has been taken over by book chains such as **Bookvoed**, but there are some smaller new and second-hand bookshops. The best are still **Dom Knigi** and the **Writers' Bookshop**. If you need a holiday novel in English, try **Anglia**, Dom Knigi or Bookvoed. More unusual, second-hand English books – usually donated by tourists – can sometimes be found in **Akademkniga** and **Na Liteynom**. **Severnaya Lira** sells sheet music – everything from classical to folk songs – as well as instruments, CDs and books on music. Art books can be bought in Dom Knigi.

DVDs of English-language films and CDs can be purchased in shops such as **Phonoteka**.

Furs and Fashion

Clothes and other accessories are mainly imported. Elegant boutiques occupy part of Gostinyy Dvor and run along streets such as naberezhnaya kanala Griboedova and ulitsa Zhukovskovo. Some local designers have their own boutiques; notably **Tatyana Parfyonova**, whose garments have been purchased by the Russian Museum.

Shapole and the **Marina Sedova Hat Salon** offer hats in everything from straw to fur. Furs are sold in **Lena**, Paloma and on the top floor of Gostinyy Dvor. Russian linen is also a good buy. Elegant shift dresses and the traditional *kosovorotka* (peasant shirt) are found in **Russky Len**. Fashion pieces are sold at **Toto**. Locally made jewellery of semi-precious stones from the Urals and amber from the Baltic is available in jewellers such as Samotsvety.

DIRECTORY

Department Stores

DLT
Bolshaya Konyushennaya ulitsa 21–23.
Map 6 E1.
Tel 648 0848.

Galeria
Галерея
Ligovskiy prospekt 30.
Map 7 C3.

Gostinyy Dvor
Гостиный двор
Nevskiy prospekt 35.
Map 6 F2.

Nevsky Centre
Nevskiy prospekt 114–116.
Map 7 B2.
Tel 313 9319.

Passazh
Пассаж
Nevskiy prospekt 48.
Map 6 F1.

Markets

Apraksin Dvor
Sadovaya ulitsa 30.
Map 6 E2.

Kuznechnyy
Кузнечный рынок
Kuznechnyy pereulok 3.
Map 7 A3.

Souvenir Market
Рынок сувениров
Naberezhnaya kanala Griboedova, by Church on Spilled Blood.
Map 2 E5.

Vernisazh
Вернисаж
Nevskiy prospekt 32–4.
Map 6 E1.

Food and Drink

Chocolate Museum
Музей шоколада
Nevskiy prospekt 17.
Map 6 E1. **Tel** 315 1348.

Gastronom 811
Гастроном 811
Nevskiy prospekt 66.
Map 7 A1.
Tel 314 8559.

Krupskaya Fabrika
Кондитерская фабрика им. Н.К. Крупской
Ulitsa Pravdy 6.
Map 7 A3.

Land
Лэнд
Vladimirskiy prospekt 19.
Map 7 A2. **Tel** 324 1324.

Stockmann Delicatessen
Гастроном Стокманн
Nevskiy prospekt 114–116. **Map** 7 B2.
Tel 313 6000.

Souvenirs and Crafts

Imperial Porcelain
Императорский фарфоровый завод
Obukhovskoy oborony prospekt 151.
Map 8 F4. **Tel** 608 4944.
Vladimirskiy prospekt 7.
Map 7 A2. **Tel** 713 1513.
Nevskiy prospekt 160.
Map 8 D3. **Tel** 717 4838.

Soviet Memorabilia

Komissionnyy Magazin
Комиссионный магазин
1-ya Sovetskaya ulitsa 12 (enter through the arch).
Map 7 C2. **Tel** 717 4932.

Udelnaya Flea Market
Fermskoye shosse 36, Metro Udelnaya.

Voennyy Kollektsioner
Военный Коллекционер
Zagorodnyy prospekt 36.
Map 7 A3. **Tel** 315 9351.

Antiques and Art

Anna Nova
Ulitsa Zhukovskovo 28.
Map 7 B1.
Tel 275 9762.

Antikvariat
Антиквариат
Bolshaya Morskaya 33.
Map 6 D2.
Tel +7 921 945 1305.

Borey
Борей
Liteynyy prospekt 58.
Map 7 A1. **Tel** 275 3837.

Marina Gisich Gallery
Fontanka 121.
Map 6 D3.
Tel 314 4380.

Pushkinskaya 10
Пушкинская 10
(The Door Gallery, Naviuila Artis, Art-Liga, New Academy of Fine Arts, Nonconformists' Museum) Ligovskiy prospekt 53.
Map 7 B3.
Tel 764 5371.

Renaissance Antiques
Pestela 8. **Map** 3 A5.
Tel 273 5404.

Russkaya Starina
Русская Старина
Nekrasova 6. **Map** 6 E1.
Tel 273 2603.

Russkie Sezony
Русские сезоны
Liteynyy prospekt 15.
Map 3 A2. **Tel** 275 1749.

S.P.A.S.
С. П.А.С.
Naberezhnaya reki Moyki 93. **Map** 5 C2.
Tel 571 4260.

Tertia
Терция
Italyanskaya ulitsa 5.
Map 6 E1. **Tel** 571 5553.

Union of Artists
Союз художников
Bolshaya Morskaya ulitsa 38. **Map** 6 D2.
Tel 314 3060.

Books, Film and Music

Akademkniga
Академкнига
Liteynyy prospekt 57.
Map 7 A1.
Tel 273 1398.

Anglia
Англия
Naberezhnaya reki Fontanki 38.
Map 7 A2.
Tel 579 8007.

Bookvoed
Буквоед
Ligovskiy prospekt 10.
Map 7 C2.
Tel 717 3086.

Dom Knigi
дом книги
Nevskiy prospekt 28.
Map 6 E1.
Tel 448 2355.

Na Liteynom
На Литейном
(Books and antiques)
Liteynyy prospekt 61.
Map 7 A2.
Tel 275 3874.

Phonoteka
Фонотека
Ulitsa Marata 28.
Map 7 B3.
Tel 712 3013.

Severnaya Lira
Северная лира
Nevskiy prospekt 26.
Map 6 E1.
Tel 312 0796.

Staraya Kollektsiya
Старая Коллекция
Naberezhnaya reki Moyki 51. **Map** 6 E1.
Tel 312 6621.

Writers' Bookshop
Лавка Писателей
Nevskiy prospekt 66.
Map 7 A2.
Tel 314 4858.

Furs and Fashion

Lena
Лена
Kronverkskaya 7.
Map 6 F1. **Tel** 244 7246.

Marina Sedova Hat Salon
Шляпный салон Марины Седовой
Ligovskiy prospekt 27/7.
Map 7 C2. **Tel** 579 3268.

Russkiye Samotsvety
Русские Самоцветы
Nevskiy prospekt 64.
Map 7 A2. **Tel** 490 6638.

Russky Len
Славянский стиль
Pushkinskaya ulitsa 3.
Map 7 B2. **Tel** 325 8599.

Shapole
Шаполе
Nevskiy prospekt 184.
Map 8 E3. **Tel** 717 8237.

Tatyana Parfyonova
Татьяна Парфенова модный дом
Nevskiy prospekt 51.
Map 7 B2.
Tel 713 3669.

Toto
Nevskiy prospekt 74.
Map 6 E1. **Tel** 579 3590.

ENTERTAINMENT IN ST PETERSBURG

St Petersburg has an impressive and varied choice of entertainment. Its ballet, opera, classical music and theatre are among the best in the world. In addition to the high culture, a thriving and vibrant nightlife is made up of numerous rock and jazz clubs, bars, art cafés, discos, nightclubs and casinos.

Increasingly, international artists are adding St Petersburg to their tours, and mainstream now exists harmoniously alongside underground in music,

theatre and cinema. The St Petersburg Philharmonia and the Mariinskiy (Kirov) ballet and opera *(see pp120–21)* deserve their impressive international reputations, though this does mean that they are often away on tour.

St Petersburg's entertainment changes with the seasons. In winter there are concerts and other traditional indoor events. Summer starts with the White Nights, followed by a mass of festivals and outdoor events.

The magnificent, gilded interior of the Yusupov Theatre

Entertainment Information

St Petersburg can be quite a difficult city to keep up with, as both official and unofficial events are organized at short notice. For example, theatre programmes are not announced more than a couple of months in advance, so it's important to keep alert in order not to miss the fun.

To find up-to-date listings in English for cultural events, visit the official website of the St Petersburg Committee for Culture (billboard.spb.ru) or look for the latest issue of *St Petersburg In Your Pocket* magazine at popular hotels and restaurants. A much broader range of information is provided in Russian in two biweekly listings magazines: *Afisha* (www.spb.afisha.com) and *Time Out* (www.spb.

timeout.ru). Tickets for a wide range of events can be booked on the Russian-language website www.bileter.ru.

Most traditional theatres and concert halls close down for July, August and part of September because their troupes go on tour. While this may deprive visitors of local performers, some theatres bring in guest troupes from Moscow and abroad. In addition, other venues such as the Hermitage *(see p86)* and Alexandrinskiy *(see p205)* theatres launch summer programmes that are aimed at tourists. It is worth noting that, although they are fun, their opera and ballet shows are sometimes not of the highest quality.

Matinees start at noon and most evening performances at 7pm. To avoid disappointment check tickets carefully so you know when to arrive.

Mariinskiy poster pillar

Buying Tickets

Most people buy their tickets with cash and in person. Theatre ticket offices and kiosks can be found all over town, offering tickets up to a month in advance. They display a full programme (in Russian) of all theatre and classical music performances for the next 20 days and are generally open daily from 10am–1pm and 4–7pm. Offices within theatres usually work from 11am–3pm and 4–7pm and sell tickets for all advertised concerts. Non-Russian-speakers should not be nervous: most ticket cashiers will be helpful and patient while you point to the date you want. Tickets can also be booked by your hotel concierge. The Mariinskiy Theatre has an excellent English-language website on which tickets can be bought (www.mariinsky.ru). Similar services for other theatres are offered on www.artis.spb.ru.

A few venues, notably the Mariinskiy Theatre *(see p121)*, have price bands, with some tickets set aside at a cheaper rate and available only to Russian citizens. Non-Russians trying to use these may be refused entry or asked to pay the difference in price. Visitors, however, may obtain tickets for sold-out performances at the Mariinskiy Theatre if they go on the day.

As in most cities, touts sell tickets for major events, but beware of possible fakes and inflated prices.

Spectacular performance of the famous *Sleeping Beauty* ballet

Late-Night Transport

The metro closes its doors soon after midnight and buses run until 12:15am (infrequently after 11pm). There is no reliable all-night public transport, so expect to take a taxi late at night. Avoid any taxis which wait outside foreign hotels and bars as they charge extortionate prices (*see pp224–5*).

Children's Entertainment

Many theatres put on plays in Russian especially for children. See the children's section of *Afisha* or *Time Out*. Unfortunately, few give English-language performances except at New Year. No language problems occur at the **Circus**, however, or at the **Dolphinarium** on Krestovskiy Island.

Some of the best shows and concerts for children are held at **Zazerkalye**, while the puppet theatres usually have several productions based on well-known fairy tales.

For the "real" Russian winter experience, try a *troika* (sleigh) ride. These are offered at Pavlovsk (*see pp160–63*) and at **Shuvalovka**, a reproduction

Russian village. Located 30 km (19 miles) out of town, Shuvalovka is open throughout the year and includes wooden houses in 17th-century Russian style, a skating rink, ice slides, a working smithy and a museum of peasant life. Take any minibus to Peterhof from Avtovo metro and ask the driver to stop at Shuvalovka.

Festivals

The various White Nights festivals (*see p53*) draw some of the big names of pop and classical music, and ticket prices go up accordingly – as do accommodation rates – during this time. But there are plenty of other worthwhile seasonal festivals. The White Days (taking in Russian Christmas on 7 January, when the city is shrouded in snow) and Shrovetide festivals place the accent on Russian culture.

Numerous jazz festivals (look out for SKIF in April), the long-standing Early Music Festival (Sep and Oct), along with feature and documentary cinema festivals ensure that the city entertainment scene thrives all year round.

The Russian Circus

Circuses first appeared in Russia in the early 19th century, but it was not until 1876–7 that Russia's first permanent circus building was erected for Gaetano Ciniselli's Italian circus. St Petersburg's circus is still based at this historic site, which was modernized in 1963, and continues to practise the traditional training, skills and animal acts which have made the Russian circus famous throughout the world.

Acrobatic performers, St Petersburg's circus

The Arts

For a city renowned worldwide for its rich tradition of ballet and classical music, it is not surprising that St Petersburg has a wide range of cultural events on offer. An evening spent at any of the three Mariinskiy Theatre venues is a highlight of any visit. It is also well worth venturing into the many other theatres, music halls and churches to absorb the city's cultural diversity. Classical music is vastly popular and local orchestras are much in demand the world over. In addition, there are the evocative sounds of church choirs, the lively ambience of folk cabarets, and numerous festivals *(see pp52–5)* held to encourage young musicians, composers, film-makers and dancers.

Mariinskiy Theatre

The **Mariinskiy Theatre** *(see p121)*, the epitome of the best in Russian ballet and opera, is a veritable performing arts complex, encompassing three separate venues. In addition to the historical stage, a nearby concert hall stages both concerts and small-scale operas, while the lavish Mariinskiy II is the city's newest stage and one of Europe's best-equipped. To see the current programme, check the website and keep an eye on the listings.

Ballet

Some of the best dancers in the world come from the **Mariinskiy** *(see p121)*. Tickets for performances by leading ballerinas Ulyana Lopatkina and Diana Vishneva are hard to come by. One of the highlights of the year is the Christmas performance of *The Nutcracker*, danced by children from the Vaganova Ballet School *(see p112)*. Ballet at the **Mikhailovsky Theatre** and the **Conservatory Opera and Ballet Theatre** *(see p122)* are of more varied quality but still provide good entertainment.

In summer, many troupes perform for tourists in various theatres, but with inconsistent levels of skill. Boris Eifmann's modern ballet company is one of the city's best, often touring abroad and winning critical praise. When at home, they perform at the **Alexandrinskiy Theatre** *(see p112)*.

Opera

Tchaikovsky's opera *Eugene Onegin* and Mussorgsky's *Boris Godunov* remain stalwarts in any repertory. Operas are performed (usually in their original language) at the **Mikhailovsky Theatre** and at the **Mariinskiy**. Look out for local stars Anna Netrebko and Olga Borodina, or the tenor Vladimir Galuzin. Less common works, including 18th-century chamber operas, are performed by **St Petersburg Opera** on their own stage, and at the **Hermitage** and tiny **Yusupov Theatres**. Look out for sparkling productions at the children's theatre **Zazerkalye** *(see p203)*.

Classical Music

The city's classical repertoire is huge. Tchaikovsky, Shostakovich, Mussorgsky and Rimsky-Korsakov lived in St Petersburg and their music is performed here frequently.

The **Great Hall of the Philharmonia** *(see p100)*, the **Small Hall of the Philharmonia** *(see p50)* and the **Academic Capella** *(see p114)* are historic venues for classical concerts. The former is the home of the St Petersburg Philharmonic Orchestra. Other historic locations used for concerts include the Hermitage *(see p86)*, and the palaces of Tsarskoe Selo *(see pp154–7)* and Sheremetev *(see p131)*. By contrast, **Dom Kochnevoy** and **Beloselskiy-Belozerskiy** are intimate spaces for chamber music.

Church Music

The music of an Orthodox choir is one of the most evocative sounds in Russia. The best are heard on Saturday evenings and Sunday mornings at the **Holy Trinity Cathedral** in Alexander Nevskiy Monastery *(see pp132–3)* and at the **Cathedral of the Transfiguration** *(see p129)*. Services in the **Cathedral of Our Lady of Kazan** *(see p113)* are also of a high standard. More formal religious music is performed in the **Smolnyy Cathedral** *(see p130)*.

Folk Music

The tourist industry encourages visits to concerts of Russian folk music and dancing, some of which are very good, especially those at the **Nikolaevskiy Palace**. Many restaurants have a folk cabaret, though these can be kitsch and loud. **Podvorye** restaurant in the grounds of Pavlovsk Palace *(see p160–63)*, however, has an excellent, small ensemble.

Street Music

Democracy has had the unexpected effect of allowing many informal activities such as busking, which has brought some highly talented musicians onto the streets. Today, as skilled players stake their pitches, the sound of music fills the city's streets. The two under-passes beneath Nevskiy prospekt by Gostinyy Dvor are busy busking spots, while other metro stations are popular sites for old ladies singing Russian love ballads.

Theatre

All performances are in Russian. For non-Russian-speakers, productions of classic plays such as *The Cherry Orchard* may be interesting to experience, but more obscure works can be difficult.

Since the days of the Soviet Union, the leading light in the drama world has been the **Bolshoy Drama Theatre** (BDT). The Alexandrinskiy Theatre is the oldest in Russia; one of the newest is the **Molodyozhnyy (Youth) Theatre**. Lev Dodin's direction of the **Malyy Drama Theatre (MDT)** has brought it international fame as the "Theatre of Europe", despite all performances being in Russian (though some are performed in English).

Cinema

Most cinemas now show Hollywood blockbusters, but these are dubbed into Russian rather than subtitled. **The Angleterre Cinema Lounge** often holds showings of undubbed films, as do a few Russian cinemas such as **Dom Kino**, **Avrora** and the

Formula Kino multiplex at Galeria. A large number of film festivals are held in the city every year, and these frequently include films in their original language.

Afisha and *Time Out* give full coverage of all festivals, including the main **Festival of Festivals** (see p53).

DIRECTORY

Tickets

Tickets are sold in city kiosks and at individual theatres unless stated otherwise.

Ballet and Opera

Conservatory Opera and Ballet Theatre
Театр оперы и балета Консерватории
Teatr opery i baleta Konservatorii
Teatralnaya pl 3.
Map 5 C3.
Tel 312 2519.

Hermitage Theatre
Эрмитажный театр
Ermitazhnyy teatr
Dvortsovaya nab 34.
Map 2 E5.
Tel 571 5059.
(Tickets from city kiosks and hotels only.)

Mariinskiy Theatre
Мариинский театр
Mariinskiy teatr
Teatralnaya pl 1.
Map 5 B3.
Tel 326 4141.
W mariinsky.ru

Mikhailovsky Theatre
Михайловский Театр
Teatr Mikhaylovsky
Pl Iskusstv 1.
Map 6 E1.
Tel 595 4305.
Closed late Jul–Aug.
W mikhailovsky.ru

St Petersburg Opera
Санкт-Петербург опера
Sankt-Petersburg opera
Galernaya ul 33.
Map 5 B2.
Tel 312 3982.

Yusupov Theatre
Юсуповский театр
Yusupovskiy teatr
Yusupov Palace, nab reki Moyki 94. **Map** 5 B3.
Tel 314 9883, 314 1991.

Classical Music

Academic Capella
Академическая Капелла
Akademicheskaya Kapella
Nab reki Moyki 20.
Map 2 E5.
Tel 314 1058.

Beloselskiy-Belozerskiy Palace
Дворец Белосельских-Белозерских
Dvorets Beloselskikh-Belozerskikh
Nevskiy pr 41.
Map 7 A2.
Tel 315 5236.

Dom Kochnevoy
Лом Кочневой
Nab reki Fontanki 41.
Map 6 F2.
Tel 710 4062.

Great Hall of the Philharmonia
Большой зал филармонии
Bolshoy zal Filarmonii
Mikhaylovskaya ul 2.
Map 6 F1.
Tel 710 4257.

Small Hall of the Philharmonia
Малый зал филармонии
Malyy zal Filarmonii
Nevskiy pr 30.
Map 6 F1.
Tel 571 8333.

Church Music

Cathedral of Our Lady of Kazan
Собор Казанской Богоматери
Sobor Kazanskoy Bogomateri
Kazanskaya ploshchad 2.
Map 6 E1.
✚ 9am & 7:30pm daily.

Cathedral of the Transfiguration
Спасо-Преображенский собор
Spaso-Preobrazhenskiy sobor
Preobrazhenskaya pl 1.
Map 3 B5.
✚ 10am & 6pm daily.

Holy Trinity Cathedral
Свято-Троицкий собор
Svyato-Troitskiy sobor
Alexander Nevskiy Monastery,
pl Aleksandra Nevskovo.
Map 8 E4.
✚ 10am & 6pm daily.

Smolnyy Cathedral
Смольный собор
Smolnyy sobor
Ploshchad Rastrelli 3.
Map 4 F4.
✚ 7am & 5pm daily..

Folk Music

Nikolaevskiy Palace
Николаевский дворец
Nikolaevskiy dvorets
Pl Truda 4.
Map 5 B2.
Tel 985 2045.

Theatre

Alexandrinskiy Theatre
Александринский театр
Aleksandrinskiy teatr
Ploshchad Ostrovskovo 6.
Map 6 F2.
Tel 312 1545.
W alexandrinsky.ru

Bolshoy Drama Theatre (BDT)
Большой драматический театр
Bolshoy dramaticheskiy teatr
Nab reki Fontanki 65.
Map 6 F2.
Tel 244 1071.
W bdt.spb.ru

Malyy Drama Theatre (MDT)
МДТ – Театр Евролы
MDT – Teatr Evropy
Ul Rubinshteyna 18.
Map 7 A2.
Tel 713 2078.

Molodyozhnyy Theatre
Молодёжный театр на фонтанке
Molodyozhnyy teatr na Fontanke
Nab reki Fontanki 114.
Map 6 D4.
Tel 316 6564.

Cinema

Angleterre Cinema Lounge
Angleterre Hotel, Malaya Morskaya ulitsa 24.
Map 6 D2.
Tel 494 5990. (Tickets from the hotel concierge.)

Avrora Cinema
Аврора
Nevskiy pr 60.
Map 7 A2.
Tel 315 5254.

Dom Kino
Дом Кино
Karavannaya ulitsa 12.
Map 7 A1.
Tel 314 5614.

Formula Kino
Формула Кино
Galeria, Ligovskiy prospekt 30.
Map 7 C3.
Tel 676 7776.

Mirage
Мираж
Bolshoy pr 35, Petrogradskaya.
Map 1 C2.
Tel 677 6060.

Live Music and Nightlife

St Petersburg was at the heart of the underground Soviet rock scene and many of the best Russian sounds originate here. The nightclub scene offers mostly techno music and mainstream pop, in vast complexes with strobe lights, and attracts the well-paid young and *nouveaux riches*. Some smaller clubs featuring an eclectic mix describe themselves as "art" clubs or cafés, and host live music one night and avant-garde fashion shows or films the next. Some large clubs and casinos accept credit cards. Where hours are not given, check programmes before heading out. Avoid places that admit foreigners or women free.

Art and Café Clubs

Fish Fabrique is probably the oldest art café in town, having survived the ups and downs of recent Russian history. **Brodyachaya Sobaka** has been frequented by poets such as Anna Akhmatova since the Silver Age, and other major poets still come here to perform their works in arts events. **GEZ-21** even manages to fit poetry and philosophy readings in among rock concerts.

Rock Venues

Under the Soviet regime, Leningrad rock was rebellious without being overtly political. Though there is now less emphasis on poetical lyrics that express a spirit of freedom from control and repression, Russian rock still owes much to its rebellious past, while also managing to incorporate the latest in Western music trends.

Kosmonavt hosts international bands, while **A2** is a popular concert venue that hosts local and international acts. Rockabilly gave birth to **Money Honey** and to the **City Club** upstairs (for older rockers), which in turn led to an explosion of rockabilly groups in the city.

Big-name, massed audience rock and pop concerts are usually held in one of the big concert halls such as the **Oktyabrskiy Bolshoy Kontsertnyy Zal**, or the largest of them all, the **Ledovyy Dvorets**. When major international stars come to town, however, they usually perform on a specially erected stage in Palace Square.

Jazz Venues

The father of Petersburg jazz is David Goloshchokin, who set up the **Jazz Philharmonic Hall**. As the name suggests, the jazz played in the hall is mainly very traditional, and, sadly, dancing or talking are prohibited. **JFC** has led the way for improvisation and innovative jazz. Guests here are often musicians with an international reputation. **G.A. Blues Club** comes a close second to JFC by virtue of its mixture of blues and rock, and its good food.

Restaurants such as **Sunduk** *(see p191)* often bring in good live performers. **48 Chairs** is a classy, intimate restaurant-club that puts on nightly shows.

Bars with Music

Live music is played in many bars around town, but on the whole a lot of the music in such places is awful. It is best to stick with the established, more reliable clubs.

Liverpool, for example, hosts live bands, not all of whom play Beatles cover versions. In addition, **Manhattan** sometimes has good jazz acts. **Fidel** is one of the most popular music bars in the city and attracts crowds of local hipsters during the weekends.

Nightclubs and Discos

There are very few large dance clubs in the city centre, and **Rossi's Club** is one of the oldest and most popular of them all. The food is highly rated as well. **Yashchik**, hidden in a maze of old warehouses just off busy Ligovskiy prospekt, offers live music as well as guest DJs. **MOD** is centrally located and attracts a student crowd at its DJ nights and performances.

Lux Club is situated in a historic building a few steps from the Church on Spilled Blood, and attracts mostly a university-aged crowd.

Smaller, more diverse clubs, such as the underground **Griboedov**, are still very much of the alternative culture trend, playing a variety of the latest hits from Europe, and hosting fashion shows and other cultural events. **Purga**, literally meaning "snowstorm", celebrates New Year's Eve every night, complete with a midnight countdown. In summer, the club takes the revelry riverside, with nightly cruises. **Zal Ozhidaniya**, which is housed in a former railway station, is one of St Petersburg's few medium-sized venues and attracts international artists.

Gay Clubs

For some reason, few gay clubs in St Petersburg manage to last more than four or five years. **Cabaret** is, however, an exception, remaining popular while other venues come and go; and **Central Station** seems to have made a go of it, too. **Priscilla** is the most recent addition to the scene, a smaller club that doesn't charge an admission fee and occasionally offers drag shows.

Billiards and Bowling

Along with bars and nightclubs, a popular night out in St Petersburg is billiards and bowling.

Billiard halls and bowling alleys are casual but upmarket affairs and always serve a full selection of alcohol as well as offering respectable restaurants with extensive menus. Many locals go to these places without ever lifting a pool cue or a bowling ball, instead preferring to enjoy the atmosphere.

DIRECTORY

Art and Café Clubs

Brodyachaya Sobaka
Бродяная Собака
Italianskaya ulitsa 4.
Map 6 F1.
Tel 312 8047.
Ⓦ vsobaka.ru

Fish Fabrique
Ligovskiy pr 53.
Map 7 B3.
Tel 764 4857.
Open 12pm–3am daily.
Ⓦ fishfabrique.ru

GEZ-21
ГЕЗ-21
Ligovskiy pr 53.
Map 7 B3.
Tel 764 5258.
Ⓦ soundmuseum spb.ru

Rock Venues

A2
Pr Medikov 3.
Tel 333 0379.
Ⓦ a2.fm

Backstage Club
Ligovskiy pr 113.
Map 7 B4.
Tel 958 3888.

Kosmonavt
Космонавт
Bronnitskaya ulitsa 24.
Map 6 E5.
Tel 303 3333.
Ⓦ cosmonavt.su

Ledovyy Dvorets
Ледовый дворец
Pr Pyatiletok 1.
Tel 718 6620.

Money Honey / City Club
Apraksin dvor block 13,
Sadovaya ul 28–30.
Map 6 E2.
Tel 310 0549.

Oktyabrskiy Bolshoy Kontsertnyy Zal
БКЗ Октябрьский
Ligovskiy prospekt 6.
Map 7 C1.
Tel 275 1300.

Yubileynyy Dvorets Sporta
Дворец спорта
юбилейный
Pr Dobrolyubova 18.
Map 1 B3.
Tel 702 3605.

Jazz Venues

48 Chairs
Ulitsa Rubinshteyna 5.
Map 7 A2.
Tel 315 7775.
Ⓦ 48chairs.com

G. A. Blues Club
Liteynyy prospekt 33.
Map 3 A5.
Tel 579 8813.
Open 2pm–midnight
daily. Concerts: 8:30pm.

Jazz Philharmonic Hall
Филармония Джазовой
музыки
Zagorodnyy prospekt 27.
Tel 764 8565.
Open 7–11pm Tue–Sun.
Ⓦ jazz-hall.spb.ru

JFC
Shpalernaya ulitsa 33.
Map 3 C4.
Tel 272 9850.
Open 7–10pm daily.
Ⓦ jfc-club.spb.ru

Bars with Music

Datscha
Дача
Dumskaya ul 9.
Map 6 E2.
Open 6pm–6am daily.

Fidel
Фидель
Dumskaya ulitsa 9.
Map 6 E2.
Tel +7 931 260 2617.
Open 6pm–6am daily.

Liverpool
Ливерпуль
Ul Mayakovskovo 16.
Map 7 B1.
Tel 579 2054.

Manhattan
Nab reki Fontanki 90.
Map 6 E3.
Tel 713 1945.
Open 1–11pm daily.
Ⓦ manhattanclub.ru

Nightclubs and Discos

Coyote Ugly
Liteynyy prospekt 57.
Map 7 A1.
Tel 416 4450.
Ⓦ coyoteugly.ru

Estrada

Ul Sadovaya 17.
Map 6 F2.
Tel 931 5101.
Open 9pm–6am daily.

Griboedov
Грибоедов
Voronezhskaya ul 2A.
Map 7 B4.
Tel 764 4355.
Open 2pm–6am.
Ⓦ griboedovclub.ru

Lux
Konyushennaya
Ploshchad 2.
Map 2 E5.
Tel 241 1953.
Open 11pm–6am daily.
Ⓦ lux-klub.ru

MOD
Nab kanala Griboedova 7.
Map 6 E1.
Tel +7 962 728 0998.
Ⓦ modclub.info

Purga
Пурга
Nab reki Fontanki 11.
Map 7 A1.
Tel 570 5123.
Ⓦ purga-club.ru

Rossi's Club
Ulitsa zodchego Rossi 1/3.
Map 6 F2.
Tel 710 4016.
Ⓦ rossis.ru

Ruki Vverkh
Руки вверх
Naberezhnaya kanala
Griboedova 28
Map 6 E2.
Tel 999 4949.

Santa Barbara
Kazanskaya ulitsa 7.
Map 6 E2.
Tel 900 0666.
Ⓦ vk.com/santa barbaraclub

Yashchik
Ящик
Ligovskiy prospekt 50,
building 13.
Map 7 B3.
Tel 964 9637

Zal Ozhidaniya
Зал Ожидания
Nab Obvodnovo
kanala 118.
Tel 913 3563.
Ⓦ clubzal.com

Gay Clubs

Cabaret (A.K.A. Matrosskaya Tishina)
Кабаре
Razezzhaya ulitsa 43.
Tel 764 0901.
Ⓦ cabarespb.ru

Central Station
Ulitsa Lomonosova 1.
Map 6 E2.
Tel 312 3600.
Ⓦ centralstation.ru

Priscilla
Ulitsa Lomonosova 1.
Map 6 E2.
Tel +7 921 332 5161.
Ⓦ priscilla.spb.ru

Billiards and Bowling

Bowling City Sennaya
Боулинг Сити Сенная
Ulitsa Yefimova 3.
Map 6 E3.
Tel 380 3090

Bowling Show
Naberezhnaya
Obvodnogo kanala 118.
Tel 380 3005
Ⓦ bowling-show.ru.

Neptun
Нептун
Naberezhnaya
Obvodnogo kanala 93A.
Map 6 F5.
Tel 324 46 93.
Ⓦ neptun.spb.ru

Santa Billiard Club
Бильярдный клуб Санта
Perekopskaya ulitsa 6/8,
M. Narvskaya.
Tel 401 4658.

SURVIVAL
GUIDE

PRACTICAL INFORMATION

The street signs and maps of St Petersburg are not as difficult to negotiate as it may first appear when confronted with daunting Cyrillic letters. Not only do hotels, restaurants and all service sectors attempt to compensate by being helpful to foreigners, but the city has English signage pointing out major sights and shops. There are also several tourist information offices located near popular places of interest. On the street, many things will seem unfamiliar, but with patience and determination everything is possible, from making international telephone calls and exchanging money to finding emergency medical treatment. The city has continued to develop along more Western lines, but still retains its exotic charms and remains a bargain due to the decline of the rouble.

The Grand Cascade of Peterhof Palace during the White Nights

When to Go

The height of the tourist season in St Petersburg is during the famed White Nights (see p53 and p203), from mid-May to mid-July, when the sun barely sets for an hour due to the city's northern location. Prices at this time are at their highest. Fewer tourists visit during the winter.

Visas and Passports

Visas are required for all visitors to Russia. Package tour companies will organize visas for you, but independent travellers need to arrange their own. Document requirements change regularly, so it is essential to check these in advance (http://ru.vfsglobal.co.uk). You will need to show proof of an invitation (visa support) from a hotel, tour company or business in Russia. Invitations can be purchased online at **ivisaonline.com** or from **Go Russia**. You can pay your travel agency to process the visa for you. Alternatively, fill in the application yourself and either post it or deliver it in person to the **Russian Visa Centre** in London.

Travel Safety Advice

Visitors can get up-to-date travel safety information from the **Foreign and Commonwealth Office** in the UK, the **State Department** in the US and the **Department of Foreign Affairs and Trade** in Australia.

Customs Information

Passports and visas are checked thoroughly at immigration. The customs official will give you a small immigration card with your personal information. This card must be kept with your passport and handed back on departure.

There are no limitations on the amount of money you can bring into Russia; Russian money to the value of 326,000 roubles may be exported. Note any items of considerable value, such as diamond jewellery, on a customs form.

All foreigners must register with **OVIR** (visa registration) within seven working days before travelling and obtain a stamp of registration on their migration card or in their passport. Tourists spending less than seven working days in the country do not need to register.

Tourist Information

Hotels are a good source of tourist information, as are Tourist information offices. **Ostwest** runs a reliable tourist information service, as well as booking accommodation and entertainment. Also try www.saint-petersburg.com, which is a useful English-language website. The bimonthly free guide St Petersburg In Your Pocket gives up-to-the-minute information.

Tourist information kiosks can be found all over the city centre: Palace Square, Smolnyy Cathedral, Ploshchad Vosstaniya, Sadovaya ulitsa and St Isaac's Square. Main offices are at the airport.

Tourists consulting a map to find their way in St Petersburg

Admission Prices

Many museums and theatres, notably the Hermitage (see pp86–95), the Russian Museum (see pp106–9) and the Mariinskiy (see p121) charge foreigners a higher entry fee than Russians. Students and schoolchildren are entitled to discounts.

The ticket office is often positioned away from the entrance, so look for the "KACCA" sign. Ticket prices vary from about 50 roubles for small state museums to 700 roubles for entrance to the Hermitage. A good-value option is to buy a Tourist Card from tourist information offices. Cards are valid for two days (3,500 roubles) to seven days (6,500 roubles), and offer free entry to many state museums, as well as discounts in some restaurants.

Opening Hours

Most sights are open from 10:30am to 6pm, with no break for lunch, and close one day a week. They also close one day each month for cleaning; see individual museum entries for this information. Last tickets are sold about 1 hour before closing. Parks are usually open from 10am to 10pm, later during White Nights.

ОТКРЫТО

Sign for open *(otkryto)*

ЗАКРЫТО

Sign for closed *(zakryto)*

Visiting Churches

Attending an Orthodox service is a fascinating experience. Since services tend to run for several hours, it is generally fine simply to drop in. Certain dress codes must be observed: no shorts; men should remove hats; women should cover their shoulders and chest and preferably wear a hat or headscarf. Women in trousers are accepted in town churches, but small monasteries outside of the city will strictly enforce the no-trousers rule. The most important services are held on Saturday evening, Sunday morning and on major religious holidays.

Most major faiths are represented in the city. Churches tend to be open all day from early morning until

St Isaac's Cathedral *(see pp80–81)*, open to visitors

late. Service times at Catholic and Protestant churches are published in *St Petersburg In Your Pocket (see p219)*, both printed and online versions.

Language

Cyrillic, the alphabet used in the Russian language, is named after the 9th-century monks Cyril and Methodius who invented it. The apparent similarity between Cyrillic and roman letters can be misleading. Some letters are common to both alphabets, others look similar but represent totally different sounds. Various systems of transliteration are in usage, but they do not differ enough to cause serious confusion.

Most people who come into contact with tourists speak some English and passers-by on the street will do their best if asked directions. Knowledge of a few Russian words *(see pp260–64)* is appreciated.

Etiquette and Smoking

On public transport, it is expected that young men should offer their seats to women with young children or the elderly.

Greetings among friends involve a handshake (between men) or a kiss, or simply saying – *"privet"* (hi).

Photographic restrictions have more or less disappeared. In museums, expect to buy a ticket for the right to photograph or film inside. Tripods and flashes are not to be used. Photography in the metro is

prohibited as it is seen as a threat to national security. If you do wish to take a photo in the metro, approach a police officer, who may allow you to for a fee, which is unlikely to exceed 100 roubles.

Smoking is prohibited in cinemas, museums, theatres and on public transport, as well as on long-distance trains, railway stations, airports and in restaurants, bars and clubs. Drinking alcohol is prohibited in the street. Russians take great pleasure in smoking and drinking and frequent toasts are required to justify the filling and draining of glasses. At a private home, always toast the hostess *(za khozyayku)* or the host *(za khozyayina)*.

Public Conveniences

The situation is improving, but most public toilets are quite basic, and a few cafés do not have any toilet facilities at all. In such cases, go to the nearest hotel or use the pay toilets located in department stores. The person who takes the money also hands out toilet paper. There are portaloos with attendants situated near several of the major tourist attractions. The fee ranges from 20 to 35 roubles. Baby-changing facilities are an extremely rare amenity in Russia and can be found only in upscale hotels, the biggest shopping malls and Western-owned stores such as IKEA, where they are usually free of charge.

Taxes and Tipping

Roubles are the sole valid currency in Russia *(see p217)*. All cash payments must be made in roubles only and all prices are given in roubles. Credit cards are accepted in most restaurants and hotels, as well as larger shops, though there are some places that will not accept them so it is best to carry cash with you.

Tipping is a matter of choice. Simply pay what you feel is right; 50 or 100 roubles is usually sufficient.

The Hermitage museum offers disabled access to visitors

Travellers with Specific Needs

While just a few years ago St Petersburg had almost no facilities for disabled visitors, the situation is gradually improving, though services remain far from ideal and transport in particular is a problem. Of the museums, only the Hermitage and the Russian Museum have disabled access. Many 4- and 5-star hotels are now equipped for disabled guests, with ramps, lifts, wider doorways, handrails and showers with removable sides. **Liberty** specializes in tours around St Petersburg and its suburbs for disabled travellers. The company uses minibuses equipped with a lift or folding ramp to transport wheelchair-users around the city, and can also advise on hotels and restaurants with disabled access and facilities.

Travelling with Children

Russians adore children, and travellers in the company of under-tens are likely to attract a good deal of attention and many compliments. Russian *babushki* (grannies) also think nothing of telling parents of their failings.

The city has many parks and during school holidays temporary playgrounds are sometimes set up around town. There are several playgrounds in the Tauride Gardens (see p130), as well as a playground in the gardens next to the Bronze Horseman (see pp80–81). Museums and public transport are free for under-sevens.

Schoolchildren pay the full fare on transport, but pay a reduced price at museums (proof of being under 18 may be required).

Attractions guaranteed to delight younger travellers are listed in the Children's Entertainment section (see p203).

Young visitors enjoying the view

Senior Travellers

St Petersburg is popular with senior travellers and many hotels offer guided coach trips around the city. Concierges can arrange tickets and transport to ballet and opera performances, as well as to the city's museums and the former imperial estates located outside St Petersburg.

Discounts for pensioners are often available at museums and for other activities such as boat trips, but not for single tickets on transport.

The hotels on St Isaac's Square, such as the Astoria (see p177) and Angleterre (see p178), are quiet and in convenient locations, as is the Belmond Grand Hotel Europe (see p178), located close to many sights.

Gay and Lesbian Travellers

Russian society is not in general very tolerant of homosexuality, and men in particular should be aware that public displays of affection may attract unwanted attention. The city does, however, have a thriving gay and lesbian scene, with several gay clubs (see p206).

The **Russian LGBT Network** provides general information on gay and lesbian life in the city. Local organizations **Coming Out** and **Gay.ru** provide information orientated to gay and lesbian visitors. *St Petersburg In Your Pocket* includes gay clubs and bars in its club guide, but there are no English-language listings of daily events.

Travelling on a Budget

St Petersburg is no longer a cheap city to visit, and it is increasingly difficult to find things to do on a budget. There are, however, many *stolovayas* (canteens) around the city, where travellers can enjoy traditional Russian food at bargain prices.

There is an increasing number of hostels in the city (see p172), such as Life Hostel on Nevskiy prospekt. **Peter's Walking Tours** are an inexpensive way to discover the city, and start from various locations. Several bike-rental offices in the city offer an affordable way to get around, and public transport is inexpensive compared to many Western European cities.

An ISIC (international student card) entitles its holder to discounts in museums and on rail and air travel, although convincing ticket sellers of this may be more trouble than its worth. A visit to the Hermitage is free upon presentation of an ISIC card, and for all visitors on the first Thursday of every month.

Entrance to all parks inside the city is free, as well as to the grounds of the Peter and Paul Fortress (see pp68–9). The Field of Mars (see p96) is popular with young people in warmer months.

Time

St Petersburg follows Moscow time, which is 4 hours ahead of Greenwich Mean Time (GMT), and 9 hours ahead of Eastern Standard Time. As of 2014, Russia decided to remain on permanent winter time and abandon the practice of changing the clocks. This decision reverses former plans, which were quite unpopular, to stay on summertime.

Electricity

The electrical current is 220 V. Two-pin plugs are required, but some of the old Soviet two-pin sockets do not take modern European plugs, which have slightly thicker pins. American appliances require a 220:110

current adaptor. Travellers are advised to bring adaptors with them because they can be difficult to find in St Petersburg.

Responsible Travel

While St Petersburg, and Russia as a whole, have a regrettably poor record with regard to the environment, it is easy to travel about the city using green transport, such as trolleybuses and trams. Bikes can be rented from companies such as **Skat Prokat** and Velotour (see p225), although it is best to stick to quieter side roads.

It is possible to visit most of the city's major attractions on foot, either independently or on a walking tour (see p224). At **Sennoi Market**, a small part of

the outdoor area is devoted to fruit and vegetables that have been grown locally in the Leningrad Oblast area.

Conversion Table

Imperial to Metric
1 inch = 2.54 centimetres
1 foot = 30 centimetres
1 mile = 1.6 kilometres
1 ounce = 28 grams
1 pound = 454 grams
1 pint = 0.6 litres
1 UK gallon = 4.6 litres

Metric to Imperial
1 centimetre = 0.4 inches
1 metre = 3 feet, 3 inches
1 kilometre = 0.6 miles
1 gram = 0.04 ounces
1 kilogram = 2.2 pounds
1 litre = 1.8 UK pints

DIRECTORY

Embassies and Consulates

Australia
14 Petrovskiy prospekt, office 22–N. **Tel** 325 7334.
W dfat.gov.au/missions/countries/rupe.html

Canada
Moscow, Starokonju-shenny per 23. **Tel** (495) 925 6000.
W canadainternational.gc.ca/russia-russie

Ireland
Moscow, Grokholski perulok 5.
Tel +7 985 928 7615.

New Zealand
Moscow, Prechistenskaya naberezhnaya 3.
Tel (495) 956 3579.
W nzembassy.com/russia

UK
Pl Proletarskoy Diktatury 5.
Map 4 E4. **Tel** 320 3200.

US
Furshtatskaya ul 15.
Map 3 B4. **Tel** 331 2600.
W stpetersburg.usconsulate.gov

Visas and Passports

Go Russia
Boundary House, Boston Road, London, W7 2QE.
Tel (020) 3355 7717.
W justgorussia.co.uk

Ivisaonline.com
Tel +7 499 653 6779.
W ivisaonline.com

Russian Visa Centre
15–27 Gee Street, London EC1V 3RD.
Tel 0905 889 0149.
W ru.vfsglobal.co.uk

Travel Safety Advice

Australia
Department of Foreign Affairs and Trade.
W smartraveller.gov.au

UK
Foreign and Commonwealth Office.
W gov.uk/foreign-travel-advice

US
US Department of State.
W gov.uk/foreign-travel-advice

Customs Information

OVIR
Овир
(Tsentralnyy district) Foreign department, Pereulok Krylova 5.
Map 6 F2. **Tel** 273 2246.
(Central) Ul Kirochnaya 4.
Map 3 B5. **Tel** 278 3486.
W visatorussia.com

Tourist Information Offices

Main Office
14 Sadovaya ulitsa.
Tel 242 3909.

Information Pavilions
Ploshchad Rastrelli (in front of Smolnyy Cathedral)
Open May–Sep: 8:30am–4pm.
Palace Square
Open 10am–7pm daily.
St Isaac's Square
Open 10am–7pm daily.
Ploshchad Vosstaniya
Open 10am–7pm daily.
Marine Facade passenger terminal
Open 9am–6pm daily (May–Sep).
Kronverkskaya Embankment (opposite Peter and Paul Fortress)
Open 10am–7pm daily.
Pulkovo airport
Open 9am–8pm daily.

Ostwest
Ulitsa Vosstania 7.
Map 7 C2. **Tel** 327 3416.
W ostwest.com

Visit Russia
Tel 309 5760.
W visitrussia.com

Travellers with Specific Needs

Liberty
12 Ulitsa Polozova.
Tel 232 8163.
W accessiblerussia.com

Gay and Lesbian Travellers

Coming Out
Tel (812) 242 5469.
W comingoutspb.com

Gay.ru
W gay.ru

Russian LGBT Network
191040, St Petersburg, Ligovsky prospekt 87, office 528. **Tel** (812) 454 6452. W lgbtnet.ru

Travelling on a Budget

Peter's Walking Tours
Tel 943 1229.
W peterswalk.com

Responsible Travel

Sennoi Rynok (Sennoi Market)
4a Moskovskiy prospekt.
Tel 310 1209.
Open 8am–7pm daily.

Skat Prokat
20 Goncharnaya ulitsa.
Map 7 C3 **Tel** 748 1407.
W skatprokat.ru.

Personal Security and Health

St Petersburg is a relatively safe city. Petty crime should be the only concern for tourists, and even this can generally be avoided if the usual precautions are taken. Make copies of your passport and visa, note Travellers' cheque and credit card numbers and, for language reasons, keep a card with the address you are staying at in Russia. A multilingual tourist helpline (303 0555) can assist with any issue and is a free number from a mobile phone by dialling 8 800 first. Medical insurance is essential, as local healthcare compares poorly with Western standards, and English-speaking services or medical evacuation via Finland are very expensive. Many medicines are readily available, but it is best to bring specific medication needed.

in the centre, and be on guard for people employing these tactics.

Women on their own are unlikely to encounter sexual harassment, though they should ignore kerb-crawlers and avoid taking a cab alone at night. When travelling around, always be alert and safety-conscious, as you would in any city. On the streets be aware of local drivers, who see all pedestrians as a nuisance. Avoid walking on manhole covers, which may rock or even collapse under your feet.

Police officer (politsiya)

Police

Several kinds of police officer operate on St Petersburg's streets. Their uniforms change according to the weather, with the very necessary addition of fur hats and big overcoats in the winter. The street officers (politsiya) wear dark-grey uniforms and many carry guns. The riot police or OMON wear blue camouflage fatigues.

Separate from both these are the traffic police, whose uniforms carry the logo ДПС (DPS) on the chest and shoulder. They have the authority to stop any vehicle to check documents.

Both the street police and traffic police supplement their income by fining people for minor infringements of the law, and have been known to stop tourists for document checks and then "forget" to return wallets

or mobile phones. This is far more likely to happen to drunk tourists. Avoid the police if possible and stay alert if stopped.

Things to be Aware Of

To avoid trouble once in St Petersburg, simple rules should be observed, such as not displaying large sums of money; carrying cash in a concealed money belt; and keeping passports, tickets and all valuables in the hotel whenever possible. Security in Western-run hotels is very high, but in all hotels it is advisable to place valuables in the safe. Travellers' cheques (see p216) may have an insurance policy but are expensive to use and are easily laundered in Russia.

Avoid the "gypsies" who occasionally group on Nevskiy prospekt, apparently begging. If they do approach, do not stop for them and keep a firm hold of your possessions. Also watch out for pickpockets on the metro and buses. A common tactic is for the culprit to (seemingly accidentally) block your exit from the metro car or bus while another goes through your pockets. Avoid the back doors on buses, which are narrower than those

In an Emergency

In the event of a fire, call 01. For police, call 02 and for an ambulance, call 03. There is also a combined emergency number, 112.

Lost and Stolen Property

The greatest danger faced by foreigners is that posed by pickpockets and petty thieves. If threatened in the streets it is advisable to hand over belongings on demand.

If you have property stolen, report it to the local police

Police car

Fire engine

Ambulance

station for insurance purposes. They are unlikely to have an interpreter, so ask your hotel for assistance or call the **Tourist Helpline**. The best place to go to for lost property is the local police station You should take all your documents with you: passport, visa and migration card. You will be required to write a statement, so it is important to call the tourist helpline first for an interpreter to be present. If you lose something on the public transport system, call the main tourist helpline. They will hold items for a limited time, so contact them immediately. If you lose your passport, inform your embassy *(see p213)*. Lost credit or debit cards should be reported to the card issuer *(see p216–17)*.

Hospitals and Pharmacies

There are pharmacies *(apteka)* located throughout the city, and many are open 24 hours. Some stronger medications can be bought over the counter, so prescriptions are not necessary. Every assistant is a trained pharmacist and can advise alternative drugs. If you have specific requirements, particularly insulin, bring sufficient supplies for your stay.

If you fall ill, seek advice at your hotel, which should have its own doctor. Several companies, notably the **Medem International Clinic** and **Euromed**, specialize in dealing with foreigners. They cover everything from minor emergencies, dental care, X-rays and pre-natal care to medical evacuation. Their charges are high, but they are used to dealing with foreign insurance policies.

If you are in need of immediate attention, head to the casualty department (Clinic No. 37) of the **Trauma Clinic of the Central District** on ulitsa Pravdy. Basic care involving stitches or injections can be given. If you are taken to a local hospital and require further treatment, contact either your consulate or one of the above medical centres. They can either have

Sign for pharmacy *(apteka)*

you moved or they can oversee your care in the hospital.

Dentists can be expensive. The medical clinics listed opposite are covered by insurance policies. **Dental Palace** will offer dental care, but costs will not be reimbursed.

Health Precautions

Neither visitors nor residents should drink tap water, which contains heavy metals and *giardia*, a parasite causing stomach problems. To be safe drink bottled water only. If you do pick up *giardia*, it can be treated with metronidazole.

Russian food is unlikely to do much harm, but avoid the meat pies sold on the streets.

Sexually transmitted diseases are on the rise, so all due caution should be exercised.

Mosquitoes *(komari)* are rife between June and late September. Burning oils or using plugs that heat chemical tablets are recommended for use at night time.

Travel and Health Insurance

Visitors to St Petersburg are advised to take out travel insurance. Check the conditions of your cover before you travel – if possessions are stolen, you will need a copy of the police report to make an insurance claim. Make a note of the 24-hour emergency medical assistance telephone number that comes with your policy – the company can give advice if you need urgent medical attention. Keep any receipts or prescriptions so that you can claim the expenses on your insurance.

DIRECTORY

In an Emergency

Combined emergency number
Tel 112.

Ambulance *(skoraya pomoshch)*
Tel 03.

Fire *(pozharnaya sluzhba)*
Tel 01.

Police *(politsiya)*
Tel 02.

Lost and Stolen Property

Tourist Helpline
Tel 303 0555 or 8 800 303 0555 from a mobile (free of charge with all local providers).

Hospitals and Pharmacies

24-Hour Pharmacy
Nevskiy pr 98.
Tel 275 8189.
Vladimirskiy pr 16.
Tel 713 2116.
Zagorodnyy pr 21.
Tel 315 2743.

American Medical Clinic
Nab reki Moyki 78. **Map** 2 E5.
Tel 740 2090.
w amclinic.com

Clinic Complex
Poliklinicheskiy compleks
Moskovskiy pr 22.
Map 6 D5.
Tel 777 9777.

Dental Palace
Petropavlovskaya ulitsa 4.
Map 2 D1.
Tel 325 7500.
w dentalpalace.ru

Euromed
Suvorovskiy pr 60.
Map 4 E4.
Tel 327 0301.
w euromed.ru

Medem International Clinic & Hospital
Ulitsa Marata 6.
Map 7 2B.
Tel 336 3333.
w medem.ru

Trauma Clinic of the Central District
Travmpunkt pri poliklinike No. 37.
Ulitsa Pravdy 18.
Map 7 A4.
Tel 315 2158.

Banking and Local Currency

Major European debit and credit cards can be used in hotels, as well as in most restaurants and shops in St Petersburg. It is advisable to carry some cash, as there are still places that do not accept credit or debit cards. Roubles are the only legal currency and the city is well equipped with exchange offices and ATMs where visitors can turn their currency into roubles. It is advisable to visit a few exchange points before exchanging money, as commission rates offered do vary.

Banks and Bureau de Change

Roubles can be obtained outside Russia, but rates are better once in the country. There are numerous exchange offices throughout St Petersburg, including at the airport.

Many exchange offices are open for 24 hours a day. A passport has to be shown when changing money. Any visible defect on foreign banknotes, especially vertical tears or ink or water stains, can make them difficult to exchange. Travellers should make sure that all the banknotes they bring into Russia are in good condition, and that any US dollars were issued after 1990.

As bank rates are so good in St Petersburg, visitors should never be tempted to change their money on the streets, however appealing the rates on offer appear to be. The unpleasant truth is that street-changers will try to cheat anyone willing to take the risk.

A few of the foreign banks in St Petersburg offer over-the-counter services. The most reliable Russian bank is **Sberbank**.

Banks are plentiful in St Petersburg. There are often branches offering both cash currency exchange, and cash advances on credit or debit cards. Some of the larger branches also cash travellers' cheques. Sberbank exchange rates are generally among the best available, and there are branches conveniently located all over the city. **Alfa-Bank**, **Citibank** and **Raiffeisen** also offer currency exchange.

A fast and safe, but also rather more expensive, way of transferring cash from abroad to Russia is through wiring via Western Union, which has offices in most major banks located in the city centre.

ATMs

There are ATMs located in major hotels such as the Belmond Grand Hotel Europe and Astoria, as well as in Dom Knigi and Gostinyy Dvor, and at regular intervals along Nevskiy prospekt and other main streets. All VISA/Maestro cards are accepted, though

DIRECTORY

Banks

Alfa-Bank
Альфабанк
Malaya Konyushennaya ulitsa 7.
Map 6 E1.
Tel +8 800 200 0000.
🌐 alfabank.ru

Citibank
Nevskiy pr 68.
Map 7 A2.
Tel 336 7575.

Raiffeisen Bank
Naberezhnaya reki Moyki 36.
Map 6 E1.
Tel 334 4343.
🌐 raiffeisen.ru
Stremyannaya ulitsa 21/5.
Map 7 B2.
Tel 334 4343.

Sberbank
Сбербанк
Dumskaya ulitsa 1–3.
Map 6 F2.
Tel 305 1515.
🌐 sberbank.ru

VTB 24
Nevskiy pr 59. **Map** 7 B2.
Tel +8 800 505 2424.
🌐 vtb24.ru

a fee of about 150 roubles per transaction is levied. As always, it is advisable to be alert to the people around you when withdrawing cash, and to cover the keypad when entering your PIN to avoid becoming the victim of credit-card fraud.

Credit and Debit Cards

It is possible to obtain roubles with a credit card through the larger banks as well as from ATMs located all over the city.

The local commission is between 2 and 5 per cent, plus credit-card charges. (This can work out as cheap or cheaper than bringing cash to change.)

The most accepted cards are VISA, MasterCard and Eurocard. Diners Club and American Express are less widely recognized. Less commission is charged for cash in roubles.

ATMs at a branch of Alfa-Bank

If your credit card is lost or stolen, you should report it immediately to the credit-card company so make sure you keep the relevant telephone number to hand.

It can be difficult to find places to cash travellers' cheques, and banks charge at least 2 per cent to do so. Only the larger banks,

such as Alfa-Bank and Sberbank, offer this service. Travellers' cheques can only be used as payment for goods or services in a few of the large hotels, and are acceptable only in US dollars and euros. You will need to present your passport whenever exchanging or paying with travellers' cheques.

Currency

The Russian currency is the rouble (or ruble), written рубль or abbreviated to р or руб. The higher denominations are available in banknotes, which bear images of Russian cities, the lower denominations in coins. The kopek, of which there are 100 in a rouble, is issued in coins.

Banknotes

There are 6 denominations of notes, with values of 10, 50, 100, 500, 1,000 and 5,000 roubles. When changing money check that the notes correspond to those shown here.

10 roubles

50 roubles

100 roubles

500 roubles

1,000 roubles

5,000 roubles

Coins

The revaluation of the Russian rouble in 1998 led to the revival of the long-redundant but much-loved kopek. Traditionally, the rouble had always consisted of 100 kopeks. As well as coins for 1, 2, 5 and 10 roubles, there are now coins for 1, 5, 10 and 50 kopeks.

 1 rouble

2 roubles

5 roubles

10 roubles

1 kopek

5 kopeks

10 kopeks

50 kopeks

Communications and Media

St Petersburg is home to many tech-savvy people and most cafés and restaurants have a Wi-Fi connection, which is usually free. There are dozens of mobile phone shops on and around Nevskiy prospekt, where a local SIM card can be purchased cheaply (for about 150 roubles) upon presentation of a passport. Unfortunately, the everyday postal service remains notoriously slow and unreliable, but St Petersburg offers several more efficient alternatives. The abundance of newspapers, magazines and TV channels on offer includes some in English.

Visitors using mobile phones at a park in St Petersburg

International and Local Telephone Calls

The local system, Rostelekom (in Cyrillic "Ростелеком"), is reliable and relatively cheap. Rostelekom phone boxes are green and located on the streets and in some metro stations. Most phone boxes have instructions in Russian only.

Local calls made from private phones are usually free of charge. International calls are much cheaper with a prepaid phonecard such as the Zebra card; these are available to buy from kiosks and post offices and also serve as Internet pay-as-you-go cards. A more efficient alternative is to buy a Russian SIM card for your mobile phone (*see opposite*).

From a payphone, the Emergency Services can be reached by dialling a two-digit number free of charge: for the fire service dial 01, for the police dial 02 and for the ambulance service dial 03.

Mobile Phones

To find out if a mobile phone will work on Russian networks, check with your local service provider before travelling. If you want to ensure your phone will work while you are away you should have a quad-band phone. Tri-band phones from the EU will usually work in Russia, but US mobile phones may not. Visitors should be aware that "roaming" in Russia is very expensive. It is also more expensive to make and receive calls while abroad.

A cheaper option is to buy a Russian SIM card from any of the mobile phone chains, such as Evroset or Svyaznoi. A SIM card costs about 150 roubles and includes the same sum in credit. A passport must be shown when you buy a SIM card.

The four networks – **MTS**, **Megafon**, **Beeline** and **Tele2** all have sufficient coverage and similar charges. Calls within St Petersburg are much cheaper than rates in Western Europe.

Reaching the Right Number

- To phone **Russia** from abroad, dial 007 followed by the local area code and individual number.
- To phone **St Petersburg**, dial 812 followed by the individual number.
- To phone **Moscow**, dial 495 or 499 followed by the individual number.
- St Petersburg directory enquiries, dial 09.
- There is no international directory enquiries.
- Inter-city call booking, dial 07.
- International call booking, dial 315 0012.
- To phone the **UK**, dial 8 (tone) 1044 followed by the number, omitting first 0 from area code.
- To phone **Canada** or the **US**, dial 8 (tone) 101 followed by the number.
- To phone the **Irish Republic**, dial 8 (tone) 10353 followed by the number.
- To phone **Australia**, dial 8 (tone) 1061 then the number.
- To phone **New Zealand**, dial 8 (tone) 1064 followed by the number.
- To phone **South Africa**, dial 8 (tone) 1027 followed by the number.

Internet

Internet access is available at cafés and clubs throughout St Petersburg such as **Cafe Max** and **5.3 GHz**. Free Wi-Fi access is available both inside the Hermitage museum and within

The interior and grounds of the Hermitage offer free Wi-Fi access

its grounds (see p86). Wi-Fi coverage is widely available in hotels, as well as at the airport. It is generally free, though some hotels may charge where Internet is only available in a specific area.

Postal Services

The state-run, international postal system is generally slow and unreliable. A more efficient, and expensive, service is run by **Westpost**, who also offer door-to-door next-day delivery to Moscow. Anything other than papers must go through customs, which can add an extra day.

DHL and **Fedex** also have offices in the city and take three days to deliver to Europe and four to Australia and the US. The Belmond Grand Hotel Europe (see p178) runs a quick postal service, taking three days to the UK via Finland, which costs about 130 roubles per letter.

Ordinary post offices, such as the **Main Post Office** (see p124), which is open daily, and those in hotels, sell normal and commemorative Russian stamps, postcards, envelopes and local phonecards. Russian postboxes are marked Почта (Pochta) and are plentiful in the city centre. Tourists should use the small, pale-blue postboxes. The yellow postboxes are used for local delivery services only.

Addresses

After 1917, when the city was renamed Leningrad, many streets and sights were renamed to avoid imperial connotations or in order to commemorate new Soviet heroes. Since the city resumed its original name after a referendum in 1991, most streets in the centre have officially reverted to their pre-1917 names. The area surrounding the city, however, is still the Leningrad Region. Many people use both the original and Soviet names; no offence is caused when one is used in preference to another. Some useful words to recognize are улица (street) and проспект (prospekt).

A kiosk selling newspapers and magazines

Newspapers and Magazines

St Petersburg doesn't have many options for printed English-language newspapers or magazines. One useful source of city information is St Petersburg In Your Pocket, a free guidebook aimed at tourists and expats that comes out every two months and can be found in hotels' restaurants and bars. The international magazine Where?, a dual Russian/English publication, focuses on high-end, luxury experiences, and can be found in upscale hotels as well as in expensive restaurants around the city.

Foreign papers can be picked up at highly inflated prices from major hotels.

Television and Radio

Russian-language television is dominated by soap operas, detective shows and talk-shows. The two St Petersburg-based channels are Channel 5 and 100TV. Russia Today, the state-run English-language channel that is widely viewed as a mouthpiece for the Kremlin, is available in most hotels. Its hourly weather forecasts can be useful for visitors. Most hotels in St Petersburg have satellite television and receive many other Western programmes.

The best English-language radio broadcast to the city on shortwave is still the BBC World Service.

DIRECTORY

Mobile Phones

Megafon
Мегафон
Nab kanala Griboedova 18.
Map 6 E1.
Tel +8 800 550 0500.
W megafon.ru

MTS
МТС
Kazanskaya ul 45.
Map 6 D2.
Tel 380 0000.
W mts.ru

Internet

5.3GHz
Nevskiy prospekt 11.
Tel 314 6705.
W 5.3ghz.ru

Cafe Max
Кафе Макс
Nevskiy prospekt 90–92.
Map 6 E1.
Tel 273 6655.
W cafemax.ru

The Hermitage
Dvortsovaya nab 38A.
Tel 710 9550.

Postal Services

DHL International Centre
Nevskiy prospekt 10.
Map 7 B2.
Tel 326 6400.

Fedex
Per Grivtsova 6.
Map 6 D2.
Tel 325 8825.

Main Post Office
Главпочтамт
Glavpochtamt Pochtamtskaya ul 9.
Map 5 C2.
Tel 315 8022.

Westpost
Nevskiy prospekt 86.
Map 7 B2.
Tel 275 0784 or 336 6352.
W westpost.ru

Newspapers and Magazines

St Petersburg In Your Pocket
W inyourpocket.com/russia/st-petersburg

TRAVEL INFORMATION

St Petersburg is growing in popularity as a tourist destination, with the local government making concerted efforts to attract foreign tourists. As the number of business travellers increases, the number of flights and alternative means of transport is on the rise. Flying remains the most popular way of travelling to St Petersburg, both for individuals and groups, with the train from Moscow or Helsinki a close second. There is a ferry link with Helsinki and Stockholm, while the Baltic capitals can be reached by coach. Independent travel in Russia is difficult for those who don't speak Russian, and for this reason it is worth considering a package tour. British companies run a variety of tours with specialist guides, which often incorporate St Petersburg and Moscow. Package tours can be expensive, but shopping around can uncover some good deals, particularly on flights with stopovers in Europe or low-season package deals.

Exterior of Pulkovo airport, the city's international airport

Arriving by Air

Direct flights from the UK to St Petersburg run seven days a week on **British Airways**. **Lufthansa**, **SAS** and **Finnair** also serve St Petersburg. There are connecting flights on other airlines departing daily and these can often be a cheaper option. **Scott's Tours** in London are particularly good for budget fares and package deals. The journey from London takes around 3 hours, or about 6 hours with a stopover in a European city.

Direct flights to St Petersburg from Ireland, US, Canada, South Africa and Australia are either very limited or simply do not exist. The usual route from these destinations is to fly via a European city or via Moscow, from where you can transfer to another flight or continue by road or rail. It is worth noting that travelling from Australia can be fairly complicated. The most usual route is to pick up a European carrier in Singapore, with a stopover in Europe. On landing, passengers are sometimes required to confirm onward flights. You can do this through the airline you are travelling with or through the **Central Air Communication Agency** on Malaya Morskaya ulitsa.

St Petersburg is served by **Pulkovo** airport, which was until recently divided between two buildings set a few kilometres apart along a single runway. In 2013, a new terminal opened that made flying in and out of the city much more convenient. Able to handle up to 7 million arrivals a year, the new Pulkovo airport has done away with the separate terminals in favour of one large central structure.

Despite its modernity and size, there are only 14 jetways, meaning that most arrivals and departures will employ buses to transfer passengers between the plane and the terminal. The greatest improvement for international passengers is that the number of passport desks has increased from 10 to 110, significantly reducing waiting times. A number of business lounges, cafés and duty-free shops offer shopping and refreshment. The Park Inn by Radisson Pulkovo Airport hotel sits just steps away, making it a convenient stop for early departures or overnight stays.

Aeroflot company logo

Transport to and from the Airport

The airport is located 17 km (11 miles) south of the city centre. The major hotels operate cars to pick up individual tourists for a cost of around 1,500 roubles, but this service is no longer as essential as it once was as there is now a regulated taxi system in the arrivals halls of both airports. Look for the stand near the exit door marked *Taxi*, and tell the attendant where you want to go. The dispatcher will state how much the journey will cost (this price will be fixed), provide you with a printed receipt and radio in a driver. You should expect to pay about 1,000 roubles to get to the city centre.

A cheaper option for those who have already changed money at the airport, is to take bus No. 39 from directly outside the arrivals hall to Moskovskaya metro station. Minibuses travel the same route and charge about twice as much (see p223).

Arriving by Rail

Rail is a convenient way to travel from Finland to Moscow and within Russia in general, although European student discount passes provide little or no reduction in fares.

More than ten trains a day run in each direction between Moscow and **Moscow Station** and **Ladozhskiy Station**. Twice daily high-speed trains connect Helsinki and **Finlyandskiy Station**. For those with time and a sense of adventure, it is possible to travel by train between London and St Petersburg via Central Europe (Warsaw, Prague, Berlin). It takes about three days and is almost always more costly than flying. Trains are comfortable and usually run on time, but carriages can be overcrowded and thefts are not uncommon. A costly transit visa is also necessary to travel through Belarus. All visitors to Russia need a visa and obtaining one can be a complicated procedure (see p210).

Trains travelling from Eastern Europe arrive and depart from **Vitebskiy Station**. Tickets for train journeys from St Petersburg should be bought from kiosks at the **Central Train Ticket Office**, **Moscow Station**, or from any other railway station in the city, regardless of destination.

An overnight sleeper compartment

Travelling Between Moscow and St Petersburg

Many visitors fly in to Moscow and out of St Petersburg, or vice versa. The most popular form of transport between the two cities is the train, of which there are ten or more a day. The fastest option is the **Sapsan** train, which takes less than 4 hours to travel between the cities, while nighttime trains take from 8 to 12 hours.

Prices vary according to the class of the train – the Sapsan being most expensive – and the type of seat. Most trains have a choice of coupé (four-person compartment), platzkart (dormitory-style carriages), or sidyachyy (open seating). For daytime travel sidyachyy is more comfortable and cheaper than platzkart. One-way prices for standard trains range from 800 roubles for sidyachyy to 2,600 roubles for coupé. Sapsan tickets start at 4,200 roubles. Food may be available but it is best to take your own.

Regular commercial flights connecting the two cities take 50–90 minutes. These are run by Aeroflot and independent companies such as S7 and Nordwind. Prices range from 2,700 roubles for an economy class one-way ticket to 4,200

roubles for business class. Tickets are sold online, at the airport, or at the **Central Air Communication Agency**. In summer, travelling by boat to and from Moscow is possible (see p222).

Rail Tickets and Reservations

Tickets can be bought both at **Moscow Station** and at the ticket office on the Griboedova Canal. Long queues are the norm, unless you are prepared to pay about 300 roubles commission to buy tickets (coupé class only) from the Service Centre at Moscow train station. E-tickets can be bought online, at www.eng.rzd.ru and www.russiantrains.com. International rail passes are not usually valid on Russian trains and foreigners are not eligible for discounts.

Arriving by Coach

Comfortable coaches run to and from Helsinki in Finland, offering a cheaper alternative to the train. **Lux-Express** runs two daytime coaches and one overnight in each direction; the journey takes around 8 hours. Coach companies do not always use the city's inconvenient coach station, but will drop off instead at various locations in St Petersburg. Dozens of coaches depart for Finland at 6 or 7am every morning and 10 or 11pm every evening from outside the Bukvoyed bookstore on Ploshchad Vosstaniya. The Baltic states can also all be reached by coach. Journey times vary from 8 to 13 hours.

Coach Tickets and Reservations

Timetables, prices and tickets to the Baltic states can all be found at www.ecolines.net and www.luxexpress.eu/ru. They are also sold at the **Eurolines** and **Ecolines** offices. It is best to book ahead as tickets regularly sell out. Students can claim a 10 per cent discount, with an ISIC card. The **Lux-Express** office also sells tickets.

Sapsan train travelling between Moscow and St Petersburg

Arriving by Sea

Arriving by boat can be one of the most exciting and novel ways to approach St Petersburg. Cruises are an increasingly popular way to visit the city, and there are regular ferry services to Helsinki and Stockholm.

Cruise ships and ferries dock at the **Marine Facade Passenger Terminal** on the north side of Vasilevskiy Island. Trolleybus No. 10 and No. 11 and bus No. 7 run from here to the centre.

In summer, river cruises between St Petersburg and Moscow run along the Volga and across to Lake Ladoga. The trips last about two weeks and make a very pleasurable way to see more of Russia. The cruises are bookable in the UK through **Noble Caledonia** or **Voyages Jules Verne**, and in the US through **Visit Russia**. Ships dock at St Petersburg's **River Terminal**, which is not near any metro

St Peter Line cruise ship visiting St Petersburg

station and requires using a taxi or bus. Cruise companies run buses to and from the city centre.

Ferry Tickets and Reservations

Tickets for the ferry to and from Stockholm and Helsinki can be bought online at www.stpeter line.com. The Princess Maria ferry travels between St Petersburg and Helsinki three to four times a week. The journey takes about 12 hours and costs for a one-way ticket range from 1,200 roubles for a berth in a four-person cabin midweek to 18,000 roubles for a spacious deluxe cabin for two at the weekend. The Princess Anastasia ferry travels once or twice a week to Helsinki, Stockholm and Tallinn before returning to St Petersburg. Ticket prices range from 600 to 20,000 roubles, depending on the timing and type of package booked.

DIRECTORY

Tour Companies

Noble Caledonia
2 Chester Close,
London SW1X 7BE.
Tel (0207) 752 0000.
🆆 noble-caledonia.
co.uk

Scott's Tours
141 Whitfield Street,
London W1T 5EW.
Tel (0207) 383 5353.
🆆 scottstours.co.uk

Visit Russia
Tel 309 5760.
🆆 visitrussia.com

Voyages Jules Verne
96 Great Suffolk Street,
London,
SE1 0BE.
Tel (0203) 131 0510.
🆆 vjv.com

Arriving by Air

Aeroflot
Ul. Rubinshteina 1/43.
Map 7 A2.
Tel 438 5583.
🆆 aeroflot.ru

Pulkovo
Пулково
Tel 337 3444.
🆆 pulkovoairport.ru

British Airways
Sotsialisticheskaya
ulitsa 14.
Map 7 A4.
Tel 313 5044.
Tel 346 8146 (Pulkovo).
🆆 britishairways.com

**Central Air
Communication
Agency**
Malaya Morskaya ul 16.
Map 6 D1. **Tel** 571 5669
🆆 cavs.ru.

Finnair
Pulkovo airport.
Tel 303 9898.

KLM
Malaya Morskaya ul 23.
Map 6 D1.
Tel 346 6864.

Lufthansa
Pulkovo airport.
Tel +7 495 411 8444.

SAS
Pulkovo airport.
Tel 324 3244.

Arriving by Rail

All Train Enquiries
Tel 055.

**Central Train
Ticket Office**
Центральные железно-
дорожные кассы
*Tsentralnye zhelezno-
dorozhnye kassy*
Nab kanala
Griboedova 24.
Map 6 E2. **Tel** 067.

Finlyandskiy Station
финляндский вокзал
Finlyandskiy vokzal
Pl Lenina 6. **Map** 3 B3.

Ladozhskiy Station
Ладожский вокзал
Ladozhskiy vokzal
Zanevskiy pr 73.

Moscow Station
Московский вокзал
Moskovskiy vokzal
Pl Vosstaniya.
Map 7 C2.

Vitebskiy Station
Витебский вокзал
Vitebskiy vokzal
Zagorodnyy prospekt 52.
Map 6 F4.

Travelling Between Moscow and St Petersburg

Sapsan
🆆 eng.rzd.ru
🆆 russiantrains.com

Arriving by Coach

Ecolines
Podezdnoi pereulok 3.
Tel 409 9410.
🆆 ecolines.ru

**Eurolines/
Lux-Express**
2 Mitrofanyevskoe shosse.
Tel 441 3757.
🆆 luxexpress.eu

Sovavto
Park Inn by Radisson
Pulkovskaya, Ploshchad
Pobedy 1.
Tel 740 3985.
🆆 bus.sovavto.com

Arriving by Sea

**Marine Facade
Passenger Terminal**
Морской фасад
пассажирский терминал
*Morskoy Fasad
passazhirskiy terminal*
Morskaya Naberezhnaya.
Tel 303 6740.
🆆 portspb.ru

River Terminal
Речкой вокзал
*Oktyabrskaya
naberezhnaya 31*
Tel 335 2196.

GETTING AROUND ST PETERSBURG

Although public transport in the city is abundant, efficient and very cheap, the most enjoyable way to get around and fully appreciate St Petersburg is on foot. A glance at a map that shows the city has a rational, organized layout, which makes it easier to negotiate. A boat cruise along the waterways can also be a wonderful way to become acquainted with St Petersburg. Nevskiy prospekt is where many of the city's transport routes and main roads meet.

Metro lines, tram, bus and trolleybus routes radiate out from here. It is possible to travel without too much difficulty to almost anywhere in town from this main avenue. Driving is not recommended due to the combination of poor road conditions, aggressive Russian driving and over-enthusiastic traffic police. Cyclists, once virtually unheard of in St Petersburg, are now becoming a common sight, and the city has several bike-rental companies.

Green Travel

The greenest ways to get around St Petersburg are on foot or by bike, both of which are perfectly viable options given the compact size of the historical centre. The public transport system is good enough to make using a car unnecessary and many forms of the transport network are also environmentally friendly, such as the extensive trolleybus and metro routes.

Buses and Minibuses

All services run every 10 minutes, sometimes less often. Bus stops in the city centre are marked either by white-and-yellow signs with a black letter "A" for *avtobus*, or by blue signs depicting a bus. Signs are placed by the side of the road or attached to lampposts. Some routes are duplicated by commercial buses, marked with a "k" before the number, or minibuses (though there are no minibus routes along Nevskiy prospekt).

Fares on these buses are higher than those on non-commercial equivalents, and are paid to the driver when getting on or off – if in doubt just follow what other passengers do. Buses can be hailed or requested to stop anywhere along the route.

Useful routes include the No. 22 bus from the Smolnyy Institute *(see p130)* via St Isaac's Square *(see p81)* to the Mariinskiy Theatre *(see p121)*. Bus numbers 3, 7, 22 and 27 run along most of Nevskiy prospekt between Ploshchad Vosstaniya and the Admiralty.

Open-top **City Tour** red buses offer sightseeing excursions from 9am to 8pm daily. Tickets can be bought on board and are valid for one day, costing 600 roubles for an adult ticket.

Trolleybuses

Trolleybuses offer convenient routes and stops around the city. Stops are marked by small blue-and-white signs suspended from wires or lampposts, indicating the trolleybus numbers. These signs show a Cyrillic "T" for trolleybus, on a white background. Trolleybuses can be boarded at the front, middle or back doors. The front eight seats are reserved for the disabled, the elderly and passengers with children. Fares are either collected by the conductor or can be paid using transport cards.

Trams

Trams are disappearing from many roads in the city centre, but some remain. Stops are marked by red-and-white signs suspended on wires above the rails. Trams can be boarded via any of the doors and tickets bought in cash from the conductor. Trams will automatically stop along the route.

Tickets and Travel Cards

A flat fare is payable on all forms of transport, whatever the length of the journey. Tickets are bought from the conductor or, on commercial transport, from the driver.

The cheapest way to travel is to buy a travel card that is applicable for all types of city transport. These cards range in price from 180 (1 day) to 680 (7 days) roubles. Monthly cards cost 2,900 roubles. Separate monthly cards are also sold for each form of transport.

A city trolleybus on Nevskiy prospekt

Walking

In some areas, particularly around Palace Embankment, sights are situated so close together that using public transport from place to place is unnecessary. A few of the more scattered sights are at some distance (20 minutes on foot) from the nearest transport and walking the last stretch is often the most practical option. Apart from the ease, getting around on foot can be a most rewarding way to explore the city, allowing you to soak up the atmosphere and appreciate the fascinating architectural and sculptural detail on many of St Petersburg's buildings.

As soon as the sun appears, in winter as well as in summer, people of all ages emerge onto the streets and into the parks. Locals are very fond of walking, whether it be promenading up and down Nevskiy prospekt, or ambling around the Neva at 2am during the White Nights (see p53). The Summer Garden (see p97) and Mikhaylovskiy Garden have long been popular with local residents. For longer walks mixed with some architectural interest, two good areas to try are Kamennyy and Yelagin islands (see pp138–9), with their official residences and *dachas*, many of them dating from the early years of the 20th century.

For a romantic stroll around the city away from the traffic, walk along the Moyka or Griboedov canals (see pp136–7). To the south of Nevskiy prospekt, majestic buildings give way to smaller, 19th-century residential blocks,

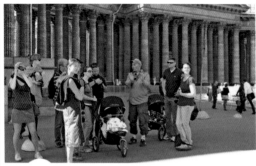
Visitors on a walking tour of St Petersburg

with trees by the waterside and leafy squares and courtyards.

Drivers have little respect for pedestrians and traffic is the main hindrance to walking. Cars drive on the right-hand side, so look left first when crossing the road. If there is a pedestrian underpass, use it and, if not, look for a light-controlled crossing with red and green figures indicating pedestrian right of way. Crossings without lights are marked by a blue sign showing a pedestrian, but although drivers are obliged by law to stop for pedestrians, this does not mean they will, so the greatest care should be taken when crossing the road.

On the main city streets, dark-blue sponsored name-plates give street names in Russian and English. Elsewhere, black-on-white street names are in Cyrillic only.

Guided Tours

Walking tours in English can be booked through **Peter's Walking Tours**, which offers themed excursions such as

A pedestrian crossing, one of the safer places to cross Russian roads

Rasputin, Dostoevsky, World War II and Style-Moderne architecture. They also offer guided cycling tours, popular during the White Nights. Liberty offer tours for disabled travellers (see p212). Many bike-hire companies provide their own tours (see p225). Other English-language excursions are available from **Anglotourismo**, who offer free daily walking tours lasting 3 hours as well as guided boat tours (see p228).

One of the taxi styles

Taxis

St Petersburg does not have a coordinated official taxi system, and private cabs come in a variety of colours. There is no uniform taxi style, but a taxi will have an orange chequered light on the top or an illuminated green light on the windscreen when it is available. The more expensive taxis have a yellow "*taksi*" sign on the roof.

Taxis can be found outside metro stations, major sights and hotels. It is usually cheaper and easier to ask hotel or restaurant staff to order you a private taxi rather than attempting to hail one on the street. Taxis can carry four people. There are no official taxi ranks in the city, but plenty on the streets to hail. Private cars and taxis that have not been pre-booked are best avoided if you are travelling alone at night.

Most convenient to use are mobile phone-based ride-sharing services such as **Uber** or **Gett**, which are very popular in Russia and offer competitive rates compared to taxis. Journeys in the city centre should cost no more than 400 roubles. After 1am some taxi companies will offer a 10 per cent discount. A journey from the airport to the city centre will cost 1,000 roubles. There may be an extra charge for passengers with large luggage.

Driving

Driving is not recommended but if you do choose to drive, be aware that local drivers tend to ignore rules of the road and do more or less as they like, so be on your guard. Drive on the right and make no left turns on main roads unless a road sign indicates that it is permitted.

In winter conditions, driving requires studded tyres as chains can be damaged on tram lines and vice versa.

There is no charge for street parking in most parts of the city centre. The Corinthia Hotel (see p178) and some hotels have

24-hour secured parking, some with an extra charge for non-guests. There are few public car parks in the city centre, with the exception of two at Ploshchad Vosstaniya and one outside **Moscow Train Station**. Car parks are identified by a white letter "P" on a blue sign. These are short-stay car parks and cost 100 roubles for one hour. Car parks are often open 24 hours.

Be aware that the traffic police can pull over drivers at any time in order to check documents and will more often than not find something wrong with your car and may ask for a bribe. Tourists are required by law to have a notarized translation of their driving licence, as producing just an international driving licence will not suffice.

Cycling

St Petersburg is flat and compact and should be a haven for cyclists. Unfortunately, it is also a city of reckless drivers. If you choose to cycle, wear a helmet and stick to quieter side roads or take part in a led cycle tour. Parts of the Neva embankment with wider pavements, such as the area near Smolnyy Cathedral (see p130), is a popular route with cyclists.

Bikes can be rented from **Skat Prokat** and **Velotour**, who also conduct cycling tours. Bike rental costs 150 roubles per hour or 600–800 roubles per day, plus a refundable deposit. Collect your bike from the office or have it delivered for 500 roubles. This delivery service is offered free of charge when you rent a bike with **Rentbike**.

Cycling, an increasingly popular means of transport in St Petersburg

DIRECTORY

Buses

City Tours
Pirogovskaya naberezhnaya 7.
Map 5 C2.
Tel 648 1228.
Ⓦ citytourspb.ru

Public Transport Agency
Ulitsa Rubinshteyna 32.
Map 7 A3. **Tel** 576 5555.
Ⓦ orgp.spb.ru

St Petersburg Coach Station
Naberegnaya Obvodnogo kanala 36
Tel 380 5248.

Trams and Trolleybuses

GorElectroTrans
Syzranskaya 15.
Tel 388 7000.
Ⓦ electrotrans.spb.ru

Guided Tours

Anglotourismo
Tel +7 921 989 4722.
Ⓦ anglotourismo.com

Peter's Walking Tours
Tel 943 1229.
Ⓦ peterswalk.com

Taxis

Gett
Ⓦ gett.com

St Petersburg Taxi
Tel 068.

Seven Million
Tel 7 000 000.

Six Million
Tel 6 000 000.

Uber
Ⓦ uber.com

Driving

Moscow Train Station
Московский вокзал
Moskovskiy vokzal
Pl Vosstaniya.
Map 7 C2.

Cycling

Rentbike
Naberazhnaya reki Fontanki 77.
Map 6 D2.
Tel 907 6409.
Ⓦ rentbike.org

Skat Prokat
Goncharnaya ulitsa 20.
Map 7 C3.
Tel 748 1407.
Ⓦ skatprokat.ru

Velotour
Stolyarnyy pereulok 10.
Map 6 D3.
Tel 981 0155.
Ⓦ velotour-spb.ru.

Travelling by Metro

Since overland transport is the most efficient means of getting around the city centre, the metro is used mainly to get to and from the outskirts of the city. As a tourist attraction, however, the metro's stunning stations, intended by Stalin to be "palaces for the people", should be high on your itinerary. The metro runs until just after midnight. Travelling in the daytime or late evening will avoid most of the two million people estimated to use the metro each day. With just five lines, negotiating the network is fairly straightforward, especially since there are now basic signs in English. Do watch out for pickpockets on the metro – gangs have particularly been known to target travellers getting off at Nevskiy Prospekt metro station.

Sculpture in Pushkinskaya metro

The Metro as a Tourist Attraction

Thousands of tonnes of marble, granite and limestone were used to face the walls, and sculptures, mosaics and chandeliers were commissioned from leading artists for the St Petersburg metro. The first line – the red line – opened in 1955, and is one of the most fascinating, being the supreme embodiment of Stalinist style and ideals. The line's crowning glory has to be Avtovo, incorporating a wealth of style and detail, even down to the moulded glass columns.

The metro now has 67 stations, ranging in style and ambience from the dim lighting and memorial atmosphere of Ploshchad Muzhestva (Courage Square, 1975) near Piskarevskoe Memorial Cemetery (see p128),

to the 1980s vulgarity of Udelnaya and the cool of Komendantskiy Prospekt (2005).

The Network

The metro is vital for getting to and from hotels outside the city centre and the airport.

The five lines run from the outskirts through the centre, where they intersect at one of six main stations.

Trains run every few minutes during the day and every 5 minutes late at night. The last train leaves the station of origin at midnight. There is no rush hour as such but the metro tends to be full at most times of day, which makes it generally safe as it is always busy. Platforms are not staffed, but there is an attendant in a booth at the bottom of each escalator who can call for assistance.

Because of the many waterways in the city, stations are buried deep underground and long escalators lead down to the platforms.

New stations are still being added to the St Petersburg metro to increase efficiency and link the centre to more areas around the city, reducing travel time.

Finding your Way

Before setting foot in St Petersburg's metro, ensure you have a network map with the Cyrillic and transliterated names to hand. There are English and Russian signs in the metro, but knowledge of the Cyrillic station names will be useful. Turnstiles are located at the top of the escalators on route to the trains, where you can touch in with a magnetic card or pay with a metro token (see Tickets and Travel Cards). Follow the signs in the metro to the platform. Once on the platform, the direction of the trains and a list of all stops along the route are marked on the wall; routes are also displayed inside the carriage.

Busy stations may have safety doors between the platform and the trains. When the train stops, these doors open, and only then do the train doors open.

Before the train doors close, an automatic announcement is made: "Ostorozhno. Dveri zakryvayutsya" (Be careful the doors are closing). As the train approaches a stop, the name of

Signs in both Cyrillic and English in the metro system

the station is announced, this will be in Russian only. Announcements are also made if the station you are approaching is an inter-connecting one, allowing you to change lines. Keep count of the stops, in case you do not catch the announcements.

To change to another line, follow the interchange signs for **переход** (*perekhod* – crossing). The exception is at Tekhnologicheskiy Institut, where the two southbound lines are on parallel platforms, as are the two northbound lines: thus to continue in the same direction on another line you simply cross the central concourse.

Exits are marked **выход** (*vykhod*). Some stations, such as Moskovskaya (for the airport) and Gostinyy Dvor, have two or more exits.

Metro tokens and a magnetic travel card

Tickets and Travel Cards

The most common means of paying for the metro is the token (*zheton*), available to buy from metro stations only. Magnetic cards, which can be topped up with as many trips as needed, are also available. There are no zones in the metro, so as with other forms of transport in the city, there is a flat charge for each journey, regardless of the distance.

Barrier machines are installed at the top of the escalators; most take both cards and tokens. Cards must be touched to the illuminated sensor on top. If you try to go through a machine without paying, an automatic barrier closes in front of you. If you have a large bag or suitcase, you must buy a special luggage token, which allows you to pass through a wider gate at the metro barrier. At the far right an

St Petersburg's Metro

Комендантский Проспект / Komendantskiy pr
Старая деревня / Staraya derevnya
Крестовский остров / Krestovskiy Ostrov
Чкаловская / Chkalovskaya
Спортивная / Sportivnaya
Беговая / Begovaya *(under construction)*
Новокрестовскама / Novokrestovskaya *(under construction)*
Приморская / Primorskaya
Василеостровская / Vasileostrovskaya
Адмиралтейская / Admiralteyskaya
Горный институт / Gorniy institut *(under construction)*
Театральная / Teatral'naya *(under construction)*
Технологический инст / Tekhnologicheskiy Inst
Балтийская / Baltiyskaya
Нарвская / Narvskaya
Броневама / Bronevaya *(under construction)*
Кировский завод / Kirovskiy Zavod
Ьуго-Западнама / Yugo-Zapadnaya *(under construction)*
Путиловская / Putilovskaya *(under construction)*
Автово / Avtovo
Ленинский пр / Leninskiy Pr
Пр Ветеранов / Pr Veteranov

Гостиный двор / Gostinyy Dvor
Невский пр / Nevskiy Pr
Сенная / Sennaya
Садовая / Sadovaya
Звенигородская / Zvenigrodskaya
Фрунзенская / Frunzenskaya
Моск ворота / Mosk vorota *(under construction)*
Заставскама / Zastavskaya *(under construction)*
Элект-росила / Elektrosila
Парк Победы / Park Pobedy
Московская / Moskovskaya
Звездная / Zvezdnaya
Купчино / Kupchino

Парнас / Parnas
Пр Просвещения / Pr Prosveshcheniya
Озерки / Ozerki
Удельная / Udelnaya
Пионерская / Pionerskaya
Черная речка / Chernaya Rechka
Петроградская / Petrogradskaya
Горьковская / Gorkovskaya
Пл Восстания / Pl Vosstaniya
Спасская / Spasskaya
Владимирская / Vladimirskaya
Достоевская / Dostoevskaya
Пушкинская / Pushkinskaya
Лиговский пр / Ligovskiy Pr
Обводный Канал / Obvodnyy Kanal
Волковская / Volkovskaya
Боровама / Borovaya
Букчарестская / Bukharestskaya
Международная / Mezhdunarodnaya
Проспект Славы / Prospekt Slavy *(under construction)*
Дунайская / Dunayskaya *(under construction)*
Шушары / Shushary *(under construction)*

Девяткино / Devyatkino
Гражданский пр / Grazhdanskiy Pr
Академическая / Akademicheskaya
Политехническая / Politekhnicheskaya
Пл Мужества / Pl Muzhestva
Лесная / Lesnaya
Выборгская / Vyborgskaya
Пл ленина / Pl Lenina
Чернышевская / Chernyshevskaya
Маяковская / Mayakovskaya
Пл Александра Невского / Pl Aleksandra Nevskovo
Елизаровская / Elizarovskaya
Ломоносовская / Lomonosovskaya
Пролетарская / Proletarskaya
Обухово / Obukhovo
Рыбацкое / Rybatskoe
Новочеркасская / Novocherkasskaya
Ладожская / Ladozhskaya
Пр болшевиков / Pr Bolshevikov
Ул дыбенко / Ul Dybenko

attendant checks passes and allows you to put your token in a machine which does not have automatic barriers. Those with magnetic cards cannot pass through this machine.

Monthly magnetic cards for the metro or for all forms of public transport are valid for 70 metro jour-neys and an infinite number of journeys on overground transport during a calendar month. Cards, which are valid for 35 metro journeys and unlimited overground transport during a two-week period, can also be bought between the 16th and the 5th of each month. Cards can be bought at any time during the month but are valid only from the 1st to the 15th of each month.

Metro token

Visitors who plan to stay in the city for a while may find it worthwhile to pur-chase a personal "smart" card – a **Podorozhnik Smart Card** – to which they can transfer credit to fund future journeys at any metro station. Such cards are placed briefly onto a sensor marked with a white circle. There are no further ticket checks once you have past through the barriers inside the metro station.

DIRECTORY

St Petersburg Metro
Tel 301 9700.
W metro.spb.ru

Podorozhnik Smart Card
Tel 576 5555.
W podorozhnik.spb.ru

Canal and River Cruises

St Petersburg's numerous natural waterways were adapted and extended, to make it resemble Peter the Great's beloved Amsterdam (see pp22–3). Indeed, it would be true to say the city vies with Amsterdam for the title "Venice of the North".

A wide selection of cruises, for small and large groups, in open and closed boats, depart from bridges along Nevskiy prospekt and other parts of the city. They offer marvellous opportunities to see more of the city, especially for those unable to walk long distances. Forming part of any cruise are the broad Fontanka river with its Neo-Classical palaces, the leafy Moyka river with its ironwork bridges, and the Griboedov Canal which twists and turns its way through southwest St Petersburg. Bring a bottle of champagne, a picnic, a warm jumper and just relax.

A river cruise passing the Rostral Columns

General Information

The weather plays a vital role in determining the exact time of year canal cruises start and finish. Most boats operate daily from mid-May to late September. Their routes also vary because regular construction work such as reinforcing the granite embankments, sometimes prevents movement along parts of the canals.

The Gulf of Finland is tidal and this affects the Neva and inland waterways. Strong winds can cause the water level to rise significantly and boat trips may be cancelled under these conditions.

Guided River and Canal Trips

Large, covered cruise boats depart every 30 minutes, between 11:30am and 8pm, from the Anichkov Bridge on Nevskiy prospekt (see p51). Tickets for the next available boat should be purchased from the kiosk on the embankment, or on board. Trips last 60 minutes and take in the Moyka and Fontanka rivers, and sometimes the Griboedov Canal. Some routes go out onto the Neva, from where there are superb views of the whole city.

Trips usually cost about 600 roubles. Guided tours are available in English from companies such as **Anglo-tourismo**, **Neptun-boat** and **Astra Marine**. Large groups are advised to book in advance, either at a kiosk or by phone, especially during school holidays. Boat trips providing guided tours in English can be booked through any of the major hotels, though this is a more expensive choice.

A popular option are the night-time boat trips along the Neva to watch the bridges opening. No commentary is usually provided on these tours, which depart from the Anichkov Bridge pier next to the Anichkov Palace at 1:30am and last for about an hour. Blankets are usually provided, but take your own food and drink, as these are rarely available.

Neva Cruises

A variety of boats cruise up and down the Neva. The trips, operating hourly between 10am and 10pm, last an hour. Tickets can be bought on the landing stage or on board for about 500 roubles. The boats leave from in front of the Admiralty (see p80) and from near the main entrance of the Hermitage (see p86–7), as well as from the pier of the Peter and Paul Fortress (see pp68–9), from where tickets can be bought for as little as 400 roubles.

Luxury catered cruises can be booked in advance. **MIR** and **Russkiye Kruizy** offer a variety of routes along the Neva and the city's other rivers and canals. Trips along the Neva are a good way to see all the majestic façades that line the river's embankment. Most trips start by going to the Blagoveshchensky Bridge before turning around. Heading back towards Palace Bridge, sights on the left-hand side include the Academy of Arts (see p65), which is easily identifed by the two Egyptian sphinxes in front of it.

The next building to come into view is the yellow Menshikov Palace (see p64), built by Peter the Great's friend Alexander Menshikov. Peter lived in the relatively humble Summer Palace, which can be seen later on the right-hand side in the Summer Gardens.

Shortly after the Menshikov Palace, the side façade of St Petersburg State University comes into view (see p63). The striking turquoise-and-white building soon after is the Kunstkammer (see p62).

On the other side of the river, the Bronze Horseman monument to Peter the Great (see pp80–81), St Isaac's Cathedral (see pp82–3) and the Admiralty (see p80) can be seen

A cruise along the Neva river

in all their glory. Back on the left, the spit of Vasilevskiy Island is crowned by the stately Stock Exchange building, and completed by the two large red Rostral Columns. Across the Neva is the spectacular Winter Palace (see pp94–5). The next sight on the left is the Peter and Paul Fortress, while shortly afterwards, the enormous blue dome of the city's first mosque can be seen.

On the right is the stunning façade of the Marble Palace (see p96), with the onion domes of the Church on Spilled Blood (see p102) peeping out above it. After the palace, the iconic intricate railings of the Summer Gardens can be admired.

Most sightseeing boats cruise up to Liteiny Bridge or beyond before doubling back to their original starting point.

Departure Points Along Rivers and Canals

Boats depart at regular intervals from the Moyka river, Griboedov Canal and Fontanka river at their intersections with Nevskiy prospekt (see pp48–51), on both sides of the street. Boats departing from the northern side may be about 50 roubles more expensive as they attract more passers-by. Boats also leave from the eastern side of St Isaac's Square, heading in the direction of Nevskiy prospekt. Other boats leave from across from the Field of Mars on the Moyka, and from many other points along all of the waterways where there are steps leading down the embankment.

Restaurant Cruises

There are several restaurant boats that sail up and down the Neva, allowing passengers to enjoy views of the city's embankments over dinner.

Favorite organizes private dinner cruises along the Neva river for couples and groups. Tickets start at 600 roubles per person, excluding food. The cruises last one-and-a-half hours and take in all the major sights along the river.

Those who like the idea of restaurants on water but fear the onset of seasickness might prefer the city's stationary floating restaurants, such as the eccentric **Flying Dutchman** (see p187), which combines several restaurants serving Russian, Japanese, French and Italian cuisine. There is also a fitness centre and beauty salon on board.

Frigate Blagodat, moored at Petrovskaya naberezhnaya, offers spectacular views over the Peter and Paul Fortress (see pp68–9) and Troitskiy most. The Veter (meaning "wind") restaurant and the Empire of Passion and Summer Garden banquet halls are the historically themed dining rooms on board.

Boats on the Griboedov

Rowing Boats

Many parks in St Petersburg have ponds and lakes that offer a great refuge to those who seek a break from city life. It is an ideal place to exercise in the open air as well.

In all the major parks, boat rental services offer various watercraft, from regular rowboats to catamarans, pedalboats and kayaks.

It is necessary to leave a deposit for the boat (either 1,500 roubles, or valuables such as cell phones and driving licenses). Rates vary from park to park, but they usually come to around 300 roubles per hour. The most enjoyable places to boat are Yelagin Park (see p128), Tsarskoe Selo (see pp154-158) and Moskovskiy Park Pobedy (near the Moskovskaya metro station).

Tickets

Tickets for all boats can be bought on board. For Neva cruises, they are sold at kiosks on the piers in front of the Admiralty and the Hermitage. Hour-long sightseeing tours along the rivers and canals usually cost about 600 roubles. Children under seven may be allowed to travel for free, while older children may be given a discount. Night boat trips, which offer the chance to see the raising of the bridges, start at 800 roubles.

Travelling Beyond St Petersburg

Every weekend during the summer, and even in winter, many locals leave the city. They head for their *dacha* or for the woods, to gather seasonal fruits and vegetables, go cross-country skiing or visit one of the former imperial summer residences. Buses and suburban trains operate frequently throughout the year and are the usual means of transport to sites out of town. Peterhof and Kronshtadt are the exceptions in being accessible by hydrofoil across the Gulf of Finland. Foreigners tend to take coach excursions out of town but, with planning, travelling independently can be part of the fun.

Hydrofoil arriving at the Hermitage landing stage

Interior view of one of St Petersburg's suburban trains

Suburban Trains

Train travel is the most comfortable way to visit the majority of the outlying sights. Tickets can be bought from the local cash desks *(prigorodnyye kassy)* at each station, where a timetable (in Russian) is displayed. Return tickets are no cheaper than two singles. Note that smoking is prohibited, and that between the hours of 10am and midday there is often a break in the timetable.

Getting to Tsarskoe Selo and Pavlovsk

Trains for Tsarskoe Selo (Pushkin) *(see pp154–7)* and Pavlovsk *(see pp160–63)* depart every 20 minutes from **Vitebskiy Station**. The line was originally built for the royal family to reach their summer residences and the station is a marvellous example of Style-Moderne architecture. The ticket office is on the right of the main building. All local trains take about 30 minutes, stopping first at Tsarskoe Selo (Detskoe Selo), then Pavlovsk.

At Detskoe Selo station, the 382 and 371 buses go to Tsarskoe Selo, stopping near the palace. On foot, it is about a 20-minute walk from the station to the estate.

At Pavlovsk, the train station is opposite the entrance to the park, through which it is a pleasant 30-minute walk to the palace.

A host of minibuses run to Tsarskoe Selo (Pushkin) and Pavlovsk from Moskovskaya metro station in St Petersburg. They provide a reliable and convenient alternative means of transport to the train.

Passengers boarding suburban train at Vitebskiy Station

Getting to Peterhof and Oranienbaum

The most enjoyable and by far the most scenic way to reach the imperial summer palace of Peterhof is the 45-minute trip across the Gulf of Finland by hydrofoil. The service runs from early June until early October and sets off from the second landing stage outside the Hermitage *(see p86)* where a weekly timetable is posted. Generally, hydrofoils operate every hour from 10am, with the last boat returning at 6pm. It is cheaper to buy a return ticket (for 1,500 roubles) than two singles. While it is much more expensive than the train or bus, it is worth the extra cost for the comfort and the view.

On arrival, a fee is charged to enter the lower park and this ticket is needed to get back into the park to return by hydrofoil.

The hydrofoils to Kronshtadt are now offered only as part of a tour costing 2,000 roubles. This includes a walking tour in Kronshtadt city centre, as well as a trip around old forts near Kronshtadt. Regular hydrofoil services no longer run to Oranienbaum.

There are suburban trains for Peterhof *(see pp150–53)* and Oranienbaum *(see pp148–9)* departing every 20 minutes from **Baltic Station.** The trains that reach Oranienbaum are those destined for Kalishche, or Oranienbaum itself. For Peterhof, get off the train at Novyy Petergof (40 minutes from town), from where it is 10 minutes to the palace on bus 348, 350, 351, 352 or 356.

At Oranienbaum, turn right out of the station and walk about 200 m (650 ft) to the main road. Almost directly opposite is the entrance to the park, and from here it is only a 5-minute walk to the Great Palace or into the heart of the park.

An efficient minibus service runs passengers to both Peterhof and Oranienbaum and is located outside Avtovo metro station.

Getting to Repino and the Gulf of Finland

For Repino (see p148) and the Gulf of Finland, trains depart every 20 minutes or so from **Finland Station**. Tickets should be bought at cash desks within the main building. Avoid any train marked Beloostrov or Krugovoy.

At Repino, cross the main road, head down the hill towards the Gulf of Finland and turn left onto the asphalt road until you reach Penaty.

Bus No. 211 also runs to Repino and stops right outside Penaty. Buses to Repino leave from Chernaya Rechka metro and tickets are bought on board.

Getting to Veliky Novgorod

Coaches leave for Veliky Novgorod (see pp164–7) every 2 hours from the **Coach Station**. The journey takes 4 hours. There are also at least two daily trains from **Moscow Station** that take 3 hours (be warned that there is no toilet on the train). An alternative is to book a guided tour (see p224).

Driving out of St Petersburg

Car hire is available from companies such as **Hertz** and **Avis**, but driving is not recommended. Firstly, there is no need, as the public transport network is excellent and inexpensive, and secondly, the local driving culture and

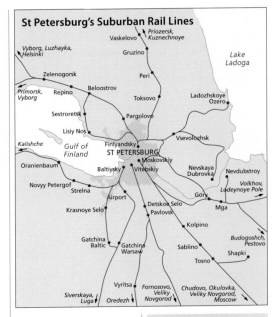

St Petersburg's Suburban Rail Lines

suspicious traffic police do not make for an enjoyable time on the road.

To drive in Russia, a notarized translation of a foreign licence is obligatory, as well as international insurance and documents proving you have the right to be driving the car: for example, registration documents or a hire agreement bearing your name.

Traffic police (see p214) have the right to stop you and check your documents. If a policeman points his baton at your vehicle and signals for you to pull over, you must do so immediately, regardless of whether you have committed any violations. The police may issue on-the-spot fines for minor infringements – such as having a dirty number plate, not having a first-aid kit – or more serious offences such as drink-driving. (Drivers are not allowed to drink any alcohol.)

The proper procedure is to issue a ticket requiring payment within a month at any branch of Sberbank, though the traffic police are notorious for preferring to receive bribes than to issue official fines. For a minor infringement, such as not wearing a seatbelt, a fine may be around 500–1,000 roubles.

DIRECTORY

Train and Coach Stations

All train enquiries
Tel 055.

Baltic Station
Балтийский вокзал
Baltiyskiy vokzal
Nab Obvodnovo kanala 120.

Coach Station
Автобусный вокзал
Avtobusnyy vokzal
Nab Obvodnovo kanala 36.
Map 7 B5.
Tel 380 5248.

Finland Station
Финляндский вокзал
Finlyandskiy vokzal
Pl Lenina 6.
Map 3 B3.

Moscow Station
Московский вокзал
Moskovskiy vokzal
Pl Vosstaniya.
Map 7 C2.

Vitebskiy Station
Витебский вокзал
Vitebskiy vokzal
Zagorodnyy pr 52.
Map 6 F4.

Car Hire

Avis
Pulkovo Arrivals.
Tel 324 6109.

Hertz
Pulkovo Arrivals. **Tel** 454 7099.

ST PETERSBURG STREET FINDER

The key map below shows the areas of St Petersburg covered by the *Street Finder*. The map references given throughout the guide for sights, restaurants, hotels, shops or entertainment venues refer to the maps in this section. All the major sights have been clearly marked so they are easy to locate. The key below shows other features marked on the maps, such as

post offices, metro stations, ferry stops and churches. The *Street Finder* index lists street names in transliteration, followed by the Cyrillic (on the maps, Cyrillic is only given for major roads). This guide uses the now reinstated old Russian street names, rather than the Soviet versions *(see p219)*. Places of interest are listed by their English name.

Key to Street Finder

Major sight	Hospital
Place of interest	Police station
Other building	Orthodox church
Railway station	Non-Orthodox church
Metro station	Synagogue
Tram stop	Mosque
Trolleybus terminus	Railway line
Bus terminus	«45 House number (main street)
River boat pier	

Scale of Map Pages

0 metres 300
0 yards 300

Street Finder Index

Abbreviations & Useful Words

ul	ulitsa	street
pl	ploshchad	square
pr	prospekt	avenue
per	pereulok	lane
nab	naberezhnaya	embankment
	most	bridge
	sad	garden
	shosse	road

General Index

Acknowledgments

Dorling Kindersley would like to thank the following people whose contributions and assistance have made the preparation of this book possible.

Main Contributors
Christopher Rice holds a PhD in Russian history from the University of Birmingham. He and his wife Melanie, also a writer, first visited Russia in 1978 and have been returning regularly ever since. Together they have written numerous travel guides to the city, and to a variety of other destinations, including Prague, Berlin and Istanbul, as well as the *Eyewitness Travel Guide to Moscow*.

Catherine Phillips is an art historian who arrived in Russia in 1985 and has lived there ever since, moving to St Petersburg in 1989. She covered major events for British and American TV and radio during the early years of *perestroika* and authored and contributed to some of the first guides to the new Russia. Today she concentrates on translating and editing scholarly texts and writing for works of reference.

Additional Contributor
Rose Baring began to study Russian at the age of 12. She has an MA in Modern History and divided her time between London, Moscow and St Petersburg for much of the early 1990s. She has written guides to St Petersburg, Moscow and other destinations, including the *Eyewitness Travel Guide to Istanbul*.

Special Assistance
Dorling Kindersley would like to thank Marc Bennetts (walks writer), Anastasia Makarova (fact checker), Hilary Bird (indexer), Ian Wizniewski (food and drink consultant), Valera Katsuba (photo permissions), Marina Maydanyuk (researcher), Oleksiy Nesnov (language consultant), Victoria Rachevskaya (language consultant), Agency Information Resources for helping with research, Yuliya Motovilova (St Petersburg Tourist Company) and the staff of Peter TiPS.

Proofreader
Stewart J Wild.

Relaunch and Revisions Team
Namrata Adhwaryu, Emma Anacootee, Gillian Allan, Douglas Amrine, Jasneet Arora, Liz Atherton, Subhashree Bharti, Stuti Tiwari Bhatia, Andrei Bogdanov, Laurence Broers, Shura Collinson, Lucinda Cooke, Vivien Crump, Dawn Davies-Cook, Hannah Dolan, Alexandra Farrell, Claire Folkard, Chris Gordon, Freddy Hamilton, Susanne Hillen, Paul Hines, Leanne Hogbin, Vicki Ingle, Cincy Jose, Bharti Karakoti, Sumita Khatwani, Priyanka Kumar, Kathryn Lane, Sam Merrell, Deepak Mittal, Shubhi Mittal, Fiona Morgan, Alexey Moskin, Jane Oliver, Reetu Pandey, Helen Partington, Marianne Petrou, Pure Content, Amir Reuveni, Ellen Root, Luke Rozkowski, Anuroop Sanwalia, Alison Stace, Avantika Sukhia, Rachel Thompson Ingrid Vienings, Matt Willis, Veronica Wood.

Additional Illustrations
Claire Littlejohn, John Woodcock.

Additional Photography
Valentin Baranovsky, Andrei Bogdanov, Victoria Buyvid, Shura Collinson, Andy Crawford, Neil Fletcher, Steve Gorton, Paul Miller, Ian O'Leary, Rough Guides/Jonathan Smith, Jon Spaull, Clive Streeter; KOMMERSANT Photo Agency: Yevgeny Pavlenko, Sergey Semyenov.

Photography Permissions
The publisher would like to thank all those who gave permission to photograph at their establishments, including hotels, museums, churches, shops and other sights, too numerous to thank individually.

Picture Credits
Key: a-above; b-below/bottom; c-centre; f-far; l-left; r-right; t-top.
The publisher would like to thank the following individuals, companies and picture libraries for their kind permission to reproduce their photographs:

123RF.com: svglass 219tc.

Aeroflot: 220cr; **AKG, London:** 18, 22bl/cl, 22–3c, 27tl, 28clb, 29c, 30br, Erich Lessing 30bl, 31ca, 39bl, 44cl/bl/bc, 45br, State Russian Museum, St Petersburg 107crb; **Alamy Images:** Art Directors & TRIP/Vladimir Sidropolev 210cl; brt Russia 83cra; Danita Delimont 116; PE Forsberg 214crb; i food and drink 184cl; ITAR-TASS Photo Agency 158-9; Jon Bower- art and museums 66; Granger Historical Picture Archive 25tl, Heritage Image Partnership Ltd 89tr, INTERFOTO 23bl, JOHN KELLERMAN 168-169, Daniel Korzeniewski 208-9; Art Kowalsky 10cl; Frans Lemmens 218cla; Dov Makabaw 223br; Medioimages 10br; Dmitry Mikhaevich 61crb, 175tl; RIA Novosti 62bl; Robert Harding Picture Library Ltd 104-105, 140cr; Robert Harding Picture Library Ltd/ Sylvah Grandadam 182cla, 183tl; Russ Images 126; Maurice Savage 227cl; Neil Setchfield 186bl; studio204 218br; Peter Titmuss 13tc, 140br, 212tl; Universal Images Group/DeAgostini 98; Patrizia Wyss 170cl; **Alfa-Bank:** 216bl; **Anglotourism.com:** 224tr; **Ancient Art & Architecture Collection:** 47cr; **APA:** Jim Holmes 95tl.

Valentin Baranovsky: 86clb, 87tl, 203tl; **Ian Bavington-Jones:** 132tc; **Baklazhan Restaurant:** 191br; **Belmond Grand Hotel Europe:** 178bc, 180cl, 189bl, 190tl; **Yuri Belinsky:** 33tl; **Bridgeman Art Library, London/New York:** Forbes Magazine Collection 30–1c; State Hermitage, St Petersburg 23cr, 26–7c, 27cl, 88cla/bc, 89bc, 90cb, 91tr/bc, 92ca/bl, 93tl/c, *La Danse*, Henri Matisse (1910) © Succession Henri Matisse/DACS 2011 89c; Private Collection *20th Century Propaganda Poster 1920*, D Moor © DACS 2011 31tr; State Russian Museum, St Petersburg *The Cyclist*, Natalya Goncharova (1913) © ADAGP, Paris and DACS, London 2011 42br, *Portrait of Princess Olga Konstantinovna Orlova*, Valentin

Alexandrovich Serov (1911) 106cla; Tretyakov Gallery, Moscow 21cla, *The Circus*, Marc Chagall, 1919 © ADAGP, Paris and DACS, London 2011 47tl.
Camera Press: Roxana Artacho 87bl; **Demetrio Carrasco:** 6b, 17b, 38cla, 55bl, 82bc, 95cra/br; **Central State Archive of Photographs and Film Documents, St Petersburg:** 44tr, 74c, 112crb, 120bl; **Corbis:** Bettmann/E. O Hoppe 120crb; Dean Conger 54cra, Antoine Gyori 141t; Rob Howard 183c; ITAR-TASS Photo/Shamukov Ruslan 220cl; Bob Krist 203bl; Library of Congress 30cla; Gianni Dagli Orti 8–9, 121bl; National Geographic Society/Jonathan Irish 2-3; Jose Fuste Raga 224bl; Steve Raymer 33crb, 120br, 140cla; State Hermitage, St Petersburg 26bl; State Russian Museum 27bl.

Dom Berga: 193tr; **Dreamstime.com:** Anoli50 144; Antartis 34; Amos Chapple 56-7; Dimbar76 110bl; Viacheslav Dyachkov 5tr; Ivanukh 76; Oleg Kovalenko 58; Denis Linine 115br; Marcorubino 4tc; Mardym 13b; Paha_i 212c ; Anna Pakutina 5cl; Renewer 140cl; Sailorr 12bl; Sborisov 4crb; Konstantin Semenov 134; Svglass 215tc.

E T Archive: Hermitage, St Petersburg 90cla, 91tl.

Fotolia: Dmitry Vereshchagin 229tl.

Getty Images: Culture Club 20cb; Fine Art 45bc; Fine Art Images 46cl; Hulton Archive 45tr, 120cla, 123c, 184tr; Photo Josse / Leemage 21cb; Sovfoto 24tl; The Image Bank/Harald Sund 11br; UniversalImagesGroup 20c; **Giraudon:** State Russian Museum 45cr, 107cra; Tretyakov Gallery, Moscow 167crb; **Gosti Restaurant:** 188tl.

Hotel Dostoevsky: 175cb.

Interior Archive: 163crb; **iStockphoto.com:** misterbike 84bc.

Kea Publishing Services: Francesco Venturi 94 tr/bc, 95bl; **David King Collection:** 31tl, 32tl, 47bc, 71bc, 131cr.

Lonely Planet Images: Jonathan Smith 11tr, 141crb.

Mary Evans Picture Library: 21br, 23tr, 24crb, 25crb, 26cl/br, 27br, 28tl, 31crb, 64bc, 163bl; **Paul Miller:** 53cra. **Neptun-boats:** 228cl; **Novosti (London):** 22br, 23tl, 28br, 29tr, 32cl, 33c, 45tl, 52c, 53br, 80bl, 167cl.

Park Inn by Radisson Veliky Novgorod: 172br, 177tr;

Plodimex Aussenhandels Gmbh, Hamburg: 180cr/bl; **Pushka INN Hotel:** 179tr.

Radisson Royal Hotel St. Petersburg: 178tr; Natasha Razina: 155tl; Renaissance St Petersburg Baltic Hotel: 174c; **Rex Features:** V. Sichov/Sipa Press 32cr; **Robert Harding Picture Library:** 86cla; **Rocco Forte Hotels, St Petersburg:** 171br; **Ellen Rooney:** 55cra, 81tr, 85br; **Russian Railways:** 221tc, 221bl.

Gregor M Schmid: 52br; **Shinok Restaurant:** 192bl; **Vladimir Sidoropolev:** 184br; **St Peter Line:** 222tr; **St Petersburg Metro:** 226br; **Skat Prokat:** 225cr; **State Russian Museum:** 7cr; *Blue Crest*, Wassily Kandinsky (1917) © ADAGP, Paris and DACS, London 2011 41br; 95tr, 106clb/br, 107tl, 108cla/br, 109tl/bc, 112bc; **SuperStock:** A. Burkatovski / Fine Art Images 19clb, 108tr, SONNET Sylvain / Hemis.fr 187tl.

Travel Library: Stuart Black 87br; **Tsar Restaurant:** 190bc; **Tsarskoye Selo State Museum and Heritage Site:** 142-3, 154tr, 154br, 155crb.

Vedensky Hotel: 176bl; **Visual Arts Library:** 46br; State Hermitage, St Petersburg *L'Homme aux bras croisés*, Pablo Picasso (1905) © Succession Picasso/DACS 2011 93br; 125cl.

Front Endpaper: Dreamstime.com: Ivanukh Rcr; Oleg Kovalenko Lcl; **Alamy Images:** Danita Delimont Lbc; Jon Bower- art and museums Rtc; Universal Images Group/ DeAgostini Rbc.

Map Cover: AWL Images: Walter Bibikow.

Cover Images: Front: AWL Images: Walter Bibikow; Back: **123RF.com:** pretoperola tc; Spine: **AWL Images:** Walter Bibikow.

All other images © Dorling Kindersley. For further information see: www.dkimages.com

Phrase Book

In this guide the Russian language has been transliterated into Roman script following a consistent system used by the US Board on Geographic Names. All street and place names, and the names of most people, are transliterated according to this system. For some names, where a well-known English form exists, this has been used – hence, Leo (not Lev) Tolstoy. In particular,

the names of Russian rulers, such as Peter the Great, are given in their anglicized forms. Throughout the book, transliterated names can be taken as an accurate guide to pronunciation. The Phrase Book also gives a phonetic guide to the pronunciation of words and phrases used in everyday situations, such as when eating out or shopping.

Guidelines for Pronunciation

The Cyrillic alphabet has 33 letters, of which only five (а, к, м, о, т) correspond exactly to their counterparts in English. Russian has two pronunciations (hard and soft) of each of its vowels, and several consonants without an equivalent. The right-hand column of the alphabet, below, demonstrates how Cyrillic letters are pronounced by comparing them to sounds in English words. However, some letters vary in how they are pronounced according to their position in a word. Important exceptions are also noted below.
On the following pages, the English is given in the left-hand column, with the Russian and its transliteration in the middle column. The right-hand column provides a literal system of pronunciation and indicates the stressed syllable in bold. The exception is in the *Menu Decoder* section, where the Russian is given in the left-hand column and the English translation in the right-hand column, for ease of use. Because of the existence of genders in Russian, in a few cases both masculine and feminine forms of a phrase are given.

The Cyrillic Alphabet

А а	a	*a*limony
Б б	b	*bed*
В в	v	*vet*
Г г	g	*get (see note 1)*
Д д	d	*debt*
Е е	e	*yet (see note 2)*
Ё ё	e	*yonder*
Ж ж	zh	*leisure (but a little harder)*
З з	z	*zither*
И и	i	*see*
Й й	y	*boy (see note 3)*
К к	k	*king*
Л л	l	*loot*
М м	m	*match*
Н н	n	*never*
О о	o	*rob (see note 4)*
П п	p	*pea*
Р р	r	*rat (rolling, as in Italian)*
С с	s	*stop*
Т т	t	*toffee*
У у	u	*boot*
Ф ф	f	*fellow*
Х х	kh	*kh (like loch)*
Ц ц	ts	*lets*
Ч ч	ch	*chair*
Ш ш	sh	*shove*
Щ щ	shch	*fresh sheet (as above but with a slight roll)*
ъ		*hard sign (no sound, but see note 5)*
Ы ы	y	*lid*
ь		*soft sign (no sound, but see note 5)*
Э э	e	*egg*
Ю ю	yu	*youth*
Я я	ya	*yak*

Notes

1) Г Pronounced as *v* in endings -oro and -ero.
2) Е Always pronounced *ye* at the beginning of a word, but in the middle of a word sometimes less distinctly (more like *e*).
3) Й This letter has no distinct sound of its own. It usually lengthens the preceding vowel.
4) О When not stressed it is pronounced like *a* in across.
5) ъ, ь The hard sign (ъ) is rare and indicates a very brief pause before the next letter. The soft sign (ь, marked in the pronunciation guide as ') softens the preceding consonant and adds a slight *y* sound: for instance, *n'* would sound like *ny* in 'canyon'.

In Emergency

Help!	Помогите! *Pomogite!*	*pamageet-ye!*
Stop!	Стоп! *Stop!*	*stop!*
Leave me alone!	Оставьте меня в покое! *Ostavte menya v pokoe!*	*astavt'-ye myenya v pakoye!*
Call a doctor!	Позовите врача! *Pozovite vracha!*	*pazaveet-ye vracha!*
Call an ambulance!	Вызовите скорую помощь! *Vyzovite skoruyu pomoshch!*	*vizaveet-ye skoru-yu pomash!*
Fire!	Пожар! *Pozhar!*	*pazhar!*
Call the fire brigade!	Вызовите пожарных! *Vyzovite pozharnykh!*	*vizaveet-ye pazharnikh!*
Police!	Милиция! *Militsiya!*	*meeleetsee-ya!*
Where is the nearest…	Где ближайший… *Gde blizhayshiy…*	*gdye bleezhaysheey…*
…telephone?	…телефон? *…telefon?*	*…tyelyefon?*
…hospital?	…больница? *…bolnitsa?*	*…bal'neetsa?*
…police station?	…отделение милиции? *…otdelenie militsii?*	*…atdyelyenye meeleetsee-ee?*

Communication Essentials

Yes	Да *Da*	*da*
No	Нет *Net*	*nyet*
Please	Пожалуйста *Pozhaluysta*	*pazhalsta*
Thank you	Спасибо *Spasibo*	*spaseeba*
You are welcome	Пожалуйста *Pozhaluysta*	*pazhalsta*
Excuse me	Извините *Izvinite*	*eezveeneet-ye*
Hello	Здравствуйте *Zdravstvuyte*	*zdrastvooyt-ye*
Goodbye	До свидания *Do svidaniya*	*da sveedanya*
Good morning	Доброе утро *Dobroe utro*	*dobra-ye ootra*
Good afternoon/day	Добрый день *Dobryy den'*	*dobree dyen'*
Good evening	Добрый вечер *Dobryy vecher*	*dobree vyechyer*
Good night	Спокойной ночи *Spokoynoy nochi*	*spakoynay nochee*
Morning	утро *utro*	*ootra*
Afternoon	день *den*	*dyen'*
Evening	вечер *vecher*	*vyechyer*
Yesterday	вчера *vchera*	*fchyera*
Today	сегодня *sevodnya*	*syevodnya*
Tomorrow	завтра *zavtra*	*zaftra*
Here	здесь *zdes*	*zdyes'*

There	там	*tam*
	tam	
What?	Что?	*shto?*
	Chto?	
Where?	Где?	*gdye?*
	Gde?	
Why?	Почему?	*pachyemoo?*
	Pochemu?	
When?	Когда?	*kagda?*
	Kogda?	
Now	сейчас	*seychas*
	seychas	
Later	позже	*pozhe*
	pozzhe	
Can I…?	можно?	*mozhna…?*
	mozhno?	
It is	можно	*mozhna*
possible/allowed	*mozhno*	
It is not	нельзя	*nyelzya*
possible/allowed	*nelzya*	

Useful Phrases

How are you?	Как Вы Поживаете?	*kak vee pozhivaete?*
	Kak vee pozhivaete?	
Very well, thank	Хорошо, спасибо	*kharasho, spaseeba*
you	*Khorosho, spasibo*	
Pleased to meet you	Очень приятно	*ochen' pree-yatna*
	Ochen priyatno	
How do I get to…?	Как добраться	*kak dabrat'sya da…?*
	до…?	
	Kak dobratsya do…?	
Would you tell me	Скажите,	*skazheet-ye,*
when we get to…?	пожалуйста,	*pazhalsta, kagda*
	когда мы	*mi pree-yedyem*
	приедем в…?	*v…?*
	Skazhite,	
	pozhaluysta,	
	kogda my	
	priedem v…?	
Is it very far?	Это далеко?	*eta dalyeko?*
	Eto daleko?	
Do you speak	Вы говорите	*vi gavareet-ye*
English?	по-английски?	*po-angleeskee?*
	Vy govorite	
	po-angliyski?	
I don't understand	Я не понимаю	*ya nye*
	Ya ne ponimayu	*paneema-yoo*
Could you speak	Говорите	*gavareet-ye*
more slowly?	медленнее	*myedlyenye-ye*
	Govorite medlennee	
Could you say it	Повторите,	*paftareet-ye,*
again please?	пожалуйста	*pazhalsta*
	Povtorite,	
	pozhaluysta	
I am lost	я заблудился	*ya zabloodeelsya*
	(заблудилась)	*(zabloodeelas')*
	Ya zabludilsya	
	(zabludilas)	
How do you say…	Как по-русски…?	*kak pa-rooskee…?*
in Russian?	*Kak po-russki…?*	

Useful Words

big	большой	*bal'shoy*
	bolshoy	
small	маленький	*malyen'kee*
	malenkiy	
hot (water, food)	горячий	*garyachee*
	goryachiy	
hot (weather)	жарко	*zharka*
	zharko	
cold	холодный	*khalodnee*
	kholodnyy	
good	хорошо	*kharasho*
	khorosho	
bad	плохо	*plokha*
	plokho	
okay/fine	нормально	*narmal'na*
	normalno	
near	близко	*bleezka*
	blizko	
far	далеко	*dalyeko*
	daleko	
up	наверху	*navyerkhoo*
	naverkhu	
down	внизу	*fneezoo*
	vnizu	

early	рано	*rana*
	rano	
late	поздно	*pozdna*
	pozdno	
vacant (unoccupied)	свободно	*svabodna*
	svobodno	
free (no charge)	бесплатно	*byesplatna*
	besplatno	
cashier/ticket office	касса	*kasa*
	kassa	
avenue	проспект	*praspyekt*
	prospekt	
bridge	мост	*most*
	most	
embankment	набережная	*nabyeryezhnaya*
	naberezhnaya	
highway/motorway	шоссе	*shasse*
	shosse	
lane/passage	переулок	*pyeryeoolak*
	pereulok	
square	площадь	*ploshat'*
	ploshchad	
street	улица	*ooleetsa*
	ulitsa	
flat/apartment	квартира	*kvarteera*
	kvartira	
floor	этаж	*etash*
	etazh	
house/block	дом	*dom*
	dom	
entrance	вход	*fkhot*
	vkhod	
exit	выход	*vikhot*
	vykhod	
river	река	*ryeka*
	reka	
summer country	дача	*dacha*
house	*dacha*	
swimming pool	бассейн	*basyeyn*
	basseyn	
town	город	*gorat*
	gorod	
toilet	туалет	*tooalyet*
	tualet	

Making a Telephone Call

Can I call abroad	Можно отсюда	*mozhna atsyooda*
from here?	позвонить за	*pazvaneet' za*
	границу?	*graneetsoo?*
	Mozhno ostyuda	
	pozvonit za	
	granitsu?	
I would like to	Позовите,	*pazaveet-ye,*
speak to…	пожалуйста…	*pazhalsta…*
	Pozovite,	
	pozhaluysta	
Could you leave	Вы можете	*vi mozhet-ye*
him/her a	передать ему/ей?	*pyeryedat'*
message?	*By mozhete peredat*	*yemoo/yay?*
	emy/ey?	
My number is…	Мой номер…	*moy nomyer…*
	Moy nomer…	
I'll ring back later	Я позвоню позже	*ya pazvanyoo*
	Ya pozvonyu pozzhe	*pozhe*

Sightseeing

castle	замок	*zamak*
	zamok	
cathedral	собор	*sabor*
	sobor	
church	церковь	*tserkaf'*
	tserkov	
circus	цирк	*tseerk*
	tsirk	
closed for cleaning	санитарный день	*saneetarnee dyen'*
"cleaning day"	*sanitarnyy den*	
undergoing	ремонт	*remont*
restoration	*remont*	
exhibition	выставка	*vistafka*
	vystavka	
fortress	крепость	*kryepost'*
	krepost	
gallery	галерея	*galeryeya*
	galereya	
garden	сад	*sad*
	sad	
island	остров	*ostraf*
	ostrov	

kremlin/fortified stronghold	кремль *kreml*	*kryeml'*
library	библиотека *biblioteka*	*beeblee-atyeka*
monument	памятник *pamyatnik*	*pamyatneek*
mosque	мечеть *mechet*	*myechyet'*
museum	музей *muzey*	*moozyey*
palace	дворец *dvorets*	*dvaryets*
park	парк *park*	*park*
parliament	дума *duma*	*dooma*
synagogue	синагога *sinagoga*	*seenagoga*
zoo	зоопарк *zoopark*	*zapark*

Shopping

open	открыто *otkryto*	*atkrita*
closed	закрыто *zakryto*	*zakrita*
How much does this cost?	Сколько это стоит? *Skolko eto stoit?*	*skol'ka eta stoeet?*
I would like to buy…	Я хотел (хотела) бы купить… *Ya khotel (khotela) by kupit…*	*ya khatyel (khatyela) bi koopeet'…*
Do you have…?	У вас есть…? *U vas yest…?*	*oo vas yest'…?*
Do you take credit cards?	Кредитные карточки вы принимаете? *Kreditnye kartochki vy prinimaete?*	*kryedeetnye kartachkee vy preeneemayetye?*
What time do you open/close?	Во сколько вы открываетесь/ закрываетесь? *Vo skolko vy otkryvaetes/ zakryvaetes?*	*Va skol'ka vy atkrivayetyes/ zakrivayetyes?*
This one	этот *etot*	*etat*
expensive	дорого *dorogo*	*doraga*
cheap	дёшево *deshevo*	*dyoshyeva*
size	размер *razmer*	*razmyer*
white	белый *belyy*	*byelee*
black	чёрный *chernyy*	*chyornee*
red	красный *krasnyy*	*krasnee*
yellow	жёлтый *zheltyy*	*zholtee*
green	зелёный *zelenyy*	*zyelyonee*
dark blue	синий *siniy*	*seenee*
light blue	голубой *goluboy*	*galooboy*
brown	коричневый *korichnevyy*	*kareechnyevee*

Types of Shop

bakery	булочная *bulochnaya*	*boolachna-ya*
bookshop	книжный магазин *knizhnyy magazin*	*kneezhnee magazeen*
butcher	мясной магазин *myasnoy magazin*	*myasnoy magazeen*
camera shop	фото-товары *foto-tovary*	*foto-tavari*
chemist	аптека *apteka*	*aptyeka*
delicatessen	гастроном *gastronom*	*gastranom*
department store	универмаг *univermag*	*ooneevyermag*
florist	цветы *tsvety*	*tsvyeti*

grocer	бакалея *bakaleya*	*bakalye-ya*
hairdresser	парикмахерская *parikmakherskaya*	*pareekma-khyerskaya*
market	рынок *rynok*	*rinak*
newspaper stand	газетный киоск *gazetniy kiosk*	*gazyetnee kee-osk*
post office	почта *pochta*	*pochta*
record shop	грампластинки *gramplastinki*	*gramplasteenkee*
shoe shop	обувь *obuv*	*oboof'*
travel agent	бюро путешествий *byuro puteshestviy*	*byooro pootyeshestvee*
bank	банк *bank*	*bank*

Staying in a Hotel

Do you have a vacant room?	У вас есть свободный номер? *U vas yest svobodnyy nomer?*	*oo vas yest' svabodnee nomyer?*
double room with double bed	номер с двуспальной кроватью *nomer s dvuspalnoy krovatyu*	*nomyer s dvoospal'noy kravat'-yoo*
twin room	двухместный номер *dvukhmestnyy nomer*	*dvookhmyestnee nomyer*
single room	одноместный номер *odnomestnyy nomer*	*adnamyestnee nomyer*
bath	ванная *vannaya*	*vana-ya*
shower	душ *dush*	*doosh*
porter	носильщик *nosilshchik*	*naseel'sheek*
key	ключ *klyuch*	*klyooch*

Eating Out

A table for two, please	Стол на двоих, пожалуйста *Stol na dvoikh, pazhalsta*	*stol na dva-eekh, pazhalsta*
I would like to book a table	Я хочу заказать стол *Ya khochu zakazat stol*	*ya khachoo zakazat' stol*
The bill, please	Счёт, пожалуйста *Schet, pozhaluysta*	*shyot, pazhalsta*
I am a vegetarian	Я вегетерианец (вегетерианка) *Ya vegeterianets (vegeterianka)*	*ya vyegyetaree-anyets (vyegyetaree-anka)*
breakfast	завтрак *zavtrak*	*zaftrak*
lunch	обед *obed*	*abyet*
dinner	ужин *uzhin*	*oozheen*
waiter!	официант! *ofitsiant!*	*afeetsee-ant!*
waitress!	официантка! *ofitsiantka!*	*afeetsee-antka!*
dish of the day	фирменное блюдо *firmennoe blyudo*	*feermenoye blyooda*
appetizers/starters	закуски *zakuski*	*zakooskee*

main course	второе блюдо	ftaroye blyooda
	vtoroe blyudo	
meat and poultry dishes	мясные блюда	myasniye blyooda
	myasnye blyuda	
fish and seafood dishes	рыбные блюда	ribniye blyooda
	rybnye blyuda	
vegetable dishes	овощные блюда	avashshniye blyooda
	ovoshchnye blyuda	
dessert	десерт	dyesyert
	desert	
drinks	напитки	napeetkee
	napitki	
vegetables	овощи	ovashshee
	ovoshchi	
bread	хлеб	khlyeb
	khleb	
wine list	карта вин	karta veen
	karta vin	
rare (steak)	недожаренный	nyedazharenee
	nedozharennyy	
well done (steak)	прожаренный	prozharenee
	prozharennyy	
glass	стакан	stakan
	stakan	
bottle	бутылка	bootilka
	butylka	
knife	нож	nosh
	nozh	
fork	вилка	veelka
	vilka	
spoon	ложка	loshka
	lozhka	
plate	тарелка	taryelka
	tarelka	
napkin	салфетка	salfyetka
	salfetka	
salt	соль	sol'
	sol	
pepper	перец	pyeryets
	perets	
butter/oil	масло	masla
	maslo	
sugar	сахар	sakhar
	sakhar	

Menu Decoder

абрикос	abreekos	apricot
abrikos		
апельсин	apyel'seen	orange
apelsin		
апельсиновый сок	apyel'seenavee sok	orange juice
apelsinovyy sok		
арбуз	arbooz	water melon
arbuz		
белое вино	byelaye veeno	white wine
beloe vino		
бифштекс	beefshtyeks	steak
bifshteks		
блины	bleeni	pancakes
bliny		
борщ	borshsh	borsch (beetroot soup)
borshch		
варенье	varyen'ye	Russian syrup-jam
varene		
варёный	varyonee	boiled
varenyy		
ветчина	vyetcheena	ham
vetchina		
вода	vada	water
voda		
говядина	gavyadeena	beef
govyadina		
грибы	greebi	mushrooms
griby		
груша	groosha	pear
grusha		
гусь	goos	goose
gus		
джем	dzhem	jam
dzhem		
жареный	zharyenee	roasted/grilled/fried
zharenyy		
икра	eekra	black caviar
ikra		
икра красная/кета	eekra krasna-ya/ kyeta	red caviar
ikra krasnaya/keta		

капуста	kapoosta	cabbage
kapusta		
картофель	kartofyel'	potato
kartofel		
квас	kvas	kvas (sweet, mildly alcoholic drink)
kvas		
клубника	kloobneeka	strawberries
klubnika		
колбаса	kalbasa	salami sausage
kolbasa		
кофе	kofye	coffee
kofe		
красное вино	krasnoye veeno	red wine
krasnoe vino		
креветки	kryevyetkee	prawns
krevetki		
курица	kooreetsa	chicken
kuritsa		
лук	look	onion
luk		
малина	maleena	raspberries
malina		
минеральная вода	mineral'naya vada	mineral water
mineralnaya voda		
мороженое	marozhena-ye	ice-cream
morozhenoe		
мясо	myasa	meat
myaso		
огурец	agooryets	cucumber
ogurets		
осетрина	asyetreena	sturgeon
osetrina		
пельмени	pyel'myenee	meat or fish dumplings
pelmeni		
персик	pyerseek	peach
persik		
печенье	pyechyen'ye	biscuit
pechene		
печёнка	pyechyonka	liver
pechenka		
печёный	pyechyonee	baked
pechenyy		
пиво	peeva	beer
pivo		
пирог	peerok	pie
pirog		
пирожки	peerashkee	small parcels with savoury fillings
pirozhki		
помидор	pameedor	tomato
pomidor		
морепродукты	moryeprodooktee	seafood
moryeproduktee		
рыба	riba	fish
ryba		
салат	salat	salad
salat		
свинина	sveeneena	pork
svinina		
сельдь	sye'ld'	herring
seld		
сосиски	saseeskee	sausages
sosiski		
сыр	sir	cheese
syr		
сырой	siroy	raw
syroy		
утка	ootka	duck
utka		
фасоль	fasol'	beans
fasol		
форель	faryel'	trout
forel		
чай	chai	tea
chay		
чеснок	chyesnok	garlic
chesnok		
шашлык	shashlik	kebab
shashlyk		
яйцо	yaytso	egg
yaytso		
слива	sleeva	plum
sliva		
фрукты	frookti	fruit
frukty		
яблоко	yablaka	apple
yabloko		

Transport

north	север *sever*	s**ye**ver
south	юг *yug*	yook
east	восток *vostok*	vast**o**k
west	запад *zapad*	z**a**pat
airport	аэропорт *aeroport*	aerap**o**rt
aeroplane	самолёт *samolet*	samal**yo**t
traffic police	Дпс *DPS*	day-pay-**ess**
bus	автобус *avtobus*	aft**o**boos
bus station	автобусная станция *avtobusnaya stantsiya*	aft**o**boosna-ya stantse**e**-ya
bus stop	остановка автобуса *ostanovka avtobusa*	astan**o**fka aft**o**boosa
car	машина *mashina*	mash**ee**na
flight	рейс *reys*	r**ye**ys
metro (station)	(станция) метро *(stantsiya) metro*	(stantse**e**-ya) my**e**tro
no entry	нет входа *net vkhoda*	nyet fkh**o**da
no exit	нет выхода *net vykhoda*	nyet v**i**khada
parking	автостоянка *avtostoyanka*	aftosto**ya**nka
petrol	бензин *benzin*	byenz**ee**n
railway	железная дорога *zheleznaya doroga*	zhel**ye**zna-ya dar**o**ga
railway station	вокзал *vokzal*	vagz**a**l
return ticket	обратный билет *obratniy bilet*	abr**a**tnee bee**lye**t
seat	место *mesto*	m**ye**sta
suburban train	пригородный поезд *prigorodniy poezd*	pr**ee**garadnee po-y**e**zd
straight on	прямо *pryamo*	pr**ya**ma
taxi	такси *taksi*	taks**ee**
ticket	билет *bilet*	bee**lye**t
token (for a single metro journey)	жетон *zheton*	zhet**o**n
to the left	налево *nalevo*	nal**ye**va
to the right	направо *napravo*	napr**a**va
train	поезд *poezd*	po-y**e**zd
tram	трамвай *tramvay*	tramv**a**y
trolleybus	троллейбус *trolleybus*	tral**ye**yboos

Numbers

1	один/одна/одно *odin/odna/odno*	ad**ee**n/adn**a**/adn**o**
2	два/две *dva/dve*	dva/dvye
3	три *tri*	tree
4	четыре *chetyre*	chyet**i**r-ye
5	пять *pyat*	pyat'
6	шесть *shest*	shest'
7	семь *sem*	syem'
8	восемь *vosem*	v**o**syem'
9	девять *devyat*	d**ye**vyat'
10	десять *desyat*	d**ye**syat'

11	одиннадцать *odinnadtsat*	ad**ee**natsat'
12	двенадцать *dvenadtsat*	dven**a**tsat'
13	тринадцать *trinadtsat*	treen**a**tsat'
14	четырнадцать *chetyrnadtsat*	chyet**i**rnatsat'
15	пятнадцать *pyatnadtsat*	pyatn**a**tsat'
16	шестнадцать *shestnadtsat*	shestn**a**tsat'
17	семнадцать *semnadtsat*	syemn**a**tsat'
18	восемнадцать *vosemnadtsat*	vasyemn**a**tsat'
19	девятнадцать *devyatnadtsat*	dyevyatn**a**tsat'
20	двадцать *dvadtsat*	dv**a**tsat'
21	двадцать один *dvadtsat odin*	dv**a**tsat' ad**ee**n
22	двадцать два *dvadtsat dva*	dv**a**tsat' dva
23	двадцать три *dvadtsat tri*	dv**a**tsat' tree
24	двадцать четыре *dvadtsat chetyre*	dv**a**tsat' chyet**i**r-ye
25	двадцать пять *dvadtsat pyat*	dv**a**tsat' pyat'
30	тридцать *tridtsat*	tr**ee**tsat'
40	сорок *sorok*	s**o**rak
50	пятьдесят *pyatdesyat*	pyadyes**ya**t'
60	шестьдесят *shestdesyat*	shes'dyes**ya**t
70	семьдесят *semdesyat*	s**ye**m'dyesyat
80	восемьдесят *vosemdesyat*	v**o**syem'dyesyat
90	девяносто *devyanosto*	dyevyan**o**sta
100	сто *sto*	sto
200	двести *dvesti*	dv**ye**stee
300	триста *trista*	tr**ee**sta
400	четыреста *chetyresta*	chyet**i**ryesta
500	пятьсот *pyatsot*	pyat's**o**t
1,000	тысяча *tysyacha*	t**i**syacha
2,000	две тысячи *dve tysyachi*	dvye t**i**syachi
5,000	пять тысяч *pyat tysyach*	pyat' t**i**syach
1,000,000	миллион *million*	meelee-**o**n

Time, Days and Dates

one minute	одна минута *odna minuta*	adn**a** meen**oo**ta
one hour	час *chas*	chas
half an hour	полчаса *polchasa*	polchas**a**
day	день *den*	dyen'
week	неделя *nedelya*	nyed**ye**l-ya
Monday	понедельник *ponedelnik*	panyed**ye**l'neek
Tuesday	вторник *vtornik*	ft**o**rneek
Wednesday	среда *sreda*	sry**e**da
Thursday	четверг *chetverg*	chyetv**ye**rk
Friday	пятница *pyatnitsa*	p**ya**tneetsa
Saturday	суббота *subbota*	soob**o**ta
Sunday	воскресенье *voskresene*	vaskrye**sye**n'ye